readings for reflective teaching

in early education

Edited by Jennifer Colwell and Andrew Pollard

B L O O M S B U R Y

LONDON • NEW DELHI • NEW YORK • SYDNEY

Bloomsbury Academic

An imprint of Bloomsbury Publishing Plc

50 Bedford Square
London
WC1B 3DP
UK

1385 Broadway
New York
NY 10018
USA

www.bloomsbury.com

BLOOMSBURY and the Diana logo are trademarks of Bloomsbury Publishing Plc

First published 2015

British Library Cataloguing-in-Publication Data
A catalogue record for this book is available from the British Library.

ISBN: HB: 978-1-4725-0526-2
PB: 978-1-4725-1264-2
ePDF: 978-1-4725-1091-4
ePub: 978-1-4725-0968-0

Library of Congress Cataloging-in-Publication Data
A catalog record for this book is available from the Library of Congress.

Series: Reflective Teaching

Typeset by Fakenham Prepress Solutions, Fakenham, Norfolk NR21 8NN
Printed and bound in Great Britain

readings for reflective teaching

in early education

Available and forthcoming titles in the *Reflective Teaching* series

Series Editors: Andrew Pollard and Amy Pollard

Reflective Teaching in Early Education, Jennifer Colwell et al.

Reflective Teaching in Further, Adult and Vocational Education, Margaret Gregson and Yvonne Hillier et al.

Readings for Reflective Teaching in Further, Adult and Vocational Education, edited by Margaret Gregson, Lawrence Nixon, Andrew Pollard and Trish Spedding

Reflective Teaching in Schools (4th edition), Andrew Pollard

Readings for Reflective Teaching in Schools (2nd edition), edited by Andrew Pollard

Reflective Teaching in Higher Education, Paul Ashwin et al.

To Jen's boys, Alex and Oscar, for their unwavering belief in her; and to Andrew's grandchildren, and others everywhere, in the hope that they will enjoy their learning.

Contents

Acknowledgements   xiii

A note on citation   xiv

Introduction   xv

Part one Becoming a reflective professional

1   Identity Who are we, and what do we stand for?   2

   1.1   Janet Moyles Passion, paradox and professionalism in early years
          education   4

   1.2   Avril Brock Perspectives on professionalism   8

   1.3   Lisa Spencer-Woodley Accountability: Tensions and challenges
          for the early years workforce   11

   1.4   Ruth Heilbron Practical judgement and evidence-informed practice   14

   1.5   Peter Moss Questioning the story of quality   17

   1.6   Sandra Mathers, Rosanna Singler and Arjette Karemaker
          Improving quality in the early years: A comparison of perspectives
          and measures   19

2   Learning How can we understand learner development?   22

   2.1   Burrhus Skinner The science of learning and the art of teaching   24

   2.2   Jean Piaget The genetic approach to the psychology of thought   28

   2.3   Lev Vygotsky Mind in society and the ZPD   32

   2.4   Jerome Bruner The spiral curriculum   35

   2.5   Carol Dweck Motivational processes affecting learning   37

3   Reflection How can we develop the quality of our practice?   40

3.1   **Jan Peeters and Michel Vandenbroeck** The role of reflection in the professionalization of the early years workforce   42

3.2   **Lawrence Stenhouse** The importance of practitioner research   44

3.3   **Richard Pring** Action research and the development of practice   46

3.4   **Denise Kingston and Jane Melvin** Measures of quality   49

3.5   **Donald Schön** Reflection-in-action   51

3.6   **John Dewey** Thinking and reflective experience   54

3.7   **Pete Watton, Jane Collings and Jenny Moon** Reflective writing   56

4   Principles What are the foundations of effective teaching and learning?   64

4.1   **Mandy Swann, Alison Peacock, Susan Hart and Mary Jane Drummond** Learning without limits   66

4.2   **Kathy Sylva, Edward Melhuish, Pam Sammons. Iram Siraj-Blatchford and Brenda Taggart** The Effective Provision of Pre-school Education (EPPE) project: Findings from pre-school to end of Key Stage 1.   70

4.3   **The Royal Society** Insights, opportunities and challenges of educational neuroscience   74

4.4   **Rodd Parker-Rees** Playful learning   79

4.5   **Cathy Nutbrown** Schemas and learning   81

Part two Creating conditions for learning

5   Contexts What is, and what might be?   86

5.1   **Qing Gu** Being an educator in times of change   88

5.2   **C. Wright Mills** The sociological imagination   91

5.3   **David Whitebread and Sue Bingham** Exploring the school readiness debate   93

5.4   **Andy Green and Jan Janmaat** Education, opportunity and social cohesion   96

5.5   **Stephen Ball** Schooling, social class and privilege   100

6 Relationships How are we getting on together?   104

6.1 **Maria Evangelou, Kathy Sylva, Maria Kyriacou, Mary Wild and Georgina Glenny** Early years learning and development literature review   106

6.2 **Carolynn Rankin and Fiona Butler** Working in teams   109

6.3 **Denis Lawrence** What is self-esteem?   114

6.4 **Sir Richard Bowlby** Attachment, what it is, why it is important?   118

6.5 **Jennifer Colwell** The role of the preschool practitioner in the development of children's social competencies   124

7 Engagement How are we managing behaviour?   128

7.1 **Ferre Laevers** Measuring involvement in the early years   130

7.2 **Pat Broadhead, Jane Johnston, Caroline Tobbell and Richard Woolley** Understanding children's behaviour in relation to their development   133

7.3 **Sonja Sheridan** Pedagogic quality and behaviour   138

7.4 **Michael Argyle** Non-verbal communication   141

7.5 **Michelle Graves and Ann Arbor** The HighScope approach to behaviour management   145

8 Spaces How are we creating environments for learning?   148

8.1 **Janet Moyles, Siân Adams and Alison Musgrove** The learning environment   150

8.2 **Marie Willoughby** The value of providing for risky play in early childhood settings   153

8.3 **Tim Loreman** Respectful environments for children   157

8.4 **Urie Bronfenbrenner** The 'ecology' of social environments   160

8.5 **Tim Waller** Digital technology and play   163

Part three Teaching for learning

9 Curriculum What is to be taught and learned?   168

9.1 **Tina Bruce, Anne Findlay, Jane Read and Mary Scarborough** Froebel's spirit and influence   170

9.2 **Sheila Nutkins, Catriona McDonald and Mary Stephen** The Reggio Emilia approach   173

9.3   **Marion O'Donnell** The Montessori approach   178
9.4   **Heiner Ullrich** Rudolf Steiner and the Waldorf Pre-School   181
9.5   **Sheila Nutkins, Catriona McDonald and Mary Stephen**
         HighScope   185
9.6   **Wendy Lee, Margaret Carr, Brenda Soutar and Linda
         Mitchell** The Te Whāriki approach   189

10 **Planning** How are we implementing the curriculum?   196
   10.1 **Lilan G. Katz** A developmental approach to the curriculum in the
            early years   198
   10.2 **Peter Moss** Listening to young children   203
   10.3 **Phil Jones** Assumptions about children and young people   207
   10.4 **Kathy Brodie** Curriculum planning   210
   10.5 **Trisha Lee** The wisdom of Vivian Paley   214

11 **Pedagogy** How can we develop effective strategies?   218
   11.1 **The General Teaching Council for England** What is pedagogy
            and why is it important?   220
   11.2 **Iram Siraj-Blatchford, Kathy Sylva, Stella Muttock, Rose
            Gilden and Danny Bell** Pedagogy in effective settings   223
   11.3 **Jerome Bruner** Folk pedagogy   227
   11.4 **Roland Tharp and Ronald Gallimore** Teaching as the assistance
            of performance   229

12 **Communication** How does language support learning?   234
   12.1 **Pat Broadhead** Interactions and social development   236
   12.2 **Julia Manning-Morton** Talking babies   238
   12.3 **Belinda Buckley** The role of the linguistic environment in early
            language development   242
   12.4 **Tözün Issa and Alison Hatt** The bilingual learner   245
   12.5 **Colin Harrison** Why is reading so important?   249
   12.6 **Sandra Smidt** Narrative in the lives of children   252

13 Assessment How can assessment enhance learning?   256
   13.1 Margy Whalley Creating a dialogue with parents   258
   13.2 Patricia Broadfoot Assessment: Why, who, when, what and how?   262
   13.3 Andrew Burrell and Sara Bubb Teacher feedback in the
   reception class   268
   13.4 Scottish Government Reporting on progress and achievement   271
   13.5 Andrew Pollard and Ann Filer The myth of objective assessment   275
   13.6 Cathy Nutbrown Watching and listening: The tools of assessment   281

Part four Reflecting on consequences

14 Outcomes How do we capture learning and achievements?   288
   14.1 Guy Claxton Learning and the development of resilience   290
   14.2 Jenny Willan Observing children   292
   14.3 Margaret Carr and Guy Claxton Learning dispositions and
   assessment   295
   14.4 Anette Emilson and Ingrid Pramling Samuelsson Observation
   and pedagogic documentation   300
   14.5 Jonathan Glazzard Involving parents and carers as partners in
   assessment   304

15 Inclusion How are we enabling learning opportunities?   308
   15.1 Anastasia Liasidou Defining inclusion   310
   15.2 Penny Borkett Supporting children with Special Educational
   Needs in the early years   313
   15.3 Gary Thomas and Andrew Loxley Difference or deviance?   316
   15.4 Jonathan Rix What's your attitude? Inclusion and early years
   settings   319

Part five Deepening understanding

16 Expertise Conceptual tools for career-long fascination   326
   16.1 Pat Collarbone Contemporary change and professional
   development   328
   16.2 Tony Eaude The development of teacher expertise   332

16.3 Marilyn Osborn, Elizabeth McNess, Andrew Pollard, Pat Triggs and Patricia Broadfoot Creative mediation and professional judgement   336

16.4 Iiris Happo and Kaarina Määttä The expertise of early childhood educators   340

17 Professionalism How does reflective teaching contribute to society?   344

17.1 Cathy Nutbrown Qualifications: The Nutbrown Review   346

17.2 Margaret Archer Thinking about educational systems   349

17.3 Frank Field The Field report: Preventing poor children becoming poor adults   351

17.4 Jones Irwin The philosophy of Paulo Freire   355

17.5 Tony Bertram and Chris Pascal The impact of early education as a strategy in countering socio-economic disadvantage   358

List of figures   363
Bibliography   365
Permissions   385
Index   391
The Reflective Teaching Series   399

Acknowledgements

The most important issue which editors face is: 'What should be included?' We have worried away at this, and imposed on a large number of people in exploring possible selections for various chapters.

In particular we would like to thank Eileen Smith and Angela Coffey for editorial support; Helen Beaumont, Helen Bradford, Julie Canavan, Denise Kingston, Holly Linklater, Sue Lynch, Catriona McDonald, Sheila Nutkins and Tim Waller for their advice and contributions to ***Reflective Teaching in Early Education***.

We would also like to thank all the publishers, editors and other publishers' representatives, both in the UK and overseas, who were kind enough to grant permission for material to be reprinted. Some provided exceptional levels of support in respect of multiple readings and in this respect we acknowledge the generosity of Routledge, Sage Publications Ltd and Bloomsbury itself. A listing for permissions for the reproduction of extracts is formally provided at the end of the book. Attempts to trace permission holders have been sustained, though a very few cases remain where replies to our enquiries have not yet been received. Any enquiries on such matters should be sent, in the first instance, to the Permissions Manager at Bloomsbury Academic.

Finally, we would like to thank all the authors whose work features in this book – and apologize to the many other researchers and educationists whose high-quality material does not! Some, of course, may be delighted to have escaped, for word-length constraints have occasionally forced detailed editing. We offer sincere apologies if any authors feel that their work has suffered in that process.

Having reviewed a wide range of publications for possible inclusion in the book, we remain enormously impressed by the richness of research and thinking which is available to practitioners; even with so many readings, it has not been possible to include all the excellent material which is available.

Jen Colwell and Andrew Pollard
February 2015

A note on citation

If wishing to quote from a reading within this book in coursework or for a publication, you will need to cite your source. Using the Harvard Convention and drawing only on this text, you should provide a bibliography containing details of the *original* source. These are provided in the introduction to each reading. You should then put: 'Cited in Colwell, J. and Pollard, A. (eds) (2015) *Readings for Reflective Teaching in Early Education.* London: Bloomsbury.

If you are building a substantial case around any reading, you are strongly recommended to go back to the original source and to check your argument against the full text. Sources will be available through the libraries of most colleges and universities and many are accessible online. If using hardcopy, you should then cite the full text only, with the specific page numbers of any material that you quote. If using an online resource, you should cite page numbers as appropriate and the date on which the site was accessed.

Introduction

This book is part of a set of professional resources. It links directly to a textbook, *Reflective Teaching in Early Education*, and to a website, **reflectiveteaching.co.uk**. They are part of a series with explicit provision for early years, schools, further, adult and higher education.

For early years education, we offer three fully integrated and complementary sources of materials:

- *Reflective Teaching in Early Education* (the core book for professional development)
- *Readings for Reflective Teaching in Early Education* (a portable library with readings linked to the core book)
- **reflectiveteaching.co.uk** (a website for supplementary, updated 'Notes for Further Reading', 'Reflective Activities', links, downloads, etc.)

Reflective Teaching in Early Education considers a very wide range of professionally relevant topics, presents key issues and research insights, suggests 'Reflective Activities' for supporting professional development, and offers notes for selected 'Key Readings'.

Readings for Reflective Teaching in Early Education provides a combination of classic and contemporary readings to support professional development. It will be useful both for those reading to extend their knowledge base and for those writing assignments at undergraduate and postgraduate levels.

reflectiveteaching.co.uk is a website supplementing the two books. For example, there are materials on how to design and carry out practitioner research and classwork-based enquiry as part of professional development. The web enables the Editorial Board to update material regularly – for example, links to recent policy developments can be easily located. There is also a glossary of terms and additional Reflective Activities, download facilities for diagrams and supplementary resources of various kinds, including observation and planning templates. The section on *Deepening Expertise* offers access to more advanced features, including a framework linking research evidence to powerful concepts for the analysis of classroom practice.

Three major aims have guided the production of *Readings for Reflective Teaching in Early Education*.

First, it is intended as a resource for busy practitioners, mentors and students who appreciate the value of educational thinking and research, and who wish to have easy access to key parts of important publications. We have drawn on a range of sources, books, journals, reports and speeches to provide 88 different readings, which provide examples of different ways of presenting information. We hope this will support those of you studying and looking to develop your own writing skills.

Second, the book provides an opportunity to showcase some of the excellent educational research from across the world which, in recent years, has been accumulating clear messages about high-quality teaching and learning. Readers may then wish to consult the full accounts in the original sources, each of which is carefully referenced.

Finally, these materials provide a unique resource for professional development activities and for those studying. The structure of the three sources is identical, so that the chapters map across from one book to the other and to the web. Thus, whether used in staff development activities, private study, mentoring conversations, workshops, staff meetings, seminars or research projects, the materials should be easily accessible. The readings both complement and expand upon the chapters in *Reflective Teaching in Early Education*.

Reflective activity is of vital importance to the teaching profession:

- It underpins professional judgement and its use for worthwhile educational purposes.
- It provides a vehicle for learning and professional renewal – and thus for promoting the independence and integrity of practitioners.
- Above all, it is a means to the improvement of teaching, the enhancement of learning and the steady growth in standards of performance for both schools and national education systems.

We hope that you will find these materials helpful in your professional work and as you seek personal fulfilment as an early years practitioner.

Jen Colwell and Andrew Pollard
February 2015

part one

Becoming a reflective professional

1 **Identity** Who are we, and what do we stand for?

2 **Learning** How can we understand learner development?

3 **Reflection** How can we develop the quality of our practice?

4 **Principles** What are the foundations of effective teaching and learning?

Identity
Who are we, and what do we stand for?

1

Readings

1.1 Janet Moyles
Passion, paradox and professionalism in early years education (p. 4)

1.2 Avril Brock
Perspectives on professionalism (p. 8)

1.3 Lisa Spencer-Woodley
Accountability: Tensions and challenges for the early years workforce (p. 11)

1.4 Ruth Heilbronn
Practical judgement and evidence-informed practice (p. 14)

1.5 Peter Moss
Questioning the story of quality (p. 17)

1.6 Sandra Mathers, Rosanna Singler and Arjette Karemaker
Improving quality in the early years: A comparison of perspectives and measures (p. 19)

The readings in this chapter assert the significance of values, perspectives and identities of early years practitioners. We see how social expectations and contemporary change – particularly the ways in which the early years and the role of the workforce are perceived in society – impact upon practitioners.

We focus on the 'professionalization' of the workforce and how the workforce is recognized as having a crucial role to play in society. We also see, however, that we must not blindly accept that which is stated by governments, policy-makers and academics and that ultimately, given the varied needs and requirements being placed upon those working within the sector, we will have to make justifiable judgements and draw upon evidence to inform our practice.

The parallel chapter in *Reflective Teaching in Early Education* is structured in a similar way – considering what it is to be an early years practitioner and the significance of the contribution early years practitioners can make to the lives of children and their families. The importance of knowing ourselves to gain an understanding of the influences on our practice also forms a key part of the chapter.

reflectiveteaching.co.uk offers notes for further reading on these issues, as well as additional reflective activities, resources and suggestions for 'deepening expertise'.

Reading 1.1

Passion, paradox and professionalism in early years education

Janet Moyles

Our first reading, taken from a paper by Janet Moyles, reminds us of the passion many early years practitioners bring to their role and contrasts this with the expectations placed upon practitioners to be professional.

Does this resonate with how you feel about your role?

Edited from: Moyles, J. (2001) 'Passion, paradox and professionalism in early years education', *Early Years: An International Research Journal,* 21 (2), 81–95.

Each of the three 'p' words—passion, paradox and professionalism—will be explored in this paper, together with their unique and often inter-related characteristics in the education of children under the age of 7 years. Throughout the article, early years educators will be referred to as 'practitioners', in order to reflect the diverse backgrounds of those who work and play in the early years.

P is for passion

Research into early years and primary teaching has shown that those who teach this age group often express a 'passion' for their role and for children which it is perhaps difficult for those in other phases of education to understand. Various research teams and individuals have written of teachers who 'love' teaching and who find teaching 'worthwhile and rewarding' because of the children, their spontaneity and the sheer joy of working in a job which brings them so close to children, families and communities (e.g. Woods, 1996; Woods and Jeffrey, 1996; Pollard and Filer, 1999; Pollard and Thiessen, 1996; Galton et al., 1999; Nias, 1989; Saltzberger-Wittenberg et al., 1983).

Disraeli (1804–81) suggested that 'Man (sic) is only truly great when he acts from the passions'. The Oxford English Dictionary suggests that to be passionate is to be 'dominated by strong feelings' or 'having strong enthusiasm' and to possess 'intense love', 'devotion', 'warmth', 'fervor' and even 'anger'. Most people who are 'work enthusiasts' become, by this definition, passionate about what they do: this passion is part of the nature of professionalism within and outside education and, as such, is continuously challenged within the current climate of accountability, particularly in the public sector.

In the early years the link between effective and affective dimensions has become an accepted part of the practitioner's role, as responses to interview questions concerning the comparative roles of Key Stage 1 (KS1) teachers and classroom assistants and nursery teachers and nursery nurses evidenced (Moyles and Suschitzky, 1997a, b):

- We want [to employ] the right people for the children, such as those who've been childminders. (Head)
- We must accept that these people primarily work for the kick they get from the job. (Head)
- Let's face it, I do this job because I love young children … the way they make you laugh and everything. You certainly wouldn't do it for the money would you? (Teacher)
- I really find working with young children worthwhile and so rewarding … they are so trusting and responsive. (Nursery Nurse)

To be an early years practitioner carries the expectation that you will like all of the children all of the time and respond to them as unique individuals: in this way, operating from the emotions is positively expected by society (Drury et al., 2000). It is hard to imagine how one could deal with the behaviours, reactions and idiosyncrasies of young children day-in-and-day-out by dealing only with lesson planning, curriculum delivery and outcome measures. With very young children, the expression 'You can take a horse to water but you can't make it drink' takes on a whole new dimension, as anyone will know who has tried to 'persuade' young children to do something they do not particularly want to do! The very nature of the work demands strong feelings towards both protecting and supporting young children and engaging empathetically with these wider family and community aspects of the child's life (Katz, 1995).

Contemporary research is increasingly establishing that feelings and emotions such as passion are acceptable, and indeed desirable, as part of educational thinking and practice. A few examples include:

- Paolo Freire (1999) whose work generates a powerful vision for education which capitalises on the very nature of humanity and emotions (the book is even called *Pedagogy of the Heart*);
- Guy Claxton (1999) writes of the importance of 'intuitive practice'. It is known that teaching demands rapid decision-making, immediate apprehension and the use of familiar behavioural patterns in order to respond to the sheer wealth of incoming information from whole classes of learners.
- Daniel Goleman (1996) produced work about 'emotional intelligence' which has prompted greater acknowledgement and understanding of thinking based in the emotions as a vital component of all human relationships and learning.
- Steinberg and Kincheloe (1998: 228) report on research into students' responses to analysing their experiences which found that 'Little … learning takes place until … our passions are engaged [and] … intellect, academic knowledge and personal experience are brought together. At this point of intersection pedagogical magic takes place—the kind of magic that produces genius, that keeps the romance of teaching alive for great teachers'.

The message from these and many other writers is that passion is never MINDLESS, but rather very mindful. To operate emotionally at a mindful level equates with significant deep level, higher-order thinking. Mindful passion also brings its own controls, concerns and conflicts.

P is for paradox

Practitioners' culture of passion can also carry associations with being anti-intellectual, idealistic, subjective, indecisive and 'feminine' (see, e.g. Stone, 1994; Yelland, 1998). It can be thought that allowing the heart to rule the head diminishes objectivity and logic, yet, paradoxically, a main characteristic of the role of early years practitioners is their ability to handle a range of events, and sometimes potential crises, in a clear-headed, rational way. Working 'not rationally but paradoxically' (Farson, 1996: 7) can, then, be a positive strength.

Heart and head can operate in tandem and, indeed, a main argument in dealing with young children is that they must if practitioners are to care sufficiently to do the job well (Anning and Edwards, 1999). What we should expect is that practitioners will reflect upon and evaluate both their role and their responses to it and to the children in their settings (Eraut, 1994) and feel professional (McCulloch et al., 2000). Instead, what has been increasingly happening is that, on the one hand, practitioners appear to feel they are regularly criticized for female caring roles inclining them towards 'non-professional' and 'woolly' thinking and, on the other hand, they are constantly urged to take on many of the perceived ills of society (e.g. low income families), high level assessments of children's existing and potential capabilities, work with a wide range of other people, for low salaries and within a context which they feel is antithetical to their role in educating and caring for small people.

Little wonder that practitioners feel a range of emotions against an education and political system which appears to demand they be all things to all people.

P for professionalism

The Oxford English Dictionary offers several definitions of 'profession': vocation/calling involving advanced learning/science; body of people thus engaged; and of 'professional': having or showing skills of a profession; worthy. These are exemplified in descriptions of being 'professional' by practitioners and early years employers (which arose in several projects) thus:

- I am a professional—conscientious and experienced. (Nursery Nurse)
- Any differences in training are equalized, in professional terms, by experience. (Nursery Teacher)
- We want people whom we can treat like teachers, who can speak knowledgeably about children. (Headteacher)
- Gosh, we're professionals here—we should know about learning! (Teacher)

There are indications here that 'professionalism' is related to thinking about the facets of one's role rather than a more proletarian view of teaching potentially espoused in prescribed educational practices (Furlong, 1999). The danger with thought is that it challenges—and not only those doing the thinking! It challenges the very nature of prescription in education (Kompf et al., 1996; Parker, 1997), but it requires high levels of professional knowledge coupled with self-esteem and self-confidence, paradoxically lacking in many early years, female, practitioners. Female practitioners are often convinced that what is 'inside' them is not valid, 'only personal' (Dadds, 1997: 31) and equated with emotional responses. They frequently perceive themselves as powerless against (often male) 'authority' (Noddings, 1994). Partly because of insecurity about professional status—after all, everyone has been a young child and therefore knows about young children!—many practitioners have learned to feel that others' visions and experiences are somehow better than their own, mindful responses.

Reading 1.2

Perspectives on professionalism
Avril Brock

In the following piece, Avril Brock considers what professionalism is, and what the
'professionalization' of the early years workforce means for practitioners in the day-to-
day. She notes how practitioners must have a voice in current debates about their role
and thus be in a position to shape policy.

Do you consider yourself to be professional? What does this mean for you?

Edited from: Brock, A. (2011) 'Perspectives on Professionalism'. In A. Brock and C. Ranken
(eds) *Professionalism in the Interdisciplinary Early Years Team.* London: Continuum, 60–5.

Professionalism has been a contentious issue for many professions during the last quarter
of a century. This debate has merited the attention of several disciplines – sociology,
philosophy, history, management and education. It is recognized as a complex changing
phenomenon located in specific cultural and historical situations (Friedson, 1994, 2001).
It 'defies common agreement as to its meaning' despite widespread use of the term
'professionalism' in the media and everyday discourse (Hoyle and John, 1995: 1). This
lack of consensus occurs because its use varies both pragmatically and conceptually
within a complex society, and there has been much debate about what constitutes 'the
professions' and how they should be defined. To 'professionalize' is to make an occupation
a profession. Does this imply that with the right conditions, any occupation could become
a profession?

Occupations seek recognition as professions, as this should lead to enhanced esteem,
status, remuneration and power. So it is important in contemporary society for occupations
to be established as professions, as there are implications for both career and personal
success.

The terms 'profession' and 'professional' are often applied to a variety of occupations
'with elusive and continual reinterpretation of the concepts' (Helsby, 1996: 135). To 'be
a professional' is a phrase often in use in the contemporary workplace and may relate
to competence and punctiliousness. Professionalism can be 'attitudinal' – there may be
professional and unprofessional garage mechanics, just as there are professional and
unprofessional teachers, lawyers and doctors. Professionalism is related to proficiency –
the knowledge, skill, competence or character of a highly trained individual, as opposed to
one of amateur status or capability. There is a distinction between 'being a professional',
which includes issues of pay, status, reward and public recognition, and 'behaving professionally', which implies dedication, commitment, standards of behaviour and a strong
service ethic. Components of pay, recognition and reward depict 'professionalization',
while characteristics of ethics, standards and commitment represent 'professionalism'

(Osgood, 2006). A definition of professionalism is complex; for Friedman (2007: 126) it is 'like a ball of knotted string' and in 'order to untangle the string, all of the other knots must be opened'. The next sections of this chapter attempt to unravel some of the complicated knots through examining the varied definitions, perspectives, dimensions and traits of professionalism.

Challenges to professionalization

Many occupational groups have faced challenges to their authority, legitimacy and inevitably their professionalization. Those already deemed to be 'professionals' resist attempts by others, whom they might deem to be less qualified, to join their high status 'fellowship'.

Traditionally professions have been a group of prestigious occupations with particular ideologies and identified by education, professional training and status. The three historically 'learned' professions of medicine, law and the clergy originated at European medieval universities and had an elite, gentlemanly status (Friedson, 1994). These origins gave rise to political influence and an economic elite in relation to the market and class system. Since the Second World War and the shift to mass education in universities, the range of careers demanding professional status increased to include accountants, veterinary surgeons and architects (Bacon et al., 2000). However, there has been an ongoing and complex struggle by some contemporary professionals to negotiate their professional status with employers, governments, administrators and other professionals, clients and the general public (Frost, 2001). Engineers, pharmacists, social workers, schoolteachers and librarians were among those who have struggled to gain status as professionals. This has also been the case for the various 'professions' within the health service – occupational therapists, physiotherapists and nurses who have all fought to 'professionalize' and gain public recognition. The challenges for professionalization have been particularly contentious for the caring professions of education, nursing and social work, where there is still a greater concentration of women. The main challenges for professionals have come from the government through reorganization, decreased autonomy, increased bureaucracy, financial controls and target setting.

According to Friedson (2001) there is a tension between government that tends to be concerned with efficiency and professionals who care mainly about providing the highest-quality service. He explores the concept of professionalism as a form of social organization where workers can organize and control their knowledge and service more freely without directives from management, as state policy often undermines the individual professional institutions. In Perkin's (2002) opinion the questioning of the status of the professions in England was concurrent with the growth of the welfare state. There was contention as the professions argued for the importance of their distinct, specialist knowledge and expertise, but their 'self-protective autonomy' was perceived by the state as their having too much power without sufficient accountability. Perkin believes there are new conceptions of professionalism developing through openness between the professions and government that create a balance between autonomy and accountability. Is this different for the diverse professions – do educators, health workers and social workers believe that they have their professional attributes recognized and their needs met?

The voices of professionals

Professionals working with young children should have a voice in shaping policy with their expertise and knowledge sought and respected. The voices of those working in the field therefore need to be elicited to create a fuller definition of professionalism. Definitions of professionalism may vary between policymakers and practitioners as they inhabit different spheres. It is therefore important that the voices of the diverse professionals are elicited for *their* perspectives on their professionalism. Any definition of professionalism should include the experiences and views of the professionals themselves to determine the qualities, dimensions and scope of professional practice to improve *being* professional (Osgood, 2006). There is therefore a need for a further analysis of the discourse of professionalism to be constructed and reconstructed within professional occupational groups (Evetts, 2009) and attempt to establish common threads that will unify their professionalism in their collective and collaborative teamwork with young children; even though their knowledge, skills and values may differ.

Reading 1.3

Accountability: Tensions and challenges for the early years workforce

Lisa Spencer-Woodley

In the piece which follows, Lisa Spencer-Woodley considers some of the factors which influence one of the drives of professionalization: accountability.

Edited from: Spencer-Woodley, L. (2014) 'Accountability: Tensions and challenges'. In Z. Kingdon and J. Gourd (eds) *Early Years Policy: The Impact on Practice.* Oxon: Routledge, 33–5.

Recognition for the early years sector

Practitioners, researchers and writers in the early years sector have argued for the sector and early years practitioners to get equal recognition of the importance of early years practice for children, and their families and carers, as schools do. However, in calling for this recognition there is a risk of mirroring the 'de-professionalisation' (Beck, 2008; Schön, 1983) experienced by teachers over the past 40 years.

Moss (2008: 122) asks:

why does British society seem to take for granted that work with young children (but also, at the other end of life, elderly people) should largely depend on poorly qualified workers earning, on average, not much above the minimum wage?

He suggests four reasons:

- That children are seen as 'incomplete human beings', and as such 'simple formulas' can be applied to their development.

- That 'care' work is perceived as largely the, biologically essentialist, natural role of women, and therefore is not in need of payment or practice development.

- The increase in private provision as a result of neoliberal, free-market ideologies has led to a competitive wage minimisation.

- Early childhood is viewed by the State in a 'positivistic paradigm', which simply 'calls for technicians trained in the right answers' (ibid.).

In arguing for more recognition of the importance of early years practice, it is therefore imperative that it is clear what is meant by 'recognition', and if this does include a focus on professionalisation, that the ideological and epistemological perspectives are also clear and transparent.

Questioning 'accountability'?

The perspective I put forward here is not one that questions whether the, at least more historical, concept of accountability is good or bad; after all, as Strathern (2000: 3) points out, '[a]s an instrument of accountability … audit is almost impossible to criticise in principle – after all, it advances values that academics generally hold dear, such as responsibility, openness about outcomes and widening of access'.

Indeed, one of my deeply held values is that I am accountable to the very people with whom I work; not because they are the tax-paying public, but rather because they are deserving of a service that is of benefit to them.

This is also not an account that suggests who early years workers should be accountable to, although my position I think will be explicit; rather, this is a recognition and analysis of the ideological positions and their associated discourses, and an exploration of ways in which early years practitioners might be able to survive within their living contradictions; to meet externally imposed requirements, alongside accountability to their own values and to those for whom they provide an important service.

It is the current State-imposed construction of accountability that I critique. The discourse of successive neoliberal governments, that those who through their professional practice 'spend' taxpayers money must be accountable for 'their' spending, has its deep roots in a particular ideological position. A new social construction, or culture of accountability as a meeting of 'financial and moral' (ibid.: 2) requirements, has meant that accountability to the State and taxpayer takes primacy over accountability to the people who use the services provided. For example, the Measuring Outcomes for Public Service Users (MOPSU) three-year government project, while in its title giving primacy to service users, had as its core aim to 'inform value for money decisions by developing new, and examining existing, measures of outcomes' (ONS, 2010). This project included a research focus on early years, the final report of which states that, 'Underpinning the project is the idea that value for money should determine who delivers public services' (Hopkin et al., 2010).

Deferring to one's own value base is important in being held accountable. State-imposed accountability justifies the use of taxpayers' money. As Biesta states:

> 'Value for money' has become a guiding principle in the transactions between the state and its taxpayers. This way of thinking is at the basis of the emergence of a culture of accountability that has resulted in tight systems of inspection and control and ever more prescriptive educational protocols.' (2006: 19)

Professional practice becomes open to scrutiny by the State on behalf of those who pay tax to the State and therefore the very parameters by which society judges professional practice becomes constructed by the State:

> These policies – performativity, privatisation and a move from government to government – do not just change the way teachers work and how they are employed and paid, they also change who they are, how we judge them and how we define a good teacher. (Ball, 2008: 50)

Ideology becomes absorbed into the everyday language of current service providers (Vincent, 2011) and thus professional accountability becomes common sense (Beck, 2008) and hegemonic (Vincent, 2011). Biesta (2009) argues that the common-sense view of what education is actually for, as academic achievement in language, science and mathematics, is relied on as an explanation because of an 'absence of explicit attention'. While there is, relative to before the last 15 or so years, a plethora of attention in early years, this attention has been focused, unsurprisingly given the neoliberal ideology, on developing evidence based practice within a modernist, positivistic, scientific paradigm, and holds a methodological fundamentalist position that gives absolute primacy to randomised experiments (House, 2005), and is itself in danger of becoming hegemonic (Smith, 2008). The notion of value for money through accountability to the State and the notion that the benchmarks that 'value' is measured against are evidence based through modernist methods, both become a 'common sense'. It is so 'common sense' that it is 'forgotten' that ideology, which is contestable and questionable, underlies it. As Vincent (2011: 336) argues, 'this can, in some contexts, be a profoundly menacing form of ideology since it masquerades as the only acceptable reality and pervades deeply into human lives, being largely unquestioned'.

Common-sense ideas and practices that have developed from ideological positions are clearly embedded within power structures that serve the interests of particular groups of people (Biesta, 2009). As much as the proponents of modernist, positivist, scientific research would argue for the objectiveness of the randomised experimental approach, post-structural, post-modern and some critical theorists, researchers, writers and practitioners have argued for multiple truths and interpretive approaches to research. The Foucaultian notion of a 'regime of truth' is useful here. A regime of truth is where truths that 'naturalise existing regimes of power' (MacNaughton, 2005: 20), where the powerful maintain what truth is (Atkinson, 2003) and where discourse 'frame[s] how we think, feel, understand and practice' (MacNaughton, 2005: 20). The discourse of saving taxpayers' money, based on practices that prepare children to become 'economically viable units' that put in to, as opposed to take out from, the State informs a highly powerful regime of truth. This is based on the 'truth' that, within the current global economic climate, this is the only option.

Reading 1.4

Practical judgement and evidence-informed practice

Ruth Heilbronn

> This reading explains the deep roots of 'practical judgement' in Aristotle's philosophy and thus confirms the enduring qualities which are required in combining experience and analysis in practical contexts. For, as we have seen in the previous readings, there are a number of expectations placed upon practitioners by different groups; thus judgements regarding practice and provision will need to be made.
>
> Heilbronn identifies three dimensions of practical judgement: ethical; flexibility; personal rootedness. In this way she affirms that teaching has moral purposes which always require personal judgement from the person who is the teacher. This is what makes it so interesting, and such a responsibility.
>
> What forms of evidence could help you in making practical judgements?
>
> *Edited from:* Heilbronn, R. (2011) 'The Nature of Practice-based Knowledge and Understanding'. In R. Heilbronn and J. Yandell (eds) *Critical Practice in Teacher Education: A Study of Professional Learning.* London: IOE Press, 7–9.

Practical judgement might be characterized as a capacity 'to do the right thing at the right time': to respond flexibly and appropriately in particular situations, whose unique correlation of variables could not be known in advance. Training for professional practice is designed to enable such expert decision making and action.

The concept of 'practical judgement' goes back to Aristotle's' concept of *phronesis*. Although this rich notion has been interpreted in a variety of ways, a relevant understanding for teachers is found in Dunne's statement that *phronesis* is: 'an *eye* for what is salient in concrete situations' (Dunne, 1993: 368). Expert practitioners know what to do in specific situations. They have what seems to be 'an intuitive sense of the nature and texture of practical engagement' (Dunne, 1993: 8).

> Phronesis does not ascend to a level of abstraction or generality that leaves experience behind. It arises from experience *and returns into experience.* It is, we might say, the insightfulness – or using Aristotle's own metaphor, 'the eye' – of a particular type of experience, and the insights it achieves are turned back into experience, which is in this way constantly reconstructed or enriched. And the more experience is reconstructed in this way, the more sensitive and insightful phronesis becomes. (Dunne, 1993: 293)

In the above quotation the key term is 'experience'. There can be no split between elements encountered in reading, research, university and schools, because these elements make no sense, have no meaning, bear no significance to the practitioner, until and unless they are integrated and able to be applied. Understanding develops through the practical situations in which novices are placed, and with which they grapple. This is true for many kinds of workplaces, where novices may be changed by experience into highly proficient practitioners (Hogan, 2003).

It is possible to outline some characteristics of practical judgement in three main dimensions.

First, there is an ethical dimension to 'the right' response. Professional practices have their codes of ethics and it is expected that practitioners follow these codes and uphold the values of the profession. If we try to think of an example of practitioner action that seems 'value free' we soon give up the attempt. Teaching, nursing, social work, are thoroughly relational practices. They have 'the other', the client, the learner, the patient, whose welfare is inextricably linked to choices and actions. So the right action at any time needs to draw on ethical considerations: a good practitioner will be someone whose actions we can trust as 'wise' or 'judicious'. In acting seemingly spontaneously practitioners draw on their own values, qualities and dispositions, as well as on technical know-how and information based on previous, relevant experiences.

Having professional values and living by them in practice are an essential part of being a practitioner involved with others. The capacity for trustworthiness is fundamental to teaching. The practice of teaching involves the ability to see things from the learners' perspective, to show 'pedagogical thoughtfulness' (van Manen, 1991) and to make adjustments accordingly. Van Manen has described 'tactful' teaching, as that which 'locates practical knowledge not primarily in the intellect or the head but rather in the existential situation in which the person finds himself or herself' (van Manen, 1995: 45–6).

Practical judgement is connected to 'virtue', in the sense that such a practitioner exercises qualities of 'practical wisdom'. A good teacher could be said to be a wise person, someone who exercises an ethical sense of doing what is right, of acting for the good. An example would be a teacher who rejects a strategy for gaining order in the classroom which would involve humiliating pupils, in favour of another, involving more effort based on developing trusting relationships. As Smith (2003) has stated, the importance of relationships between pupils, and between them and their teacher cannot be over-emphasised. Teaching is 'thoroughly relational' (Noddings, 2003: 249) and many of the virtues are exercised in relation to others in a pedagogical space of trust (van Manen, 1991).

A second dimension of practical judgement is its flexibility. Expert practitioners can respond flexibly to changing situations. We cannot know in advance what individual situations will throw up in the way of stimuli requiring response. Experts respond flexibly. Since there cannot be a definitive, right way to respond in every circumstance, it follows that any expert response might not be the best one for the circumstance. Therefore, reflecting on practice, interrogating aims, purposes and outcomes of particular choices in particular situations, can be a fruitful source of knowledge and understanding, and can support the development of practical judgement. It follows too that there can be no universally applicable, infallible theory or pedagogical intervention, given the contingency of individual situations of practice. This is significant if there are government promoted pedagogical strategies and educational changes and control over the school curriculum.

A third feature of judgement is its rootedness within an individual person, with a particular character, dispositions and qualities. When a teacher decides what is to be done in any situation, for example with a recalcitrant pupil, even if her decisions seem intuitive they are informed by the teacher's prior experiences and values. There is always more than one available course of action and individual teachers make choices of what they consider the right action in the circumstances. These choices may be based on a number of different factors, involving practical and ethical considerations. A teacher's character, dispositions and capacities underlie the exercise of practical judgement.

Good teachers can be said to exercise sound practical judgement, which involves exercising virtues such as justice, tolerance and courage, and qualities such as patience and optimism. We think of good teachers as acting with integrity and trustworthiness, being open-minded and able to learn from experience. It is an interesting exercise to think of all the qualities required, desired and expected, an exercise fruitfully revisited at various points in a teaching career (Burbules, 1997).

Reading 1.5

Questioning the story of quality

Peter Moss

> In the reading which follows, Peter Moss reminds us that we must question the rhetoric put to us by governments, politicians and academics; that education can lose its potential for wonder and joy if we focus on outcomes; and ultimately, that practitioners must be involved in the debate offering other ways of thinking. To do this one must be able to reflect upon personal beliefs, the beliefs of others, practice and policy.
>
> *Edited from:* Moss, P. (2014) *Transformative Change and Real Utopias in Early Childhood Education: A Story of Democracy, Experimentation and Potentiality.* London: Routledge, 4–5.

From local beginnings, emerging from a particular spatial and temporal context, to be precise from the English-speaking world in the 1980s, the story of quality and high returns has been borne far and wide by the economic zeitgeist, positivistic science and the English language. It has crossed borders and gained international credibility in a process of hegemonic globalisation, 'the successful globalisation of a particular local and culturally-specific discourse to the point that it makes universal truth claims and "localises" all rival discourses' (Santos, 2004: 149). A local story has gone viral, become an international best seller. Now all sorts of people, from politicians to practitioners, academics to media commentators, talk the same talk around the world, telling themselves and others the same story over and over and over again. So this discourse, this story of quality and high returns, has abandoned its local roots, forgotten it is just another local tale, claiming instead to tell a universal truth as if its way of talking about things is natural, neutral and necessary. In so doing, the story drowns out other stories about early childhood education, alternative ways of making meaning of the world, rendering them unimaginable and unspeakable, limiting what it is possible to think. Whether in high profile research reviews, official reports or conference presentations, certain privileged voices are heard time and again re-iterating the story. while other voices telling other stories are heard not at all or only faintly. This, much-told story has made some things familiar and others strange, whilst stifling critical thinking and questioning by its pretensions to being self-evident, proven and undeniable. I am troubled, therefore, by the way this story, of quality and high returns, marginalises other story-telling about early childhood education, striving to impose DONA – a 'dictatorship of no alternatives' (Unger, 2005a: 1) – on early childhood education. (DONA is the first cousin of TINA – 'there is no alternative' – much beloved of Margaret Thatcher and other politicians when seeking to impose their views, rubbish those of others and head off democratic debate.) But I am troubled in other ways. The story seems to me incredible: which would not matter since magic realism has its place in story-telling, only the story tellers insist they tell objective truth, that they really do have the one right answer, and others act on this claim. Nor do I like the politics that pervades the story, expressed in the answers it assumes or espouses to the political questions that define education. Last but not least, I fear its consequences, arising from the will to control and govern children and adults alike that is inscribed in the story.

But I am not only troubled. I am left deeply unsatisfied by the story itself and the way it is told; by its lack of curiosity, imagination and originality; by its instrumental rationality and reductionist logic that eschews complexity and context; and by the banality and dullness of its language. Told repeatedly, the story of quality and high returns has drained education of its potential to amaze and surprise, to invoke wonder and passion, to emancipate and experiment, leaving instead a lifeless husk of facile repetition and clichéd vocabulary: 'evidence-based'…'programmes'…'quality'…'investment'…'outcomes'… 'returns'…'assessment scales'…'human capital'. This is a story told in the desiccated language of the managerial memo, the technical manual and the financial balance sheet. Not to put too fine a point on it, the story of quality and high returns dulls and deadens the spirit, reducing the potentially exciting and vibrant subject of early childhood education to 'a one-dimensional linear reductive thinking that *excludes and closes off* all other ways of thinking and doing' (Lenz Taguchi, 2010a: 17; original emphasis).

Reading 1.6

Improving quality in the early years: A comparison of perspectives and measures

Sandra Mathers, Rosanna Singler and Arjette Karemaker

We noted in *Reflective Teaching in Early Education* that what constitutes high-quality provision can vary between different stakeholders: parents or providers, for example. In this summary of research findings Sandra Mathers, Rosanna Singler and Arjette Karemaker note how different stakeholders perceive quality and how quality can be measured.

Do you rely on Ofsted inspections for quality measures? Do you undertake other quality measures? Do you find different stakeholder groups note different strengths and challenges facing your setting? How useful is it to reflect upon any differences of opinion? Where they stem from? What different individuals want and/or expect from ECEC?

Edited from: Mathers, S., Singler, R. and Karemaker, A. (2012) *Improving Quality in the Early Years: A Comparison of Perspectives and Measures. Final Report.* London: Daycare Trust and Oxford: University of Oxford. Research funded by the Nuffield Foundation, 85–8.

The quality of early education and care matters, not only because it affects the everyday experiences of children but because the benefits are only realised if the provision used is high quality (Peisner-Feinberg and Burchinal, 1997; NICHD, 2000; Sylva et al., 2008). To achieve this, effective tools are needed to help different stakeholder groups identify high quality provision, and support them in improving it:

- Parents need tools to help them to select high quality providers for their children, and drive quality improvement through market forces;

- Providers need effective tools to identify their own strengths and possible areas for development, in order to improve the quality of provision offered to children;

- Local authorities need to be able to prioritise funding, support and training using evidence based decisions, and to encourage providers in quality improvement; and

- Policy-makers in central government need to be able to identify where investment is needed to improve outcomes for young children.

A number of measures exist for assessing quality, many of them validated by research as capturing elements of quality which are predictive of improved child outcomes (e.g. Sylva et al., 2004; Harms, Clifford and Cryer, 2005; Pianta, La Paro and Hamre, 2007). However, the fact that a measure captures quality effectively does not guarantee that it will be a practical and usable tool for quality improvement. Likewise, tools which are accessible and easy to use may not necessarily have been validated by research. This study, funded by the Nuffield Foundation, set out to consider some of these issues and explore three well-known measures used:

- The inspection reports of the regulatory body Ofsted (Office for Standards in Education, Children's Services and Skills);
- The Environment Rating Scales (ECERS-R, ECERS-E and ITERS-R); and
- Quality assurance schemes.

Our starting point for considering these different measures was that each stakeholder group should have access to tools which:

- capture elements of quality shown to be predictive of children's outcomes;
- reflect a definition of quality which they value and recognise; and
- are accessible and usable.

This study focused on the first three stakeholder groups (parents, providers and local authorities) but is also intended to inform and guide policy-makers at national level. Where we refer to parents, providers and local authority staff, we are referring to those who took part in this study. A summary of two of the key findings is provided below.

Key finding 1: How do the different stakeholders perceive quality in early years education and care?

Stakeholders primarily valued what we might call 'process quality', defined as 'actual experiences that occur in [early years settings] including children's interaction with caregivers and peers and their participation in different activities' (Vandell and Wolfe, 2000):

- The quality of the staff team was seen as the most important factor in determining quality of provision.
- Stakeholders agreed that practitioners need to be able to meet children's social, emotional and developmental needs, and have a good understanding of child development.
- All three stakeholder groups recognised the importance of engaging with parents, and involving them as partners in their children's learning.

In relation to the more structural aspects of provision, differences between the three stakeholder groups were more evident, with their emphasis varying according to specific priorities, roles and knowledge:

- Providers and local authorities, with their deeper understanding of the aspects which lead to high quality provision, were more likely to mention dimensions such as training and qualifications, and the importance of leadership and management.
- Parents were more likely than providers to list structural aspects such as health, safety and supervision as essential components of quality.
- In many cases, stakeholders differed less in their concepts of quality than in the

ways in which these were articulated. Different understandings were particularly evident in the use of the word 'education' as it relates to early years, with parents tending to equate this with a rigid and 'school-like' approach.

Key finding 2: To what extent do the concepts of quality embodied in the measures considered here align with stakeholder perceptions of quality?

Our research focused primarily on Ofsted and ECERS/ITERS. Both these approaches consider the extent to which settings provide for children's social, emotional and cognitive needs, and therefore align strongly with stakeholder perceptions of quality. Both also cover 'structural' aspects of provision such as the quality of the physical environment, and the extent to which providers meet basic welfare requirements such as health, safety and supervision.

The key differences between the two approaches, and their alignment with stakeholder perceptions of quality, relate to their differing purposes. Neither tool completely fulfilled all the requirements set out by stakeholders for identifying quality; rather, they were complementary:

While ECERS and ITERS have a more explicit focus on the observations of 'process quality', valued highly by all stakeholders, Ofsted inspectors cover a broader range of dimensions and therefore spend less time directly observing practice. Stakeholders agreed that Ofsted inspections could not fully capture the depth of information needed to reflect all elements of quality they valued, particularly complex aspects such as staff-child interactions.

However the broader focus of Ofsted encompasses setting-level dimensions valued by providers and local authority staff but not covered by ECERS/ITERS (e.g. the effectiveness of leadership, management and self-evaluation).

Parents valued the ability of providers to help their children progress and achieve 'key milestones'. While Ofsted has an explicit focus on children's outcomes, ECERS and ITERS consider the extent to which settings provide effectively for children, assessing key aspects shown by research to lead to improved child outcomes.

Our findings highlight the limitations of any evaluation completed at one time-point (whether Ofsted, or an external ECERS/ITERS audit) in providing a rich and complete picture of quality. Providers and local authorities said this required regular observations, and consultation with professionals who have worked with a setting over a period of time (e.g. local authority advisers).

Quality assurance schemes reflected both of these features: schemes tend to work on a more continuous basis, and generally provide the support of a mentor (e.g. local authority adviser) who works with the setting over time. Local authorities and providers were positive about the coverage of the schemes they used, saying that they enabled them to look at everyday practices, but also to focus on the effectiveness of leadership and the individual needs of the staff team.

Learning
How can we understand learner development?

2

Readings

2.1 Burrhus Skinner
The science of learning and the art of teaching (p. 24)

2.2 Jean Piaget
The genetic approach to the psychology of thought (p. 28)

2.3 Lev Vygotsky
Mind in society and the ZPD (p. 32)

2.4 Jerome Bruner
The spiral curriculum (p. 35)

2.5 Carol Dweck
Motivational processes affecting learning (p. 37)

The first readings in this chapter illustrate some major approaches to learning. Behaviourism is represented by Skinner, while Piaget's contribution reviews key elements of his constructivist psychology. Modern theories of social cognition derive from in the work of Vygotsky, as illustrated by his classic account of the 'zone of proximal development', and this idea is evident in the spiral curriculum promoted by Bruner. Having knowledge of these positions is vital for anybody wanting to understand early years policy and curriculum and how they have been influenced by some of the major approaches to learning.

In our final reading Carol Dweck considers how children come to think of themselves, and how this impacts upon their futures. A key tenant of the Reflective Teaching Series is how do we enable all children and young people to be positive about their learning, to be curious and resilient.

There are suggestions for Key Readings and other ideas for more detailed study on the companion website. To access these, please visit *reflectiveteaching. co.uk* – then navigate to this book, this chapter and Notes for Further Reading.

Reading 2.1

The science of learning and the art of teaching
Burrhus Skinner

B. F. Skinner made a very important contribution to 'behaviourist' psychology, an approach based on the study of the ways in which animal behaviour is shaped and conditioned by stimuli. In this reading, Skinner applies his ideas to the learning of pupils in schools. Taking the case of learning arithmetic, he highlights the production of correct 'responses' from children and considers the forms of 'reinforcement' which are routinely used in classrooms. He regards these as hopelessly inadequate.

What do you see as the implications of behaviourism for the role of the teacher?

Edited from: Skinner, B. F. (1954) 'The science of learning and the art of teaching', *Harvard Educational Review*, 24, 86–97.

Promising advances have been made in the field of learning. Special techniques have been designed to arrange what are called 'contingencies of reinforcement' – the relations which prevail between behaviour on the one hand the consequences of that behaviour on the other – with the result that a much more effective control of behaviour has been achieved. It has long been argued that an organism learns mainly by producing changes in its environment, but it is only recently that these changes have been carefully manipulated.

Recent improvements in the conditions which control behaviour in the field of learning are of two principal sorts. The Law of Effect has been taken seriously; we have made sure that effects *do* occur and that they occur under conditions which are optimal for producing the changes called learning. Once we have arranged the particular type of consequence called a reinforcement, our techniques permit us to shape up the behaviour of an organism almost at will. It has become a routine exercise to demonstrate this in classes in elementary psychology by conditioning such an organism as a pigeon. Simply by presenting food to a hungry pigeon at the right time, it is possible to shape up three or four well-defined responses in a single demonstration period – such responses as turning around, pacing the floor in the pattern of a figure-8, standing still in a corner of the demonstration apparatus, stretching the neck or stamping the foot. Extremely complex performances may be reached through successive stages in the shaping process, the contingencies of reinforcement being changed progressively in the direction of the required behaviour. The results are often quite dramatic. In such a demonstration one can *see* learning take place. A significant change in behaviour is often obvious as the result of a single reinforcement.

A second important advance in technique permits us to maintain behaviour in given states of strength for long periods of time. Reinforcements continue to be important, of course, long after an organism has learned how to do something, long after it has acquired behaviour. They are necessary to maintain the behaviour in strength. Of special interest is the effect of various schedules of intermittent reinforcement. We have learned how to maintain any given level of activity for daily periods limited only by the physical exhaustion of the organism and from day to day without substantial change throughout its life. Many of these effects would be traditionally assigned to the field of motivation, although the principal operation is simply the arrangement of contingencies of reinforcement.

These new methods of shaping behaviour and of maintaining it in strength are a great improvement over the traditional practices of professional animal trainers, and it is not surprising that our laboratory results are already being applied to the production of performing animals for commercial purposes.

From this exciting prospect of an advancing science of learning, it is a great shock to turn to that branch of technology which is most directly concerned with the learning process – education. Let us consider, for example, the teaching of arithmetic in the lower grades. The school is concerned with imparting to the child a large number of responses of a special sort. The responses are all verbal. They consist of speaking and writing certain words, figures and signs which, to put it roughly, refer to numbers and to arithmetic operations. The first task is to shape up these responses – to get the child to pronounce and to write responses correctly, but the principal task is to bring this behaviour under many sorts of stimulus control. This is what happens when the child learns to count, to recite tables, to count while ticking off the items in an assemblage of objects, to respond to spoken or written numbers by saying 'odd', 'even', 'prime' and so on. Over and above this elaborate repertoire of numerical behaviour, most of which is often dismissed as the product of rote learning, the teaching of arithmetic looks forward to those complex serial arrangements of responses involved in original mathematical thinking. The child must acquire responses of transposing, clearing fractions and so on, which modify the order or pattern of the original material so that the response called a solution is eventually made possible.

Now, how is the extremely complicated verbal repertoire set up? In the first place, what reinforcements are used? Fifty years ago the answer would have been clear. At that time educational control was still frankly aversive. The child read numbers, copied numbers, memorized tables and performed operations upon numbers to escape the threat of the birch rod or cane. Some positive reinforcements were perhaps eventually derived from the increased efficiency of the child in the field of arithmetic and in rare cases some automatic reinforcement may have resulted from the sheer manipulation of the medium – from the solution of problems or the discovery of the intricacies of the number system. But for the immediate purposes of education the child acted to avoid or escape punishment. It was part of the reform movement known as progressive education to make the positive consequences more immediately effective, but anyone who visits the lower grades of the average school today will observe that a change has been made, not from aversive to positive control, but from one form of aversive stimulation to another. The child at his desk, filling in his workbook, is behaving primarily to escape from the threat of a series of minor aversive events – the teacher's displeasure, the criticism or ridicule of his classmates, an ignominious showing in a competition, low marks, a trip to the office 'to be talked to' by the principal, or a word to the parent who may still resort to the birch rod. In this welter of aversive consequences, getting the right answer is in itself an insignificant event, any effect of which is lost amid the anxieties, the boredom and the aggressions which are the inevitable by-products of aversive control.

Secondly, we have to ask how the contingencies of reinforcement are arranged. When is a numerical operation reinforced as 'right'? Eventually, of course, the pupil may be able to check his own answers and achieve some sort of automatic reinforcement, but in the early stages the reinforcement of being right is usually accorded by the teacher. The contingencies she provides are far from optimal. It can easily be demonstrated that, unless explicit mediating behaviour has been set up, the lapse of only a few seconds between response and reinforcement destroys most of the effect. In a typical classroom, nevertheless, long periods of time customarily elapse. The teacher may walk up and down the aisle, for example, while the class is working on a sheet of problems, pausing here and there to say right or wrong. Many seconds or minutes intervene between the child's response and the teacher's reinforcement. In many cases – for example, when papers are taken home to be corrected – as much as 24 hours may intervene. It is surprising that this system has any effect whatsoever.

A third notable shortcoming is the lack of a skilful program which moves forward through a series of progressive approximations to the final complex behaviour desired. A long series of contingencies is necessary to bring the organism into the possession of mathematical behaviour most efficiently. But the teacher is seldom able to reinforce at each step in such a series because she cannot deal with the pupil's responses one at a time. It is usually necessary to reinforce the behaviour in blocks of responses – as in correcting a work sheet or page from a workbook. The responses within such a block must not be interrelated. The answer to one problem must not depend upon the answer to another. The number of stages through which one may progressively approach a complex pattern of behaviour is therefore small, and the task so much the more difficult. Even the most modern workbook in beginning arithmetic is far from exemplifying an efficient program for shaping up mathematical behaviour.

Perhaps the most serious criticism of the current classroom is the relative infrequency of reinforcement. Since the pupil is usually dependent upon the teacher for being right, and since many pupils are usually dependent upon the same teacher, the total number of contingencies which may be arranged during, say, the first four years, is of the order of only a few thousand. But a very rough estimate suggests that efficient mathematical behaviour at this level requires something of the order of 25,000 contingencies. We may suppose that even in the brighter student a given contingency must be arranged several times to place the behaviour well in hand. The responses to be set up are not simply the various items in tables of addition, subtraction, multiplication and division; we have also to consider the alternative forms in which each item may be stated. To the learning of such material we should add hundreds of responses concerned with factoring, identifying primes, memorizing series, using shortcut techniques for calculation, constructing and using geometric representations or number forms and so on. Over and above all this, the whole mathematical repertoire must be brought under the control of concrete problems of considerable variety. Perhaps 50,000 contingencies is a more conservative estimate. In this frame of reference the daily assignment in arithmetic seems pitifully meagre

The result of this is, of course, well known. Even our best schools are under criticism for the inefficiency in the teaching of drill subjects such as arithmetic. The condition in the average school is a matter of widespread national concern. Modern children simply do not learn arithmetic quickly or well. Nor is the result simply incompetence. The very subjects in which modern techniques are weakest are those in which failure is most conspicuous, and in the wake of an ever-growing incompetence come the anxieties, uncertainties and aggressions which in their turn present other problems to the school. Most pupils soon claim the asylum of not being 'ready' for arithmetic at a given level or, eventually, of not having a mathematical mind. Such explanations are readily seized upon by defensive teachers and parents. Few pupils ever reach the stage at which automatic reinforcements follow as the natural consequences of mathematical behaviour. On the contrary, the figures and symbols of mathematics have become standard emotional stimuli. The glimpse of a column of figures, not to say an algebraic symbol or an integral sign, is likely to set off – not mathematical behaviour – but a reaction of anxiety, guilt or fear.

The teacher is usually no happier about this than the pupil. Denied the opportunity to control via the birch rod, quite at sea as to the mode of operation of the few techniques at her disposal, she spends as little time as possible on drill subjects and eagerly subscribes to philosophies of education which emphasize material of greater inherent interest.

There would be no point in urging these objections if improvement were impossible. But the advances which have recently been made in our control of the learning process suggest a thorough revision of classroom practices and, fortunately, they tell us how the revision can be brought about. This is not, of course, the first time that the results of an experimental science have been brought to bear upon the practical problems of education. The modern classroom does not, however, offer much evidence that research in the field of learning has been respected or used. This condition is no doubt partly due to the limitations of earlier research, but it has been encouraged by a too hasty conclusion that the laboratory study of learning is inherently limited because it cannot take into account the realities of the classroom. In the light of our increasing knowledge of the learning process we should, instead, insist upon dealing with those realities and forcing a substantial change in them. Education is perhaps the most important branch of scientific technology. It deeply affects the lives of all of us. We can no longer allow the exigencies of a practical situation to suppress the tremendous improvements which are within reach. The practical situation must be changed.

There are certain questions which have to be answered in turning to the study of any new organism. What behaviour is to be set up? What reinforcers are at hand? What responses are available in embarking upon a program of progressive approximation which will lead to the final form of behaviour? How can reinforcements be most efficiently scheduled to maintain the behaviour in strength? These questions are all relevant in considering the problem of the child in the lower grades.

Reading 2.2

The genetic approach to the psychology of thought

Jean Piaget

The presented reading provides a concise overview of Piaget's constructivist psychology, but is necessarily packed with ideas. The distinction between formal knowledge and the dynamic of transformations is important, with the latter seen as providing the mechanism for the development of thought. Successive 'stages' of types of thinking are reviewed and are related to maturation, direct experience and social interaction. Finally, attention is drawn to the ways in which children 'assimilate' new experiences and 'accommodate' to their environment, to produce new levels of 'equilibration' at successive stages of learning.

Interpretations of Piaget's work have been of enormous influence on the thinking of ECEC practitioners. Indeed, his ideas were specifically used as a rationale for the policy recommendations contained in the Plowden Report, which emphasized the importance of providing a rich, experiential learning environment which would be appropriate for the 'stage' of each child.

What importance do you attach to concepts such as 'stages of development', 'readiness' and 'learning from experience'?

Edited from: Piaget, J. (1961) 'A genetic approach to the psychology of thought', *Journal of Educational Psychology,* 52, 151–61.

Taking into consideration all that is known about the act of thinking, one can distinguish two principal aspects:

The *formal* viewpoint which deals with the configuration of the state of things to know,

The *dynamic* aspect, which deals with transformations

The study of the development of thought shows that the dynamic aspect is at the same time more difficult to attain and more important, because only transformations make us understand the state of things. For instance: when a child of 4 to 6 years transfers a liquid from a large and low glass into a narrow and higher glass, he believes in general that the quantity of the liquid has increased, because he is limited to comparing the initial state (low level) to the final state (high level) without concerning himself with the transformation. Towards 7 or 8 years of age, on the other hand, a child discovers the preservation of the liquid, because he will think in terms of transformation. He will say that nothing has been taken away and nothing added, and, if the level of the liquid rises, this is due to a loss of width etc.

The formal aspect of thought makes way, therefore, more and more in the course of the development to its dynamic aspect, until such time when only transformation gives an understanding of things. To think means, above all to understand; and to understand means to arrive at the transformations, which furnish the reason for the state of things. All development of thought is resumed in the following manner: a construction of operations which stem from actions and a gradual subordination of formal aspects into dynamic aspects.

The operation, properly speaking, which constitutes the terminal point of this evolution is, therefore, to be conceived as an internalized action bound to other operations, which form with it a structured whole.

So defined, the dynamics intervene in the construction of all thought processes; in the structure of forms and classifications, of relations and serialization of correspondences, of numbers, of space and time, of the causality etc.

Any action of thought consists of combining thought operations and integrating the objects to be understood into systems of dynamic transformation. The psychological criterion of this is the appearance of the notion of conservation or 'invariants of groups'. Before speech, at the purely sensory-motor stage of a child from 0–18 months, it is possible to observe actions which show evidence of such tendencies. For instance: From 4–5 to 18 months, the baby constructs his first invariant, which is the schema of the permanent object (to recover an object which escaped from the field of perception).

When, with the beginning of the symbolic function (language, symbolic play, imagery etc.), the representation through thought becomes possible, it is at first a question of reconstructing in thought what the action is already able to realize. The actions actually do not become transformed immediately into operations, and one has to wait until about 7–8 years for the child to reach a functioning level. During this preoperative period the child, therefore, only arrives at incomplete structures characterized by a lack of logic.

At about 7–8 years the child arrives at his first complete dynamic structures (classes, relations and numbers), which, however, still remain concrete – in other words, only at the time of a handling of objects (material manipulation or, when possible, directly imagined). It is not before the age of 11–12 years or more that operations can be applied to pure hypotheses.

The fundamental genetic problem of the psychology of thought is hence to explain the formation of these dynamic structures. Practically, one would have to rely on three principal factors in order to explain the facts of development: maturation, physical experience and social interaction. But in this particular case none of these three suffice to furnish us with the desired explanations – not even the three together.

Maturation

First of all, these dynamic structures form very gradually. But progressive construction does not seem to depend on maturation, because the achievements hardly correspond to a particular age. Only the order of succession is constant. However, one witnesses innumerable accelerations or retardations for reasons of education (cultural) or acquired experience.

Physical experience

Experiencing of objects plays, naturally, a very important role in the establishment of dynamic structures, because the operations originate from actions and the actions bear upon the object. This role manifests itself right from the beginning of sensory-motor explorations, preceding language, and it affirms itself continually in the course of manipulations and activities which are appropriate to the antecedent stages. Necessary as the role of experience may be, it does not sufficiently describe the construction of the dynamic structures – and this for the following three reasons.

First, there exist ideas which cannot possibly be derived from the child's experience – for instance, when one changes the shape of a small ball of clay. The child will declare, at 7–8 years, that the quantity of the matter is conserved. It does so before discovering the conservation of weight (9–10 years) and that of volume (10–11 years). What is the quantity of a matter independently of its weight and its volume? This abstract notion is neither possible to be perceived nor measurable. It is, therefore, the product of a dynamic deduction and not part of an experience.

Second, the various investigations into the learning of logical structure, which we were able to make at our International Centre of Genetic Epistemology, lead to a unanimous result: one does not 'learn' a logical structure as one learns to discover any physical law.

Third, there exist two types of experiences:

Physical experiences show the objects as they are, and the knowledge of them leads to the abstraction directly from the object. However, logico-mathematical experience does not stem from the same type of learning as that of the physical experience, but rather from an equilibration of the scheme of actions, as we will see.

Social interaction

The educative and social transmission (linguistic etc) plays, naturally, an evident role in the formation of dynamic structures, but this factor does not suffice either to entirely explain its development.

Additionally, there is a general progression of equilibration. This factor intervenes, as is to be expected, in the interaction of the preceding factors. Indeed, if the development depends, on one hand, on internal factors (maturation), and on the other hand on external factors (physical or social), it is self-evident that these internal and external factors equilibrate each other. The question is then to know if we are dealing here only with momentary compromises (unstable equilibrium) or if, on the contrary, this equilibrium becomes more and more stable. This shows that all exchange (mental as well as biological) between the organism and the environment (physical and social) is composed of two poles: (a) of the *assimilation* of the given external to the previous internal structures, and (b) of the *accommodation* of these structures to the given ones. The equilibrium between the assimilation and the accommodation is proportionately more stable than the assimilative structures which are better differentiated and coordinated.

To apply these notions to children's reasoning we see that every new problem provokes a disequilibrium (recognizable through types of dominant errors) the solution of which consists in a re-equilibration, which brings about a new original synthesis of two systems, up to the point of independence.

Reading 2.3

Mind in society and the ZPD
Lev Vygotsky

Vygotsky's social constructivist psychology, though stemming from the 1930s, underpins much modern thinking about teaching and learning. In particular, the importance of instruction is emphasized. However, this is combined with recognition of the influence of social interaction and the cultural context within which understanding is developed. Vygotsky's most influential concept is that of the 'zone of proximal development' (ZPD), which highlights the potential for future learning which can be realized with appropriate support.

Thinking of a particular area of learning and a child you know, can you identify an 'actual developmental level' and a 'zone of proximal development' through which you could provide guidance and support?

Edited from: Vygotsky, L. S. (1978) *Mind in Society: The Development of Higher Psychological Processes.* Cambridge, MA: Harvard University Press, 84–90.

That children's learning begins long before they attend school is the starting point of this discussion. Any learning a child encounters in school always has a previous history. For example, children begin to study arithmetic in school, but long beforehand they have had some experience with quantity – they have had to deal with operations of division, addition, subtraction, and determination of size. Consequently, children have their own pre-school arithmetic which only myopic scientists could ignore.

It goes without saying that learning as it occurs in the preschool years differs markedly from school learning, which is concerned with the assimilation of the fundamentals of scientific knowledge. But even when, in the period of her first questions, a child assimilates the names of objects in her environment, she is learning. Indeed, can it be doubted that children learn speech from adults; or that, through asking questions and giving answers, children acquire a variety of information; or that through imitating adults and through being instructed about how to act, children develop an entire repository of skills? Learning and development are interrelated from the child's very first day of life.

In order to elaborate the dimensions of school learning, we will describe a new and exceptionally important concept without which the issue cannot be resolved: the zone of proximal development.

A well-known and empirically established fact is that learning should be matched in some manner with the child's developmental level. For example, it has been established that the teaching of reading, writing and arithmetic should be initiated at a specific age level. Only recently, however, has attention been directed to the fact that we cannot limit ourselves merely to determining developmental levels if we wish to discover the actual relations of the developmental process to learning capabilities. We must determine at least two developmental levels.

The first level can be called the *actual developmental level*, that is, the level of development of a child's mental functions that has been established as a result of certain already *completed* developmental cycles. When we determine a child's mental age by using tests, we are almost always dealing with the actual developmental level. In studies of children's mental development it is generally assumed that only those things that children can do on their own are indicative of mental abilities. We give children a battery of tests or a variety of tasks of varying degrees of difficulty, and we judge the extent of their mental development on the basis of how they solve them and at what level of difficulty. On the other hand, if we offer leading questions or show how the problem is to be solved and the child then solves it, or if the teacher initiates the solution and the child completes it or solves it in collaboration with other children – in short, if the child barely misses an independent solution of the problem – the solution is not regarded as indicative of his mental development. This 'truth' was familiar and reinforced by common sense. Over a decade even the profoundest thinkers never questioned the assumption; they never entertained the notion that what children can do with the assistance of others might be in some sense even more indicative of their mental development than what they can do alone.

The zone of proximal development is the distance between the actual developmental level as determined by independent problem solving and the level of potential development as determined through problem solving under adult guidance or in collaboration with more capable peers.

If we naively ask what the actual developmental level is, or, to put it more simply, what more independent problem solving reveals, the most common answer would be that a child's actual developmental level defines functions that have already matured, that is, the end products of development. If a child can do such-and-such independently, it means that the functions for such-and-such have matured in her. What, then, is defined by the zone of proximal development, as determined through problems that children cannot solve independently but only with assistance? The zone of proximal development defines those functions that have not yet matured but are in the process of maturation, functions that will mature tomorrow but are currently in an embryonic state. These functions could be termed the 'buds' or 'flowers' of development rather than the 'fruits' of development. The actual developmental level characterizes mental development retrospectively, while the zone of proximal development characterizes mental development prospectively.

The zone of proximal development furnishes psychologists and educators with a tool through which the internal course of development can be understood. By using this method we can take account of not only the cycles and maturation processes that have already been completed but also those processes that are currently in a state of formation, that are just beginning to mature and develop. Thus, the zone of proximal development permits us to delineate the child's immediate future and his dynamic developmental state, allowing not only for what already has been achieved developmentally but also for what is in the course of maturing. The state of a child's mental development can be determined only by clarifying its two levels: the actual developmental level and the zone of proximal development.

A full understanding of the concept of the zone of proximal development must result in re-evaluation of the role of imitation in learning. Indeed, human learning presupposes a specific social nature and a process by which children grow into the intellectual life of those around them.

Children can imitate a variety of actions that go well beyond the limits of their own capabilities. Using imitation, children are capable of doing much more in collective activity or under the guidance of adults. This fact, which seems to be of little significance in itself, is of fundamental importance in that it demands a radical alteration of the entire doctrine concerning the relation between learning and development in children.

Learning which is oriented toward developmental levels that have already been reached is ineffective from the viewpoint of a child's overall development. It does not aim for a new stage of the developmental process but rather lags behind this process. Thus, the notion of a zone of proximal development enables us to propound a new formula, namely that the only 'good learning' is that which is in advance of development.

The acquisition of language can provide a paradigm for the entire problem of the relation between learning and development. Language arises initially as a means of communication between the child and the people in his environment. Only subsequently, upon conversion to internal speech, does it come to organize the child's thought, that is, become an internal mental function.

We propose that an essential feature of learning is that it creates the zone of proximal development; that is, learning awakens a variety of internal developmental processes that are able to operate only when the child is interacting with people in his environment and in cooperation with his peers. Once these processes are internalized, they become part of the child's independent developmental achievement.

From this point of view, learning is not development; however, properly organized learning results in mental development and sets in motion a variety of developmental processes that would be impossible apart from learning. Thus, learning is a necessary and universal aspect of the process of developing culturally organized, specifically human, psychological functions.

Reading 2.4

The spiral curriculum

Jerome Bruner

Bruner's classic text, *The Process of Education* (1960), is premised on the idea that learners construct their own knowledge and understanding. Challenging the constraining effects of those advocating developmental progression, he argued that all knowledge can 'be taught in some intellectually honest form to any child at any stage of development' (p. 33). It is then revisited, successively, at further levels of difficulty. He drew particular attention to the place of narrative in learning and in 'making sense' through life.

If there is value in these ideas, they have significant implications for progression in curriculum planning.

Edited from: Bruner, J. S. (2006) *In Search of Pedagogy Volume II: The Selected Works of Jerome* S. Bruner. New York: Routledge, 145–6.

A very long time ago I proposed something which was called a spiral curriculum (1960). The idea was that when teaching or learning a subject, you start with an intuitive account that is well within the reach of the student, then circle back later in a more powerful, more generative, more structured way to understand it more deeply with however many recyclings the learner needs in order to master the topic and turn it into an instrument of the mind, a way of thinking. It was a notion that grew out of a more fundamental view of epistemology, about how minds get to know. I stated this view almost in the form of a philosophical proverb: Any subject could be taught to any child at any age in some form that was honest. Another way of saying the same thing is that readiness is not only born but made. You make readiness.

The general proposition rests on the still deeper truth that a domain of knowledge can be constructed simply or complexly, abstractly or concretely. The kid who understands the intuitive role of the lever and can apply it to the playground see-saw is getting within reach of knowing the meaning of quadratic functions. He now has a grasp of one instantiation of an idea that makes teaching him about quadratics a cinch. I'm saying this because we have done it. Give me a balance beam with hooks placed at equal distances along it, some weights that you can hang on the hooks of the balance beam to make it balance, and I will show you. A ten-year-old I was working with once said to me: 'This gadget knows all about arithmetic'. That gave me pause, and I tried to convince him that it was he who knew arithmetic, not the balance beam. He listened politely, but I don't think I succeeded; maybe that will come later along the curriculum spiral. Anyway, he had learned a meaning of expressions like $x^2 + 5x + 6$ and why they balance – mean the same – as ones like $(x + 2)(x + 3)$.

The research of the last three decades on the growth of reasoning in children has in the main confirmed the rightness of the notion of the spiral curriculum in spite of the fact that we now know about something called domain specificity. It is not true now, nor was it ever true, that learning Latin improves your reasoning. Subject matters have to be demonstrably within reach of each other to improve each other. There isn't infinite transfer. On the other hand, there is probably more than we know, and we can build up a kind of general confidence that problems are solvable. That has a huge transfer affect. The kid says, 'Now how would we do that?' using a kind of royal 'we'. A good intuitive, practical grasp of the domain at one stage of development leads to better, earlier, and deeper thinking in the next stage when the child meets new problems. We do not wait for readiness to happen. We foster it by making sure they are good at some intuitive domain before we start off on the next one.

However, it's interesting that we don't always do it. It is appalling how poorly history, for example, is taught at most schools and at most universities. Teachers need to give students an idea that there are models for how events happened historically, even if we give them a sort of Toynbeyan model, to the effect that there is challenge and response, or the kind of Paul Kennedy model of what happens to wealthy nations. The particular model doesn't matter, just so it is clear and coherent so that kids can say, 'Pretty smart, but it doesn't work'. We need models that can be given some basic sense even though they are rejected later. One way to do it is by placing emphasis upon what is story-like about the model. For what we grasp better than anything else are stories, and it is easy for children (or adults) to take them apart, retell them, and analyse what's wrong with them.

The most natural and earliest way in which we organize our experience and our knowledge is by use of narrative. It may be that the beginnings, the transitions, the full grasps of ideas in a spiral curriculum depend upon embodying those ideas initially into a story of narrative form in order to carry the kid across any area where he is not quite grasping the abstraction. The story form is the first one grasped by kids, and is the one with which they all seem most comfortable.

Reading 2.5

Motivational processes affecting learning
Carol Dweck

A child's motivation and approaches in new learning situations is obviously crucial to outcomes and this has been the focus of Carol Dweck's research for many years. In this reading, she shows how children's view of intelligence (as fixed or something that can be developed) may lead them to adopt relatively pragmatic performance goals or more developmental learning goals. These are associated with different beliefs in themselves (helpless or mastery-orientated), different forms of behaviour and different learning outcomes.

How can we help children to really believe in themselves and their potential? To create curious confident learners?

Edited from: Dweck, C. S. (1986) 'Motivational processes affecting learning', *American Psychologist*, October, 1040–6.

It has long been known that factors other than ability influence whether children seek or avoid challenges, whether they persist or withdraw in the face of difficulty and whether they use and develop their skills effectively. However, the components and bases of adaptive motivational patterns have been poorly understood. As a result, commonsense analyses have been limited and have not provided a basis for effective practices. Indeed, many 'commonsense' beliefs have been called into question or seriously qualified by recent research – for example, the belief that large amounts of praise and success will establish, maintain, or reinstate adaptive patterns, or that 'brighter' children have more adaptive patterns and thus are more likely to choose personally challenging tasks or to persist in the face of difficulty.

In the past 10 to 15 years a dramatic change has taken place in the study of motivation. This change has resulted in a coherent, replicable, and educationally relevant body of findings – and in a clearer understanding of motivational phenomena. During this time, the emphasis has shifted to a social-cognitive approach – away from external contingencies, on the one hand, and global, internal states on the other. It has shifted to an emphasis on cognitive mediators, that is, to how children construe the situation, interpret events in the situation, and process information about the situation. Although external contingencies and internal affective states are by no means ignored, they are seen as part of a process whose workings are best penetrated by focusing on organizing cognitive variables.

Specifically, the social-cognitive approach has allowed us to (a) characterize adaptive and maladaptive patterns, (b) explain them in terms of specific underlying processes, and thus (c) begin to provide a rigorous conceptual and empirical basis for intervention and practice.

The study of motivation deals with the causes of goal-oriented activity. Achievement motivation involves a particular class of goals – those involving competence – and these goals appear to fall into two classes: (a) *learning goals*, in which individuals seek to increase their competence, to understand or master something new, and (b) *performance goals*, in which individuals seek to gain favourable judgments of their competence.

Adaptive motivational patterns are those that promote the establishment, maintenance, and attainment of personally challenging and personally valued achievement goals. Maladaptive patterns, then, are associated with a failure to establish reasonable, valued goals, to maintain effective striving toward those goals, or, ultimately, to attain valued goals that are potentially within one's reach.

Research has clearly documented adaptive and maladaptive patterns of achievement behaviour. The adaptive ('mastery-oriented') pattern is characterized by challenge seeking and high, effective persistence in the face of obstacles. Children displaying this pattern appear to enjoy exerting effort in the pursuit of task mastery. In contrast, the maladaptive ('helpless') pattern is characterized by challenge avoidance and low persistence in the face of difficulty. Children displaying this pattern tend to evidence negative affect (such as anxiety) and negative self-cognitions when they confront obstacles.

Although children displaying the different patterns do not differ in intellectual ability, these patterns can have profound effects on cognitive performance. In experiments conducted in both laboratory and classroom settings, it has been shown that children with the maladaptive pattern are seriously hampered in the acquisition and display of cognitive skills when they meet obstacles. Children with the adaptive pattern, by contrast, seem undaunted or even seem to have their performance facilitated by the increased challenge.

If not ability, then what are the bases of these patterns? Most recently, research has suggested that children's goals in achievement situations differentially foster the two patterns. That is, achievement situations afford a choice of goals, and the one the child preferentially adopts predicts the achievement pattern that child will display.

Figure 2.5.1 Achievement goals and achievement behaviour

Theory of intelligence	Goal orientation	Confidence in present ability	Behaviour pattern
Entity theory – Intelligence is fixed	Performance goal (Goal is to gain positive judgments/avoid negative judgments of competence)	If high →	Mastery-orientated Seek challenge High persistence
		but	
		If low →	Helpless Avoid challenge Low persistence
Incremental theory (Intelligence is malleable)	Learning goal (Goal is to increase competence)	If high or low →	Mastery-oriented Seek challenge (that fosters learning) High persistence

Figure 2.5.1 summarizes the conceptualisation that is emerging from the research. Basically, children's theories of intelligence appear to orient them toward different goals: Children who believe intelligence is a fixed trait tend to orient toward gaining favourable judgments of that trait (performance goals), whereas children who believe intelligence is a malleable quality tend to orient toward developing that quality (learning goal). The goals then appear to set up the different behaviour patterns.

Much current educational practice aims at creating high-confidence performers and attempts to do so by programming frequent success and praise. How did this situation arise? I propose that misreadings of two popular phenomena may have merged to produce this approach. First was the belief in 'positive reinforcement' as the way to promote desirable behaviour. Yet a deeper understanding of the principles of reinforcement would not lead one to expect that frequent praise for short, easy tasks would create a desire for long, challenging ones or promote persistence in the face of failure.

Second was a growing awareness of teacher expectancy effects. As is well known, the teacher expectancy effect refers to the phenomenon whereby teachers' impressions about students' ability actually affect students' performance, such that the students' performance falls more in line with the teachers' expectancies (Rosenthal and Jacobson, 1968). The research on this 'self-fulfilling prophecy' raised serious concerns that teachers were hampering the intellectual achievement of children they labelled as having low ability. One remedy was thought to lie in making low-ability children feel like high-ability children by means of a high success rate.

The motivational research is clear in indicating that continued success on personally easy tasks is ineffective in producing stable confidence, challenge seeking and persistence (Dweck, 1975). Indeed, such procedures have sometimes been found to backfire by producing lower confidence in ability. Rather, the procedures that bring about more adaptive motivational patterns are the ones that incorporate challenge, and even failure, within a learning-oriented context and that explicitly address underlying motivational mediators. For example, retraining children's attributions for failure (teaching them to attribute their failures to effort or strategy instead of ability) has been shown to produce sizable changes in persistence in the face of failure, changes that persist over time and generalize across tasks (Andrews and Bebus, 1978).

Motivational processes have been shown to affect (a) how well children can deploy their existing skills and knowledge, (b) how well they acquire new skills and knowledge, and (c) how well they transfer these new skills and knowledge to novel situations. This approach does not deny individual differences in present skills and knowledge or in 'native' ability or aptitude. It does suggest, however, that the use and growth of that ability can be appreciably influenced by motivational factors.

Reflection
How can we develop the quality of our practice?

3

Readings

3.1 Jan Peeters and Michel Vandenbroeck
The role of reflection in the professionalization of the early years workforce (p. 42)

3.2 Lawrence Stenhouse
The importance of practitioner research (p. 44)

3.3 Richard Pring
Action research and the development of practice (p. 46)

3.4 Denise Kingston and Jane Melvin
Measures of quality (p. 49)

3.5 Donald Schön
Reflection-in-action (p. 51)

3.6 John Dewey
Thinking and reflective experience (p. 54)

3.7 Pete Watton, Jane Collings and Jenny Moon
Reflective writing (p. 56)

The quality of early years provision has been at the heart of much research and many policy developments in recent years. The readings in this chapter illustrate both conceptions of quality and the key ideas about the meaning of reflection and its role in providing and defining high-quality provision. We then move on to consider the importance of practitioners engaging in research and enquiry in their own settings for the improvement of practice.

The readings provided include excerpts from the highly influential work of Dewey and Schön. Dewey contrasts routinized and reflective thinking, and suggests that 'to be genuinely thoughtful, we must be willing to sustain a state of doubt'. Schön identifies the capacity of skilled practitioners to engage in 'reflection-in-action'. The final reading provides support for identifying levels of reflection and examples of what deep reflection 'looks like' in practice.

The relevant parts of *reflectiveteaching.co.uk* maintain this focus and provide links to further work.

Reading 3.1

The role of reflection in the professionalization of the early years workforce

Jan Peeters and Michel Vandenbroeck

> In this first reading we rejoin the professionalization debate covered in Chapter 2 and consider the role reflection plays in early years teaching and learning.
>
> *Edited from:* Peeters, J. and Vandenbroeck, M. (2011) 'Childcare Practitioners and the Process of Professionalization'. In L. Miller and C. Cable (eds) *Professionalization, Leadership and Management in the Early Years.* London: Sage Publications Ltd, 62–77.

Academic attention to the professionalization of the early years workforce is relatively new and is dominated by studies in the United States of America, Australia and the United Kingdom. As a result, the academic discussion on professionalism in early childhood is dominated by contexts, marked by a history of significant differences in staff qualifications, large shares of care work provided by private providers, and little government regulation regarding staff qualifications, though in the case of the UK this has recently changed (OECD, 2006; UNICEF, 2008). Notwithstanding this bias in published research, some consensus emerges from the literature regarding the relationship between quality and professionalization. Higher levels of qualifications correlate positively with better childcare quality as well as with better developmental outcomes for children (e.g. Cameron and Moss, 2007; Fukkink and Lont, 2007; Sylva et al., 2004). Research also shows that in-service training (on the job) may be as important as pre-service (initial) qualifications, provided it is of sufficient length and intensity (e.g. Fukkink and Lont, 2007). However, this does not mean that qualifications can be considered in isolation, nor that the professionalization of the workforce is in itself sufficient to predict the quality of provision. First, it is important to note educators with higher levels of qualification tend to choose to work in higher quality provision. Second, more highly qualified practitioners can bring about quality results only when the staff is supported in implementing the insights gained through training in their practice and when the working conditions (including salaries) do not jeopardize the continuity of the workforce (Early et al., 2007).

In addition, there is also a considerable degree of consensus on how this professionalism may be understood. There is general agreement that a specific body of knowledge, as well as a series of skills, are necessary but that these do not suffice. Indeed, reflection is considered by many writers to be the most important part of professionalism (Dunn et al., 2008; Urban, 2008). However, the concept of the 'reflective practitioner', although frequently mentioned in the literature, remains rather underdeveloped and the apparent consensus on the need for reflection may very well disguise a lack of consensus on what it actually means. We can distinguish between reflection-for-action (what will I do?);

reflection-in-action (what am I doing?) and reflection-on-action (what have I done?) (Cheng, 2001). Overall, however, the concept of reflection that is most dominant in academic literature is about 'doing things right'. As Coussée, Bradt, Roose and Bouverne-De Bie (2008) rightly argue, this is quite different in nature to reflection on 'doing the right things'. The reflective practitioner moves towards becoming reflexive by questioning taken-for-granted beliefs and by understanding that knowledge is contestable (Kuisma and Sandberg, 2008; Kunneman, 2005; Miller, 2008; Urban and Dalli, 2008). While the first approach focuses on documenting and evaluating one's practice within a fixed paradigm, the second approach questions the very paradigms in which one is operating. A recent thematic monograph published by the *European Early Childhood Education Research Journal* (Urban and Dalli, 2008), is one of the few international publications exploring this second approach. A second observation is that practitioners are virtually absent from the discussion about their reflexive professionalism. The result is that – paradoxically – the literature on reflexive practitioners risks reducing the practitioners to objects, rather than including them as reflexive and agentic subjects. According to Sorel and Wittorski (2005), it is essential that the individuals who are 'professionalizing' themselves are not reduced to the role of a 'consumer' of the knowledge that is presented to them. Yet, little is known about the practitioner's views on this emerging role transformation, with its new emphasis on negotiating and networking competencies (Oberhuemer, 2000). As a result, important questions of how individuals develop their professionalism remain. This may imply a need for participative action research in this field. Leitch and Day (2000) have argued that action research can play an important role in increasing professionalism, providing that it is oriented towards change, critical reflection and participation. Action research, as opposed to pragmatic research, raised the possibility of questioning the social position of research. According to Roose and De Bie (2003), participative research may be a driving force for cultural action, a process of searching for new definition of reality, leading to a commitment to critical thinking.

Reading 3.2

The importance of practitioner research
Lawrence Stenhouse

> Lawrence Stenhouse led the Humanities Project during the late 1960s that revolutionized thinking about professional development. One of his central concerns was to encourage teachers as 'researchers' of their own practice, thereby extending their professionalism.
>
> Do you think early years practitioners ought to research their own practice and the work that takes place in their setting? What role do you think practitioner research has to play in ensuring the workforce has a strong voice in debates around professionalism, regulation or curriculum?
>
> *Edited from:* Stenhouse, L. (1975) *An Introduction to Curriculum Research and Development.* London: Heinemann, 143–57.

All well-founded curriculum research and development, whether the work of an individual teacher, of a school, of a group working in a teachers' centre or of a group working within the co-ordinating framework of a national project, is based on the study of classrooms. It thus rests on the work of teachers.

It is not enough that teachers' work should be studied: they need to study it themselves. My theme is the role of the teachers as researchers in their own teaching situation. What does this conception of curriculum development imply for them?

The critical characteristics of that extended professionalism which is essential for well-founded curriculum research and development seem to me to be:

The commitment to systematic questioning of one's own teaching as a basis for development;
The commitment and the skills to study one's own teaching;
The concern to question and to test theory in practice.

To these may be added as highly desirable, though perhaps not essential, a readiness to allow other teachers to observe one's work directly or through recordings – and to discuss it with them on an open and honest basis. In short, the outstanding characteristics of the extended professional is a capacity for autonomous professional self-development through systematic self-study, through the study of the work of other teachers and through the testing of ideas by classroom research procedures.

It is important to make the point that teachers in this situation are concerned to understand better their own classroom. Consequently, they are not faced with the problems of generalizing beyond his or her own experience. In this context, theory is simply a systematic structuring of his or her understanding of such work.

Concepts which are carefully related to one another are needed both to capture and to express that understanding. The adequacy of such concepts should be treated as provisional. The utility and appropriateness of the theoretical framework of concepts should be testable; and the theory should be rich enough to throw up new and profitable questions.

Each classroom should not be an island. Teachers working in such a tradition need to communicate with one another. They should report their work. Thus a common vocabulary of concepts and a syntax of theory need to be developed. Where that language proves inadequate, teachers would need to propose new concepts and new theory.

The first level of generalization is thus the development of a general theoretical language. In this, professional research workers should be able to help.

If teachers report their own work in such a tradition, case studies will accumulate, just as they do in medicine. Professional research workers will have to master this material and scrutinize it for general trends. It is out of this synthetic task that general propositional theory can be developed.

Reading 3.3

Action research and the development of practice
Richard Pring

Richard Pring, a leading educational philosopher, takes stock of some key characteristics of 'action research', which is a useful way for practitioners to think about the ongoing development of practice. The reading makes useful comparisons with the characteristics of conventional academic research. Although there are important differences in key objectives, there are also many similarities in the issues that must be faced in any enquiry. Pring emphasizes the need for openness, the importance of dialogue with colleagues and of critical reflection on practice. Action research may thus involve scrutiny of values, including those which might be embedded in centrally prescribed curricula, pedagogies or forms of assessment.

Edited from: Pring, R. (2000) *Philosophy of Educational Research.* Continuum: London, 130–4.

Respect for educational practitioners has given rise to the development of 'action research'. This may be contrasted with conventional research. The goal of research is normally that of producing new knowledge. There will, of course, be many different motives for producing such knowledge. But what makes it research is the systematic search for conclusions about 'what is the case' on the basis of relevant evidence. Such conclusions might, indeed, be tentative, always open to further development and refinement. But the purpose remains that of getting ever 'nearer the truth'. Hence, it makes sense to see the outcomes of research to be a series of propositions which are held to be true.

By contrast, the research called 'action research' aims not to produce new knowledge but to improve practice – namely, in this case, the 'educational practice' in which teachers are engaged. The conclusion is not a set of propositions but a practice or a set of trans-actions or activities which is not true or false but better or worse. By contrast with the conclusion of research, as that is normally conceived, action research focuses on the particular. Although such a practical conclusion focuses on the particular, thereby not justifying generalization, no one situation is unique in every respect and therefore the action research in one classroom or school can illuminate or be suggestive of practice elsewhere. There can be, amongst networks of teachers, the development of a body of professional knowledge of 'what works' or of how values might be translated into practice – or come to be transformed by practice. But there is a sense in which such professional knowledge has constantly to be tested out, reflected upon, adapted to new situations.

Research, as that is normally understood, requires a 'research forum' – a group of people with whom the conclusions can be tested out and examined critically. Without such openness to criticism, one might have missed the evidence or the counter argument which casts doubt on the conclusions drawn. Hence, the importance of dissemination through publications and seminars. To think otherwise is to assume a certitude which cannot be justified. Progress in knowledge arises through replication of the research activity, through criticism, through the active attempt to find evidence *against* one's conclusions.

Similarly, the growth of professional knowledge requires the sympathetic but critical community through which one can test out ideas, question the values which underpin the shared practice, seek solutions to problems, invite observation of one's practice, suggest alternative perspectives and interpretation of the data.

This is an important matter to emphasize. The temptation very often is to seek to justify and to verify, rather than to criticize or to falsify, one's belief, and to protect oneself by not sharing one's conclusions or the way in which one reached them.

With action research, reflection upon practice with a view to its improvement needs to be a public activity. By 'public' I mean that the research is conducted in such a way that others can scrutinize and, if necessary, question the practice of which it is part. Others become part of the reflective process – the identification and definition of the problem. the values which are implicit within the practice, the way of implementing and gathering evidence about the practice, the interpretation of the evidence. And yet teacher research, in the form of action research, is so often encouraged and carried out as a lonely, isolated activity. Those who are concerned with the promotion of action research – with the development in teachers of well-tested professional knowledge – must equally be concerned to develop the professional networks and communities in which it can be fostered.

There is a danger that such research might be supported and funded with a view to knowing the most effective ways of attaining particular goals – goals or targets set by government or others external to the transaction which takes place between teacher and learner. The teacher researches the most efficient means of reaching a particular educational objective (laid out, for instance. in the National Curriculum or a skills-focused vocational training). But this is not what one would have in mind in talking about research as part of professional judgement or action research as a response to a practical issue or problem. The reflective teacher comes to the problem with a set of values. The problem situation is one which raises issues as much about those values as it does about adopting an appropriate means to a given end. Thus, what makes this an educational practice is the set of values which it embodies – the intrinsic worth of the activities themselves, the personal qualities which are enhanced, the appropriate way of proceeding (given the values that one has and given the nature of the activity).

One comes to science teaching, for example, with views about the appropriate way of doing science – evidence based enquiry, openness to contrary evidence, clarity of procedures and conclusions. The practice of teaching embodies certain values – the importance of that which is to be learnt, the respect for the learner (how he or she thinks), the respect for evidence and the acknowledgement of contrary viewpoints. Therefore, when teacher researchers are putting into practice a particular strategy or are implementing a curriculum proposal, then they are testing out the values as much as the efficaciousness of the strategy or proposal. Are the values the researchers believe in being implemented in the practice? If not, does this lead to shifts in the values espoused or in the practice itself? Action research, in examining the implementation of a curriculum proposal, involves, therefore, a critique of the values which are intrinsic to the practice. Such a critique will reflect the values which the teacher brings to the practice, and those values will in turn be refined through critical reflection upon their implementation in practice. 'Action research' captures this evershifting conception of practice through the attempt to put into practice certain procedures which one believes are educational.

However, such constant putting into practice, reflecting on that practice, refining of beliefs and values in the light of that reflection, subjecting the embodied ideas to criticism, cannot confine itself to the act of teaching itself. It cannot but embrace the context of teaching – the physical conditions in which learning is expected to take place, the expectations of those who determine the general shape of the curriculum, the resources available for the teachers to draw upon, the constraints upon the teacher's creative response to the issues, the scheme of assessment. It is difficult to see how the clash between the 'official curriculum' and the 'teacher researcher' can be avoided when the latter is constantly testing out the values of the teaching strategies. One can see, therefore, why the encouragement of teacher research is so often defined within official documents in a rather narrow sense.

Action research, therefore, is proposed as a form of research in which teachers review their practice in the light of evidence and of critical judgement of others. In so doing, they inevitably examine what happens to the values they hold, and which they regard as intrinsic to the transaction they are engaged in. Such critical appraisal of practice takes in three different factors which impinge upon practice, and shape the activities within it – the perceptions and values of the different participants, the 'official expectations and values' embodied within the curriculum, and the physical conditions and resources. To do this, various methods for gathering data will be selected – examination results, classroom observation, talking with the pupils. And the interpretation of what is 'working' will constantly be revised in the light of such data. But, of course, others too might, in the light of the data, suggest other possible interpretations. Thus, the dialogue continues. There is no end to this systematic reflection with a view to improving practice.

Reading 3.4

Measures of quality

Denise Kingston and Jane Melvin

We have referred to high-quality provision on numerous occasions in the book so far, but we have not yet considered what 'high quality' is. While there are studies which have helped build our understandings of what constitutes high-quality provision, 'high quality' means different things to different people and, of course, is measured by different groups in different ways. In the reading below, Denise Kingston and Jane Melvin consider some of the measures of quality and what quality means to different stakeholders.

Edited from: Kingston, D. and Melvin J. (2012) 'Quality and Effectiveness in Working with Young People'. In N. Edmond and M. Price (eds) *Integrated Working With Children and Young People.* London: Sage Publications Ltd, 60–79.

Different approaches to quality management

Different contexts have resulted in the development of differing approaches to quality management and we explore three here – quality control, total quality management (TQM) and quality assurance (QA).

Quality control

Quality control is a set of activities intended to ensure that quality requirements are actually being met. Quality control is one part of quality management and 'requires the setting of standards and is essentially a process of inspection, rejection and correction. Quality control is a widely-used method for ensuring quality' (Bone, 1991, as cited by Ford et al., 2002: 167) An example of this approach is the Ofsted inspection. Ofsted, in their publication *Raising Standards, Improving Lives* (2009: 3), state: Inspection entails assessing a service against a published framework and criteria. It involves close observation by trained and experienced inspectors with knowledge of the sector concerned, informed by a range of data, and dialogue with staff and users of services. The output of inspection is normally the publication of judgements set out in a report. Over the years, Ofsted has increasingly been reliant on information and evidence relating to the impact of services, which they collect primarily from service users. For example: what difference has attending this play centre or youth project made to you? What is the benefit to your child of attending this provision? The intention behind such inspection is to identify when quality standards are not being met.

Total quality management (TQM)

TQM is a more wide-ranging and holistic approach to quality because it relies on all staff in an organisation interacting with each other to meet the expressed goal of continual improvement; this is done by constantly monitoring and evaluating their own work, rather than being inspected or audited (Murgatroyd and Morgan, 1994). West-Burnham (1997) also comments that staff need to be passionate about this way of working, as well as systematically following the principles through. The Japanese word 'kaizen' has become associated with the term 'continuous improvement', which is at the heart of the TQM model, and this was based on Deming's 14 Points theory (1982) which was key in relation to the transformation of American and Japanese post-war manufacturing industries. Deming maintained that leadership was as important as ownership and that the manufacturing process should be seen as a whole system, rather than discrete, separate parts

Deming (1982) took these principles and converted them into a cycle of PLAN (establish objectives and define methods to reach them), DO (implement what you have planned), CHECK (measure and compare results obtained against results expected) and ACT (take action to improve what you have implemented). These simple steps were designed to encourage organisations to work in a planned yet adaptable way that accepts and flexes to the constant improvement agenda.

Quality assurance (QA)

Quality assurance is a process that sits somewhere between quality control and TQM. QA processes are based on prevention not cure, and work on the principle of getting it right in the first place, rather than getting things wrong and then putting them right. It involves the development of a structure where everyone agrees on the standards to be reached, by enabling all involved to discuss, understand, own and embed the standards. Leadership and management are then tasked with the following: ensuring that appropriate action is taken, and that processes and procedures for action-planning, reflection, review and evaluation are in place and accessible to all. Quality assurance relates to an agreed set of activities that are intended to monitor that quality requirements are being met, and quality improvement refers to anything that enhances an organisation's ability to meet the identified quality requirements. Both elements form part of an overall quality management strategy.

Quality improvement or self-evaluation/assessment is the process that is conducted within and for the setting. If it forms part of team development and is conducted in collaboration with all of the stake holders, it can be a powerful and empowering process. Quality improvement is linked to effective practice and as such is encouraged by many government agencies. The Self-Evaluation Form (SEF) used in the Ofsted inspection has been developed to encourage and evidence this approach.

Reading 3.5

Reflection-in-action
Donald Schön

> Donald Schön's analysis of reflective practice has influenced training, development and conceptions in many professions. His key insight is that there are forms of professional knowledge which, though often tacitly held, are essential for the exercise of judgement as the complexities and dilemmas of professional life are confronted. Such knowledge is in professional action, and may be developed by reflection-in-action.
>
> *Edited from:* Schön, D. A. (1983) *The Reflective Practitioner: How Professionals Think in Action.* London: Maurice Temple Smith, 50–68.

When we go about the spontaneous, intuitive performance of the actions of everyday life, we show ourselves to be knowledgeable in a special way. Often we cannot say what it is that we know. When we try to describe it we find ourselves at a loss, or we produce descriptions that are obviously inappropriate. Our knowing is ordinarily tacit, implicit in our patterns of action and in our feel for the stuff with which we are dealing. It seems right to say that our knowing is *in* our action.

Similarly, the workaday life of the professional depends on tacit knowing-in-action. Every competent practitioner makes innumerable judgments of quality for which he cannot state adequate criteria, and he displays skills for which he cannot state the rules and procedures. Even when he makes conscious use of research-based theories and techniques, he is dependent on tacit recognitions, judgments, and skilful performances.

On the other hand, both ordinary people and professional practitioners often think about what they are doing, sometimes even while doing it. Stimulated by surprise, they turn thought back on action and on the knowing which is implicit in action. They may ask themselves, for example, 'What features do I notice when I recognize this thing? What are the criteria by which I make this judgment? What procedures am I enacting when I perform this skill? How am I framing the problem that I am trying to solve?' Usually reflection on knowing-in-action goes together with reflection on the stuff at hand. There is some puzzling, or troubling, or interesting phenomenon with which the individual is trying to deal. As he tries to make sense of it, he also reflects on the understandings which have been implicit in his action, understandings which he surfaces, criticizes, restructures, and embodies in further action.

It is this entire process of reflection-in-action which is central to the 'art' by which practitioners sometimes deal well with situations of uncertainty, instability, uniqueness, and value conflict.

Knowing-in-action

There is nothing strange about the idea that a kind of knowing is inherent in intelligent action. Common sense admits the category of know-how, and it does not stretch common sense very much to say that the know-how is *in* the action.

There are actions, recognitions, and judgments which we know how to carry out spontaneously; we do not have to think about them prior to or during their performance. We are often unaware of having learned to do these things; we simply find ourselves doing them. In some cases, we were once aware of the understandings which were subsequently internalized in our feeling for the stuff of action. In other cases, we may usually unable to describe the knowing which our action reveals. It is in this sense that I speak of knowing-in-action, the characteristic mode of ordinary practical knowledge.

Reflecting-in-action

If common sense recognizes knowing-in-action, it also recognizes that we sometimes think about what we are doing. Phrases like 'thinking on your feet,' 'keeping your wits about you,' and 'learning by doing' suggest not only that we can think about doing but that we can think about doing something while doing it. Some of the most interesting examples of this process occur in the midst of a performance.

Much reflection-in-action hinges on the experience of surprise. When intuitive, spontaneous performance yields nothing more than the results expected for it, then we tend not to think about it. But when intuitive performance leads to surprises, pleasing and promising or unwanted, we may respond by reflecting-in-action. In such processes, reflection tends to focus interactively on the outcomes of action, the action itself, and the intuitive knowing implicit in the action.

A professional practitioner is a specialist who encounters certain types of situations again and again. As a practitioner experiences many variations of a small number of types of cases, he is able to 'practice' his practice. He develops a repertoire of expectations, images and techniques. He learns what to look for and how to respond to what he finds. As long as his practice is stable, in the sense that it brings him the same types of cases, he becomes less and less subject to surprise. His knowing-in-practice tends to become increasingly tacit, spontaneous, and automatic, thereby conferring upon him and his clients the benefits of specialization.

As a practice becomes more repetitive and routine, and as knowing-in-practice becomes increasingly tacit and spontaneous, the practitioner may miss important opportunities to think about what he is doing. He may find that he is drawn into patterns of error which he cannot correct. And if he learns, as often happens, to be selectively inattentive to phenomena that do not fit the categories of his knowing-in-action, then he may suffer from boredom or 'burn-out' and afflict his clients with the consequences of his narrowness and rigidity. When this happens, the practitioner has 'over-learned' what he knows.

A practitioner's reflection can serve as a corrective to over-learning. Through reflection, he can surface and criticize the tacit understandings that have grown up around the repetitive experiences of a specialized practice, and can make new sense of the situations of uncertainty or uniqueness which he may allow himself to experience.

Practitioners do reflect *on* their knowing-in-practice. Sometimes, in the relative tranquillity of a postmortem, they think back on a project they have undertaken, a situation they have lived through, and they explore the understandings they have brought to their handling of the case. They may do this in a mood of idle speculation, or in a deliberate effort to prepare themselves for future cases. But they may also reflect on practice while they are in the midst of it. Here they reflect-in-action.

When a practitioner reflects in and on his practice, the possible objects of his reflection are as varied as the kinds of phenomena before him and the systems of knowing-in-practice which he brings to them. He may reflect on the tacit norms and appreciations which underlie a judgment, or on the strategies and theories implicit in a pattern of behaviour. He may reflect on the feeling for a situation which has led him to adopt a particular course of action, on the way in which he has framed the problem he is trying to solve, or on the role he has constructed for himself within a larger institutional context.

Reflection-in-action, in these several modes, is central to the art through which practitioners sometimes cope with the troublesome 'divergent' situations of practice. When the phenomenon at hand eludes the ordinary categories of knowledge-in-practice, presenting itself as unique or unstable, the practitioner may surface and criticize his initial understanding of the phenomenon, construct a new description of it, and test the new description by an on-the-spot experiment. Sometimes he arrives at a new theory of the phenomenon by articulating a feeling he has about it.

When he is confronted with demands that seem incompatible or inconsistent, he may respond by reflecting on the appreciations which he and others have brought to the situation. Conscious of a dilemma, he may attribute it to the way in which he has set his problem, or even to the way in which he has framed his role. He may then find a way of integrating, or choosing among, the values at stake in the situation.

When someone reflects-in-action, he becomes a researcher in the practice context. He does not separate thinking from doing. Because his experimenting is a kind of action, implementation is built into his inquiry. Thus reflection-in-action can proceed, even in situations of uncertainty or uniqueness.

Although reflection-in-action is an extraordinary process, it is not a rare event. Indeed, for reflective practitioners it is the core of practice.

Reading 3.6

Thinking and reflective experience

John Dewey

The writings of John Dewey have been an enormous influence on educational thinking. Indeed, his distinction of 'routinised' and 'reflective' teaching is fundamental to the conception of professional development through reflection. In the two selections below Dewey considers the relationship between reflective thinking and the sort of challenges which people face through experience.

Do you feel that you are sufficiently open-minded to be really 'reflective'?

Edited from: Dewey, J. (1933) *How We Think: A Restatement of the Relation of Reflective Thinking to the Educative Process.* Chicago: Henry Regnery, 15–6; and Dewey, J. (1916) *Democracy and Education.* New York: Free Press, 176–7.

The origin of thinking is some perplexity, confusion, or doubt. Thinking is not a case of spontaneous combustion; it does not occur just on 'general principles'. There is something that occasions and evokes it. General appeals to a child (or to a grown-up) to think, irrespective of the existence in his own experience of some difficulty that troubles him and disturbs his equilibrium, are as futile as advice to lift himself by his boot-straps.

Given a difficulty, the next step is suggestion of some way out – the formation of some tentative plan or project, the entertaining of some theory that will account for the peculiarities in question, the consideration of some solution for the problem. The data at hand cannot supply the solution; they can only suggest it. What, then, are the sources of the suggestion? Clearly, past experience and a fund of relevant knowledge at one's command. If the person has had some acquaintance with similar situations, if he has dealt with material of the same sort before, suggestions more or less apt and helpful will arise. But unless there has been some analogous experience, confusion remains mere confusion. Even when a child (or grown-up) has a problem, it is wholly futile to urge him to 'think' when he has no prior experiences that involve some of the same conditions.

There may, however, be a state of perplexity and also previous experience out of which suggestions emerge, and yet thinking need not be reflective. For the person may not be sufficiently *critical* about the ideas that occur to him. He may jump at a conclusion without weighing the grounds on which it rests; he may forego or unduly shorten the act of hinting, inquiring; he may take the first 'answer,' or solution, that comes to him because of mental sloth, torpor, impatience to get something settled.

One can think reflectively only when one is willing to endure suspense and to undergo the trouble of searching. To many persons both suspense of judgment and intellectual search are disagreeable; they want to get them ended as soon as possible. They cultivate an over-positive and dogmatic habit of mind, or feel perhaps that a condition of doubt will be regarded as evidence of mental inferiority. It is at the point where examination and test enter into investigation that the difference between reflective thought and bad thinking comes in.

To be genuinely thoughtful, we must be willing to sustain and protract that state of doubt which is the stimulus to thorough inquiry.

The general features of a reflective experience are:

perplexity, confusion, doubt, due to the fact that one is implicated in an incomplete situation whose full character is not yet determined;

a conjectural anticipation – a tentative interpretation of the given elements, attributing to them a tendency to effect certain consequences;

a careful survey (examination, inspection, exploration, analysis) of all attainable consideration which will define and clarify the problem in hand;

a consequent elaboration of the tentative hypothesis to make it more precise and more consistent, because squaring with a wider range of facts;

taking one stand upon the projected hypothesis as a plan of action which is applied to the existing state of affairs; doing something overtly to bring about the anticipated result, and thereby testing the hypothesis.

It is the extent and accuracy of steps three and four which mark off a distinctive reflective experience from one on the trial and error plane. They make *thinking* itself into an experience. Nevertheless, we never get wholly beyond the trial and error situation. Our most elaborate and rationally consistent thought has to be tried in the world and thereby tried out. And since it can never take into account all the connections, it can never cover with perfect accuracy all the consequences. Yet a thoughtful survey of conditions is so careful, and the guessing at results so controlled, that we have a right to mark off the reflective experience from the grosser trial and error forms of action.

Reading 3.7

Reflective Writing
Pete Watton, Jane Collings and Jenny Moon

The guidance for students wanting to develop their reflective practice provided by Watton, Collings and Moon (below) provides some very clear examples of reflection. The focus is on reflective writing but the same guidance applies to all reflective practices. The examples of writing they offer allow us to see the differences between surface level reflection and deep reflection, the difference between giving something a little thought and really considering how things came to be and your own personal thoughts, feelings and beliefs.

Can you see the differences between these different levels of reflection? Where do you think your current level of reflection stands?

Edited from: Watton, P., Collings, J. and Moon, J. (2001) *Reflective Writing: Guidance for Students.* Exeter: University of Exeter, available at: exeter.ac.uk/fch/work-experience/reflective-writing-guidance.pdf

Introducing reflection

An excellent description of reflection can be found in the Harry Potter novel *The Goblet of Fire*. In the paragraph below Dumbledore the chief wizard and head teacher is talking to Harry about having excess thoughts!

Harry stared at the stone basin. The contents had returned to their original, silvery white state, swirling and rippling beneath his gaze.
" What is it?" Harry asked shakily.
"This? It is called a Pensieve," said Dumbledore. " I sometimes find, and I am sure you know the feeling, that I simply have too many thoughts and memories crammed into my mind."
"Err," said Harry who couldn't truthfully say that he had ever felt anything of the sort.
"It becomes easier to spot patterns and links, you understand, when they are in this form." (Rowling, 2000: 518–19).

What is required in reflective writing

Have an experience does not automatically mean you will in learn from it. Gibbs (1988) states that unless an experience is reflected upon it may quickly be forgotten, and/or its learning potential lost. It is the feelings and thoughts arising from the reflection that generalizations or concepts can be generated that allow new situations to be tackled effectively (Gibbs, 1988). Reflective writing provides an opportunity for you to gain further insights from your work through reflection on your experiences, and through further consideration of other perspectives from people and theory.

The nature and content of reflection

So what do we mean by reflection? One tentative definition of reflection is offered by Moon (1999):

> ... a form of mental processing with a purpose and/or anticipated outcome that is applied to relatively complex or unstructured ideas for which there is not an obvious solution. (Moon, 1999: 23)

She continues by outlining some of the purposes for reflection:
To:

- Consider the process of our own learning – a process of metacognition
- Critically review something – our own behaviour, that of others or the product of behaviour (e.g. an essay, book, painting etc.)
- Build theory from observations: we draw theory from generalisations – sometimes in practical situations, sometimes in thoughts or a mixture of the two
- Engage in personal or self development
- Make decisions or resolve uncertainty ...
- Empower or emancipate ourselves as individuals (and then it is close to self-development) or to empower/emancipate ourselves within the context of our social groups.' (Moon, 1999: 23)

Deepening reflection – three models of Reflection

'Deep' reflective writing is more than a superficial review of your experience it requires moving beyond the descriptive, and subjecting your experience to greater scrutiny.

In *Learning by Doing*, Gibbs (1988) outlines the stages for a 'Structured Debriefing', which are based on Kolb's (1984) Experiential Learning Cycle and which encourage deeper reflection:

Description: What is the stimulant for reflection? (incident, event, theoretical idea) What are you going to reflect on?

Feelings: What were your reactions and feelings?

Evaluation: What was good and bad about the experience? Make value judgements.

Analysis: What sense can you make of the situation? Bring in ideas from outside the experience to help you. What was really going on?

Conclusions: What can be concluded, in a general sense, from these experiences and the analyses you have undertaken? What can be concluded about your own specific, unique, personal situation or ways of working?

Personal action plans: What are you going to do differently in this type of situation next time? What steps are you going to take on the basis of what you have learnt?

Hatton and Smith (1995) identified four levels in the development of teacher reflection from teaching practice.

Descriptive writing: This is a description of events or literature reports. There is no discussion beyond description. The writing is considered not to show evidence of reflection.

Descriptive reflective: This is basically a description of events, but shows some evidence of deeper consideration in relatively descriptive language. There is no real evidence of the notion of alternative viewpoints in use.

Dialogic reflection: This writing suggests there is a 'stepping back' from the events and actions which leads to different level of discourse. There is a sense of 'mulling about', discourse with self and an exploration of the role of self in events and actions. There is consideration of the qualities of judgements and possible alternatives for explaining and hypothesising. The reflection is analytical or integrative, linking factors and perspectives.

Critical reflection: This form of reflection, in addition, shows evidence that the learner is aware that actions and events may be 'located within and explicable by multiple perspectives, but are located in and influenced by multiple and socio– political contexts'

Bloom (1964) identified different levels of thinking processes, which he presented in a hierarchy (Figure 3.6.1); these can also be used as a framework for more thorough reflection. They move from knowing, evidenced through recalling information, through to evaluating, evidenced through making systematic judgements of value.

Figure 3.6.1
Bloom's hierarchy of thinking processes

Increasing Difficulty

Process	Explanation
Knowledge	Recognition and recall of information – describing events
Comprehension	Interprets, translates or summarises given information – demonstrating understanding of events
Application	Uses information in a situation different from original learning context
Analysis	Separates wholes into parts until relationships are clear – breaks down experiences
Synthesis	Combines elements to form new entity from the original one – draws on experience and other evidence to suggest new insights
Evaluation	Involves acts of decision making, or judging based on criteria or rationale – makes judgements about

Exercise in reflective writing

Read the four different accounts of the same story below. Consider how are they written against the factors provided by Hatton and Smith (1995) and Bloom (1965).

The park (1)

I went to the park today. The sun shone and clouds floated across the sky in a gentle breeze. It was really quite hot – so much nicer than the day before when it rained. When I got there, I went over to the children's playing field. There were several children there and one, in particular, I noticed, was in too many clothes for the hot day. The children were running about and this child became red in the face and began to slow down and then he sat. He must have been about 10. Some of the others called him up again and he got to his feet. He stumbled into the game for a few moments, tripping once or twice. It appeared that he had just not got the energy to lift his feet. Eventually he stumbled down and did not get up but he was still moving and he shuffled into a half sitting and half lying position watching the other children and I think he was calling out to them. I don't know.

Anyway, I walked on after a few minutes. I had to get to the shop to buy some fresh chilli peppers for the chilli-con-carne that my children had asked for tonight's party. The twins had invited many friends round for an end-of-term do to celebrate the beginning of the summer holidays. They might think that they have cause to celebrate but it makes a lot more work for me when they are home. James, my partner, often says that we should celebrate when they go back to school but I would not like to tell them that.

It was the next day when the paper came through the door – in it there was a report of a child who had been taken seriously ill in the park the previous day. He was fighting for his life in hospital and they said that the seriousness of the situation was due to the delay before he was brought to hospital. The report commented on the fact that he had been lying unattended for half an hour before one of the other children decided to do something about him. It said that that several passers-by might have seen him looking ill and the report went on to consider why passers-by do not take action when they see that something is wrong. The article was headed 'Why do they 'Walk on by'?'

The park (2)

The event took place in the park. There was a child playing with others. He looked hot and unfit. I watched the children for a while and walked on. Next day it was reported in the paper that the child had been taken to hospital seriously ill – very seriously ill. The report said that there were several passers-by in the park who had seen the child looking ill and who had done nothing.

Reading the report, I felt very guilty and I have found it difficult to shift the feelings.

I did not stop because I was on my way to the shops to buy food for a meal that I had to cook. Though I saw that the child was ill, I chose not to act. If I had realized that he was so ill, I would have acted differently. I guess I did really know, but I did not want to do anything about it. I know that.

I should have gone over and asked him what was wrong – and even got one of the other children to call for help. I am not sure if the help would have been ambulance or doctor at that stage – but it does not matter now. If he had been given help then, he would not be fighting for his life.

I guess this situation has really shocked me. It reminds me of when my uncle died – but then again I don't really think that that is relevant. He was going to die anyway. My bad feelings about that situation were due to sheer sadness at his death and some irrational regrets that I did not visit him on the day before.

This event has really shaken me to my roots – more than I would have expected. It is making me think about actions in all sorts of areas of my life. Maybe it is the culmination of many events that have been happening recently and I need to consider what is going on in my life in a big way. I need to think about how to sort out all the different things that this has made me think about in my life.

The park (3)

I went to the park today. The light reminded me of a time that I was walking on St David's Head in Wales – when there was a hard and bright light and anything I looked at was in silhouette. Unlike on that occasion, this time, things were generally very satisfactory in my life I thought. In fact I was going to the supermarket to get some chilli peppers to make the chile-con-carne that I had promised the children. They were having one of their end of term celebrations with friends. I always thought that they were unfair on me when they did this. I find that their holiday time makes a lot more work. If I were to celebrate anything about their school terms, it would be the end of the holidays when they are about to go back to school. No – I joke (or do I? – I am not sure that I really joke. How I could do with a little less pressure on my life just at the moment).

Anyway, I was walking across the park and came to a group of children. I don't know why I stopped to look at them. I don't usually look at other people's children – I just did. Anyway there were a number of kids there. I noticed, in particular, one child who seemed to be very overdressed for the weather. His face was red. He was a boy of around 10 – not unlike Charlie. He was running around with the others but was beginning to look distressed. I felt uneasy about him but I did not do anything. What could I have done?

Anyway, I remember thinking, I had little time and the supermarket would get crowded. I suppose that in retrospect I wish I had acted – but I still do not know quite how, at that point. Anyway he sat down, looking absolutely exhausted and as if he had no energy to do anything. A few moments later, the other children called him up to run about again. I felt more uneasy and watched as he got up and tried to run, then fell, ran again and fell and half sat and half lay. Still I did nothing more than look – what was going on with me?

Eventually I went on – it was to get to the shops, and to get the meal and all the other things I had to do, I told myself. It was the next day when the paper came through the door that I had a real shock. It made me feel as guilty as that awful trauma all those years ago. I do not usually do wrong, in fact I think of myself as a good person. In the paper there was a report of a child who had been taken seriously ill in the park the previous day. He was fighting for his life in the hospital and the situation was much more serious because there had been such a delay in getting him to hospital. The report commented on the fact that he had been lying unattended to for half an hour before one of the other children decided to do something about him. One of my many reactions was to ask why the other children had not been more responsible. However, it went on to say that several passers-by might have seen him playing and looking ill and the report considered why passers-by do not take action when they see that something is wrong. The article was headed 'Why do they 'Walk on by'?'

The event affected me for some days afterwards but I did not know where to go or whom to tell. I did want to own up. I assumed that the bad feelings would eventually fade and they did – thank goodness. Next time I will not walk on by – I hope!

The park (4)

I went past the park on the way to the shops. There were children playing there. I thought I knew some of them. They are a gang of kids who are perpetual bullies to other children who are younger or weaker than themselves. They have caused problems to my children quite recently. I stopped and watched them and I thought that they seemed to become a bit nervous – they must have realized who I was. I suppose there was a bit of intimidation intended on my part. I guess they were worried about what I might do.

They were running about. The sun was hot. One boy – probably a bit older than Charlie's age – seemed more bothered and nervous than the others – rightly too – he was the main trouble-maker from what I recalled. He seemed to fall over – faking it in front of me I guessed. The others left him there anyway. That made me think even more that his was acting – I think he wanted me to feel sorry for him. I did not. Eventually the others called to him and he got up slowly – still faking it – then he fell again and I got fed up with his acting and went on to do my shopping. I felt cross. Thank goodness he was not coming to the party that my children were planning – though I am surprised that he had not managed to play-act his way into their sympathy given his current performance of manipulation.

Well yes – there was a bit more to the story. The next day's paper said that a child had been taken ill in the park the previous day – and that he had been lying there for some time and he was very ill. It did also mention that there had been passers-by who had seen him there and had not done anything about it. Even the headline referred to that – 'Why do they 'Walk on by'?' – what a silly headline!

Well what could I have done? I thought things were different – he couldn't still be faking it at the hospital could he – or maybe the paper is short of news today and is exaggerating. Maybe he fell asleep on the ground and got cold and the other children eventually panicked – and maybe he decided to go on with his play-acting at the hospital. Knowing the family he comes from, I wouldn't be surprised.

That is how I thought about it on the day afterwards anyway. I wrote it all down in my journal – but I was a bit plagued by it. It kept coming back in my mind and gradually

– over the next few days – I begun to think of him differently. Maybe he was ill when I saw him. Maybe I was caught up in the anger that the bullying activities of those kids had caused among some of us other parents and I could only see the boy in that light. Thinking of it in that way makes me realize that I should perhaps have acted differently. Bully though he might have been, I think now that he was ill – and maybe he was even coming near me in the hope that I might take pity on him.

But of course, I do not know the truth of the situation. I am sure that I would have acted differently if I had seen the situation as I did later. My reactions the next day would have been different and I would not be plagued as I am now by the feelings of irresponsibility. I guess I just hope that other parents don't misconstrue my children's actions in the way I misunderstood his – if I did.

This has all made me think about how we view things. The way I saw this event at the time was quite different to the way I see it now. It is a year later. The story ran in the paper for some time because the boy was very ill indeed and he nearly died and the paper kept going back to the theme of people who do not take action and just stand and stare when there is an incident.

Thinking back to the time, the bullying was on my mind – mainly because we had been talking about it at breakfast. It had actually happened a while before – but the conversation had brought all the anger and upset to my mind – and then seeing them there– well I thought they were the same children – it is even possible that they were not. It was just so much on my mind at the time.

So I can see how I looked at that event and interpreted it in a manner that was consistent with my emotional frame of mind at the time. Seeing the same events without that breakfast conversation might have led me to see the whole thing in an entirely different manner and I might have acted differently. The significance of this whole event is chilling when I realize that my lack of action nearly resulted in his death. But how could I have seen it differently when I was caught up in that set of emotions? What mechanism could I have used in order to see if there were any other ways of construing it? How can I know that my perceptions in respect of some event are not distorted in such a way that I act in an inappropriate manner?

When practising reflective writing:

- Be aware of the purpose of your reflective writing and state if it is appropriate.
- Reflective writing requires practice and constant standing back from oneself.
- Practice reflecting writing on the same event/incident through different people's viewpoints and disciplines.
- Deepen your reflection/reflective writing with the help of others through discussing issues with individuals and groups, getting the points of others.
- Always reflect on what you have learnt from an incident, and how you would do something differently another time.
- Try to develop your reflective writing to include the ethical, moral, historical and socio-political contexts where these are relevant.

Principles

What are the foundations of effective teaching and learning?

4

Readings

4.1 Mandy Swann, Alison Peacock, Susan Hart and Mary Jane Drummond
Learning without limits (p. 66)

4.2 Kathy Sylva, Edward Melhuish, Pam Sammons, Iram Siraj-Blatchford and Brenda Taggart
The Effective Provision of Pre-school Education (EPPE) project: Findings from pre-school to end of Key Stage 1. (p. 70)

4.3 The Royal Society
Insights, opportunities and challenges of educational neuroscience (p. 74)

4.4 Rodd Parker-Rees
Playful learning (p. 79)

4.5 Cathy Nutbrown
Schemas and learning (p. 81)

The readings in this chapter draw out some of the key issues raised in Chapter 4 of *Reflective Teaching in Early Education* in which we consider the TLRP principles for teaching and learning. The first reading encourages practitioners to think about the expectations they hold of children and how this can impact upon the opportunities children receive and the ways in which they come to view learning. This is followed by a summary of the key findings of the first phase of the Effective Provision of Pre-school Education (EPPE) project. The work of the EPPE team has been highly influential in the development of policy and practice in the UK in recent years and thus understanding how this data was collected and reported is of importance for any early years practitioner. We then turn to neuroscience and consider what is known in this relatively new field and how this influences how we view learning.

The final two readings provide more detailed information on the issues raised throughout the *Reflective Teaching in Early Education* book: play and schemas. These readings have been included here as we recognized that their influence can be traced through effective early years practice.

There are suggestions for Key Readings and other ideas for more detailed study at *reflectiveteaching.co.uk*. To access these, please visit *reflectiveteaching.co.uk* – then navigate to this book, this chapter and Notes for Further Reading.

Reading 4.1

Learning without limits

Mandy Swann, Alison Peacock, Susan Hart and Mary Jane Drummond

For any educator, there is a crucial choice. Deeply embedded in our culture are views about the nature of 'abilities' and ideas about genetic inheritance, social class, ethnicity, gender, etc. Such taken-for-granted ideas emerge and have serious consequences in the form of restricted expectations of what children can achieve.

Swann and her colleagues throw down a gauntlet. Abilities can be developed, and learning has no limits if approached in appropriate ways. Every child has learning capacities. The task of the teacher is to unlock and nurture these capacities. It is also argued that building on learner capacities is the enlightened way to improve standards, but that some national requirements can, ironically, inhibit this.

So where do you stand?

Edited from: Swann, M., Peacock, A., Hart, S. and Drummond, M. J. (2012*) Creating Learning Without Limits.* Maidenhead: Open University Press, 1–7.

We began our research drawn together by some unshakeable convictions:

- that human potential is not predictable;
- that children's futures are unknowable;
- that education has the power to enhance the lives of all.

Few would argue with these simple truths, and yet they are at odds with the prevailing spirit of the age – a time in which teachers are required to use the certainty of prediction as a reliable tool in their planning and organization of opportunities for learning. Targets, levels, objectives, outcomes – all these ways of conceptualizing learning require teachers to behave as if children's potential is predictable and their futures knowable far in advance, as if their powers as educators can have only a limited impact on the lives of many children and young people. Furthermore, closely associated with this view of learning is an equally damaging view of the children who do the learning, who can themselves be known, measured and quantified in terms of so-called ability, a fixed, internal capacity, which can readily be determined.

This determinist thinking is not limited to those of any particular political persuasion. Nor is it an issue of transient significance. It is the legacy of a longstanding and ongoing, deep-rooted and damaging orthodoxy about the nature of 'ability' and how best to set about educating children. This legacy has given rise to limited and limiting thinking on the part of policy makers about children and about how to structure and organize learning and schooling.

Teachers need a much more complex understanding of learning and of the many inter-acting influences that underlie differences of attainment if they are to be able to use their powers as educators to transform children's life chances.

So, what if teachers were to jettison the linear model of learning? What if, instead of being constantly compared, ranked, and fettered by labels, children's learning capacity was enabled to flourish and expand in all its rich variety and complexity? What if planning for preordained and predicted levels was replaced with planning experiences and opportu-nities for learning that promote deep engagement, that fill children with a sense of agency, that endow them with motivation, courage and belief in their power to influence their own futures? And what if school development were to be driven by a commitment on the part of a whole-school community to creating better ways for everybody to live, work and learn together, in an environment free from limiting beliefs about fixed abilities and fixed futures?

In our book, *Creating Learning Without Limits,* we argue that school development inspired by this alternative vision is both necessary and possible. We present the findings of our research study of one primary school which, in just a few years, moved out of 'special measures' to become a successful, vibrant learning community (also rated 'outstanding' by Ofsted). This was not achieved through the use of targets, planning, prediction and exter-nally imposed blueprints for pedagogy, but through a focus on learning (rather than simply attainment) which was nourished by deep belief in the learning capacity of everybody.

The principles which informed developments in this school had their origins in previous work which had explored alternatives to ability-based pedagogy – the *Learning Without Limits* project (Hart et al., 2004). Nine teachers had worked with young people aged from 5 to 16 and drew on expertise across a range of curriculum areas. While their practices were distinctively individual, the research team found that they shared a particular mindset – a way of making sense of what happens in classrooms. This was based on an orientation to the future that came to be called 'transformability'. Rather than accepting apparent differences in ability as the natural order of things, and differentiating their teaching accordingly, these teachers did not see the future of their students as predictable or inevi-table. They worked on the assumption that there is always the potential for change: things can change for the better, sometimes even dramatically, as a result of what both teachers and learners do in the present.

For these teachers the concept of inherent ability, an inaccessible inner force respon-sible for learning, residing in the individual and subject to the fixed, internal limits of each individual learner, had no currency or value. In its place, the research team discerned a powerful alternative concept of *learning capacity*, which resides both in the individual learner and in the social collective of the classroom, and is by no means fixed and stable. This concept of learning capacity, evidenced in the various daily practices of these teachers, released the teachers from the sense of powerlessness induced by the idea of inherent ability. Furthermore, they realized that the work of transforming learning capacity does not depend on what teachers do alone, but on what both teachers *and* learners do together – a joint enterprise, the exercise of co-agency. Convinced of their own (and their students') power to make a difference to future learning, they used their rich fund of knowledge about the forces – internal and external, individual and collective – that shape and limit learning capacity to make transforming choices. Working on the principle that classroom decisions must be made in the interests of all students, not just some – a principle the research team called 'the ethic of everybody' – and rooting their work in the fundamental trust in their students' powers as learners, the project teachers made good their commitment to the essential educability of their learners.

The study amassed convincing evidence that teaching for learning without limits is not a naïve fantasy, but a real possibility, in good working order, accessible to observation and analysis. The research team developed a practical, principled pedagogical model (see Figure 4.1.1), arguing that elements of this model would be recognizable to other teachers who shared similar values and commitments and had themselves developed classroom

Figure 4.1.1
Principled
Pedagogic Model

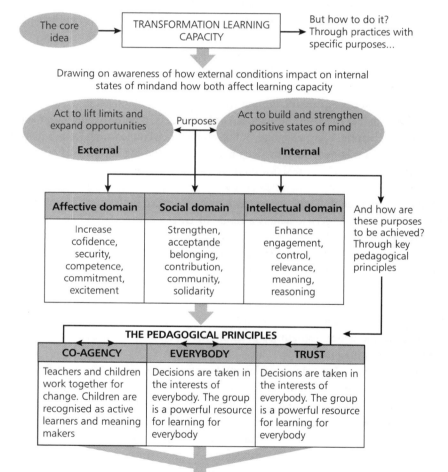

practices in line with their convictions. They hoped that their work would convince more teachers that the alternative 'transformability' model is a practical and empowering way of realizing their commitment to young people's learning.

The nine teachers in the original study were all working in different schools, in different parts of the country. The focus was inevitably limited to what teachers found themselves able to do individually, within their own classrooms. The teachers thus recognized that there was so much more that could be done to lift limits on learning if groups of teachers, departments, whole-school staffs or even whole school communities were to work together towards a common vision.

When one of these teachers, Alison Peacock, took up a headship in a primary school, a wonderful opportunity presented itself to explore these wider possibilities. Alison was committed to leading staff in adopting teaching and learning practices devoted to strengthening and transforming children's learning capacity and free from all forms of ability labelling. A new research project was set up, *Creating Learning Without Limits*, to carry out a two-year in-depth study of the work of the staff of The Wroxham School, in Hertfordshire.

Our book thus tells the story of what we learned from this school community about how to create 'learning without limits'. Our enquiry focused on the learning that went on, individually and collectively, as the whole staff worked together, day by day, to create in reality their vision of an education based on inclusive, egalitarian principles, including an unshakeable bedrock belief in everybody's capacity to learn.

Reading 4.2

The Effective Provision of Pre-school Education (EPPE) project: Findings from pre-school to end of Key Stage 1

Kathy Sylva, Edward Melhuish, Pam Sammons, Iram Siraj-Blatchford and Brenda Taggart

This research briefing summarizes the key findings of the initial findings of the EPPE project. This project has been extended to become the Effective Pre-school, Primary and Secondary Education (EPSE) project, the findings of which we also recommend that you read. This research has been a key influence on policy and practice in the UK and beyond in recent years. It is one of the few studies to use a normative sample – that is, a sample which represents the whole population of children, rather than focusing on children from particular groups. As such, the findings are particularly useful and interesting for those considering early years policy and practice.

Edited from: Sylva, K., Melhuish, E., Sammons, P., Siraj-Blatchford, I. and Taggart, B. (2004) *The Effective Provision of Pre-school Education (EPPE) Project: Findings from Pre-school to end of Key Stage 1.* Nottingham: DfES.

The Aims of EPPE

EPPE explored five key questions:

1 What is the impact of pre-school on children's intellectual and social/behavioural development?
2 Are some pre-schools more effective than others in promoting children's development?
3 What are the characteristics of an effective preschool setting?
4 What is the impact of the home and childcare history on children's development?
5 Do the effects of pre-school continue through Key Stage 1 (ages 6 and 7 years)?

EPPE studied a range of different types of preschools and 3,000 children from differing social backgrounds. An important element in the study has been to ensure that fair comparison can be made between individual settings and types of provision. The study has taken into account the contribution to children's development

Key findings over the preschool period
Impact of attending a pre-school

- Preschool experience, compared to none, enhances all-round development in children.

- Duration of attendance (in months) is important; an earlier start (under age 3 years) is related to better intellectual development.

- Full time attendance led to no better gains for children than part-time provision.

- Disadvantaged children benefit significantly from good quality pre-school experiences, especially where they are with a mixture of children from different social backgrounds.

- Overall disadvantaged children tend to attend preschool for shorter periods of time than those from more advantaged groups (around 4–6 months less).

- Does type of pre-school matter?

- There are significant differences between individual preschool settings and their impact on children, some settings are more effective than others in promoting positive child outcomes.

- Good quality can be found across all types of early years settings; however quality was higher overall in settings integrating care and education and in nursery schools.

Effects of quality and specific 'practices' in preschool

- High quality preschooling is related to better intellectual and social/behavioural development for children.

- Settings that have staff with higher qualifications have higher quality scores and their children make more progress.

- Quality indicators include warm interactive relationships with children, having a trained teacher as manager and a good proportion of trained teachers on the staff.

- Where settings view educational and social development as complementary and equal in importance, children make better all-round progress.

- Effective pedagogy includes interaction traditionally associated with the term "teaching", the provision of instructive learning environments and 'sustained shared thinking' to extend children's learning.

The importance of home learning

For all children, the quality of the home learning environment is more important for intellectual and social development than parental occupation, education or income. What parents do is more important than who parents are.

Key findings at the end of Key Stage 1
Lasting effects

The beneficial effects of preschool remained evident throughout Key Stage 1, although some outcomes were not as strong as they had been at school entry.

Duration and quality

- The number of months a child attended preschool continued to have an effect on their progress throughout Key Stage 1, although this effect was stronger for academic skills than for social behavioural development.
- Preschool quality was significantly related to children's scores on standardised tests of reading and mathematics at age 6. At age 7 the relationship between quality and academic attainment was somewhat weaker but still evident, and the effect of quality on social behavioural development was no longer significant. High quality preschool provision combined with longer duration had the strongest effect on development.

Effective settings

Individual preschools varied in their 'effectiveness' for influencing a child's development. The advantages for a child's development of attending a particularly 'effective' preschool centre persists up to age 7. Of course this does not mean that contemporaneous experiences at primary school have no impact on children's lives – only that the individual pre-schools attended continued to have an influence.

Vulnerable children

A small group of children continued to be at risk of special educational needs (2.3 per cent of the EPPE sample had full statements), with more of the home children falling into this group even after taking into account background factors.

Multiple disadvantage continued to have a negative affect on intellectual and social development up to the end of Key Stage 1. However, the impact of English as an additional language (EAL) is much reduced at age 7, compared to the strength of the effect at age 3 and 5.

Home learning environment

The effect of home learning activities during the preschool period continues to be evident in children's developmental profiles at the end of Key Stage 1.

Social mix

Disadvantaged children do better in settings with a mixture of children from different social backgrounds rather than in settings catering mostly for children from disadvantaged families. This has implications for the siting of centres in areas of social disadvantage.

The EPPE research indicates that preschool can play an important part in combating social exclusion and promoting inclusion by offering disadvantaged children, in particular, a better start to primary school. The findings indicate preschool has a positive impact on children's progress over and above important family influences. The quality of the pre-school setting experience as well as the quantity (more months but not necessarily more hours/day) are both influential.

The results show that individual preschool centres vary in their effectiveness in promoting intellectual progress over the pre-school period, and indicate that better outcomes are associated with certain forms of provision. Likewise, the research points to the separate and significant influence of the home learning environment. These aspects (quality and quantity of preschool and home learning environment) can be seen as more susceptible to change through policy and practitioner initiatives than other child or family characteristics, such as SES.

The EPPE project has become well known for its contribution to 'evidence based policy' in early years education and care. Its findings are robust because they are based on sound and innovative research methods. The implications for policy of the EPPE project have been spelled out clearly and are being discussed – and acted upon – at national and local level. EPPE set out to contribute to the debate about the education and care of young children; the EPPE mixed-method research design targeted issues that could 'make a difference' to the lives of young children and their families.

Reading 4.3

Insights, opportunities and challenges of educational neuroscience

The Royal Society

> The text in this reading reflects the work of the Royal Society in promoting greater public understanding of the significance of neuroscience. *Brain Waves* is a series of reports which apply neuroscientific insights to a range of contemporary issues. Module 2 focuses on education.
>
> The reading begins with eight bullet points from the executive summary of the report, and continues with elaboration and discussion of some of the evidence and issues arising. The full text, with copious citation of evidence, is available at royalsociety.org and **reflectiveteaching.co.uk**. Membership of the Working Party which produced Brain Waves Module 2 was Uta Frith (Chair), Dorothy Bishop, Colin Blakemore, Sarah-Jayne Blakemore, Brian Butterworth, Usha Goswami, Paul Howard-Jones, Diana Laurillard, Eleanor Maguire, Barbara Sahakian and Annette Smith.
>
> *Edited from:* The Royal Society (2011) *Brain Waves Module 2: Neuroscience: Implications for Education and Lifelong Learning.* London: The Royal Society.

The brain is the organ that enables us to adapt to our environment – in essence, to learn. Neuroscience is shedding light on the influence of our genetic make-up on learning over our life span, in addition to environmental factors. This enables us to identify key indicators for educational outcomes, and provides a scientific basis for evaluating different teaching approaches.

Education is concerned with enhancing learning, and neuroscience is concerned with understanding the mechanisms of learning. This common ground suggests a future in which educational practice is transformed by science, just as medical practice was transformed by science about a century ago. In this report we consider some of the key insights from neuroscience that could eventually lead to such a transformation.

- The brain changes constantly as a result of learning, and remains 'plastic' throughout life. Neuroscience has shown that learning a skill changes the brain and that these changes revert when practice of the skill ceases. Hence 'use it or lose it' is an important principle for lifelong learning.

- Neuroscience research suggests that learning outcomes are not solely determined by the environment. Biological factors play an important role in accounting for differences in learning ability between individuals.

- By considering biological factors, research has advanced the understanding of specific learning difficulties, such as dyslexia and dyscalculia. Likewise, neuroscience is uncovering why certain types of learning are more rewarding than others.

- Research also shows that resilience, our adaptive response to stress and adversity, can be built up through education with lifelong effects into old age.

- Research also shows that both acquisition of knowledge and mastery of self-control benefit future learning. Thus, neuroscience has a key role in investigating means of boosting brain power.

- Some insights from neuroscience are relevant for the design of adaptive digital technologies. These have the potential to create more learning opportunities inside and outside the classroom, and throughout life. This is exciting given the knock-on effects this could have on wellbeing, health, employment and the economy.

- There is great public interest in neuroscience, yet accessible high quality information is scarce. We urge caution in the rush to apply so-called brain-based methods, many of which do not yet have a sound basis in science. There are inspiring developments in basic science although practical applications are still some way off.

- The emerging field of educational neuroscience presents opportunities as well as challenges for education. It provides means to develop a common language and bridge the gulf between educators, psychologists and neuroscientists.

Both nature and nurture affect the learning brain

Individuals differ greatly in their response to education, and both genes and the environment contribute to these differences. Work with identical twins, who have the same genetic make-up, has shown that they are more similar in, for instance, personality, reading and mathematical ability, than non-identical twins, who differ in their genetic make-up. While it is widely agreed that individual differences can have a genetic basis, genetic influences on brain development and brain function are not yet well understood.

Genetic make-up alone does not shape a person's learning ability; genetic predisposition interacts with environmental influences at every level. Human learning abilities vary, in the same way that human height and blood pressure vary.

The brain is plastic

The brain is constantly changing and everything we do changes our brain. These changes can be short lived or longer lasting. When we sleep, walk, talk, observe, introspect, interact, attend, and learn, neurons fire. The brain has extraordinary adaptability, sometimes referred to as 'neuroplasticity'. This is due to the process by which connections between neurons are strengthened when they are simultaneously activated. This process is often summarised as, 'neurons that fire together wire together'. The effect is known as experience-dependent plasticity and is present throughout life.

Neuroplasticity allows the brain continuously to take account of the environment. It also allows the brain to store the results of learning in the form of memories. In this way, the brain can prepare for future events based on experience. On the other hand, habit learning, which is very fast and durable, can be maladaptive and difficult to overcome, as for example in addiction.

Key findings based on neuroplasticity include the following:

- Changes in the brain's structure and connectivity suggest there are sensitive periods in brain development extending beyond childhood into adolescence. Plasticity tends to decrease with age and this is particularly evident when we consider learning of a second language.

- The overall pattern of neural development appears to be very similar between genders, but the pace of brain maturation appears to differ, with boys on average reaching full maturation at a slightly later age than girls.

- Dynamic changes to brain connectivity continue in later life. The wiring of the brain changes progressively during development for a surprisingly long time.

- Just as athletes need to train their muscles, there are many skills where training needs to be continued to maintain brain changes. The phrase 'use it or lose it!' is very apt. Changes in the adult brain following the acquisition of specific skills has also been shown for music, juggling and dance. This illustrates what we mean by experience-dependent plasticity. The genetic specification of our brains only partly determines what we know and how we behave; much depends on environmental factors that determine what we experience. Education is prominent among these factors.

The brain has mechanisms for self-regulation

Together with findings from cognitive psychology, neuroscience is beginning to shed light on self-regulation and self control, that is, the inhibition of impulsive behaviour.

Recent research has shown that the ability to inhibit inappropriate behaviour, for example, stopping oneself making a previously rewarded response, develops relatively slowly during childhood, but continues to improve during adolescence and early adulthood. This is probably because the brain regions involved in inhibition, in particular the prefrontal cortex, continue to change both in terms of structure and function, during adolescence and into the twenties. In addition, there are large individual differences in our ability to exert self-control, which persist throughout life. For example, by age three, some children are much better than others at resisting temptation, and the ability to resist temptation (delayed gratification) at this age has been found to be associated with higher education attainment in later childhood and adolescence. Research is under way to investigate to what extent cognitive training programmes can strengthen this ability.

Understanding mechanisms underlying self-control might one day help to improve prospects for boosting this important life skill. In addition, it is important to learners and teachers who are dealing with lack of discipline or antisocial behaviour. Given that the self-reported ability to exert self-control has been found to be an important predictor of academic success, understanding the neural basis of self-control and its shaping through appropriate methods may be valuable.

Education is a powerful form of cognitive enhancement

Cognitive enhancement usually refers to increased mental prowess, for instance, increased problem-solving ability or memory. Such enhancement is usually linked with the use of drugs or sophisticated technology. However, when compared with these means, education seems the most broadly and consistently successful cognitive enhancer of all. Education provides, for instance, access to strategies for abstract thought, such as algebra or logic, which can be applied in solving a vast range of problems and can increase mental flexibility. Literacy and numeracy change the human brain, but also enable human beings to perform feats that would not be possible without these cultural tools, including the achievements of science. The steady rise in IQ scores over the last decades is thought to be at least partially due to education. Findings from neuroscience and cognitive enhancement include the following:

- *Education* can build up an individual's cognitive reserve and resilience, that is, their adaptive response to stressful and traumatic events and illness, including brain injury, mental disorder, and normal ageing. Cognitive reserve and resilience can be built up at any point during life. Research on cognitive reserve has found an inverse relationship between educational attainment and risk of dementia, which means that keeping the mind active slows cognitive decline and improves cognitive abilities in older adults.

- *Physical health, exercise, sleep and nutrition* are crucial to physical and mental wellbeing and their effects on cognitive functions are mediated by the brain. For example, neuroscience research on sleep and sleep deprivation can explain some highly specific effects on memory and other mental functions.

Individual differences in learning ability and the brain

There is wide variation in learning ability; some individuals struggle to learn in all domains, whereas others have specific difficulties for instance, with language, literacy, numeracy or self control. There is ample evidence that these individuals are at increased risk of poor social adaptation and unemployment. The costs to society are thus substantial and there is an urgent need to find educational approaches that will work.

Current work in neuroscience is directed toward identifying the brain basis of learning difficulties. As this research advances, prospects are raised for identification and diagnosis, and for designing interventions that are suitable for different ages and may overcome or circumvent the learning difficulties. Even for those with severe learning difficulties, improved understanding of specific cognitive and neurological correlates of disorder can be harnessed to make education more effective.

Future challenges

There are major cultural and vocabulary differences between the scientific research and education communities.

Critics of neuroscience fear that it represents:

- a reductionist view that overemphasises the role of the brain at the expense of a holistic understanding of cultural life based on interpretation and empathy

- a determinist view that our neurological inheritance sets us on a path that is unchangeable

However, a neuroscience perspective recognises that each person constitutes an intricate system operating at neural, cognitive, and social levels, with multiple interactions taking place between processes and levels. Neuroscience is a key component of this system and is therefore a key contributor to enriching explanations of human thought and behaviour. Furthermore, it is a mistake to regard biological predispositions as deterministic; their impact is probabilistic and context-dependent. The important point is that there are educational difficulties that have a biological basis, and cannot be attributed solely to parents', teachers' or society's expectations. If in these cases the biological risk factors are not taken into account, important opportunities to optimize learning will be missed.

A web search using Google with the keywords 'Learning', 'Teaching', and 'Brain' indicates that there is a huge demand for applications of brain science to education. Thus despite philosophical reservations, there is considerable enthusiasm for neuroscience and its applications. This can, however, lead to problems. For example, commercial interests have been quick to respond to the demand of the enthusiasts and promote their credibility with testimonials of reportedly trustworthy individuals. There is already a glut of books, games, training courses, and nutritional supplements, all claiming to improve learning and to be backed by science. This is problematic because the sheer volume of information from a range of sources makes it difficult to identify what is independent, accurate and authoritative. At worst, this industry creates 'neuro-myths' that can damage the credibility and impact of authentic research.

The idea that 'Knowledge needs to go in both directions' typifies the sentiments expressed by neuroscience, policy and teaching communities.

If educational neuroscience is to develop into an effective new discipline, and make a significant impact on the quality of learning for all learners, we need a long-term dialogue between neuroscientists and a wide range of other researchers and professionals from a variety of backgrounds in education.

Reading 4.4

Playful learning
Rod Parker-Rees

Rod Parker-Rees uses his insights as an early years educator to make some powerful points about the significance of playfulness in learning. In particular, he locates play within a Vygotskian framework, demonstrating how it enables interaction between social and personal meanings. Play with sand, water, dough, etc. is thus matched by playfulness with words, concepts, roles and identities. It can be a way of experimentally transforming ourselves, transcending problems, imagining possibilities and of learning throughout life.

Do the children in your care have appropriate opportunities for play, in a form appropriate to their age? And what about yourself? Beyond 'what is', can you imagine 'what might be'?

Edited from: Parker-Rees, R. (1999) 'Protecting Playfulness'. In L. Abbott and H. Moylett (eds) *Early Education Transformed: New Millennium Series.* London and New York: Falmer Press, 64–6.

The Piagetian model of the child as 'little scientist' smoothing the tangle of everyday experience into increasingly tidy, cool and formal concepts is itself only one of many possible ways of mapping the complexity of cognitive development. Vygotsky insisted that this 'natural line' of development was accompanied by a 'cultural line' (Wertsch, 1991: 25) because we construct our ways of interpreting experience within a cultural environment which is deeply rutted by the social process of communication. The flow of our perceptions is channelled into shared forms as we tune our interpretations and adopt common ways of organizing what we know.

Communication both generates and depends upon common ways of simplifying and making sense of experience; words mean what people mean when they use them. But communication also depends on a certain amount of play in the cultural machine; word meanings are far from fixed or static. Our personal sense-making can never correspond exactly with another person's because, although we may share a broad system of simple definitions, the colour, richness and warmth of the meanings and connotations which we attach to these is rooted in our own, unique, subterranean tangle of experience. This inevitable looseness of meaning is what makes conversation both interesting and emotionally rewarding; it is 'just what is needed to allow change to happen when people with different analyses interact' (Newman et al. in Bliss et al., 1996: 62).

Children play with sand, water, dough and construction kits, forming and transforming materials and exploring their possibilities, but they can also transform the more abstract, cultural properties of objects, playing with what things are meant to mean. When a child uses a leaf to represent a plate in her play she can observe similarities and differences between her direct perception of the leaf and remembered information about plates, becoming more aware of physical properties such as flatness, smoothness, hardness and rigidity. She may also, if only implicitly, inform her understanding of the metaphorical, transformational nature of representation.

Playful transformation of experience depends on, and gives access to, the '100 languages of children' (Edwards et al., 1993), the patterned forms of representation which make communication possible. Adults are responsible for 'making and protecting the child's space' but also for 'introducing into it appropriate structural elements which derive from the surrounding culture' (Hodgkin, 1985: 26): 'open materials leave the most room for children to create their own ideas in play' (Jones and Reynolds, 1992: 20). Jones and Reynolds emphasize the importance of a plentiful supply of 'loose parts' which can be combined and recombined in different ways (ibid.: 23) and this is precisely what the languages of representation provide (Parker-Rees, 1997). Children who have been encouraged to use these languages in playful ways, as construction kits which can be deconstructed, transformed and reassembled, may feel more confident about choosing how to make sense of problem situations by remembering possible ways of responding:

> Transfer seems to involve grasping the structural features of a task, comparing these with analogous tasks, and taking the risk of 'going beyond the information given' and applying the old skills to the new situation where they may possibly be useful. (Meadows, 1996: 93)

This sort of risk taking requires both confidence and flexibility; the mastery orientation which children are more likely to develop if they have opportunities to practise and represent decision making in play situations (Sylva, 1992). Children can also be encouraged to transform artefacts and situations in their imaginations: How else might things be done? What else could be used? What else might have caused this? Playing with 'what might be' helps children to escape from the shackles of 'what is' but it also deepens their understanding of why things are the way they are (Parker-Rees, 1997). By holding open a space within which we are protected from the stresses and pressures of 'everyday life', playful activities can allow us to wander between the well-trodden paths which we must use when we are hurried. The looser, more complicated and more interconnected knowledge which results from this sort of wandering (or wondering) prepares us to cope more creatively when we find our path blocked: instead of giving up, we are able to strike out in a different direction, using both our implicit knowledge of the terrain and our explicit mental map of established tracks to remember another route (Claxton, 1997).

Reading 4.5

Schemas and learning

Cathy Nutbrown

The following reading explains schemas, the learning patterns of babies and young children. Understanding schemas is important for all early years practitioners as schemas are the behaviours which foster children's early foundations of learning.

Do you observe schemas in the children you work with? Do you use these observations to inform your planning?

Edited from: Nutbrown, C. (2011) *Key Concepts in Early Childhood Education and Care.* London: Sage Publications Ltd, 133–6.

It is generally understood in present early childhood pedagogy, a schema is 'a pattern of repeatable behaviour into which experiences are assimilated and that are gradually co-ordinated'. The work of Athey (2007) made popular the incorporation of schemas into early childhood pedagogy in the learning of three to five year olds. More recent work has extended understanding of schematic learning to work with babies and toddlers.

There is no single or definitive definition of the term 'schema' and, although the current use of the term in early childhood education and care is that given above, earlier work (Piaget, 1953) identifies schemas as part of the study of cognitive structures of young children's developing minds. Athey (2007) gives a thorough explanation of the various roots and definitions of the term as derived from the work of Piaget (1969), Bartlett (1932) and Neisser (1976).

We now know more about the learning patterns (or schemas) of babies and how they might think and learn. Goldschmied (1989) demonstrates how babies, given safe, stimulating and supportive opportunities, will use their senses and their developing physical skills to learn about the objects they encounter. Babies, as they suck, handle and smell are in a world of discovery – they puzzle, enjoy social interactions with others and make attempts to communicate their feelings and their needs. Those who watch young babies see some of the early patterns of gazing and following with their eyes, and some of those basic patterns of behaviour (or schemas) are quite obvious to the observer. As babies suck and grasp they work on, develop and refine the early schematic behaviours which foster their early foundations of learning. Early patterns of behaviour seen in babies become more complex and numerous, eventually being connected so that babies and young children coordinate their actions.

Toddlers work hard, collecting a pile of objects in the lap of their consistent carer, walking to and fro, backwards and forwards, bringing one object at a time. They are working on a pattern of behaviour which has a consistent thread running through it. Their patterns of action and thought at this point are related to the consistent back-and-forth movement. The early schemas of babies form the basis of the patterns of behaviour which children show between the ages of two and five years, and these in turn become established foundations of learning.

Athey (2007) maintains that children will notice elements in their environment, depending upon their interests at the time, and that they have their own intrinsic motivation which must be facilitated by materials and support from adults. Athey focused on how two to five year old children also work on particular patterns of behaviour, referring to each of these patterns as a schema and defining a schema as 'a repeatable pattern of behaviour into which experiences are assimilated and that are gradually co-ordinated' (Athey, 1990: 37). A number of patterns of behaviour were identified by Athey as part of the Froebel Early Education Project (which collected and analysed over 5,000 observations of 20 two-to five-year-olds over two years). These were named according to their characteristics. For example, a 'vertical schema' is so called because it relates to up-and-down movements. Athey discusses children's learning and development in terms of the following schemas:

- dynamic vertical;
- dynamic back and forth;
- dynamic circular;
- going over and under;
- going round a boundary;
- enveloping and containing space;
- going through a boundary.

The actions and marks related to these descriptions of movement can be identified in young children's drawing and mark-making, but Athey illustrates how such patterns can be represented in children's play, their thinking and their language. Athey argues that patterns pervade children's actions and speech as well as their mark-making. Detailed description and discussion on ways in which different patterns of learning can be represented through action, speech and mark-making are given by Athey, who further illustrates in theoretical and practical terms how forms of thought (schemas) once identified can be nourished with worthwhile content. If a child is focusing on a particular schema related to 'roundness' we could say that she or he is working on a circular schema. The form is roundness' and the content can be anything which extends this form: wheels, rotating machinery, rolling a ball, the spinning of planets. Similarly, a child interested in 'up and down ness' could be working on a vertical schema, The form is 'up and down'; related content can involve using ladders, using the climbing frame, riding in a lift or on an escalator. In the same way, if a child is interested in enclosing and enveloping schemas, the form is 'insideness' and related content may include wrapping presents hatching chick eggs, *encroute* cookery, mining and burrowing.

The main task for research is to provide further evidence of how children's schemas might be used to nourish children's thinking and how practitioners can develop their pedagogy to incorporate working with children's schemas. Educators can provide a more appropriate curriculum which matches the developmental levels and interests of the children by using their knowledge of schemas and their skills as observers to develop greater awareness of children's patterns of learning. Practitioner research of this kind, which illuminates the fine detail of individual children's learning can add to the bank of research studies which will, in turn, enable practitioners to reflect on their own strategies for helping young children to learn in developmentally appropriate ways. There is space for further research which considers how assessment – through observation of children's schemas – can be incorporated into required assessment procedures and assist practitioners in making decisions about next steps in teaching and learning.

Belinda's enclosing schema

Belinda was three years old and she seemed to be tuned into spotting or seeking out opportunities to enclose or be enclosed, and objects which enclosed. At home she enjoyed emptying and filling the washing and in the garden and in the bath she filled numerous containers with water to the point that they overflowed. She and her mother built up a collection of tins and boxes that she enjoyed fitting inside one another in different combinations and she often enjoyed sitting inside cardboard boxes sometimes pretending that the box was a car, bus, boat or rocket. Some of Belinda's favourite books included stories like *Where's Spot?* (Hill, 1980). At her sessional group Belinda particularly enjoyed playing in the house and hiding the farm animals inside the little wooden farm buildings. She dressed up and liked to play in the tunnel and hidey boxes outside.

Exploring her enveloping/containing schema, Belinda encountered much learning which linked with different areas of learning and experience. She learned about being with others and being apart, cooperating when equipment needed to be shared and dealing with her emotions when she wanted to be the only person to play in the house and was told to allow other children to play too. Opportunities at home and in the group enabled Belinda to explore her schema and develop her knowledge. The adults around her, sensitised to her interests, provided encouragement where a lack of knowledge may have led some adults to stop Belinda doing some of the things she found interesting. All the adults who lived or worked with Belinda were able to support and extend her learning. She encountered situations which required her to develop and refine mathematical skills of collecting, sorting, selecting, counting, ordering, reordering, grading, categorising and placing. She puzzled over ideas of shape and size and how things fitted together. She asked questions such as: 'Why does the washing have to get covered in water before it is clean?', 'Why do we have to wrap the potatoes before they go in the oven?' and 'Why won't this one [big tin] fit inside this one here [smaller tin]?' Her mother extended her interest, and in doing so provided more connections between experiences, such as involving her in baking, washing, writing letters and posting them. They looked at holes and hiding places, talked about being inside a lift and packed the shopping into boxes in the supermarket. She began to learn more about space and place relationships, finding out about relative size. Belinda's mother acted on what she saw and what she understood.

part two

Creating conditions for learning

5 **Contexts** What is, and what might be?

6 **Relationships** How are we getting on together?

7 **Engagement** How are we managing behaviour?

8 **Spaces** How are we creating environments for learning?

Contexts
What is and what might be?

5

Readings

5.1 Qing Gu
Being an educator in times of change (p. 88)

5.2 C. Wright Mills
The sociological imagination (p. 91)

5.3 David Whitebread and Sue Bingham
Exploring the school readiness debate (p. 93)

5.4 Andy Green and Jan Janmaat
Education, opportunity and social cohesion (p. 96)

5.5 Stephen Ball
Schooling, social class and privilege (p. 100)

These readings address the broad contexts in which all educators work – contexts which impact upon children's access and experiences within ECEC settings and throughout their education.

On ourselves as educators, Gu reviews some contemporary studies of teacher careers and the ways in which professional commitment is sustained. The second reading draws from a classic text, in which Mills analyses the relationship between individuals and society. He accounts for social change through the continuous interaction of biography and history. This analysis underpins a reflective and questioning attitude towards taken-for-granted structures, policies and assumptions – for 'personal troubles' can often be seen in relation to more enduring 'public issues'.

The third reading considers what is meant by the term 'school readiness', how this term is used in society, and how alternative interpretations of school readiness impact upon our expectations of children and, as such, their early educational experiences.

We then move on to a reading by Green and Janmaat which demonstrates how public policies vary in particular countries, and highlights the underlying assumptions upon which taken-for-granted thinking is based. International comparison shows how things can be thought about, and developed, in a variety of ways.

The final reading from Ball highlights the influence of social class on education. Across the UK, this remains powerful and pervasive. The focus of this paper is on how some families are able to respond to their circumstances, and on policies and educational practices which may enhance opportunities for more children and young people.

The parallel chapter in *Reflective Teaching in Early Education* engages with many additional issues. The 'social context' of education is analysed in terms of the concepts of ideology, culture, resources and accountability, as these influence schools in each country within the UK. Practitioners, children and families are considered, both as individuals and as groups, with particular attention to how they act within their circumstances. Extensive notes for further reading on such factors are available at *reflectiveteaching.co.uk*.

Reading 5.1

Being an Educator in times of change
Qing Gu

> Qing Gu outlines some of the challenges facing teachers in contemporary societies. In particular, she points out the way in which teachers are positioned as mediators between society's past, present and future – as realized in a very wide range of expectations. And yet teachers are simply people who occupy a particular role on behalf of society.
>
> To meet these challenges, teachers need a robust sense of personal identity and a commitment to professional development and reflective practice – and these must be sustained throughout their career. Even so, it is often the case that a strong sense of moral purpose generates personal and emotional challenges. This reading supports the readings in Chapter 1, reaffirming that, since early years practitioners are increasingly acknowledged as playing a key role in children's development and in their futures, self-assurance and confidence are required.
>
> How confident do you feel as a person in the role of practitioner?
>
> *Edited from:* Gu, Q. (2007) *Teacher Development: Knowledge and Context.* London: Continuum, 7–12.

Current changes in the global and local context pose profound implications for the teaching profession:

> An education system needs to serve the needs of society. When that society is undergoing profound and accelerating change, then particular pressures emerge for improvement in the alignment between the education system and these changing societal needs. The teaching profession is a key mediating agency for society as it endeavours to cope with social change and upheaval. (Coolahan, 2002: 9)

Teachers thus play a mediating role in bridging the past, the present and the future, the traditions and the innovations, the old and the new. Hargreaves (2003: 15) describes teachers as catalysts of successful knowledge societies who 'must be able to build special knowledge of professionalism'. This new professionalism means that teachers may not have the autonomy to teach in the way they wished, that they have to learn to teach in a way they were not taught, and that they need to build and develop a capacity for change and risk (Hargreaves, 2003; see also Robertson, 1996, 1997).

Teachers' knowledge, values and beliefs are subjected to constant re-examination and testing by the process of change in modern society.

For these reasons, continuing professional learning and development has become a necessary condition for teachers to sustain commitment and maintain effectiveness. OECD (2005: 14) calls to transform teaching into a knowledge-rich profession:

Research on the characteristic of effective professional development indicates that teachers need to be active agents in analysing their own practice in the light of professional standards and their own students' progress in the light of standards for student learning.

Teachers' professional identities – the way teachers perceive themselves as professionals in the classroom, the school, the community and the society – are undergoing profound change. In between the tensions embedded in the context where teachers work and live are their struggles to negotiate their understanding of what it means to be a teacher and their endeavours to 'integrate his various statuses and roles, as well as his diverse experiences, into a coherent image of self' (Epstein, 1978: 101). Castells (2004: 6–7) defines identity as people's source of meaning and experience. He distinguishes identities from roles:

> Roles … are defined by norms structured by the institutions and organizations of society. Their relative weight influencing people's behaviour depends upon negotiations and arrangements between individuals and these institutions and organizations. Identities are sources of meaning for the actors themselves, and by themselves, constructed through a process of individuation … In simple terms, identities organize the meaning, while roles organize the functions. I define *meaning* as the symbolic identification by a social actor of the purpose of her/his action. I also propose the idea that, *in the network society*, … for most social actors, meaning is organized around a primary identity (that is an identity that frames the others), which is self-sustaining across time and space.

However, teachers' roles are an indispensable part of their professional identities. Teachers play a variety of roles within the classroom: an authority, facilitator, parent, friend, judge and counsellor. Their strong sense of moral purpose and the immense satisfaction derives from the academic and personal progress of their students and makes a major contribution to the teacher's professional outlook. Outside the classroom, a teacher may also have additional managerial responsibilities. These managerial roles often give teachers a broader view of the education system, and help to promote the quality of their teaching in the classroom. In their national study of 300 teachers, Day et al. (2006, 2007) found that teachers' identity is a composite construct consisting of interactions between personal, professional and situated factors. Teachers' personal lives influence, positively or negatively, the construction of teachers' professional identities. For example, a teaching family background, being a parent, and taking on active roles in the local community may all affect how teachers view the part they play in the classroom; marriage breakdown, ill health and increased family commitments can, on the other hand, become sources of tensions 'as the individual's sense of identity could become out of step' (Day et al., 2006: 149).

In contrast to many other professions, teaching is emotionally attached and value-laden. Teachers' intense feelings in the job are not 'merely intrapersonal, psychological phenomena' (Kelchtermans, 2005: 996):

> Emotions are understood as experiences that result from teachers' embeddedness in and interactions with their professional environment. They are treated as meaningful experiences, revealing teachers' sense making and showing what is *at stake* for them …

In other words, a teacher's emotions are contextually embedded and highly rationalized with their values, beliefs and philosophies of education. They are inextricably bound up with their *moral purposes* and their ability to achieve those purposes (Hargreaves 1998). Hargreaves reminds us that for teachers, students are an 'emotional filter'. The OECD's study on attracting and retaining effective teachers also suggests that seeing children achieve remains a major, intrinsic source of teachers' job satisfaction and fulfilment. Roles for teachers are not merely associated with functions, duties and responsibilities. They are filled with positive emotions:

> Good teaching is charged with positive emotion. It is not just a matter of knowing one's subject, being efficient, having the correct competences, or learning all the right techniques. Good teachers are not just well-oiled machines. They are emotional, passionate beings who connect with their students and fill their work and their classes with pleasure, creativity, challenges and joy. (Hargreaves, 1998: 835)

For many teachers their jobs consist of far more than fulfilling routine requirements that are externally imposed upon them. Numerous studies suggest that this is also the case for the millions of teachers working in all the corners of the world. The sense of calling urges them to take actions in seeking ways of improving their teaching practice and service for the students, sustaining their sense of efficacy, promoting their sense of agency, commitment and resilience, and ultimately their effectiveness. Teachers have to play a range of roles to fulfil their commitment and internal calling to serve in education, such as a facilitator, an encourager, a parent, an authority and a friend. All of these roles contribute to the formation of teachers' identities and any change in context leads to further change in these professional and personal identities.

Reading 5.2

The sociological imagination
C. Wright Mills

This reading comes from a classic sociological text. Wright Mills focused on the inter-action between individuals and society, and thus on the intersection of biography and history. All educators have particular responsibilities because, although acting in particular historical contexts, we shape the biographies of many children and thus help to create the future. Mills poses several questions which can be used to think about our society and the role of education within it.

How do you think what you do today may influence what children might do in the future?

Edited from: Mills, C. W. (1959) *The Sociological Imagination.* New York: Oxford University Press, 111–13.

The sociological imagination enables its possessor to understand the larger historical scene in terms of its meaning for the inner life and the external career of a variety of individuals. It enables him (sic) to take into account how individuals, in the welter of their daily experience, often become falsely conscious of their social positions. Within that welter the framework of modern society is sought, and within that framework the psychologies of a variety of men and women are formulated. By such means the personal uneasiness of individuals is focused upon explicit troubles and the indifference of publics is transformed into involvement with public studies.

The first fruit of this imagination – and the first lessons of the social science that embodies it – is the idea that the individual can understand his own experience and gauge his own fate only by locating himself within his period, that he can know his own chances in life only by becoming aware of those of all individuals in his circumstances. In many ways it is a terrible lesson; in many ways a magnificent one. We do not know the limits of man's capacities for supreme effort or willing degradation, for agony or glee, for pleas-urable brutality or the sweetness of reason. But in our time we have come to know that the limits of 'human nature' are frighteningly broad. We have come to know that every individual lives, from one generation to the next, in some society; that he lives out a biography, and that he lives it out within some historical sequence. By the fact of his living he contributes, however minutely, to the shaping of this society and to the course of its history, even as he is made by society and by its historical push and shove.

The sociological imagination enables us to grasp history and biography and the relations between the two within society. That is its task and its promise. To recognize this task and this promise is the mark of the classic social analyst. And it is the signal of what is best in contemporary studies of man and society.

No social study that does not come back to the problems of biography, of history, and of their intersections within a society, has completed its intellectual journey. Whatever the specific problems of the classic social analysts, however limited or however broad the features of social reality they have examined, those who have been imaginatively aware of the promise of their work have consistently asked three sorts of questions:

- *What is the structure of this particular society as a whole?*
  What are its essential components, and how are they related to one another? Within it, what is the meaning of any particular feature for its continuance and for its change?

- *Where does this society stand in human history?*
  What are the mechanics by which it is changing? What is its place within and its meaning for the development of humanity as a whole? How does any particular feature we are examining affect, and how is it affected by, the historical period in which it moves? And this period – what are its essential features? How does it differ from other periods? What are its characteristic ways of history-making?

- *What varieties of men and women now prevail in this society and in this period?*
  And what varieties are coming to prevail? In what ways are they selected and formed, liberated and repressed, made sensitive and blunted? What kinds of 'human nature' are revealed in the conduct and character we observe in this society in this period? And what is the meaning for 'human nature' of each and every feature of the society we are examining?

Reading 5.3

Exploring the school readiness debate
David Whitebread and Sue Bingham

The following reading is taken from a larger report produced by the Association for the Professional Development of Early Years Educators (TACTYC) and written by David White-bread and Sue Bingham. It explores the emergence and underlying perspectives behind the use of the term 'school readiness'. The authors argue that despite the term being contested, it is one which is used on an almost daily basis. They note that, historically, being 'ready for school' places the onus on the child, and their family, to ensure the child is indeed ready. But they question this and consider an alternative: that the child is ready to learn. They also ask whether 'schools are ready for children'.

Edited from: Whitebread, D. and Bingham, S. (2012) 'School Readiness: A Critical Review of Perspectives and Evidence'. TACTYC. Available from http://scmeyegroup.weebly.com/uploads/1/8/4/9/1849450/readiness_review_12312.pdf

Many early childhood educationalists have called into question the very concept of 'readiness' but there is no denying that the term is used on a daily basis in policy and practice within the UK. What is 'readiness for school'? Historically, the onus for 'readiness' has been placed squarely upon the child; however much of the work related to 'readiness' has confounded two distinct concepts: readiness to learn and readiness for school.

Readiness to learn

Clearly all children, at all ages, are 'ready to learn'. So the significant question is not whether a child is ready to learn, but rather what a child is ready to learn. Originally advanced by leading child developmentalists, 'ready to learn' in relation to any particular skill or area of understanding is generally acknowledged as the developmental level at which an individual theoretically has the capacity to undertake learning of that specific material (usually the age at which the average group of individuals achieves the specified capacity). While beliefs regarding precisely which factors affect readiness to learn in particular areas vary widely, there is agreement, from this perspective, that readiness is situated in the domains of physical development, intellectual ability, social and emotional maturity and health.

'Readiness for school'

'Readiness for school' is a more finite construct and implies a fixed standard of physical, intellectual, and social development that enables children to meet school requirements and assimilate curriculum, typically embracing specific cognitive and linguistic skills. Within England, the combination of policy changes over recent years, such as encouraging parents to start their child in a Reception class in the September following their fourth birthday (DfE, 2011) and the use of the phrase 'ready for school', has led to multi-interpretations of when a child actually starts school. Misunderstandings arise because, although the statutory age for a child to start in Year 1 remains five years (or the term following their fifth birthday), in practice, most children start their school career at the age of four, when they join a Reception class in a maintained school, as recognised by the Tickell report (p. 19). Proponents of this view interpret the Reception year as the start of school and understand that, although still included in the Foundation Stage curriculum, this is a 'transition' year, in which a child is prepared for entry into Year 1. Opponents of this view, on the other hand, argue that policy endorsing the preparation of children for starting school is based on the premise that the curriculum (National Curriculum) in Year 1 is 'set' and children must be fit into it as it stands. They argue that a more appropriate strategy is to adapt the curriculum to the developmental and experiential levels of the children who enter Year 1, whatever their cognitive and social skills. They take the position that if children are faring poorly there, the solution needs to be found in the school 'offering', including perhaps a recognition that the National Curriculum is inappropriate, rather than assessing the child as 'inadequate'. In this view, ideally, the transition from pre-school programmes to Reception and then into Year 1 schooling should be seamless and continuous, not the abrupt shift to a completely different social context and set of academic demands that the notion of 'readiness' implies. Many early years educationalists believe that the important issue is not where young children's educational needs are met, but whether the types of curriculum they are offered are of high quality, appropriate for their developmental needs and offered through appropriate teaching methodologies.

Assessing children's diverse skills related to the school curriculum, and tailoring appropriate teaching and learning opportunities to the variety of understandings, learning styles, and social skills that the children in any given class will exhibit requires well-trained teachers. Anything less than this will not serve the educational needs of children who, regardless of the age for school entry, will vary considerably in their social, emotional, and intellectual skills. Early childhood educationalists suggest that a much greater service would be provided to children if the focus was more on making school ready for children than on making children ready for school.

The readiness of schools

Many early childhood educationalists have turned the issue of 'readiness' on its head to focus on schools rather than children (see Fabian and Dunlop, 2002; Dunlop and Fabian,

2003), Certainly, some children are not 'ready' to sit at desks and do paper-and-pencil activities for long periods of time when they turn five or even six years old. But that does not mean that they cannot benefit from any kind of education appropriately delivered. The pertinent policy question here, therefore, relates not to what children need to know or be able to do when they get to school, but what schools need to do to meet the social and educational needs of the children who walk through their doors. A growing number of educationalists and teachers have therefore adopted a broadened conceptualization of 'readiness', in which it is regarded as a condition of institutions, as well as individuals. 'Readiness' here is understood as the match between the readiness of the child and the readiness of the environments that serve young children. This contemporary understanding of readiness acknowledges that the sources of readiness are not only the child's emotional, cognitive, linguistic, and social abilities but also the contexts in which children live and interact with adults, teachers, and other community members. In order to affect a child's school readiness, multiple contexts including families, schools, neighbourhoods and early childhood settings must be involved.

Reading 5.4

Education, opportunity and social cohesion
Andy Green and Jan Janmaat

> This reading is based on analysis of data on inequality and social attitudes in over 25 developed countries. The study shows how educational inequality undermines key aspects of social cohesion, including trust in institutions, civic cooperation and the rule of law. The authors argue that more egalitarian education systems tend to promote both economic competitiveness and social cohesion. The work highlights the significance for social cohesion of the distribution of opportunities and the nature of the values that people acquire.
>
> Through its work with children and young people, education influences the future and is infused with moral purpose. We must recognize 'What is', but may also ask 'What should be?' and what is our role in realizing this vision?
>
> *Edited from:* Green, A. and Janmaat, J. G. (2011) *Education, Opportunity and Social Cohesion.* Centre for Learning and Life Chances in Knowledge Economies and Societies. London: Institute of Education, 2–5.

Regimes of social cohesion

Different traditions of thought and policy on social cohesion have evolved within the western world. Comparative analysis identifies three distinctive types of social cohesion in contemporary states. These can be characterised as 'liberal', 'social market' or 'social democratic'. We refer to these as 'regimes of social cohesion' to emphasise their systemic properties, which are relatively durable over time.

Liberal (English-speaking countries, e.g. particularly the UK and the USA)
In liberal societies, such as the United Kingdom and the United States, social cohesion has traditionally relied on the triple foundations of market freedoms, an active civil society, and core beliefs in individual opportunities and rewards based on merit. A wider set of shared values has not been regarded as essential for a cohesive society – and nor, in the British case at least, has a tightly defined sense of national identity. The state was not, historically, considered the main guarantor of social cohesion, beyond its role in the maintenance of law and order.

Social Market (NW continental Europe, e.g. Belgium, France, Germany and the Netherlands)
The social market regime, by contrast, has relied on a strong institutional embedding of social cohesion. Solidarity has depended relatively more on the state and less on civil society, and rates of civic participation have generally been lower. Trade union coverage and public spending on welfare and social protection are high. These factors, along with

concerted and centralized trade union bargaining, have helped to reduce household income inequality. Maintaining a broad set of shared values – and a strong national identity – has also, historically, been considered important for holding societies together.

Social Democratic (The Nordic countries, e.g. Denmark, Finland, Norway and Sweden) The social democratic regime, like the social market regime, institutionalises social solidarity. However, here, egalitarian and solidaristic values make a greater contribution to social cohesion. Levels of social and political trust are also much higher. This cannot be attributed solely to greater ethnic homogeneity in these societies, although this may have once played a part in Denmark and Norway. Sweden is both ethnically diverse and highly trusting.

Social cohesion during economic crisis

Every country is affected by the challenges of globalisation and particularly so during periods of economic crisis. However, societies differ in what holds them together.

The core beliefs of liberal societies, such as the UK (e.g. active civil society and individual opportunities), are seen to be embodied in the 'free market' which has become more dominant under globalisation. However, social cohesion in such societies is likely to be undermined by the rapid erosion of people's faith in individual opportunity and fairness.

The UK has high levels of income inequality and relatively low rates of social mobility. Inequality and lack of mobility are likely to grow due to the disproportionate effects of the economic crisis (in unemployment and public expenditure cuts, for example) on young people, women, the low paid and those in areas of socio-economic disadvantage. As the prospects of secure jobs and home ownership diminish for many people, belief in the core unifying values of opportunity, freedom and just rewards are likely to decrease, causing social and political trust to diminish further.

Education, inequality and social cohesion

Education systems play a key role in determining future life chances and in mitigating or exacerbating social inequalities. These have been linked with various negative health and social outcomes, including high rates of depression, low levels of trust and cooperation, and high levels of violent crime.

We found that education systems which select students to secondary schools by ability and make extensive use of ability grouping within schools tend to exhibit more unequal educational outcomes than non-selective comprehensive systems with mixed ability classes.

The four education systems in the UK perform somewhat differently. Those in Scotland and Wales produce slightly more equal educational outcomes at 15 than those in England and Northern Ireland, according to the OECD Programme for International student Assessment (PISA).

The 2009 PISA study of literacy skills amongst 15 years olds shows that educational outcomes in the UK are more unequal than in most of the OECD countries where tests were conducted (Green and Janmaat, 2011).

The gap between the mean scores of UK students in the 90th and 10th percentiles was 246 points – the equivalent of six years of schooling on the average across OECD countries. PISA 2009 showed that the variance in scores in the UK have only reduced marginally since the 2000 survey. Amongst the 34 countries tested, the UK had the 11th highest total variance in scores.

The UK is also notable for the degree to which the average performance within a school is influenced by the social characteristics of its intake. Across all OECD countries, on average, 57 per cent of the performance difference between schools can be attributed to the social character of the intake. In the UK (and in Luxembourg, New Zealand and the USA) the social intake accounts for over 70 per cent of performance difference between schools.

Skills distribution and social cohesion

Variation in performance among school students is one of the factors which, over time, determines the overall distribution of skills within the adult population. We found strong links between social cohesion and the distribution of adult skills.

The more unequal the skills distribution among adults, the higher the rates of violent crime and civic unrest, and the lower the levels of social trust and civil liberties. For several of the indicators, these correlations also hold over time, suggesting that the relationships may be causal. It seems likely that wide educational disparities generate cultural gaps and competition anxieties which undermine social bonds and trust.

Our research suggests that it is not so much the average level of education in a country which matters most for social cohesion, but rather how the skills acquired are spread around.

Education systems and civic competences

Civic competences are an important component of social cohesion. These refer to the knowledge, skills and values that people need to participate effectively in a liberal democratic society. We examined the links between education system characteristics and the levels and distributions of civic competences across countries.

When compared with comprehensive systems, selective education systems have:

- higher levels of social segregation across classrooms
- greater disparities in civic knowledge and skills and
- larger peer effects on civic knowledge and skills (meaning that the latter are strongly affected by the social backgrounds and achievement levels of other students in the class).

Implications for policy

We urge policymakers in the UK to take account of the potentially negative impact that educational inequality can have on social cohesion.

Social cohesion in the UK has always depended on high levels of civic participation and a widespread belief in the availability of individual opportunities and rewards based on merit. In the current period of austerity, where opportunities for young people are substantially reduced, there is a serious danger that these shared beliefs will be eroded, thus weakening social bonds. In such circumstances it is particularly important that the education system is seen to offer opportunities for all students.

Reading 5.5

Schooling, social class and privilege
Stephen Ball

This reading illustrates and analyses how social class inequalities are reproduced, in part, by the strategies adopted by some families to secure educational advantage. It suggests that, behind arguments about the efficacy of quasi-markets and choice of school, there are significant social consequences which deepen inequalities within our societies. Ball suggests that parental investment in children by middle-class families, through broadening their experiences and understanding, creates 'abilities' which schools then develop further.

How does this analysis illuminate patterns of attendance and performance at schools you know? What role do you play in supporting transitions into statutory schooling? Are you aware that different children in your setting face different futures because of family circumstances?

Edited from: Ball, S. (2003) 'The more things change: Educational research, social class and 'interlocking' inequalities'. Professorial Inaugural Lecture, Institute of Education, University of London, 12 March.

I see sociological theories as a toolbox which provides levers and mechanisms for analysis and interpretation. This is particularly important, I think, in the understanding of social class.

I am interested in the pro-active tactics of certain families as a way of understanding 'success' rather than failure in education. This enables the construction of a theory of privilege rather than a theory of deficits – a distinction which is crucial to my endeavours here.

Class is never more potent and damaging than when inequality is no longer explained in its terms, when classed policy is naturalised, becomes common sense – when class policy is simply good policy. The naturalisation of policy makes possible the tracing back of social problems, and the allocating of blame, to social subjects. This kind of transference is centrally embedded in policies which allocate resources through systems of choice, within which families are expected to act as 'risk managers'. Such choice systems call for particular resources and skills which are unevenly distributed across the population.

If we want to understand the production of social inequalities in and through education we thus need to take families seriously. Greater attention has to be given to the ways in which inequalities are produced in the complex interactions between the cultural, social and material sites of home, school and policy – to the interlocking of inequalities.

Education policy, school choice and social practices

Choice policies and a market system of education, in the current socio-economic context, are a response to the current interest anxieties of the middle class.

In effect education policy is a focus of class struggles: very immediate and down-to-earth struggles for opportunity, advantage and closure, and over the distribution of scarce resources. The policies in play at any point in time bear the hallmarks of those struggles. They may be overt, through campaigns and interventions – particularly those articulated around curriculum, modes of instruction, student grouping and the distribution of rewards and success roles; or through the privileging of opportunity over and against equity; or through the mechanism of the market itself which values some qualities and some kinds of students and devalues others.

The anxieties, concerns and efforts which underlie these struggles are of an enduring nature, but the middle classes are particularly anxious and active. Current social and economic conditions have raised the stakes of competition for educational success; and moves to empower parents have given a specific legitimacy to diverse forms of intervention and participation. For these, middle-class parents possess the relevant skills and resources.

Additionally, there is an overlap of interests from the two sides of the market: parental consumers and school providers.

In a performative system of education, this process is also driven by the differential valuing of students by schools needing to compete within league tables of achievement and to reach exam and test targets. Middle-class students, on the whole, are cheaper and easier to teach in relation to achieving targets and performance improvements, and many schools will do whatever they can to woo them (Woods et al., 1998).

On the consumer side, it is interesting to note examples of the efforts of middle-class parents in socially diverse metropolitan settings to colonise and capture particular schools of choice. Butler and Robson (2001) note examples in their research into gentrification in six London settings. One is a 'success' story in Telegraph Hill, where they report a primary school which has been '"made" by the middle class and transformed' ; the second, in Brixton, is, at least for the time being, a failure. Here, despite concerted efforts, 'the middle classes have not been successful in establishing hegemony over any particular primary school'. Ball, Vincent and Kemp (2003) found similar, and successful 'captures' of primary schools, as class 'enclaves', in Stoke Newington and Battersea.

Clearly, in all of this the most distinct and decisive strategy of choice is for private schooling. Private schools offer a cultural milieu which is coherent and undiluted, and constitutes a 'protected enclave for class formation' (Sedden, 2001: 134).

As I have noted already, middle-class families work hard and deploy their resources to establish a monopoly over routes of and locations of privilege, ensuring for their children high-status trajectories through the education system, and insulating them from the untoward influence of social 'others'. This is a process of drawing and maintaining lines of distinction, between and within schools: it is a process of social closure.

Loads of children there had special needs and they have lots of children who are refugees who really didn't speak English, and I just thought, it's not appropriate for a bright little girl who, you know, is going to need quite a lot of stimulation. (Mrs Henry)

I liked the fact that they catered specifically for children's abilities in subjects that I think are difficult to teach in a mixed-ability group. … It was one of the points we thought were positive. … They set in maths and languages straight off. (Mrs McBain)

The state school down the road would have been lovely, except that *nobody* sends their children there. (Mrs Henry, my emphasis)

The 'nobody' referred to in the final extract is striking and telling – the school in question, the 'state school down the road' has children in it, but it is full of 'nobodies', the point is here that 'nobody' is 'not us'. People like us do not send our children to a school like that. It is a school 'of' and 'for' 'others'. These sorts of cultural and calculative evaluations, and their concomitant recognitions and rejections, the 'us's' and 'others', are part of the parents' 'reading' of schools in the process of making choices between them.

Access to routes of privilege and success roles and their associated identities ensures the storing up of valuable cultural capital 'within' the student.

Parenting and investment in the child

Within the educational life of the middle-class family enormous effort is devoted to the assembly and maintenance of a well-adapted educational subject, a 'reasoning and reasonable' child, as Vincent puts it (2001). In a risk society the prudent family can no longer leave their child's fate to the state. This may be thought of as a process of investment in the child and involves the deployment of a range of capitals – economic, social, cultural and emotional – and 'the gratuitous expenditure of time, attention, care and concern' (Bourdieu, 1986b: 253). Let me offer some glimpses of these capitals at work.

A couple of months ago I got a studies skills teacher and I started working, it's through my mum's friends, so I've been seeing this woman weekly, and she's helping me, you know, how to work, when to work and actually getting down and doing it [Anick wants to be a lawyer]. Neither of my parents are lawyers, we have lawyer friends but I mean at school, my parents just saw me, because I argue, they said that would just fit a lawyer. … I think I am going to America this summer. I've got the opportunity of working at McDonald's law firm in Chicago. Because one of my Dad's best friends is head lawyer at McDonalds. So I could go there for a couple of months. (Anick: Hemsley Girls)

…. yeah, but A level's beyond my field. A level maths. So sort of like, six months ago we got him a tutor anyway. And he was happy talking to him. So I think he sort of … LAUGHS … overcame a lot of the problems. He didn't have many, I must say, actually. But anything he did have, the tutor sorted out with him, and he felt happier doing that than actually speaking to them. And I said – do you want me to talk to them? And he said no. So I thought I wouldn't interfere, especially as he seemed all right about it. (Carl's mother: Maitland Union)

Part of this process of social formation, the support and encouragement, the bought-in expertise and supplementary activities, the long-term sculpting of decision-making, is focused on the child's needs – but it also establishes for the child a sense of their best interests. They are made clear about what is important and possible, and what is not. 'Cultural scripts' are acted out with little scope for improvisation – and where improvisations do occur they can lead to family crises and thence to organised remediation. Again, at these points of crisis and potential failure the deployment of relevant capitals is crucial to the maintenance of trajectories. Emotional resources are particularly important at times of uncertainty (Devine, 1998: 33), but so too is the ability to 'buy in' specialist support or to lobby for special services.

These experiences develop in the child a particular orientation to schooling and develop certain skills and capabilities – a role readiness. They also work to constitute the child as able.

In this sense we can see 'ability' and 'achievement' partly at least as a social assembly achieved within the family, as a collective endeavour, which often extends beyond the family itself (through, for example, the employment of tutors) and requires various forms of capital investment in order to be maintained. This is a point made by Bourdieu: 'ability or talent is itself the product of an investment of time and cultural capital' (Bourdieu, 1986b: 244). Viewed in this way ability and achievement can be understood as the composite productions of families, which at times involve enormous emotional exertions and capital expenditures – rather than either a natural or individual phenomenon.

Only a part of this activity is visible in the classroom: the middle-class child in the classroom is in part a cipher of attentive, surveillant, participant parenting – or, to borrow a phrase, 'intensive parenting' – or more often and more accurately 'intensive mothering'. The vast majority of the work of assembly and support is done in the vast majority of middle-class families by mothers. Responsibility weighs heavily on the mother in a whole variety of senses.

In such ways, the values and incentives of market policies being pursued and celebrated by the states of almost all western societies give legitimation and impetus to certain actions and commitments – enterprise, competition, excellence – and inhibit and de-legitimise others – social justice, equity, tolerance.

I am a sociologist and as such, for me, the task is 'to show that things are not as self-evident as one believed; to see that what is accepted as self-evident will no longer be accepted as such' (Foucault, 1988: 154). 'Thinking otherwise' is thus possible.

Relationships
How are we getting on together?

6

Readings

6.1 Maria Evangelou, Kathy Sylva, Maria Kyriacou, Mary Wild and Georgina Glenny
Early years learning and development literature review (p. 106)

6.2 Carolynn Rankin and Fiona Butler
Working in teams (p. 109)

6.3 Denis Lawrence
What is self-esteem? (p. 114)

6.4 Sir Richard Bowlby
Attachment, what it is, why it is important (p. 118)

6.5 Jennifer Colwell
The role of the preschool practitioner in the development of children's social competencies (p. 124)

Good relationships support learning. The readings in this group confirm this significance, analyse underlying processes and suggest practical strategies for developing excellent relationships between colleagues, adults and children, and children and their peers.

The first reading outlines the importance of relationships for children's development. The second considers team-working; team members who can recognize what other members bring to the team are able to work well together.

We then offer a clear account of self-esteem. For children, this may be enhanced or diminished by a great many influences, but the actions of educators are among the most significant. The attachments children form have also been shown to impact upon social and emotional development, and this is the focus of Bowlby's extract.

The final reading provides a summary of what research has shown to be the key factors pre-school practitioners ought to be aware of when supporting and planning to support children to develop the skills to maintain positive relationships.

The parallel chapter of *Reflective Teaching in Early Education* addresses similar issues and provides more practical guidance and further suggestions for Key Readings. On *reflectiveteaching.co.uk* there are additional ideas on the issues raised in this chapter.

Reading 6.1

Early years learning and development literature review

Maria Evangelou, Kathy Sylva, Maria Kyriacou, Mary Wild and Georgina Glenny

The reading which follows considers the importance of children's relationships for their learning and development, identifying five key facets which warrant our attention and consideration.

Edited from: Evangelou, M., Sylva, K., Kyriacou, M., Wild, M. and Glenny, G. (2009) *Early Years Learning and Development Literature Review.* DCSF and University of Oxford, 76–9.

Enabling children's development by building positive relationships

Children's development is influenced by rich relational experiences that take place both at home and at settings with parents and the staff around them. The research evidence in this report identifies five key facets of relationships: the warmth of relationships; the contingency of relationships; the use of talk in building and maintaining such relationships; the recognition of the uniqueness and agency of the child; the importance of mutually responsive relationships in facilitating pro-social thinking and behaviour. In addition to adult-child relationships it is important to remember the key role of others e.g. siblings and extended family in a child's social world. Similarly children's friendships become increasingly important to children through the early years.

Warm relationships

Children's socio-emotional development is enhanced by secure attachment through development of nurturing relationships with at least one key person who identifies with them strongly. Characteristics of these relationships include the presence of responsive parent-child interactions; supportive caregiver feedback and the establishment of routines. The familiarity with and the presence of a caring adult in life thus provides children with a safe and secure environment. Opportunities for children to affirm their feelings through positive conversations with caring adults are critical in the development of children's self esteem and of their understanding of social expectations.

Contingency of relationships

High levels of contingent response by the adults help infants' gain a sense of self during the first year of life. Contingent responses can also reinforce the child's understanding of the social world around them, serving to reinforce social expectations and the socialisation of the child within particular contexts. It is important for the development of a child's understanding of themselves and others that the responses of parents and other adults is underpinned by warmth and positivity but also that responses to the child are contingent to the child's desires and specific behaviours in particular contexts. Some degree of non-compliance may also be important in development, particularly around the second year of life when the children are learning to assert their own autonomy and independence. Adults can assume different roles in different situations, for example, negotiating group conflicts or protecting individual children's needs may require different responses to the child.

Use of talk and narrative in building and maintaining relationships

A further factor that supports children's building of relationships and the development of social understandings is the opportunity for rich communication, both between adults and children as well as between children. Rich conversations about children's feelings with important adults in their lives enhance their self-esteem. Such conversations can stem from stories and fictional scenarios, as well as real-life contexts and can promote trusting relationships that further build children's emotional awareness and self-regulation. These conversations can also transmit culturally appropriate ways of expressing emotional displays and behaviours. The research literature suggests that an "elaborative narrative style" is likely to be most effective. Narrative can be simply descriptive but an elaborative narrative style implies a deeper structuring of events and relational contexts as they are recounted with opportunities for children to reflect on the experiences, both real and fictional, and to hypothesise about alternative outcomes and consequences.

Recognising the uniqueness and agency of the child

The recent literature indicates that children's development is an active rather than a passive process; it is a dynamic process within which the pattern of relationships can vary as the unique characteristics of each child interacts with the unique characteristics of those around them. The child's individual temperament affects their social behaviours and inter-actions in both their home and the setting. The choice of a key worker within settings thus becomes very important since the personal dynamics of individuals is constantly shaping their interactions.

Facilitating pro-social thinking and behaviour

The role of relationships in children's social and emotional understanding is already known to be important. Research has suggested that children's socialisation is best supported within a 'social relational model'. Children's pro-social thinking and behaviour is facilitated by internalising rules through mutually responsive relationships between themselves and their mother. This mutual responsiveness combined with explicit focus on behaviours through the kind of narrative described earlier helps to shape the development of conscience. It is important to promote both aspects of compliance with social norms to become 'committed compliance' as opposed to the more superficial 'situational compliance'. Recognising the uniqueness and agency of the child Children's pro-social behaviours are also facilitated by play with their peers in which children are engaged in mutual exchanges and learn how to interact with each other and others.

Reading 6.2

Working in teams
Carolynn Rankin and Fiona Butler

Working with others is both rewarding and challenging. Carolynn Rankin and Fiona Butler consider what we know about team roles and the management of teams, before considering what this means for the early years practitioner.

Do the roles identified help you to see where you fit within your team and what you offer to the group? Can you recognize the roles some of your colleagues contribute?

Edited from: Rankin, C. and Butler, F. (2011) 'Issues and Challenges for the Interdisciplinary Team in Supporting the Twenty-first-century Family'. In A. Brock and C. Rankin (eds) *Professionalism in the Interdisciplinary Early Years Team.* London: Continuum, 41–3.

Back to basics – theory of teamwork

Before we look further at how practitioners are required to work together to support the child, let us consider the basic elements of teamwork and why this is an effective way to achieve objectives. In an organizational setting, a team can be regarded as a number of individuals working together to achieve a particular outcome, often tackling difficult, interdependent and complex tasks. Salas et al. (2008) defines a team as a set of two or more individuals that adaptively and dynamically interact through specified roles as they work toward shared and valued goals. Team members can also have different specializations in knowledge and skills, and it is this diversity of expertise that creates the potential for teams to complete work outside the scope of any one individual's capabilities. This is why teams and work groups continue to be such an important asset to organizations. Belbin (2010) discusses how professionals must fulfil not only their functional roles, but also their roles as team members. Belbin began researching management teams in the 1970s with an interest in finding out why some teams worked successfully and others did not. In researching management team dynamics, each participant undertook a range of psychometric tests so that the effects of attributes such as behaviour and personality could be considered. The research revealed that the differences between success and failure for teams was more dependent on behaviour and not on factors such as intellect. Separate clusters of behaviour were identified by Belbin and his research team. These became known as Team Roles and were defined as 'a tendency to behave, contribute and inter-relate with others in a particular way'. A total of nine different Team Roles were identified, indicating the strengths or contributions they provided and the summary descriptions are in Figure 6.2.1. Each Team Role was also found to have 'allowable weaknesses', the flipside of the behavioural characteristics allowable in the team because of the strength which goes with it. The 'specialist' role was identified as the final Team Role and the value of

Figure 6.2.1 Belbin Team Role summary descriptions

Team Role Summary Descriptions

Team Role	Contribution	Allowable Weakness
Plant	Creative, imaginative, unorthodox. Solves difficult problems.	Ignores incidentals. Too pre-occupied to communicate effectively.
Resource Investigator	Extrovert, enthusiastic, communicative. Explores opportunities. Develops contacts.	Over-optimistic. Loses interest once initial enthusiasm has passed.
Coordinator	Mature, confident, a good chairperson. Clarifies goals, promotes decision-making, delegates well.	Can be seen as manipulative. Offloads personal work.
Shaper	Challenging, dynamic, thrives on pressure. Has the drive and courage to overcome obstacles.	Prone to provocation. Offends people's feelings.
Monitor Evaluator	Sober, strategic and discerning. Sees all options. Judges accurately.	Lacks drive and ability to inspire others.
Teamworker	Cooperative, mild, perceptive and diplomatic. Listens, builds, averts friction.	Indecisive in crunch situations.
Implementer	Disciplined, reliable, conservative and efficient. Turns ideas into practical actions.	Somewhat inflexible. Slow to respond to new possibilities.
Completer Finisher	Painstaking, conscientious, anxious. Searches out errors and omissions. Polishes and perfects.	Inclined to worry unduly. Reluctant to delegate.
Specialist	Single-minded, self-starting, dedicated. Provides knowledge and skills in rare supply.	Contributes on only a narrow front. Dwells on technicalities.

an individual with in-depth knowledge of a key area was recognized as an essential team contribution. The allowable weakness for specialists is the tendency to focus narrowly on their own subject of choice and to prioritize this over the team's progress. The Team Roles identified by Belbin are used widely in organizations all over the world based on the premise that by identifying preferred Team Roles, individuals can use their strengths to advantage and try to manage weaknesses in their behaviour.

The social dynamics of effective teamwork are key to achieving the potential benefit for the parent organizations. Salas et al. (2008: 41) discuss task work competencies that are the knowledge, skills, attitudes and other characteristics used to accomplish individual task performance. However, team members must have individual-level expertise relevant to their own tasks, and also expertise in the social dynamics of teamwork in order to work effectively in an interdependent team. Salas et al. (2008: 39) write about the 'wisdom of collectives' as the increased capacity for performance of various types afforded by the interactions of team members. A further level of complexity is provided by an individual's cultural knowledge, acquired knowledge that we use to interpret experience and generate social behaviour, which will have an influence on the social dynamic of the team as cultural knowledge forms values, creates attitudes and influences behaviour (Salas et al., 2008: 532). Team building and effective working practices can take time to develop. In our twenty-first-century society there is constant flux and change in organizations and institutions. Organizational restructuring has the potential to damage a team. In a formal structure the job requirements will be clear and common goals shared, but this may only hold until the next reorganization when a team may be dismantled and a new team formed and the team building process needs to start all over again.

Looking at this from a functional viewpoint, teams endeavour to perform their tasks and achieve objectives in a complex, context-rich environment. Teams do not operate in a vacuum and many organizational and environmental factors can have a significant impact on how effectively they function. New forms of organizational structures are evolving to replace the more traditional hierarchical structures; this provides the opportunity and challenge for individuals to play an effective part in a range of settings with a different mix of practitioners.

So what makes an effective team in a context-rich environment?

There is an extensive body of literature on the theory, principles, tools and practical know-how about leading, managing and developing effective teams. In the Towards Interprofessional Partnerships (TIPS) research project Brock et al. (2009) found communication, assertive leadership, a supportive culture, individual qualities and organizational issues to be crucial factors for effective team working. Effective teams are characterized by a caring, compassionate approach. Where an atmosphere of openness and trust pervades, there is a sharing of responsibility, accountability and ownership of actions; commitment to the team is strong and strengths and weaknesses are known. The whole team acknowledges and deals with situations of potential conflict. This reinforces the concept of a healthy team in which no members are frightened or, when asking questions, made to feel inadequate because of their status (Brock et al., 2009: 20). Bertram et al. (2002: 10) argue that successful multi-professional practice requires shared philosophies and agreed working principles:

A successful team is one that demonstrates professionalism, shared beliefs, common identity and vision and a breadth of experience and skills, and feels secure enough within the management system to take on new activities without fear and to operate within a professional climate which balances openness to new ideas with pragmatic critique. (Bertram et al., 2002: 10)

Certain team processes and behaviour can help teams to perform effectively. A key factor is the need for clear goals and direction and clarity about what needs to be done and who is responsible for doing it. This can be supported by having regular meetings and opportunities to share information and by setting and working to agreed standards. Anticipating problems, having contingency plans and challenging complacency will also create and foster an environment in which team performance has effective outcomes.

> We have actions and targets to meet and we have quarterly planning sessions where I get the whole team together and we look at our actions and outcomes against the five ECM headings. That helps the team to understand why I keep banging on about outcomes, why they are important and make sustainable changes in families' lives. It helps them think creatively about why they deliver stuff and the bigger picture. We've just changed the sessions from half day to full day sessions and we now also look at safeguarding across the whole spectrum. And we look at budgeting and resource management.
>
> This gives a team focus on what we deliver, why we do what we do, and also makes it not a me and them situation when I'm banging on about the SEF and asking them for the information I need. They're already aware of how they fit into the bigger picture. (Children's Centre Manager, professional background: education)

The settings – where the connections might be made and partnerships developed

Having considered some of the basic teamwork theory, let us look at the variety of settings where children and families might interact with a broad range of professionals and the services they offer. It is important to remember that many twenty-first-century children and their families will carry out their everyday lives without being regarded as having a problem, being at risk or needing particular additional specialist support.

> Obviously working really closely with Children's Centres and family outreach workers there are a lot of vulnerable families and you become aware of issues that may be arising. Also if you have groups in for story time sessions over a period of twelve weeks and you have the same people you build up relationships with them and you do find out what is going on in their lives. (Children's Librarian).

A young child may have early childhood education and care experiences at home within the family, and outside her immediate environment, where she may encounter a combination of childminder, private day care, Children's Centre, foundation stage unit, nursery class or special needs school, nursery nurses, early years professionals and teachers. She may visit a health centre or medical practice and require the services of various health professionals such as midwives, health visitors, physiotherapists, paediatrician, dietician or speech and language therapist. The health visitor will introduce her to Bookstart and present her with a complementary book and library card and her parents may take her to meet librarians at their local library, mobile library or the one attached to a nearby Children's Centre. She may come into contact with a social worker or social services throughout her early years or may have one brief connection for a temporary problem. The young child may therefore encounter a range of different professionals who all have particular roles and expertise. These professionals will come together at different points in time to provide support – some are in constant contact with the child and her family, or this may be intermittent when the need or opportunity arises.

Reading 6.3

What is self-esteem?
Denis Lawrence

> Denis Lawrence provides an account of the collection of ideas associated with self-esteem. Distinguishing between self-concept, self-image and the sense of ideal self, he describes self-esteem in terms of an individual's evaluation of their personal worth.
>
> Self-esteem is a vital issue in respect of the formation of identity and self-confidence. However, it also has a direct effect on the ways in which learners approach challenges. Clearly, practitioner expectations are a particularly significant influence on the ways in which children see themselves.
>
> How could you build the self-esteem of the children in your care?
>
> *Edited from:* Lawrence, D. (2006) *Enhancing Self-Esteem in the Classroom.* London: Paul Chapman, 1–9.

What is self-esteem? We all have our own idea of what we mean by the term, but in any discussion of self-esteem amongst a group of teachers there are likely to be several different definitions. The chances are that amongst these definitions the words *self-concept, ideal self* and *self-image* will appear.

Self-concept

Firstly, the term *self-concept* is best defined as the sum total of an individual's mental and physical characteristics and his/her evaluation of them. As such it has three aspects: the cognitive (thinking); the affective (feeling) and the behavioural (action). In practice, and from the teacher's point of view, it is useful to consider this self-concept as developing in three areas – self-image, ideal self and self-esteem.

The self-concept is the individual's awareness of his/her own self. It is an awareness of one's own identity. The complexity of the nature of the 'self' has occupied the thinking of philosophers for centuries and was not considered to be a proper topic for psychology until James (1890) resurrected the concept from the realms of philosophy. As with the philosophers of his day, James wrestled with the objective and subjective nature of the 'self' – the 'me' and the 'I' – and eventually concluded that it was perfectly reasonable for the psychologist to study the 'self' as an objective phenomenon. He envisaged the infant developing from 'one big blooming buzzing confusion' to the eventual adult state of self-consciousness. The process of development throughout life can be considered, therefore, as a process of becoming more and more aware of one's own characteristics and consequent feelings about them. We see the *self-concept* as an umbrella term because subsumed beneath the 'self' there are three aspects: self-image (what the person is); ideal self (what the person would like to be); and self-esteem (what the person feels about the discrepancy between what he/she is and what he/she would like to be).

Each of the three aspects of self-concept will be considered in turn. Underpinning this theoretical account of the development of self-concept will be the notion that it is the child's *interpretation* of the life experience which determines self-esteem levels. This is known as the phenomenological approach and owes its origin mainly to the work of Rogers (1951). It attempts to understand a person through empathy with that person and is based on the premise that it is not the events which determine emotions but rather the person's interpretation of the events. To be able to understand the other person requires therefore an ability to empathize.

Self-image

Self-image is the individual's awareness of his/her mental and physical characteristics. It begins in the family with parents giving the child an image of him/herself of being loved or not loved, of being clever or stupid, and so forth, by their non-verbal as well as verbal communication. This process becomes less passive as the child him/herself begins to initiate further personal characteristics. The advent of school brings other experiences for the first time and soon the child is learning that he/she is popular or not popular with other children. He/she learns that school work is easily accomplished or otherwise. A host of mental and physical characteristics are learned according to how rich and varied school life becomes. In fact one could say that the more experiences one has, the richer is the self-image.

The earliest impressions of self-image are mainly concepts of *body-image*. The child soon learns that he/she is separate from the surrounding environment. This is sometimes seen amusingly in the young baby who bites its foot only to discover with pain that the foot belongs to itself. Development throughout infancy is largely a process of this further awareness of body as the senses develop. The image becomes more precise and accurate with increasing maturity so that by adolescence the individual is normally fully aware not only of body shape and size but also of his/her attractiveness in relation to peers. Sex-role identity also begins at an early age, probably at birth, as parents and others begin their stereotyping and classifying of the child into one sex or the other.

With cognitive development more refined physical and mental skills become possible, including reading and sporting pursuits. These are usually predominant in most schools so that the child soon forms an awareness of his/her capabilities in these areas.

This process of development of the self-image has been referred to as the 'looking-glass theory of self' (Cooley, 1902) as most certainly the individual is forming his/her self-image as he/she receives feedback from others. However, the process is not wholly a matter of 'bouncing *off* the environment' but also one of 'reflecting *on* the environment' as cognitive abilities make it possible for individuals to reflect on their experiences and interpret them.

Ideal self

Side by side with the development of self-image, the child is learning that there are ideal characteristics he/she should possess – that there are ideal standards of behaviour and also particular skills which are valued. For example, adults place value on being clean and tidy, and 'being clever' is important. As with self-image the process begins in the family and continues on entry to school. The child is becoming aware of the mores of the society. Peer comparisons are particularly powerful at adolescence. The influence of the media also becomes a significant factor at this time with various advertising and show-business personalities providing models of aspiration.

So, what is self-esteem?

Self-esteem is the individual's *evaluation* of the discrepancy between self-image and ideal self. It is an affective process and is a measure of the extent to which the individual cares about this discrepancy. From the discussion on the development of self-image and ideal self it can be appreciated that the discrepancy between the two is inevitable and so can be regarded as a normal phenomenon.

Indeed, there is evidence from clinical work that without this discrepancy – without levels of aspiration – individuals can become apathetic and poorly adjusted. For the person to be striving is therefore a normal state.

What is not so normal is that the individual should worry and become distressed over the discrepancy. Clearly, this is going to depend in early childhood on how the significant people in the child's life react to him/her. For instance, if the parent is overanxious about the child's development this will soon be communicated and the child, too, will also become overanxious about it. He/she begins first by trying to fulfil the parental expectations but, if he/she is not able to meet them, he/she begins to feel guilty.

The subject of reading is probably the most important skill a child will learn in the primary school and normally will come into contact with reading every day of school life. It is not surprising therefore, that the child who fails in reading over a lengthy period should be seen to have developed low self-esteem, the end product of feeling guilt about his/her failure. The child then lacks confidence in him/herself.

It can be appreciated from the foregoing description of the development of self-concept that teachers are in a very strong position to be able to influence self-esteem. It is not failure to achieve which produces low self-esteem, it is the way the significant people in the child's life react to the failure. Indeed, it could be argued that failure is an inevitable part of life. There is always someone cleverer or more skilful than ourselves. This must be accepted if we are to help children develop happily without straining always to be on top. Eventually, of course, children become aware of their own level of achievement and realize that they are not performing as well as others around them. Then they can develop low self-esteem irrespective of the opinion of others; they have set their own standards. It is probably true to say, however, that the primary schoolchild is still likely to be 'internalizing' his/her ideal self from the significant people around him/her.

Self-esteem as defined so far refers to a 'global self-esteem' – an individual's overall feeling of self worth. This is relatively stable and consistent over time. In addition to this overall, or global, self-esteem we can have feelings of worth or unworthiness in specific situations. Accordingly we may feel inadequate (low self-esteem) with regard to mathematics or tennis playing. However, they do not affect our overall feeling of self-worth as we can escape their influences by avoiding those situations. If, of course, we cannot avoid them and regularly participate in these activities which make us feel inadequate they may eventually affect our overall self-esteem. Also if we continue to fail in areas which are valued by the significant people in our lives then our overall self-esteem is affected. It is worth reflecting on how children cannot escape school subjects which is why failure in school so easily generalizes to the global self-esteem.

In summary, self-esteem develops as a result of interpersonal relationships within the family which gradually give precedence to school influences and to the influences of the larger society in which the individual chooses to live and to work. These extraneous influences lose their potency to the extent to which the individual becomes self-determinate. For the student of school age, however, self-esteem continues to be affected mainly by the significant people in the life of the student, usually parents, teachers and peers.

Reading 6.4

Attachment, what it is, why it is important?

Sir Richard Bowlby

Sir Richard Bowlby, son of John Bowlby, has continued his father's work on attachment. Sir Richard gave a presentation on the theme of attachment to the Quality of Childhood Group in the European Parliament on 8 January 2008; a summary of the notes made from his speech is provided below. The speech provides an overview of attachment theory, what it means for babies and young children and how it impacts upon them in later life.

The dawn of attachment theory had an impact on how families are seen, on the expectations that were placed on women to remain in the home from the 1950s onwards. What does this theory mean for your practice? How do you feel about babies and young children entering ECEC? What do you understand your role to be?

Edited from: Bowlby, R. (2008) 'Attachment, what it is, why it is important and what we can do about it to help young children acquire a secure attachment'. *Summary of the Seventh Session on 8 January 2008 in Brussels of the Working Group on the Quality of Childhood within the European Parliament.* The European Council for Steiner Waldorf Education.

What is attachment theory?

Before talking about attachment theory, I need to tell you what attachment is. My father used the term "attachment" to describe the affectional bonds that develop between babies and their mothers. Most people call these family bonds "love" – the sort of family love that's different from sexual love.

Based on empirical research

Attachment theory is based on findings from empirical research, from observational studies and from clinical examples; it's a framework for understanding the nature of the enduring family bonds that develop between children and their parents – their attachment figures. The theory focuses mainly on relationships during early childhood, and the impact that these have on the emotional development and mental health of children as they grow up.

In times of danger babies and toddlers seek their mother/primary attachment figure

Babies and toddlers have a powerful survival reaction to sense danger whenever they are in unfamiliar places and have no access to an attachment figure, preferably to their primary attachment figure (who is usually but not necessarily their biological mother). This sense of danger frightens children and triggers their attachment seeking response, and this response will be terminated only when they reach proximity to their attachment figure. Attachment seeking is a specific response requiring a specific termination – proximity to an attachment figure. Similar behaviours (usually called imprinting) can be observed in the young of many other species and it's a very successful survival strategy. For example, if you watch a herd of elephants protecting newly born baby elephants from a group of lions, they do such a good job that the lions do not have not a chance.

Attachment response: when it starts and when it peaks

The attachment response starts at about 6 months, peaks between 12 and 24 months, and by 36 months the intensity has reduced sufficiently that most children can tolerate a few hours separation from attachment figures without distress – during pre-school nursery for example.

The quality of this enduring mother/child bond will have a significant impact on the child's developing personality and future social, emotional and mental wellbeing

By their fifth birthday most children can manage five short days of school. Attachment theory concentrates mainly on the bond that a mother has with her child, and on the attachment that a child has with their mother or the person who raises them. The quality and nature of this enduring mother/child bond will have a significant impact on the child's developing personality and future social, emotional and mental wellbeing – for better or for worse.

The quality of the attachment has a very significant influence on how children build future relationships

A child's primary attachment figure is usually the biological mother, but the biological link is not essential. In many cases someone else raises the child and becomes the primary attachment figure. But most people have an enduring attachment bond with their mother that lasts a lifetime, and the quality of this relationship has a very significant influence on how they build future relationships.

The development of babies' primary attachment bond can be compared to the development of speech

Human babies have a natural propensity to talk, but they need to have the experience of hearing speech in order to acquire the words and to learn to speak the language of the adult. Similarly, babies have a natural propensity to become attached, but they need to have regular interactions with a consistent adult in order to develop an attachment relationship with them. The quality of the relationship will depend on the adult's capacity for making secure or insecure attachments.

Secondary attachment figures can promote self-esteem in children

In appropriate circumstance and given sufficient time and attention, children can develop enduring secondary attachment bonds to affectionate and responsive people such as grand-mothers, nannies, aunts, neighbours or child-minders. Three or more secondary attachment figures in addition to a primary attachment figure can promote self-esteem in children, and is a psychological protective factor that can reduce the probability of mental health problems in the future. Being part of a big family is a protective factor.

Why is attachment theory important?

Attachment theory has helped researchers to identify the causal links between people's childhood experiences of adverse attachment relationships, and their subsequent social, emotional and mental health problems. Understanding the nature and effects of childhood attachments has been extremely valuable to health care professionals who try to promote good parenting practice.

Attachment is a characteristic of the relationship

A child can form a secure attachment to one parent, and an insecure attachment to the other parent. Attachment is not a characteristic of either the child or the parent, it is a characteristic of the relationship. The parent's sensitivity to the needs of the child is a major determinant in whether a secure or insecure attachment will develop. It has been found that the parent's ability to provide a secure attachment will be heavily influenced by the quality of care that they received during the first two or three years of their own life.

How do babies develop a primary attachment?

From birth, babies are learning to recognise different people and are developing their mental capacity to form attachments. By about 6 months most babies are beginning to show a preference for one person, and by about 9 months their primary attachment bond to this person – usually the birth mother – is well advanced, and by about 12 to 14 months the primary attachment is usually well established. At the same time the baby's ability to differentiate between familiar people they know and unfamiliar strangers they don't recognise will have developed.

There are many features of care that influence babies' choice of who becomes their primary attachment figure, but the two main ones are:

- being comforted when they cry,
- being played with.

These two experiences help babies select the one person who most frequently and predictably brings them both comfort and joy, and that person becomes the baby's primary attachment figure. In the English language there is a saying which illustrates the above:

"Families that play together stay together."

How do babies develop a secure primary attachment?

A secure attachment is likely to develop when an adult is sensitive and attuned to the baby's communications, and when the adult provides consistent and predicable care which meets the needs of the baby quickly and reliably.

An insecure attachment is likely to develop when the adult is insensitive and not well attuned to the baby's communications, and when the care is inconsistent and unpredictable and does not satisfy the baby's needs quickly or reliably.

Playing – providing positive feelings

A secure attachment is likely to develop when an adult engages sensitively in playful inter-active games that hold the baby's attention and bring them joy. The adult's play needs to be appropriate to the baby's capacity to enjoy the game, and the adult must be sufficiently attuned to know when to start, stop, repair or re-engage with the baby.

An insecure attachment is likely to develop when the adult is not sufficiently sensitive when playing interactive games and does not engage with the baby or bring them joy. The activities may be beyond the baby's capacity for excitement, or the adult may be careless, neglectful or intrusive and misjudge the baby's abilities or mood, and not know when to start, stop, repair or re-engage with the baby.

NOTE. At the same time that babies are developing their primary attachment (either secure or insecure), they are usually developing secondary attachments to other familiar people. These secondary attachments can be either secure or insecure depending again on the adult's ability to relate, so a baby can develop a secure attachment to one adult and an insecure attachment to another adult.

How to maintain a secure attachment

One of the most important and complex tasks for parents of securely attached children is to maintain boundaries that are realistic and appropriate to the child's developing competence and within the parents' resources. Considerable time and attention is required to maintain these limits for children who have grown to expect supportive and sensitive care and are eager to explore and learn about their environment. The challenge for parents is to find a balance between restraint and safety on one hand, and encouraging new and challenging experiences on the other.

How to avoid harming a baby's and a child's attachment

The key to maintaining secure attachments throughout childhood is to avoid any experience, however well intentioned, that overwhelms the attachment bond. Maintaining children's security of attachment requires that their attachment figure provides them with a sense of safety and protection at all times. Children who are frightened, whether by parents who are abusive, neglectful or violent, or by being separated from their attachment figures for an inappropriate amount of time (even when they're in perfectly "safe" situations) can become insecurely attached.

I believe that many babies and toddlers develop a risk factor in daycare without an attachment figure. Babies with an insecure attachment at home, who then spend time in daycare without an attachment figure, will have their negative model of relationships reinforced.

These babies need daycare from a long-term secondary attachment figure who is consistent throughout the years of daycare, is sensitive to their individual needs, and is always available to them. In this way a more positive model of relationships can develop. Although we know that this is what babies need, it seems to be extremely difficult to provide this in group daycare settings.

How to change from insecure to secure attachment

Attachment theory is concerned with the quality of the relationships that babies and toddlers develop with their primary attachment figures. Although the security of the babies' attachment may be influenced by their temperament, the greatest influence will come from the adult's ability to form secure relationships. Therefore changing the adult's ability to relate to the baby is going to be the focus of early intervention programmes.

Changing from insecure to secure attachment is slow, expensive and takes very skilful therapists, and the cure is never complete – at times of stress, "ghosts from the nursery" return to haunt people. Prevention is infinitely preferable to cure.

Neuroscientists discover the impact of a good early childhood environment on the brain

Today neuroscientists are discovering that they cannot explain the rapid neurological developments in the brain of a child without reference to the interaction between the baby and his/her environment. This discovery was triggered by research on the Romanian orphans from the Ceausescu regime, which were intensely studied. These orphans had been severely deprived of interactions with a primary caregiver. It turned out that certain parts of their brains were non-existent (black holes on the brain scans). It furthermore turned out that the harm was least for those children who had endured this for a shorter period. Professor Mike Rutter is one of the people who carried out this research.

Reading 6.5

The role of the preschool practitioner in the development of children's social competencies

Jennifer Colwell

In the previous readings and in Chapter 6 of *Reflective Teaching in Early Education*, we firmly establish that positive relationships are key to learning and that children must be supported to develop the skills needed to maintain such relationships and work with others. The following reading provides an overview of the key factors early years practitioners must be aware of when supporting the development of children's social competencies.

Edited from: Colwell, J. (2012) *The Relational Approach to Group Work: The Role of the Preschool Practitioner in the Development of Children's Social Competencies.* Unpublished PhD, University of Brighton.

A framework for understanding the role of the preschool practitioner in the development of children's social competencies

Research was undertaken to explore the development of children's social competencies with children aged thirty to sixty months within one preschool. A series of five complex mediating factors, which together provide a framework for understanding the role of the preschool practitioner in the development of children's social competencies, were identified.

Factor one: Practitioners should understand the theoretical and conceptual underpinnings of relational programmes and activities

Having a clear and developed understanding of the theoretical framework of any programme will be crucial for the practitioner to be able to develop their practice and fulfil the other factors identified in this framework. For example, to be able to reflect upon the development and use of any programme one must understand its theoretical underpinnings.

In addition, where time is at a premium and there are many programmes and theories available to practitioners, it will be crucial that practitioners understand the potential benefits to maintain their motivation, as the time and dedication needed to modify one's practice is substantial (Stevens, 2007). Thus any programmes and activities used by practitioners to support the development of children's social competencies must have a clear theoretical underpinning which is available to all staff.

Factor two: Practitioners should provide a suitable environment in which positive relationships and the development of social competencies can thrive

There are a number of facets to providing a suitable environment in which working relationships can thrive in preschools. These include: creating a suitable physical environment (Baines, Blatchford and Kutnick, 2007); developing a culture which promotes positive relations, and providing children with opportunities for collaboration (Blatchford et al., 2003). Research has shown that in order to create such an environment adopting a whole staff team approach to a new initiative is more likely to lead to positive gains than one practitioner acting alone (e.g. Banerjee, 2010).

Factor three: Practitioners should reflect upon their practice, observe children's behaviours and use the information gathered to inform their practice

Without reflecting upon practice practitioners will not be able to identify positive changes which can be made, for example to the environment, or to their practice. This links back to factor one, that without the underpinning of an understanding of the theoretical and conceptual framework of the approach being taken, meaningful reflection will be difficult to achieve. Without an understanding of what you are doing and why you are doing it, it is not possible to identify areas of practice which require consideration.

As practitioners reflect upon their own practice it will also be necessary for them to observe the children to ensure that they have a clear understanding of their needs (Johnson and Johnson, 2008). Practitioners need to be aware of the children's needs to inform their planning and ensure children receive the support they need to develop their social competencies (Gura, 1992).

Combining an awareness of practitioner action with an understanding of the needs of the children, practitioners will be able to plan to support the development of children's social competencies.

Factor four: The practitioner should hold expectations that the children are capable of developing social competencies and make these expectations explicit

Practitioners must believe that all children are capable of developing the skills needed to work and learn together. It may be believed that children of this age are too egocentric to develop the social competencies required to work collaboratively (Kutnick at al., 2008) and if this is the case opportunities for children to develop and practise these skills will be limited.

Factor five: Practitioners should model the desired social competencies

Bandura in his model of Social Learning Theory (1969) recognises the potential for modelling to impact upon children's actions. He states however that simply having a behaviour modelled is insufficient for learning to take place. He recognises a number of processes which the expert and novice must be engaged in for learning to occur:

- **Attentional Processes** – the novice must be paying attention
- **Retention Processes** – the novice must be able to retain the information gleaned and be able to act on the information as required at a later stage
- **Moteric Reproduction Processes** – the novice must have opportunities to practise the behaviour and develop its application
- **Motivation Processes** – for a behaviour to be imitated there must be a motivation to do so.   (Bandura, 1977)

I would make an addition to Bandura's processes, that modelling needs to be cognitive in nature. By this I mean that practitioners should make the meanings behind the decisions they take explicit to the children. Allowing the children to 'hear what the practitioner is thinking', as they say they thoughts aloud, so that the children can begin to understand and develop their own thought processes.

These five reciprocal and dynamic factors provide a framework for supporting practice which presents an understanding of the complexity of the role of the practitioner in supporting children to develop the skills required to work and learn collaboratively. To achieve these in practice will require time and effort.

Engagement
How are we managing behaviour?

7

Readings

7.1 Ferre Laevers
Measuring involvement in the early years (p. 130)

7.2 Pat Broadhead, Jane Johnston, Caroline Tobbell and Richard Woolley
Understanding children's behaviour in relation to their development (p. 133)

7.3 Sonja Sheridan
Pedagogic quality and behaviour (p. 138)

7.4 Michael Argyle
Non-verbal communication (p. 141)

7.5 Michelle Graves and Ann Arbor
The HighScope approach to behaviour management (p. 145)

The following readings expand upon some of the key issues related to behaviour management. We begin with a reading by Ferre Laevers, which considers what involvement is, what it looks like and how it can be measured. This reading is presented first, as we believe that ensuring the environment is one which supports children to be relaxed and engaged in their learning is at the heart of good behaviour management.

The following three readings consider the role of the practitioner in behaviour management, in particular how certain behaviours convey messages to children and what the potential consequences of these behaviours may be. Finally, we end with a reading which provides some practical ideas for supporting behaviour management and, specifically, how to support children who are presenting as a cause for concern.

Reading 7.1

Measuring involvement in the early years
Ferre Laevers

The following reading considers what is meant by the term 'involvement' and the use of the respected Leuven Scale of Involvement. As discussed in the parallel chapter in *Reflective Teaching in Early Education*, ensuring that children are engaged, happy and relaxed in the setting is one of the most crucial aspects of behaviour management. Prevention is better than cure. The Leuven Scale provides a tool for supporting reflections regarding children's involvement in activities in the setting.

Edited from: Laevers, F. (2003) 'Experiential Education: Making Care and Education More Effective Through Well-being and Involvement'. In F. Laevers and L. Heylen (eds) *Involvement of Children and Teacher Style.* Leuven: Leuven University Press, 15–17

Involvement, the key word

The concept of involvement refers to a dimension of human activity. Involvement is not linked to specific types of behaviour nor to specific levels of development. Both the baby in the cradle playing with his voice and the adult trying to formulate a definition can share that quality. Csikszentmihayli (1979) speaks of the 'state of flow'.

One of the most predominant characteristics of this state of flow is concentration. An involved person is narrowing his attention to one limited circle. Involvement goes along with strong motivation, fascination and total implication: there is no distance between person and activity, no calculation of the possible benefits. Because of that, time perception is distorted (time passes by rapidly). Furthermore there is an openness to (relevant) stimuli and the perceptual and cognitive functioning has an intensity, lacking in activities of another kind. The meanings of words and ideas are felt more strongly and deeply. Further analysis reveals a manifest feeling of satisfaction and a bodily felt stream of positive energy. The 'state of flow' is sought actively by people. Young children find it most of the time in play.

Of course one could describe a variety of situations where we can speak of satisfaction combined with intense experience, but not all of them would match our concept of involvement. Involvement is not the state of arousal easily tuned by the entertainer. The crucial point is that the satisfaction stems from one source: the exploratory drive, the need to get a better grip on reality, the intrinsic interest in how things and people are, the urge to experience and figure out. Only when we succeed in activating the exploratory drive do we get the intrinsic type of involvement and not just involvement of an emotional or functional kind. Finally, involvement only occurs in the small area in which the activity matches the capabilities of the person, that is in the 'zone of proximal development'.

To conclude: involvement means that there is intense mental activity, that a person is functioning at the very limits of his or her capabilities, with an energy flow that comes from intrinsic sources. One couldn't think of any condition more favourable to real development. If we want deep-level-learning, we cannot do without involvement.

Measuring involvement

However much involvement may seem to be subjective, it is very well possible to assess in a reliable way the levels of involvement in children and adults. For this the "Leuven Involvement Scale" has been developed, encompassing seven variants for different settings, ranging from childcare to adult education.

The LIS is a 5-point rating scale. At level I, there is no activity. The child is mentally absent. If we can see some action it is a purely stereotypic repetition of very elementary movements. Level 2 doesn't go further than actions with many interruptions. At level 3 we can without a doubt label the child's behaviour as an activity. The child is doing something (e.g. listening to a story, making something with clay, experimenting in the sand table. interacting with others. writing. reading, finishing a task…). But we miss concentration, motivation and pleasure in the activity. In many cases the child is functioning at a routine level. In level 4 moments of intense mental activity occur. At level 5 there is total involvement expressed by concentration and absolute implication. Any disturbance or interruption would be experienced as a frustrating rupture of a smoothly running activity.

The core if the rating processes consists of an act of empathy in which the observer has to get into the experience of the child. This gives the information to draw conclusions concerning the mental activity of the child and the intensity of his experience.

Research with the Leuven Involvement Scale has shown that the levels of involvement within a setting tend to be more or less stable (Laevers, 1994). They are the result of the interactions between the context (including the way teachers handle their group) and the characteristics of the children. We can expect that the more competent the teacher, the higher the level of involvement can be, given a particularly composed group of children. We find indications for this in our own research, but also in the large scale Effective Early Learning project in the UK, where more than 3,000 adults learned to use the scale and more than 30,000 children at the pre-school age have been observed with it (Pascal and Bertram, 1995; Pascal et al., 1998).

The scales

The Leuven Scale of Well-being

Level	Well-being	Signals
1	Extremely low	The child clearly shows signs of discomfort such as crying or screaming. They may look dejected, sad, frightened or angry. The child does not respond to the environment, avoids contact and is withdrawn. The child may behave aggressively, hurting him/herself or others.
2	Low	The posture, facial expression and actions indicate that the child does not feel at ease. However, the signals are less explicit than under level 1 or the sense of discomfort is not expressed the whole time.
3	Moderate	The child has a neutral posture. Facial expression and posture show little or no emotion. There are no signs indicating sadness or pleasure, comfort or discomfort.
4	High	The child shows obvious signs of satisfaction (as listed under level 5). However, these signals are not constantly present with the same intensity.
5	Extremely high	The child looks happy and cheerful, smiles, cries out with pleasure. They may be lively and full of energy. Actions can be spontaneous and expressive. The child may talk to him/herself, play with sounds, hum, sing. The child appears relaxed and does not show any signs of stress or tension. He/she is open and accessible to the environment. The child expresses self-confidence and self-assurance.

The Leuven Scale of Involvement

Level	Well-being	Signals
1	Extremely low	Activity is simple, repetitive and passive. The child seems absent and displays no energy. They may stare into space or look around to see what others are doing.
2	Low	Frequently interrupted activity. The child will be engaged in the activity for some of the time they are observed, but there will be moments of non-activity when they will stare into space, or be distracted by what is going on around.
3	Moderate	Mainly continuous activity. The child is busy with the activity but at a fairly routine level and there are few signs of real involvement. They make some progress with what they are doing but don't show much energy and concentration and can be easily distracted.
4	High	Continuous activity with intense moments. The child's activity has intense moments and at all times they seem involved. They are not easily distracted.
5	Extremely high	The child shows continuous and intense activity revealing the greatest involvement. They are concentrated, creative, energetic and persistent throughout nearly all the observed period.

Reading 7.2

Understanding children's behaviour in relation to their development

Pat Broadhead, Jane Johnston, Caroline Tobbell and Richard Woolley

This reading considers how understanding child development is a vital part of behaviour management. Through such understandings practitioners can support children to develop self-control and recognize appropriate and accepted behaviours. In the parallel chapter in *Reflective Teaching in Early Education*, we note that it is important to have realistic expectations of children that are clearly expressed, as this will help establish a child's ability to manage their behaviour.

Edited from: Broadhead, P., Johnston, J., Tobbell, C. and Woolley, R. (2010) *Personal, Social and Emotional Development.* London: Continuum, 69–72.

Understanding development in relation to behaviour and self-control

Understanding how children develop emotionally, socially, cognitively, physically and morally can help practitioners support children in developing appropriate and acceptable behaviour and self-control. Feelings and emotions underpin most behaviour and therefore practitioners need to support children emotionally and help them understand their emotions and how they may affect their behaviour (Goleman, 1996).

Behaviour and self-control from birth to 3 years of age

Children under the age of 12 months need to feel safe and secure with the adults they come into contact with. Therefore it is important that the adults spend time with the child and become familiar with the child's needs and moods. They will eventually be able to recognize when a child needs feeding or sleep, or if they need to be soothed or reassured. They will communicate with the child by touch and facial expressions and talk. They will become attuned to the needs of the child and by meeting these needs they will be able to care and support the child within a routine that is flexible enough to do so and in which the child feels safe and secure. If the practitioner understands the importance of getting to know and respond to babies in their care and then builds a close and trusting relationship with them and their parents this will provide a good foundation for children to start to understand their own behaviour and develop self-control (DCSF, 2008b).

As children start to grow and become more mobile and start to talk they become more aware of others. However they are still unsure of what they can do and their physical skills are still developing. So a child may drop things or spill things or bump into things. At this stage the practitioner needs to be aware of the environment and provide safety and security but still allow children freedom to explore and develop. Sometimes practitioners can become frustrated or annoyed with children who drop things or bump into others and interpret it as unacceptable behaviour when in fact it is to do with physical immaturity. This can be particularly true when children are able to run but find it difficult to navigate or stop. The practitioner must think carefully about the environment and how it can be adapted to the needs of the child in order to help the child to interact in the best way.

As children start to develop language they may be able to start expressing simple needs such as wanting a biscuit. However it takes time for children to be able to fully communicate their needs (Rodd, 1996) and they may continue to cry and throw tantrums if they feel their needs are not being met. Again, this can be interpreted as unacceptable behaviour rather than the frustration it is, so it is still important that adults take time to get to know the child and to be able to respond to their needs as sensitively as possible. Even though children may be starting to develop more complex sentences by the age of 3, they may not be able to respond to adults talking to them about their behaviour, as they are not always able to comprehend meaning.

Emotionally they need the security of a familiar adult and comfort when things go wrong. The reassurance of a familiar adult in sight can act as a calming influence for many children. Children of 2 to 3 years old are starting to recognize themselves as individuals and start to assert their independence and try to control (Erickson, 1963). For example if you ask them to put on their coat they may refuse. Again this may be interpreted as unacceptable behaviour and a battle of wills may follow but if a choice is offered, for example, 'Do you want to put on your coat or wellies first?' it allows for some choice.

Socially children are starting to be much more aware of others and gravitate towards other children. However, they have not learned many of the social skills they need to always mange this successfully so they may snatch toys if they want them. They find it difficult to wait or take turns at this stage without adult support (Lindon, 1997). They may become frustrated and hit people or throw things. Practitioners in this situation need to put boundaries in place but they also need to start helping children understand that such actions can hurt. Simple stories can be a good way to do this. For example using a persona doll to tell the story of what happened when someone threw some lego and it hit the doll and how it made it feel. The practitioner can discuss with the character what the more appropriate behaviour would be and encourage the children to join in the discussion. They can also play with children to model appropriate behaviour and support turn taking (Pre-school Learning Alliance, 2007). For example in role play the practitioner may model appropriate ways of using please and thank you. By doing this they are starting to help children to acquire the social skills they need in a safe way. Sometimes practitioners may recognize a situation before it develops and distract or divert the child to play with something else; in this way they may help children avoid a situation which could result in conflict or distress and as a result avoiding an incident of inappropriate behaviour.

Behaviour and self-control from 3 to 5 years of age

As children start to become more physically adept and are able to run and climb they often seem to have a lot of energy and need opportunities to move around and a range of physical challenges. It is important for practitioners to recognize this and provide opportunities for children to be able to do this. Often children who are full of energy and run around a lot and engage in boisterous play (often, though not always, boys) (Papatheodorou, 2005) can be seen as overactive and a danger to others. Practitioners may try to stop this and where children continue to engage in this behaviour they can be labelled difficult. However practitioners need to consider the physical needs of children and provide activities and space which allow children to use this energy in a positive way but also help them to understand how running in confined spaces or hurting others is not acceptable and children get hurt.

While children do have lots of energy at this age they also can become tired, hungry and thirsty quite quickly which will have an effect on how they manage their behaviour (Lindon, 1997). Often children are unable to recognize their physical needs and associated feelings in this way so it's important for practitioners to be sensitive to children's needs and so should explore and provide for these rather than interpret a child's behaviour as a problem.

Between 3 and 5 children's language develops rapidly but at different rates for different children and it may well be that they do not always understand or are able to interpret what practitioners are saying to them. So telling children what to do does not always lead to them doing what you may have intended and this may be interpreted as a child misbehaving. So it is important that practitioners think about the language they use and check how the child has understood, or model what they want the child to do. Communication with children at this stage is not just about using language; actions can be very useful as well. This is also true of rules and routines. Children need help in understanding them and applying them, modelling them, practising them, using songs and props helps children know what they need to do and how to follow them.

As children approach 5, they are starting to be able to engage with both adults and peers and can express their needs through language and listen to a response so practitioners can start to encourage children to resolve any issues and conflicts using language but will need to ensure that children have the necessary vocabulary and support them in this process. Vygotsky, a social constructivist theorist, believed that children develop and learn in a social context and it is the interaction between the child and the person who has the skills and understanding of what they need to do (in this case the practitioner) which guides them in their learning. This joint approach to helping children think about their behaviour and solve problems enables children to gain a better understanding of their own behaviour and also how to deal with others and resolve conflicts (Vygotsky, 1962).

Emotionally children are starting to be aware of themselves and their feelings. Positive feelings and a good self-concept are very important in determining appropriate behaviour. They need to have trusting relationships with practitioners who help them to feel good about themselves. They need to feel valued and that they belong and they need assistance to be successful and to receive support, encouragement and praise in response to their actions. They need their feelings to be recognized and acknowledged. If children feel that practitioners approval depends on them always being good they may start to feel insecure, anxious and even guilty. They may not be able to separate the response of the adult to their behaviour and interpret it as being about them; they may then start to see themselves as naughty or worthless. It is very important for practitioners not to emotionally distance themselves from a child as a response to them if they do behave inappropriately (DCSF, 2008a).

Behaviour and self-control from 5 to 7 years of age

When children move into Year 1 at 5 to 6 years old there can be many presures on practitioners to make children conform to a very different environment. Timetables become more formal as do ways of working and sometimes children are expected to make big adaptations with little recognition of their readiness. Teachers and parents can sometimes make assumptions about children's levels of development and experience; they may expect children to fit into their practices rather than responding to the child as an individual and supporting them appropriately. This can lead to children feeling confused and anxious, feelings they are unlikely to be able to express directly, and so can lead to inappropriate behaviour. It is important for teachers to be familiar with what children can do and support them in a sensitive manner.

Physically children are starting to develop more control but they still need opportunities to run and use their energy and to be active in their learning. Long periods in confined spaces and limited opportunities for children to move around can be very difficult for many children and may result in poor behaviour. This may be particularly true when children are asked to sit on the carpet and concentrate without moving for 20 minutes, which can seem like a long time for many children. Children still become tired and may need time to rest and access to snacks and water.

At this stage teachers may expect children to have the cognitive abilities to reason and make sensible choices about behaviour and while children are starting to develop this capacity they still need help and guidance in doing this. This represents a challenge where staff to child ratios are 1:30. They may also be expected to engage in a curriculum and a way of learning which they find difficult. These may include lots of tasks sitting at tables where they are required to remember and follow instructions, organize themselves and their resources,. These expectations can be very daunting and where children are unable to manage the tasks they may feel angry or frustrated and this may damage their self-esteem. This may lead to children using avoidance behaviour and disrupting others. If the task itself is too difficult for the child they may feel inferior and if this happens frequently it can damage their confidence which may lead to seeing themselves as a failure. This in turn will have a negative impact on children's behaviour and their behaviour may become withdrawn or they may display behaviours practitioners see as difficult such as clowning, or being disruptive or aggressive. Practitioners need to be open to the idea that they can influence and mange children's behaviour by providing learning activities which are active, appropriate and accessible for children in which they can successfully engage in them.

Emotionally, children are able to start to recognize their emotions and with adult help can start to describe them. They are beginning to understand that others have feelings and to empathize with others. However, they will still need adults to help them. They are starting to be able to control their feelings, for example by waiting their turn. But in some situations they may still find it difficult to control their emotions, for example if they are tired or feel anxious. They still need to feel safe and valued and it is important for practitioners to get to know children as individuals and respond to them in that way. This can be a challenge in a class of 30, but if a practitioner does not see this as being important then children who struggle to conform to the expectations may receive a negative response from adults and this can lead to low self-esteem.

Children will have much more understanding of rules and the consequences of breaking rules. They will also be increasingly able to recognize their own thoughts and feelings and be able to understand that others may also have similar thoughts and feelings. For example feelings of distress if something they value is lost or broken (Kohlberg, 1996). However they will still not be able to apply rules consistently or think through the consequences of the actions they take and how they may affect others. Teachers need to help children understand why we need rules and involve them in creating them. When children break rules they need help to discuss what happened and how it may have affected others.

Reading 7.3

Pedagogic quality and behaviour
Sonja Sheridan

Four dimensions of quality are identified in the following reading, which focuses upon the dimension of the teacher. Through a discussion of her research, Sonja Sheridan describes the influences practitioner behaviour has on the quality of the early years environment and how this behaviour impacts upon children's behaviours and their interactions.

Edited from: Sheridan, S. (2007) *Dimensions of pedagogical quality in preschool,* International Journal of Early Years Education, 15:2, 197–217

In recent decades, a considerable amount of research has been focused on the interrelation between preschool quality and children's learning experiences. In this paper I consider four empirical studies based on a pedagogical perspective of quality. This multidimensional phenomenon focuses on children's opportunities for learning and development in relation to the overall goals of preschool. Based on interactionistic theories, pedagogical quality does not exist in itself but takes shape and develops in pedagogical processes through the interaction between people, and people and objects, in the learning contexts of preschool (Sheridan, 2001). It is a broad perspective that takes into account the norms, values, traditions, cultural specifics, contextual specifics and heritage of society. At the same time, it closes in and focuses on how various pedagogical processes in preschool are formed to support the right of the child to learn and develop, to participate and influence on-going processes and activities, to be respected, listened to and counted on as a worthy member of society. The overall aims of these studies were to define and describe characteristics and values of pedagogical quality and to deepen the understanding of quality by exploring how different aspects of quality are experienced, expressed and valued from diverse perspectives, contexts and time.

The analysis led to the identification of four dimensions of quality. The four quality dimensions are: (1) the dimension of society, (2) the dimension of teachers, (3) the dimension of children, and (4) the dimension of settings/learning contexts. It should be pointed out, however, that these dimensions of evaluation and analysis are inseparable in pedagogical quality as a whole. The dimension of society is the macro level, which constitutes the frame of the educational system in a societal context. It clarifies values, educational intentions, resources, structures and pedagogical processes in the educational environment from a broad perspective. The other three dimensions are on meso- and micro-levels within the preschool context. For the purpose of this edited piece the second dimension, the dimension of the teacher is discussed.

The dimension of the teacher

The focus of the second dimension of evaluation and analysis was how the teachers approach and interact with the children, their pedagogical awareness and educational strategies in relation to the learning process of the child and the content from which a child has to constitute knowledge. Evaluating quality in this dimension includes external evaluations of what takes place in the meeting between teacher and child as well as self-evaluations, which mirror the teacher's own perspective (Sheridan, 2001). Several studies indicate that it is the competence and the approach of the teacher that seem to have a crucial impact on the quality in preschool (Kärrby, 1992; Pramling, 1994; Sheridan, 2001; Johansson, 2003; Sylva et al., 2004). The meta-analysis of the four empirical studies highlights four teaching strategies in which the teachers interact with and approach the children: the strategy of abdication in which the teacher has given up his/her professionalism, the strategy of dominance overriding the children's initiatives, the democratic strategy, which is an engaged, sensitive, social and negotiating teaching strategy and the democratic/learning-oriented strategy. The latter approach has a clear learning orientation in addition to what distinguishes the democratic approach (Sheridan, 2001).

Consequently, different teaching strategies will lead to different possibilities for children's participation and influence. The teaching strategies of abdication and dominance seemed to either restrict or limit the children's possibilities for learning and experiencing. Significant was the attitude of harsh control and the demand for obedience, or no control at all. In these preschools there were conflicts and less sharing among the children. There was little space for children's own initiatives and participation, and the quality was evaluated as low.

It was the democratic approaches that promoted interplay, participation, communication and cooperation between the teachers and the children and among the children. Characteristic of this interplay was mutual respect, trust, open-mindedness and reciprocity. Teachers with a democratic learning-oriented strategy encouraged the children to ask questions, to learn and participate, and the children seemed quite contented, helped each other and solved conflicts through negotiation. The distinguishing quality in this educational approach was that the teachers had a clear direction of learning and focused on the child's possibility of developing an understanding of various phenomena, such as the principle of democracy and skills to practise it. The variety of understanding among the children was made visible both to themselves and others, as a tool for learning.

Let us examine ECERS evaluations of the quality of the six preschools participating in the third study. The range of the preschools' quality as externally evaluated is 2.88–6.13 (the minimum is 1.00 and the maximum 7.00). The variation in quality depended on how the teacher used his or her competence to interact, communicate with and approach the child, and whether the child was made part of what was going on in preschool, e.g. if he/she was involved in the organization of the physical environment, in the planning of the content and activities, etc.

Observable in the self-evaluations is the tendency for preschool teachers to evaluate higher than the external evaluator in low-quality preschools and vice versa (Sheridan,

2000). Analysis of the self-evaluations indicates that in low-quality preschools there seems to be a pedagogical unawareness compared to high-quality preschools. Different reasons for difficulties in interplay with the children were given by the teachers from high- and low-quality preschools. External factors were seen as obstacles hindering the teachers from low-quality preschools from interacting. They said that it was the large number of children in the groups that prevented them from communicating with individual children, and from making children part of the planning of on-going activities, etc. They also explained: 'if we had an extra room, the children could paint more often and when they want to'. In these preschools a meal situation was not seen as an opportunity for social-izing or as a time to engage in a stimulating conversation. Instead, the teachers' comments emphasize the importance of rules and keeping quiet during meals. They write: 'We try to place the children so it is as quiet as possible. Unfortunately, there are always some children who talk loudly and need to be told off all the time.'

The teachers from high-quality preschools were self-critical and held themselves responsible for missing opportunities to communicate, to extend children's learning, and to make children part of what was going on. They said: 'I need to discuss and reason more with the children in conflict situations.' In these preschools, the focus in the meal situation is on the provision of a pleasant atmosphere and the opportunity for learning. They write: 'The atmosphere at the table is pleasant, we talk all the time and try to make all children express their points of view during the on-going conversation.'

We may thus conclude that the teacher's competence can be seen from two intertwined perspectives: first, how they use their competence when trying to approach the perspective of the child in relation to participation and influence, which is the object of learning here. Second, the awareness of their professional role and the task of preschool to provide the foundation for children's understanding of democracy.

Evaluations of quality in this dimension highlight that the core of pedagogical quality is in the interplay. According to interactionistic theories, it is constituted in, takes shape and develops in the meeting between the child and the teacher. How this meeting turns out depends on the competence of the teacher to combine the short- and long-term goals of society with the child's own intentions and goals for learning in a positive manner. The challenge is to combine them in such a way that the child maintains his or her curiosity to explore the world and develops an urge for lifelong and life-wide learning (Sheridan, 2001).

Reading 7.4

Non-verbal communication

Michael Argyle

> Michael Argyle's work, presented in this reading, draws attention to the ways in which we communicate with others through the way we speak, our expressions, gestures and even clothes. When thinking about behaviour, it is important to consider the messages we are sending to others. Facial expressions, gestures and posture will provide cues to children about the way you feel towards them, their behaviour, their families.
>
> A valuable activity would be to consider the messages you are sending to those around you and how they are being interpreted.
>
> Edited from: Argyle, M. (1994) The Psychology of Interpersonal Behaviour. 5th edn. London: Penguin, 22–8.

People make use of a variety of verbal and non-verbal elements of behaviour. In conversation, for example, there are alternating utterances, together with continuous facial expressions, gestures, shifts of gaze and other non-verbal acts on the part of both speaker and listener. All social signals are encoded and decoded by a sender receiver. Often the sender is unaware of his or her own social signals, though it is plainly visible to the decoder. Sometimes neither is aware of it. Social skills training or reading this book will increase sensitivity to the social signals of others and control over the social signals which are emitted. There are a number of different channels, we will look at seven and we will start with the face.

1 Facial expression

The face is an important communication area, and can indicate emotional reactions, and attitudes to other people, as well as moment-to-moment commentaries on conversation. People smile and produce other expressions because they have facial muscles. The facial muscles are activated by the facial nerve. Sometimes people smile because they feel happy or like someone, but they can also smile when in quite different moods, when it may be advantageous to do so. The facial nerve is activated by areas in the mid-brain producing genuine emotional expressions, and it is also activated by the motor cortex, which can produce socially correct or other bogus expressions; the upshot may reflect a battle between the two. The origins of these processes are entirely different: the mid brain system has its roots in evolution; the influences from the motor cortex system derive from socialization in the culture and cultural history. The evolution of facial expressions can clearly be seen in apes and monkeys, who communicate a great deal in this way. Izard

(1975) cut the facial muscles of some infant monkeys and their mothers and found that the pairs failed in develop any relationship with each other.

One of the main functions of facial expression is to communicate emotional states, and attitudes such as liking and honesty. It must be admitted that the origins of smiling are rather obscure. Ekman and others (1972) have found that there are six main facial expressions, corresponding to the following emotions: happiness, surprise, fear, sadness, anger, disgust and contempt. These six emotions have an innate, physiological basis: they are found in all cultures, correspond to distinctive patterns of physiological arousal and are found in young children, while similar expressions are found in non-human primates, The six emotions can be discriminated quite well, though similar ones can be confused, such as anger and fear, or surprise and happiness. In addition, unlike monkeys, we often conceal our true feelings; it is not always easy to decode a smiling face, for example. These facial expressions seem to be much the same in all cultures, though Ekman has shown that there are 'display rules' which specify when an emotion may be shown – whether to cry at funerals or to show pleasure when you have won. The final verdict is that facial expressions are partly deliberate social signals, but they also true emotional states.

2 Gaze

Gaze is of central importance in human social behaviour. It acts as a non-verbal signal, showing, for example, the direction of the gazer's attention; at the same time it opens a channel, so that another person's non-verbal signals, and particularly their facial expression, can be received. Gaze, then, is both a signal for the person looked at and a channel for the person doing the looking. It is linked with the social skill model, since this channel is the main one for receiving feedback. Consequently the timing of gaze, in relation to speech, for example, is important. During conversation and other kinds of interaction individuals look at each other, mainly in the region of the eyes, intermittently and for short periods. For some of the time two people are doing this simultaneously. Gaze is used as a social signal very early in life: mutual gaze with the mother first occurs at the age of three or four weeks. Visual interaction between mother and infant plays an important part in forming the bond between them: by six months infants are upset when eye contact is broken, by eight months it plays an important part in games with the mother. Gaze is an important signal for liking and disliking; we look more at people we like.

3 Voice

The voice communicates a lot in addition to words. Animals and small children communicate their emotions by cries, shrieks, grunts, but when we have learned to speak we do it by the way words are spoken. Scherer (1981) and other have studied the voices produced by people in different emotional states. Voices also vary in speech spectrum, for example angry voices are discordant, happy voices have purer tomes. Voices are 'leakier' than the face, true emotions tend to show through.

4 Gestures

While a person speaks he [sic] moves his hands, body and head continuously; these movements are closely coordinated with speech and form part of the total communication. He may:

1 display the structure of the utterance by enumerating elements or showing how they are grouped

2 point to people or objects

3 provide emphasis

4 give illustrations of shapes, sizes or movements, particularly when these are difficult to describe in words.

These 'illustrators' are iconic, i.e. resemble their referents, and can convey useful information. Graham and Argyle (1975) found that shapes could be conveyed much better, in one minute of speech, if hand movements were allowed. The effect was greater for those shapes for which there were no obvious words, and more information was conveyed in gestures by Italian subjects than by British ones. There is also evidence that gestures are part of the act of speaking and serve to help the speaker (p. 50).

Johnson, Ekman and Friesen (1975) found seventy-six gestures which were widely used and understood in the USA. Head nods are a rather special kind of gesture and have two distinctive roles. They act as 'reinforcer', i.e. they reward and encourage what has gone before and encourage people to keep talking and they are also used to give permission for somebody to talk.

5 Posture

Attitudes to others are indicated, in animals and humans, by posture. A person who is trying to assert himself stands erect, with chest out, squaring his shoulders, and perhaps with hands on hips. A person in an established position of power or status, however, adopts a very relaxed posture, for example leaning back in his seat or putting his feet on the table. Positive attitudes to others are expressed by leaning towards them (together with smiling, looking, etc.). If two people are getting on well with each other they often adopt similar, mirror-image postures. Posture does not show emotions very clearly, though Bull (1987) found that boredom and interest were clearly shown. Perhaps the main dimension of meaning is tense to relaxed.

6 Touch, bodily contact

This is a very powerful social signal. There are many ways of touching people, but only a few are used in any one culture, in ours, for example, shaking hands, and kissing and embracing, though in India and Japan non-touch greetings are used. The general meaning of touch is a combination of warmth and assertiveness, so there is a certain ambiguity about it. Touch often has quite a strong positive effect. In general, touch leads to liking and often to social influence. Touch is governed by strict rules about who may be touched, on which parts of their body, in what way and on which occasions. Bodily contact is encouraged between people in certain relationships, discouraged in others. Common observation suggests that there are a number of situations in which bodily contact is more acceptable: sport, dancing, games, crowds, medical and other professional attention, encounter groups, greeting and partings. In all of these situations different rules apply; a specialized kind of touch is used, with no implication of great intimacy. Shaking hands in greeting does not have the same significance as holding hands by courting couples; nor does embracing of football players who have scored goals.

7 Spatial behaviour

Encounters are usually started by people moving sufficiently close and into the right orientation to see and hear one another (and are ended by moving away again). Closer distances are adopted for more intimate conversations; at the closest distances, different sensory modes are used – touch and smell come into operation, and vision becomes less important (Hall, 1966). We move closer to people whom we like, and proximity is an important cue for liking. Argyle and Dean (1965) proposed that proximity is the outcome of a balance between approach and avoidance forces, so people will seek just the right degree of proximity with a particular individual, and may lean forwards or back to attain it. Dominance, however, is signalled neither by proximity nor orientation, but by the symbolic use of space. Manipulating the physical setting itself is another form of spatial behaviour – placing a desk to dominate the room or arranging seats for intimate conversation. There are considerable cultural differences in spatial behaviour. In some cultures people like to sit or stand nearer and more directly facing than in other cultures, and this can cause obvious problems in inter-cultural contacts. A European or Asian may back away, turning, to establish the preferred angle and distance, but be pursued in a spiral by an Arab or Latin American.

8 Appearance

Clothes are not just for keeping warm: they also send information about the wearer – his or her job, status, personality, political attitudes, group membership, even mood. Uniforms are a very clear example, for example in a hospital or lawcourt, but to a lesser extent in most places of work, indicating rank or job. Different personalities prefer different clothes – more or less colourful – for example. Different social groups wear different clothes. hippies, artists, politicians, country gentlemen and football hooligans all have their special costumes. They are used to present both differences and conformity.

Reading 7.5

The HighScope approach to behaviour management

Michelle Graves and Ann Arbor

> The following reading provides both some practical guidance for behaviour management, in the form of the 'six steps for conflict resolution', and a case study example of supporting a child with challenging behaviours. As stated in the paper, while most children will respond well to these six steps and function happily and well in the setting, others will need more targeted support which can often be challenging for the adults and the children in the setting.
>
> *Edited from:* Graves, M. and Arbor, A. (2002) *Working With a Challenging Child.* HighScope, 17 (1), www.highscope.org

The High/Scope Curriculum recommends a preventive approach to child behavior problems in which team members work to avert difficulties and conflicts by creating a supportive classroom environment and an orderly daily routine. When prevention fails, we advise adults to help children resolve their own conflicts and frustrations through problem solving rather than through adult-imposed control or punishment. The goal of this approach is to help children become aware of how their own actions affect others and of how the choices they make can help them overcome difficulties and conflicts.

Six steps in conflict resolution

Children with challenging behaviour can learn the following six-step process to resolve conflicts with other children, but you will need to use the steps below with extra patience and persistence. Note that each step is also a general interaction strategy that can be used in many situations to encourage positive behaviour.

1 Approach calmly, stopping any hurtful actions.
2 Acknowledge children's feelings.
3 Gather information.
4 Restate the problem.
5 Ask for ideas for solutions and choose one together.
6 Be prepared to give follow-up support.

While this approach enables most children to function fairly smoothly in most early childhood settings, sometimes staff find themselves spending a disproportionate amount of time dealing with the problems created by one or two challenging children. When faced with one child's severe behaviour problems, they often ask themselves whether they, as program staff, are the 'real problem'. They may first try to lessen the child's troublesome behaviour by altering the environment, but when such efforts fail repeatedly, they may wonder whether the child needs an entirely different approach.

Each challenging child is a different individual, and we don't claim to have answers for every child; however, we have dealt successfully with such problems in the High/Scope Demonstration Preschool. Following is a description of one such difficult situation we experienced and the process the staff went through in coping with it.

Jeremy was 3½ years old when he entered our program. We soon noticed that when Jeremy could not have exactly what he wanted, he would react violently: biting, kicking, screaming curses, throwing things, and occasionally making a 'mad dash' out of our classroom space. These outbursts, which occurred once or twice each morning, were so severe and disruptive that it often took 10–45 minutes of a staff member's time to calm Jeremy down.

During the next few months of school, much of our time together as a team was spent in discussions about Jeremy. Here are some of the strategies we developed for working with him.

- We took turns being the adult who stopped the behaviors when they occurred – spreading this difficult task around helped us be more patient with Jeremy. Even though we wanted Jeremy to develop inner controls, it was usually necessary at first to physically supply the control that Jeremy lacked. For example, we would separate Jeremy from the person being bitten or the object being thrown, and we would hold him inside the classroom when he tried to run out. As we held Jeremy, we would calmly and patiently explain why we could not let him do what he was doing, labeling the feelings that we thought were causing the behavior. In restraining Jeremy, we tried to avoid sending mixed messages. For example, if the adult spoke in a calm voice but her body was tense as she held him, Jeremy might not feel that we were confident that he would learn to control his own behavior.

- We made an effort to spend time with Jeremy during his calmer moments, playing next to him or describing his behavior and the positive reactions he was getting from other children: 'When you built together with Sally today, the house you made was big enough to fit three people inside'.

- We recorded our observations of Jeremy. We kept track of the frequency of his outbursts and looked for patterns: Did the problems tend to occur at certain times of the day? Were they related to changes in the classroom routine? Much later in the year, with the help of his family, we kept track of how much he was sleeping and what kinds of foods he was eating.

- We used the daily routine as a vehicle for helping Jeremy control his behavior. If Jeremy refused to do something that the group was doing (such as clean up after work time) we could remind him of the many choices that would be possible at other parts of the routine. 'It's time to for you to clean up and get your jacket on, but when we get outside, you can decide what you want to play with there'.

When Jeremy understood the schedule better, he was sometimes able to cope more appropriately with frustration.

- We tried to help the other children understand their own feelings about Jeremy in the classroom and the ways they could deal with his unpredictable behaviors: 'I know it scares you when Jeremy comes close to you. Tell him: "It hurts me when you try to bite. Stop it."'

- We looked for ways for Jeremy to take responsibility for his behavior. For example, when he pulled the arms out of a doll, we helped him find a way to repair it before he chose another activity.

- We involved Jeremy's parents in the process of finding ways to deal with him. This was perhaps the most difficult part of dealing with this situation. We tried to balance our reports on Jeremy's challenging behavior with some positive comments. It took several meetings and phone calls before the parents realized that we were not passing judgement on them. Once they trusted us, they were able to provide us with a great deal of support, both by continuing our classroom behavior strategies with Jeremy at home and by telling us about outside stresses that might be affecting Jeremy's behavior in preschool.

- As a team, we talked about and set time limits (for example, 'We'll try this for three weeks. If we don't see any improvement, we will…'). Knowing that we wouldn't have to endure the situation indefinitely helped us over the rough spots with Jeremy. We anticipated that we might have to repeat our behavior strategies many more times with Jeremy than we have to with most children before we would see results. However, we didn't want to spend so much time and effort on Jeremy that the rest of the class suffered or that staff members got burned out.

- When we felt stretched (by about week three) we looked to community resources for support. We contacted a local Foster Grandparent Program and accepted volunteer workers in our classroom. They helped with the other children so staff members could spend more time working directly with Jeremy. We also asked a social worker from the local social services department to observe in the classroom. She gave us some much-needed encouragement by confirming that we were on the right track with Jeremy.

As it turned out, our patience and persistence with Jeremy were eventually rewarded. Slowly, Jeremy's development progressed; as he grew older, the techniques we were modeling gradually became a part of him instead of something that came from us. He hit others less often, used language more often to describe his anger, and he stopped running out of the classroom.

Reflecting on this experience, we realize that we used the same basic strategies with Jeremy that we use with most children, but we used them with more intensity, frequency, and patience. We're glad that we did not 'throw in the towel' too early and we believe that the patience we displayed helped Jeremy find control within himself. We realize, however, that such efforts are not always successful. If we had felt that all involved were losing too much by continuing in the situation, our next step would have been to help Jeremy's parents find a more appropriate placement for him.

Spaces
How are we creating environments for learning?

8

Readings

8.1 Janet Moyles, Siân Adams and Alison Musgrove
The learning environment (p. 150)

8.2 Marie Willoughby
The value of providing for risky play in early childhood settings (p. 153)

8.3 Tim Loreman
Respectful environments for children (p. 157)

8.4 Urie Bronfenbrenner
The 'ecology' of social environments (p. 160)

8.5 Tim Waller
Digital technology and play (p. 163)

The readings in this chapter are intended to help with understanding ECEC settings as 'learning environments'. We begin with a reading which identifies the features of the learning environment, including both space and relationships. Two readings then focus on children as capable beings who deserve to be respected, and provided with enabling learning environments that afford opportunities for them to take risks.

Bronfenbrenner's classic analysis of layered contexts for development and learning offers a way of looking at the world of the child and the role ECEC practitioners play in their worlds. In the final reading, Waller illustrates how technology has impacted upon children's play, and thus their learning environments.

The parallel chapter of *Reflective Teaching in Early Education* addresses similar issues and suggests activities to increase the effectiveness of the learning environment with suggestions of Key Readings. *Reflectiveteaching.co.uk* offers many further ideas and activities.

Reading 8.1

The learning environment
Janet Moyles, Siân Adams and Alison Musgrove

> The SPEEL framework, devised by Janet Moyles, Siân Adams and Alison Musgrove following extensive research, provides an overview of the facets of effective pedagogy in the early years. In this reading they focus upon the ways in which practitioners provide for children's learning.
>
> *Edited from:* Moyles, J., Adams, S. and Musgrove, A. (2002) *SPEEL Study of Pedagogical Effectiveness.* Norwich: Stationery Office. Department for Education and Skills.

Within the SPEEL Framework, the learning and teaching context is constructed through:

- Creating a supportive, enquiring and respectful ethos within the setting;
- Making provision for learning, including playful learning;
- Maintaining relationships.

It is considered that the learning environment within settings influences the quality of children's learning (Day, 1999). However, Muijs and Reynolds (2001) found that many practitioners are more concerned with children's emotional and social needs than their cognitive development. Fisher (1997) considered that decisions made by teachers regarding curriculum issues also include consideration of their confidences and affective and social needs. It has been established that ensuring that children's learning is promoted within a context of care and security is more challenging and highly complex. In his research, Woodhead (1998) questions indicators of quality that inevitably contribute to children's development and care suggesting that quality judgments are related to cultural goals and expectations. Many of these cultural goals are represented in the nature and use of buildings, materials and staffing, as well as the day-to-day processes such as children's experiences, and varied approaches to teaching, learning, control and discipline. Turner-Bissett (2001) acknowledges that the cultural context is reflected in the primary classroom including many of the tensions and contradictions about teaching and learning, curriculum and play and the needs of the individual, a group or society. In total, these contribute to a setting's ethos. Ethos, however, is also argued to be a fashionable but an unsubstantiated concept (Donnelly, 2000). Donnelly suggests it is used to describe the distinctive range of values and beliefs which contribute to philosophy or atmosphere – the materials, resources and routines which construct the learner's patterns of behaviours and thinking. Ethos is too important to ignore yet difficult to define (Donnelly, 2000). Donnelly suggests there are three levels of considerations involved in creating a setting's ethos. First is a superficial level, which is apparent, for example, in documentation from settings. Although referred to as superficial, it is also considered to be 'aspirational' in its content. Second is conceived of as an outward, tangible attachment, visible in organizational structures that may be informed by policies. The final level is deeper, leading to inward attachment with genuine priorities and vision.

Within the context of the SPEEL project, the outward and visible structures, such as displays or documentation, have been identified and provide evidence of the ways in which effective pedagogues make provision for supportive, enquiring and respectful ethos within their settings. The deeper, inward attachments were often revealed during the reflective dialogues.

Ethos is sometimes characterised by beliefs about the role of the child, within pedagogy. There are frequent references, in the Framework and in literature, to the desirability of a child-centred approach to learning that contributes to a playful ethos within a setting (Bredekamp and Copple, 1997).

The concept of 'child-centredness' is subject to much debate (Chung, 2000). A child-centred ideology suggests that in play, children reveal their needs and interests on which curriculum may then be based. Malaguzzi (1996) declares that:

> There is an inner force that pushes children on, but this force is greatly multiplied when they are convinced that facts and ideas are resources, just as their friends and the adults in their lives are precious resources. It is especially at this point that children expect...the help and thoughtfulness of grownups. These are the important offerings of children. Their own timing and rhythms demand enormous respect. Children need the support of adults (p. 30).

Only recently has a coherent framework been developed to support practitioners' ideological basis of learning through play (Moyles et al., 2001). Through studying the framework it is possible to understand how practitioners' underlying values and beliefs regarding the place of play in children's learning determine the way in which the learning environment is organised, planned, resourced, maintained and accessed. Wood and Attfield (1996: 153) also found that:

> Play acts as an integrating mechanism that enables children to draw on experiences, represent them in different ways, make connections, explore possibilities, and create sense and meaning. It integrates cognitive processes and skills that assist in learning. Some of these develop spontaneously, others have to be learnt consciously in order to make learning more efficient.

Providing a playful ethos within the setting demands understanding of how children learn. The adult must take the responsibility for providing an environment that will promote children's active construction of concept development and new understandings (Bowman et al., 2001). The environment will reflect children's interests, past experiences, prior learning and current cognitive development; it will also have provision for developing children's construction of ideas and ways of thinking and learning. The quality of the 'integrating mechanisms' and the ways in which children are able to 'make connections' will be influenced by the context in which their play occurs – hence the importance and significance, to their learning and development, of the learning environment.

Research has shown that young children learn best when they are actively interacting with others and the environment (David et al., 1993). Providing materials and opportunities for experiences must be accompanied by appropriate intervention from informed and supportive adults (Moyles and Adams, 2001). Provision alone, 'providing opportunities' does not automatically promote learning or development.

The ethos is affected by the resources that are made available for children (Beardsley and Harnett, 1998). For example, the accessibility of materials and the ways in which they are organised and presented to children will determine the extent to which children's autonomy, independence and initiative are promoted and effective learning established (Wood and Bennett, 1999).

The importance of the environment is emphasised by Siraj-Blatchford (1999), for instance, the ways in which practitioners can honour children's cultural experiences and the ways in which anti-racist materials contribute sensitively to the curriculum (Siraj-Blatchford, 1992) Embedding a multicultural approach also ensures that children learn about and celebrate cultural differences.

Practitioners incorporate play activities in their planning and often use them as a basis for furthering children's understandings of different aspects of curriculum. However, promoting learning through play in reception class has been found to be problematic (Beardsley and Harnett, 1998). Sestini (1987) suggests that few play activities have criteria for cognitive challenge.

The ethos within the learning environment is socially constructed. McLaughlin (1993) emphasizes the social aspect of settings:

> The school workplace is a physical setting, a formal organisation, an employer. It is also a social and psychological setting in which teachers construct a sense of practice, of professional efficacy, and of professional community. This aspect of the workplace – the nature of the professional community that exists there – appears more critical than any other factor to the character of teaching and learning for teachers and the students.

Above all, the most important aspect is the nature and quality of the dynamic relationships between teacher and learner. At a pragmatic level, this will involve ensuring seating is appropriate to support the development of relationships, that clear rules are established, guidelines, whole school behaviour policies are developed by all staff and implemented with enthusiasm (Muijs and Reynolds, 2001; Brophy, 1981). Informed by knowledge of children, the practitioners will ensure the environment supports further learning and promotes 'comfortable collaboration' (Day, 1999). They argue that generating a collaborative ethos supports practitioners and promotes a more inclusive approach to individual needs of children.

Evans et al. (1994) discuss ways in which collaboration may lead to positive effects within and between schools and pupils. They argue that generating a collaborative ethos supports practitioners and promotes a more inclusive approach to individual needs of children. Some concern has been noted that although promoting collaborative work amongst children has many advantages, it might encourage dependency on others in peer groups and does not necessarily also foster independence (MEP, 2001). Generating and sustaining an appropriate ethos is highly complex and demands on-going reflection, evaluation and assessment of children's progress through development and learning as reflected in the SPEEL framework.

Reading 8.2

The value of providing for risky play in early childhood settings

Marie Willoughby

Risk is a concern for all those working with children. We have a moral and legal obligation to protect and care for children, yet we also have a duty to support children's learning and development. The reading which follows considers the benefits of providing risky play for young children and how we can reconcile this with our concerns to protect them.

Edited from: Willoughby, M. (2011) in A. Conroy (ed.) *Childlinks, Barnardos, Issue 3.* Available from http://www.barnardos.ie/assets/files/publications/free/childlinks_body27.pdf

Everyday life always involves a degree of risk and children need to learn how to cope with this from an early age. They need to learn how to take calculated risks and, for this learning to happen, they need opportunities for challenging and adventurous play and to move and act freely. Their actions are very often constrained by adults.

Adults who don't fully appreciate children's need to experience challenge constantly express doubts about children's competence. In addition to undermining children's efforts, simply being told about possible dangers is inadequate – children need to see or experience the consequences of not being careful. By engaging in exploration, adventure, taking risks and meeting challenges they can learn what they are able to do as well as the limits of their physical capabilities.

Providing opportunities to experience challenge is particularly important in the early years when young children's brains are still developing. Early experiences determine whether a child's developing brain architecture provides a strong or weak foundation for all future learning, behavior and (both physical and mental) health (Center on the Developing Child, Harvard University).

Jennie Lindon warns that 'adults who analyse every situation in terms of what could go wrong, risk creating anxiety in some children and recklessness in others' (Lindon, 1999: 10). Many adults, who are afraid that children might hurt themselves, simply remove objects, furniture and equipment rather than allow children time and opportunities to learn how to use them safely. Children are competent, confident and capable learners, able to make choices and decisions. If adults don't allow or don't provide children with opportunities for worthwhile risks they also prevent children from developing the decision-making skills necessary to make accurate risk judgements (Little and Wyver, 2008). Children's skill levels and competencies are changing constantly as they grow and develop so it is difficult for them to know just what they are capable of.

'When they have the opportunities to explore, risk, and try and try again in an environment that is both safe and challenging, babies can engage in motor practice play that leads to advanced physical abilities, mobility, agility, dexterity, and as a result, confidence, independence and learning.' (Kernan, 2007: 30).

Children are competent, confident and capable learners, able to make choices and decisions. Early years providers can and should offer children the opportunities and experiences to learn about risk in an environment that is designed for that purpose and in so doing help children to become capable of dealing with the hazards they will encounter in the wider world including when they start school.

What do we mean by risk?

It is important to distinguish between a 'risk' and a 'hazard':

The easiest way to think of it is that a risk is something you can judge, how high can you go and still safely jump off the swing and fly through the air. This is good. Children learn 'physical literacy' this way by starting small and then becoming more adventurous.

A hazard is something you cannot judge, is the swing pivot almost worn right through and about to give way unexpectedly? This cannot be judged by a child, so this is bad and must be avoided by good management practices.

Balancing the need for safety with the benefits of allowing for risk

The 'Managing Risk in Play Provision' position statement issued by the UK's Play Safety Forum in 2002 challenged the tendency to focus on safety at the expense of other concerns including health and well-being. Not focusing entirely or solely on safety does not mean ignoring safety, but rather carrying out a risk-benefit assessment which considers the benefits to children as well as the risks. The Play Safety Forum outlined the objectives that are fundamental in any play provision: to offer children challenging, exciting, engaging play opportunities while ensuring they are not exposed to unacceptable risk of harm. When carrying out any risk assessment it is essential then to balance the benefits of an activity with the likelihood of coming to harm and the severity of that harm.

Approaches to managing risk

Bearing in mind the distinction between a risk and a hazard, one approach to risk management outlined by the Play Safety Forum is to make the risks as apparent as possible to young children. This means designing spaces where the risk of injury arises from hazards that children can readily appreciate (such as heights), and where hazards that children may not appreciate (such as equipment that can trap heads or for children under three small sharp stones that they could swallow) are eliminated.

Regular inspection and maintenance of equipment is essential. When equipment or tools which could be dangerous are introduced, children need to be shown how to use them safely and how this is to be done needs to be considered as part of activity planning. It is also essential for services to have clear policies and procedures which outline the service's position on risk assessment and safety. These must be shared and discussed with parents.

Another important aspect of any approach to safety and risk is teaching children about risk and encouraging them to make their own risk assessments and to think about the possible consequences of their actions – asking questions like 'What do you think might happen if you hold the knife like this?'

Clear and evidence-informed policies and procedures on approaches to children's behaviour are not only legally required but also essential to ensure all of the adults have a consistent approach in allowing children to experience appropriate risk taking and being appropriately supported.

What young children need in their play spaces

Children need movement. Over-protecting young children from experiences out of a concern for their safety (especially outdoors) has become a serious issue in crèches, pre-schools and schools, with some not allowing children to run. As well as being free to run, jump, climb, swing and touch, children need to experience nature in the environments where they spend so much of their young lives. Many schools where children as young as four spend many hours have no access to nature or to opportunities to explore, to experience adventure, to use their imaginations. Such environments, in my view, present a far greater risk to children than the risk of falling – the risk of not developing to their fullest potential.

Planning opportunities for children to experience appropriate challenges

Inclusive practice means providing for all children what are risky play opportunities for them. What may be physically challenging, interesting and risky for a two-year-old may not provide four-year-olds with sufficiently satisfying or physically challenging experiences. It is important to observe the children closely and identify those who need either greater challenge or specific support.

As well as children's age, their individual dispositions are an important consideration when planning appropriate activities. Having a key worker system facilitates an individualized approach to assessing the risks and benefits of a particular piece of equipment or a planned activity. Part of the role of a key worker is to observe changes in each of the children to whom they are assigned and how their interests and abilities are developing. They can then ensure that experiences are matched to their key child's abilities, interests, disposition and developmental needs and are appropriately challenging for them.

We know from research that early childhood is an important time for developing children's ability to:

- Persevere
- Take risks
- Solve problems
- Develop confidence and independence
- Nurture their curiosity
- Develop an identity as a learner

It is important to plan children's play environments and the experiences they facilitate with these outcomes as the goals.

Constraints for providers to overcome

In Tim Gill's view it is often the risks to adults – blame, loss of reputation, liability – that too often cloud providers' judgements when it comes to allowing children to take risks (Gill, 2007). Risk benefit assessment means that the provider weighs the duty to protect children from avoidable serious harm against the duty to provide them with stimulating, adventurous play opportunities – allowing children to take risks while protecting them from serious harm.

The goal for early years educators should be to help children learn how to cope with the everyday challenges that they will inevitably be presented with as they grow older. The best way to keep children safe is to be willing, as adults, to take more risks on their behalf. The real risk is ... there is 'no risk' (Bundy et al., 2009).

Reading 8.3

Respectful environments for children

Tim Loreman

> If we believe that children are capable beings we must provide learning environments which reflect this, which respect their needs and their capabilities. In the following reading Tim Loreman considers the features of respectful indoor and outdoor learning environments.
>
> *Edited from:* Loreman, T. (2009) *Respecting Childhood*. London: Continuum, 60–3.

Respectful interior physical environments

The fostering of environments that will nurture a child's abilities and capacities in cognitive, physical, emotional, and spiritual ways is paramount. The environments in which we allow children to live their lives reflect our levels of respect for their individual variations and capacities. However, Tarr (2001, 2004) argues that many of the commercially available decorations for classroom walls (and, it can be assumed, other contexts, including the home) serve to silence children rather than acknowledging and promoting their creativity. Describing one classroom which was visually busy with commercial materials on the walls and hanging from the ceiling, Tarr (2004) observed that 'Almost mute amid the visual din were children's drawings and written work on the walls' (p. 88). Tarr goes on to say that

> The image of the learner embedded in these materials is that of a consumer of information who needs to be entertained, rather than a child who is curious and capable of creating and contributing to the culture within this environment. (p. 89)

The alternative to this is the maintenance or creation of more enabling envionments for children. Posters of cartoon characters on bedroom or classroom walls can be replaced by children's own creative efforts which would demonstrate a higher regard for their products. Ceppi and Zini (1998) led a team of Italian researchers examining children's spaces and their relationships with these spaces. This project deconstructed some exemplary pre-school environments and examined what is important in terms of lighting, colour, furniture, functionality, and other aspects of overall design. The implications of this study reach beyond the pre-school and into all environments in which children spend time. Rinaldi (1998), in summing up the project, concludes that

The objective is thus to construct and organize spaces that enable children:

- to express their potential, abilities, and curiosity;
- to explore and research alone and with others, both peers and adults;

- to perceive themselves as constructors of projects and of the overall educational project carried out in the school;
- to reinforce their identities (also in terms of gender), autonomy, and security;
- to work and communicate with others;
- to know that their identities and privacy are respected. (p. 120)

Bruner (1998) adds that a pre-school needs to be somewhere 'where the young discover the uses of mind, of imagination, of materials, and learn the power of doing these things together. It is as much like a stage, a self-made museum, or a forum as it is a classroom' (p. 137). This idea of an environment which respects children's capacity to create could be said to be a requirement of any of the spaces children regularly inhabit, including the home and public spaces in the community.

Respectful exterior physical environments

Views that children have limited abilities and capacities are reflected in more than wall decorations and interior spaces which surround them. If, as Gandini (1998) says, the environment is itself an educator, then some exterior environments constructed especially for children provide evidence of a disrespect for children's capacities. Children's playgrounds, for example, are now usually designed so as to reduce the risk of children hurting themselves, and while these design changes have been effective in reducing playground injuries (Howard et al., 2005), caution needs to be exercised when modifying existing playgrounds or building new ones. While nobody would advocate unsafe playgrounds for children (in the United States 205,000 playground injuries are treated annually; see American School and University, 2007), the creation of sterile, limiting environments where children can engage in few other activities than swinging or sliding above rubber mats leaves little room for experimentation and adventure. The fundamental idea behind the design and construction of such playgrounds is that children are clumsy, weak, and incapable of good judgement. Therefore, environments must be created in which such judgements do not need to be made. Furthermore, the real reason behind the construction of such playgrounds may be adult rather than child-oriented. McKendrick, Bradford, and Fielder (2000) argue that in some instances such playgrounds are constructed so as to give adults a break from children, rather than focusing on child needs and interests. Adults in these environments can relax in the knowledge that little harm can come to the children in their care, even if they are inattentive to them.

There are, however, alternatives to the creation of limiting play environments. The alternatives both reduce the risk of playground injury, and at the same time respect children's capacities to make good decisions about how they use such facilities. Schwebel (2006) found that effective adult supervision of children in playgrounds is likely the most promising means of reducing injury. The approach as suggested by Schwebel involves a component of teaching children how to use playgrounds in a safe manner, and then supporting their ability to do so. Later research demonstrated that such teaching was effective in producing behaviours likely to reduce playground injury (Schwebel,

Summerlin, Bounds and Morrongiello, 2006). Schwebel et al. focused on the playground supervisors, and promoted greater engagement with children and rewards for safe playground behaviour. In this way the adults were scaffolding (supporting) the learning for the children of safe playground behaviour. Rather than assuming children are essentially incompetent and incapable of playing safely (and therefore changing the playground to limit their play), this approach respects children's capacity to learn safe behaviour, and play in ways which would be less likely to result in injury. In an inherently unsafe world, if generalized, this approach might have positive benefits to a child's life outside the playground. It has the potential to expand the possible environments in which children can live and play.

While it is important to avoid harm, children need to be presented with opportunities to experience adventure on the playground and elsewhere, and they are certainly resilient enough to withstand a certain amount of this. Erikson (1980) argued that a certain level of challenge is important in the social and emotional development of young children. Those who do not experience some challenges which they need to overcome at a young age are less likely to be able to cope with them in a healthy way later in life. Overcoming challenges teaches children to develop their own competencies, and contributes to their notions of identity. It helps them to understand their own limitations, and if adults can help them to decide ways of possibly overcoming these limitations or alternate routes to the same goal, then a healthy attitude towards challenges and even failure to meet them can be preserved. According to Malone (2007)

> by not allowing children to engage in independent mobility and autonomous environmental play in their community, parents are denying their children important aspects of learning including psychological, social, cultural, physical and environmental. This could lead children to be lacking in environmental competence, sense of purpose, social competence, self worth and efficacy and resilience. (p. 523)

Reading 8.4

The 'ecology' of social environments
Urie Bronfenbrenner

Bronfenbrenner's work on the 'ecology' of social environments and their effects on child development and learning has been extremely influential since publication of his *The Ecology of Human Development* (1979). His model highlights life-wide and life-long dimensions in the contexts which learners experience. In the summary below, four terms are used to describe layers of life-wide context. These range from the direct interaction of significant others in a child's life (microsystem) to the characteristics of broader culture, social and economic circumstances (macrosystem). The final term adds the life-long dimension of time (chronosystem).

Can you see, with or without these terms, the key dimensions which Bronfenbrenner represents?

Edited from: Bronfenbrenner, U. (1993) 'Ecological Models of Human Development', *International Encyclopedia of Education*. Vol. 3, 2nd edn. Oxford: Elsevier, 37–43.

Environments as contexts of development

The ecological environment is conceived as a set of nested structures, each inside the other like a set of Russian dolls. Moving from the innermost level to the outside, these structures are described below.

Microsystems

A microsystem is a pattern of activities, social roles, and interpersonal relations experienced by the developing person in a given face-to-face setting with particular physical, social, and symbolic features that invite, permit, or inhibit engagement in sustained, progressively more complex interaction with, and activity in, the immediate environment. Examples include such settings as family, school, peer group, and workplace.

It is within the immediate environment of the microsystem that proximal processes operate to produce and sustain development, but as the above definition indicates, their power to do so depends on the content and structure of the microsystem.

Mesosystems

The mesosystem comprises the linkages and processes taking place between two or more settings containing the developing person (e.g., the relations between home and school, school and workplace, etc.). In other words, a mesosytem is a system of microsystems.

An example in this domain is the work on the developmental impact of two-way communication and participation in decision-making by parents and teachers. Pupils from classrooms in which such joint involvement was high not only exhibited greater initiative and independence after entering high school, but also received higher grades. The effects of family and school processes were greater than those attributable to socioeconomic status or race.

Exosystems

The exosystem comprises the linkages and processes taking place between two or more settings, at least one of which does not contain the developing person, but in which events occur that indirectly influence processes within the immediate setting in which the developing person lives (e.g., for a child, the relation between the home and the parent's workplace; for a parent, the relation between the school and the neighbourhood peer group).

Research has focused on exosystems that are especially likely to affect the development of children and youth indirectly through their influence on the family, the school, and the peer group.

Macrosystems

The macrosystem consists of the overarching pattern of micro-, meso-, and exosystems characteristic of a given culture or subculture, with particular reference to the belief systems, bodies of knowledge, material resources, customs, life-styles, opportunity structures, hazards, and life course options that are embedded in each of those broader systems. The macrosystem may be thought of as a societal blueprint for a particular culture or subculture.

This formulation points to the necessity of going beyond the simple labels of class and culture to identify more specific social and psychological features at the macrosystem level that ultimately affect the particular conditions and processes occurring in the microsystem.

Chronosystems

A final systems parameter extends the environment into a third dimension. Traditionally in the study of human development, the passage of time was treated as synonymous with chronological age. Since the early 1970s, however, an increasing number of investigators have employed research designs in which time appears not merely as an attribute of the growing human being, but also as a property of the surrounding environment not only over the life course, but across historical time.

A chronosystem encompasses change or consistency over time not only in the characteristics of the person but also of the environment in which that person lives (e.g. changes over the life course in family structure, socioeconomic status, employment, place of residence, or the degree of hecticness and ability in everyday life).

An excellent example of a chronosystem design is found in Elder's classic study *Children of the Great Depression* (1974). The investigation involved a comparison of two otherwise comparable groups of families differentiated on the basis of whether the loss of income as a result of the Great Depression of the 1930s exceeded or fell short of 35 per cent. The availability of longitudinal data made it possible to assess developmental outcomes through childhood, adolescence, and adulthood. Also, the fact that children in one sample were born eight years earlier than those in the other permitted a comparison of the effects of the Depression on youngsters who were adolescents when their families became economically deprived with the effects of those who were still young children at the time.

The results for the two groups presented a dramatic contrast.

Paradoxically, for youngsters who were teenagers during the Depression years, the families' economic deprivation appeared to have a salutary effect on their subsequent development, especially in the middle class. As compared with the non-deprived, deprived boys displayed a greater desire to achieve and a firmer sense of career goals. Boys and girls from deprived homes attained greater satisfaction in life, both by their own and by societal standards. These favourable outcomes were evident among their lower-class counterparts as well, though less pronounced.

Analysis of interview and observation protocols enabled Elder to identify what he regarded as a critical factor in investigating this favourable developmental trajectory: the loss of economic security forced the family to mobilize its own human resources, including its teenagers, who had to take on new roles and responsibilities both within and outside the home and to work together toward the common goal of getting and keeping the family on its feet.

Reading 8.5

Digital technology and play

Tim Waller

> In this reading Tim Waller considers how the influx of new technologies has changed children's play and thus their learning environments. Waller notes that Prensky (2005) developed the terms 'digital natives' to describe the generation who have grown up with digital technology and 'digital immigrants' to refer those who have not.
>
> Do you consider yourself to be a digital native or a digital immigrant?
> How does this impact on how the children in your care experience ICT in your setting?
>
> *Edited from:* Waller, T. (2010a) 'Digital Play in the Classroom: A Twenty-first Century Pedagogy?'. In S. Rogers (ed.) *Rethinking Play and Pedagogy in Early Childhood Education: Concepts, Contexts and Cultures.* Abingdon: Routledge Falmer, 139–41.

The impact of digital technology on childhood, children's lives and children's play and communicative practices

Digital technology is now a significant part of many children's everyday lives and as McPake et al. (2007) point out, children grow up as part of an 'e-society' in which digital connectivity (use of the internet, mobile phones and other interactive technologies) is essential to daily life. Consequently, from birth many children across the world are immersed in a way of life where this digital technology is used for a range of complex cultural, social and literacy practices (Marsh, 2007). These practices, which are constantly changing, include using a range of hand held devices such as mobile phones, multimedia players (iPods) and games consoles, playing interactive games on digital and satellite television and accessing the internet to communicate images and text, hold telephone conversations and play games with participants across the world. Currently, social network websites (shared databases of photographs which facilitate group discussion) and blogging (contributing to online web diaries) are very popular, but as the technology develops new and different communicative possibilities and practices will evolve (Waller, 2008). It is clear therefore, that many young children develop dispositions and competences with and through digital technology in the context of social interaction with their families and peers. For example, Marsh (2007) describes a number of cases which show that mobile phone use was firmly part of some families' communication practices with their young children, including the children's involvement in texting. Indeed, the BECTA (2006) survey of access and use of digital technology found that social interaction with peers, friends and family is emerging as the major driver for children's increasing use of Information and Communication Technologies (ICT). As Beastall (2008) surmises there can be little argument against the claim that (a significant number of) children and young people now have an advanced relationship with technology that has been developed right from birth. Given that many children are immersed in a world where digital technology is increasingly used for a range of social and communicative practices it is inevitable that they will incorporate this technology in their play. As Wood (2009: 37) argues, 'play can be seen as a social practice that is distributed across a range of contexts and co-participants and is influenced by the tools and symbols of community cultures'. Here a key question needs to be posed: is play with and through digital technology the same as play in other contexts or is play transformed by the context? Also, what are the features of digital play that make it different from non-digital play? Salonius-Pasternak and Gelfond (2005: 6) assert that, computer play is, perhaps, 'the first qualitatively different form of play that has been introduced in at least several hundred years … it merits an especially careful examination of its role in the lives of children'. The main focus of research conducted on digital technology so far has concentrated on the use of computers by older children and young people and not with the range of digital technologies or with children under five. Despite these concerns four factors are evident from recent studies. First, it is clear that many young children develop significant competence with technology at home well before they attend an early years setting or school (Marsh et al., 2005). Prensky (2005) developed the term 'digital natives' to describe the generation who have grown up with digital technology and 'digital immigrants' to refer those who have not. Similarly, Lankshear and Knobel (2004) use the phrase 'digitally at home' to describe a generation comfortable with and competent in the use of new technologies. Prensky (2005) argues that these 'digital natives' think differently from other generations due to the types of technology they have been exposed to and the ways in which they are exposed to these technologies. For digital natives, ways of acting and being in the social world are framed by their experiences with the technology. This involves not only the exploration of buttons on devices such as a remote control or mobile phone, but crucially, interacting in social worlds where devices are used for communication and young children re-construct this in their play. For example, I recently observed my grandson Hari aged 18 months playing with a mobile phone by exploring the buttons, pretending to have a conversation by holding the phone to his ear and talking and rushing to answer the phone when it rang. He also regularly incorporates an old disabled phone (that is part of his toy box) in his play. Yelland (2007: 1) makes an important point here when she observes that 'in much of the literature technologies are regarded merely as tools'. Yelland cites Castells (1996) who contends that technologies are also processes that affect how we can make sense of the world and communicate our views to others about it. Second, children's play and participation in the use of digital technology helps to transform cultural, social and literacy practices (Marsh, 2005) and third, young children are deliberately targeted by global software and games manufacturers (Verenikina et al., 2008). Finally, as Zevenbergen (2007) and McPake et al., (2005) point out, exposure to such digital tools creates different experiences and orientations to learning and thinking and offers significantly different ways of playing from what had been possible in non-digital worlds. Verenikina, et al. (2008) argue that for many children digital play and, in particular, computer games are a significant part of their daily experience. This experience has recently been given much greater recognition within an emerging literature, which they review. They draw attention to numerous studies that examine the value of computer play for learning and discuss arguments that this experience can impact positively on their academic achievements. Verenikina et al. (2008) conducted research (in Australia with children aged 5 to 7) to investigate the affordances and limitations of computer games and the features of children's traditional play that can be supported and further enhanced by different kinds of computer play. Usefully, they provide a classification of computer games according to game characteristics that support higher order thinking. Verenikina et al. (2008) showed that the games involved in the research afforded young children plenty of opportunity explore the environments in imaginative and make-believe ways, both within the games and beyond them to their everyday play. Interestingly, this research suggests that make believe play is at its best when children participate as a group. Additionally, Plowman and Luckin (2003) who studied the use of interactive 'smart' toys by children aged between four and eight at home and in school, found that social interactions were significantly increased for the children participating in the research with the 'smart' toys. Consequently Plowman and Luckin argue that 'this increase in social interactions around technology is an appealing contradiction of the popular belief that technology leads to reduced socialisation' (2003: 2). As a result of their research, Verenikina et al. also argue that computer games do not necessarily constrain children's play to movements pre-determined by the game designer and that 'while it is possible that some games do inhibit imaginative play, the games chosen for the study appeared to enable developmental play in often unintended ways' (2008: 7). Further, as Zevenbergen (2007) has pointed out, new and emerging play experiences are not restricted to digital media as there is an ever increasing amount of supporting matter. For example, many games are supported by television programmes, magazines, websites, trading cards and movies. As a result, children and young people have many worlds to explore that are separate but linked to these virtual games. Also Yelland (2007: 55) argues that, 'for young children the linking of three dimensional play things or television or movie characters with computer software provides a valuable context for learning that should not be underestimated'. There is, however, much research to be done in order to distinguish the conditions under which computer games best facilitate play and higher order thinking in very young children (Verenikina et al., 2008) and to also identify the features of digital play that make it different from non-digital play.

part three

Teaching for learning

9   **Curriculum** What is to be taught and learned?

10   **Planning** How are we implementing the curriculum?

11   **Pedagogy** How can we develop effective strategies?

12   **Communication** How does language support learning?

13   **Assessment** How can assessment enhance learning?

Curriculum

What is to be taught and learned?

9

Readings

9.1 Tina Bruce, Anne Findlay, Jane Read and Mary Scarborough
Froebel's spirit and influence (p. 170)

9.2 Sheila Nutkins, Catriona McDonald and Mary Stephen
The Reggio Emilia approach (p. 173)

9.3 Marion O'Donnell
The Montessori approach (p. 178)

9.4 Heiner Ullrich
Rudolf Steiner and the Waldorf Pre-School (p. 181)

9.5 Sheila Nutkins, Catriona McDonald and Mary Stephen
HighScope (p. 185)

9.6 Wendy Lee, Margaret Carr, Brenda Soutar and Linda Mitchell
The Te Whāriki approach (p. 189)

A curriculum reflects the values and understanding of those who construct it; the parallel text in *Reflective Teaching in Early Education* considers the development of early years curricula in the UK. There are also additional readings at *reflectiveteaching.co.uk*.

Given the degree of flexibility with curricula designed for the early years, and the focus on supporting the unique child, the beliefs of those implementing and delivering the curriculum are key to the experiences that young children and their families have within ECEC.

The readings in this chapter provide an overview of some the key influences of early years curricula, provision and practice, including the work of Froebel, Montessori and Waldorf Steiner and the approaches taken in the USA by HighScope.

Do you identify with any of these approaches? Can you identify any aspects of these approaches which have influenced your practice or the design of the curriculum you implement?

Reading 9.1

Froebel's spirit and influence

Tina Bruce, Anne Findlay, Jane Read and Mary Scarborough

> Froebel's mother had died before he reached the age of one. He was brought up, along with siblings, by his father. He was a neglected child, until an uncle took an interest in him and sent him to school. Froebel spent much of his time alone in his garden and this is where it is thought his love of nature blossomed. Influenced by the teachings of Johann Heinrich Pestalozzi while working as a teacher in Frankfurt, Froebel wrote numerous articles and in 1826 published his most important treatise, *The Education of Man* – a philosophical presentation of principles and methods pursued at Keilhau, a school he had founded with friends. Froebel went on to found his own school in 1837, calling it the Kindergarten: the children's garden.
>
> The following reading, taken from *Recurring Themes in Education* by Tina Bruce, Anne Findlay, Jane Read and Mary Scarborough (1995), was an address by Cockburn to London teachers over century ago, illustrating the spirit of Froebelian teaching and the 'essence' of Froebelian philosophy. It may be useful to bear in mind what education – and indeed life – was like for many children in England at this time, only four years after the 1901 Factory and Workshop Act raised the minimum working age to 12, and only three years after the 1902 Education Act (Balfour Act).
>
> *Edited from:* Bruce, T., Findlay, A., Read, J. and Scarborough, M. (1995) *Recurring Themes in Education.* London: Paul Chapman Publishing, 105–8.

I think all educationalists recognise that if a truth is to be judged by its fruits the highest possible rank in practical education must be awarded to Froebel. Everywhere we see the results of his teaching throughout our educational system doubtless he is best known in connection with the Kindergarten, but the fruits of Froebel's efforts do not end with the kindergarten, they penetrate throughout the whole of school life. One may say that his efforts begin on the lowest rung of the educational ladder, but continue right up to the very summit of the highest development of the faculties of which human nature is capable. Child study may be regarded as an offshoot from Froebel's work, and manual training as one of the fruits of his teaching. Nature study, the latest and one of the most valuable acquisitions to systematic education may be traced, also direct to Froebel's influence.

We recognise that Froebel took his stand on nature; that he regarded man as conditioned in nature, and he acted on the well known maxim which I think Bacon was the first to formulate – that nature could only be overcome by obedience to her laws. Froebel again gave expression to the great truth that there is no true education except through activity; that we best learn things by doing them; and he it was who first gave shape to the idea of self-activity – that is to say, that the education of the child must be sought in watching carefully totally and following and ministering to an impulse which comes from within.

The child's mind is not wax or putty. The child has a little will of its own and develops according to its own laws, which are God's laws, and not the laws of any pedagogic system. And it was Froebel who laid stress on the fact – it is true, that Aristotle had already laid stress on it – that we must watch the nature of the child, and train the various faculties in the proper order of their development. The child's own nature must be studied, and nothing like premature attempts at development undertaken. Recent science has shown that it is probably better to allow the mind to lie fallow for a time than to prematurely force a crop.

It is now recognised that the child comes into the world in a very immature condition; that the child is not a little man; that he is altogether different; that 'by the child's ways are not the ways of the adult, but that the child thinks quite differently from the adult – not only falls short in powers of thought, but employs other methods – that one might as well try to make an insect fly before it has wings, as to try to make children of tender years embark in processes of abstract thought before the power of abstract thought is developed.

The true secret of the kindergarten is that the child knows just what it wants in its own development. The child knows the sequence of its own development, and I imagine that the latest kindergarten teaching is coming towards the truest application of Froebel's principles by placing the infants in favourable conditions in an environment favourable for their own development and leaving them to do the rest. They know just what is good for them, and in their early education children's games provide the very best possible form of training.

We know now also that a great portion of the brain is composed of motor centres, and it has been realised that the best way to develop the brain is to the muscles and infants know themselves that the best way to develop the muscles is by play of all sorts; and the advantage of free, unrestrained play is that there is always a very much better supply of blood to the muscles and organs when the actions are unrestrained and take place spontaneously.

There is of course true and a false application of Froebel's principles and there are some who of late have been introducing practices in attempting to carry out Froebel's principles which would never have received the approval of the master mind. The process of construction throughout the course of all development should be, as it were, pyramidal, that is to say the broad base should be established before the attempt is made to attain height. Now in all development of the muscles, we know that the massive fundamental muscles should be exercised first – that they should form the base as it were of the pyramid of muscular action, and that the more delicate movements should come later. But I am afraid there has been a tendency in kindergartens to reverse this process, and the endeavour is made to teach children of very tender years most delicate operations in drawing, for example, those shocking microscopic squares.

This is not training, it is torture, it is putting weight on the top of the pyramid before the base is secure, and that leads to an unstable equilibrium in the mental world just as much as it does in the physical world; and the result of this unstable equilibrium, brought about by the endeavour to train the delicate muscles before you have got the solid massive muscular foundation shows itself in all sorts of convulsive and irregular discharges of muscular force. There is always a tendency to forget the spirit that underlies the teaching of a great genius, and to take hold of the letter – to think as it were only of the skeleton and to lose sight of the living flesh that should clothe it. There is a tendency always to turn every-thing to grammar – to systematise too much. Of course a certain amount of system is all right, but you must be very careful how you systematise your babies in the kindergarten. Anything in the form of grammar – I do not care whether it is kindergarten grammar, or manual, any other sort of grammar – is bad, anything like premature specialisation is fatal. We know it was through specialisation death came into the world.

Let us bear in mind that Froebel was essentially one who laid down general principles and that it does not necessarily follow that everything that any individual mind or any number of minds collectively deduce from Froebel's principles is correctly deduced from them, and therefore, we must always endeavour to draw a distinction between what is true and what is false in the application of Froebel's principles. I take it Froebel stood firmly on two things. He took his stand on nature, he held that education must be a natural process, that you can only rise as it were, above nature by pursuing nature's methods, and above all he took his stand on self-activity and anything that contradicts those two fundamental axioms is a false and not a true interpretation of Froebel's teaching.

Reading 9.2

The Reggio Emilia approach
Sheila Nutkins, Catriona McDonald and Mary Stephen

Reggio Emilia, synonymous with 'early years', is a region in Northern Italy. The 'Reggio approach' began as a community-centred, culture-inspired educational model. It was developed by a teacher, Loris Malaguzzi and parents, who felt that after the devastation and destruction of World War II a new approach was needed towards their children's learning. This reading looks at some of the key elements of the 'Reggio approach', including family and social context, the importance of participation and collaboration of all parties, and the environment – 'the third teacher'.

Edited from: Nutkins, S., McDonald, C. and Stephen, M. (2012) *Early Childhood Education and Care.* London: Sage Publications Ltd, 187–90.

Reggio Emilia is a region in northern Italy where, after the ravages of the Second World War, parents in this area wanted to provide a better future for their children. They felt that fascism had taught them the dangers of conforming to rules and wanted to nurture a generation of children who could act and think for themselves. They were dynamically led by Loris Malaguzzi and together they began an innovative pre-school system which has become synonymous with early years.

Loris Malaguzzi, already disenchanted with the public school system had left his post to study psychology in Rome. He was inspired by Vygotsky, Dewey, Piaget and Bruner and brought their thinking about how children learn together in a social context, how capable and competent children are, how important culture and expressive arts are to developing the mind and particularly Dewey's belief in democratic principles that evidently matched his own. The development of these pre-schools arose and has been sustained, as perhaps with all such educational initiatives, by a political movement or 'will'. Initially this was a reaction to fascism and war and as is often the case with matters concerning young children, changes to the lives of women after the war played an important part. Women moving to the city and leaving their homes to work in industry wanted good quality childcare and they came from a rural culture where family was important, Valentine (1999). It was natural perhaps that the pre-schools set up reflected this. Parental involvement is a key feature.

Other key features of this approach must include:

- Participation and collaboration – all parties involved in the children's education participate equally and collaborate, including families, children and teachers. There is no hierarchical system for staff so no promoted staff structure but a teacher and an *atelierista* (professional artist) to a class of 24 children that stay together for the whole three years.

- Image of the child – the view of the child as competent, strong, powerful, full of potential and 'connected' to adults and other children – part of society with 'rights' rather than 'needs'.

- An 'emergent curriculum' – meaning that the curriculum is fluid, allowed to be uncertain, without prescribed outcomes, arises from and follows children's interests.

- Documentation – children's activities are closely observed, extensively and continually documented and reviewed with the child, teacher and parents.

- The environment – parents are considered to be the child's first teacher, then there is the 'teacher' in school, which here means all staff including an *atelierista* and the environment is seen as the 'third teacher'.

- The importance placed on the expressive arts – the presence of the full-time *atelierista* attests to this.

What is perhaps most remarkable about the Reggio Approach is that a relatively small initiative has sustained and grown over many years. Some factors that have helped sustain it might include the fact that Jerome Bruner, Howard Gardner, Lillian Katz and others became interested and wrote about it spreading the word. Loris Malaguzzi, who died in 1994, lived long enough to continue the momentum of the project he began in 1947.

Parental involvement

The Reggio Emilia pre-schools were started essentially by parents as a reaction to political events and the family and social context have remained central to the approach. It is interesting to note however that in Reggio Emilia parents are **not** encouraged to become involved in work in the classroom as this is seen as disruptive to routines and children's learning. It would be a mistake to think that the approach is entirely flexible or non-prescriptive. Some aspects are quite rigid. The mere mention of 'disruption to routine' seems at odds with everything we see, read and hear about the Reggio Approach. However, there is certainly a very special relationship with parents and if it is not built around their involvement in the classroom it is well worth examining how it is established and maintained. Key factors appear to be:

- it is developed over time particularly through the same two teachers working with children over three years;

- parents receive lots of detailed information about what their child is doing and learning daily;

- parents collaborate in documenting children's learning;

- parents are involved with the administration including being on the school council and establishing policy;

- parents are involved in the upkeep of the buildings, repairs, as well as helping with outings and organising celebrations;

- contact begins before the child starts and parents stay with their child for at least a week gradually withdrawing for smooth transition;
- the school provides adult learning opportunities such as talks on child health or practical guidance for diet with cookery sessions;
- parents are involved in research;
- there is plenty of personal contact and interaction.

It has been suggested that to talk of 'home-school links' as we might just does not do justice to this special relationship and the child/family/teachers are the school, Valentine (1999).

Participation and collaboration

The Reggio Approach has been described (by those who provide it) as *'a pedagogy of relationships'*. Participation and interaction at every level by all parties including families, children, teachers and the whole community is seen as centrally important. They have created a 'Charter of Rights' for children and parents that confirms the right to participate and describes the child as *'entrusted to the public institution'*. The politics and culture of this part of Italy play an important part.

The lack of hierarchical structure is interesting. There are no principals or head teachers or promoted members of staff. There is a teacher and an atelierista (professional artist also seen as a teacher) for every 24 children. The ratio of 2:12 is slightly higher than in the UK but this is between two members of staff deemed to be equally well qualified – they are however differently qualified. Rinaldi (1994) describes staff development as a *'vital and daily aspect of our work'* about *'interaction with children and among ourselves'* as *'a right'* and *'a new concept of didactic freedom ... to discuss and challenge ideas, to have an interactive collegial relationship'*.

The image of the child as 'competent'

Children are imagined as competent, full of potential, curious and imaginative. They are seen as capable of expressing emotions, feelings and ideas, not as empty vessels. Children are seen to be searching for meaning with *'tenacity and effort'* from birth, Rinaldi, (2005). This is a positive model not a deficit model. The period of early childhood is seen as valuable in its own right not as a stepping stone to later childhood or adulthood, not as a preparation for education or working life. Children are not seen as the only learners in the school as teachers and parents are also learning. All are learning together, co-constructing knowledge and understanding and this 'ethos' under-pins everything. Our education system and each setting everywhere has an under-pinning ethos but it is rarely so explicitly expressed. It seems to me that the approaches we admire and study and write about most often have an explicit ethos that is clearly expressed, reviewed and discussed openly.

Documentation

Within the Reggio Approach documentation is seen as a tool for recalling and reflection. It is clearly an important part of the 'pedagogy of listening', Rinaldi (2006). It is essentially a collected and collated narrative that is then interpreted initially by the person recording it and then shared with others including the 'subject' (the child) and is open to reinterpretation. It could be the end point of a learning experience but is often the starting point. This approach allows the teacher (or adult) to give value to the meaning the child has made and hence value it. It is a way of listening to children. It gives the child a voice. They are not anonymous. The child is seen and heard.

The 'third teacher' – the environment

The environment in which children learn in a *scuole dell'infanzia* is designed (many but not all are purpose built) to encourage participation by having a series of linked spaces rather than separate spaces for certain groups or classes or for particular activities. These spaces work around a central 'piazza' or atelier just as their town environment centres around the squares. The focus is on creating a light, multi-functional space that is open to change. The design allows and encourages children to operate independently integrating inside and outside and allowing access to resources. They are intended to be multi-sensory and make much use of windows, mirrors, see through storage containers and white walls. This is in stark contrast to the vast majority of pre-school settings that I visit where there is usually an eye-boggling mix of bright often primary colours; windows are often plastered with pictures, posters etc. or covered by blinds; the lack of space is emphasised and exacerbated by clutter and the children only stand out because they are contrastingly dressed in an often drab school uniform.

The Reggio Approach is founded on the belief that children are entitled to a *'rich, complex'* environment with a *'wealth of sensory experiences'* and this is written into their Charter of Rights. The intention is to create an environment in which children, teachers and parents – everyone, feels at ease. The spaces both internal and external are linked together and all are free for all to access and use. Each space has a purpose but is flexible and takes on the 'identity' of the children according to how they choose to use it. Colours are subtle and resources are natural and largely recycled. These are sourced through the ReMida Creative Recycling Centre; a joint project that collects and distributes surplus and recycled materials (Thornton and Brunton, 2005). Thirty years ago under the Inner London Education Authority (ILEA) there was a similar project serving all the schools in London. This was obviously a much larger undertaking servicing a population of millions and many schools but nevertheless made good use of recycled and reclaimed paper, polystyrene, fabric etc. for creative use in schools. This is an approach that might be usefully revived in your area if it does not exist.

Conclusions

Understanding the Reggio Approach requires and deserves broader and more in depth study than can be provided here. However, the critical issues as with study of any alternative approaches are around how the ideas, approaches, strategies or theories can be applied in another context or culture. There is clearly much to be learned and some elements that could be more easily adopted or adapted. A key feature of the Reggio Approach that could impact quite easily and quite quickly on any culture or setting is the attitude to and influence of the environment. The physical environment can be changed, even if it is just small changes. Style and use of documentation might be influenced but more slowly. The amount and quality of communication with parents may be more problematic given that it is so heavily influenced by cultural attitudes but is important enough to merit further sustained attention.

Reading 9.3

The Montessori approach

Marion O'Donnell

> The following reading, taken from Marion O'Donnell's book which details the life and work of Maria Montessori, describes how the Montessori approach was born out of a developing understanding of children – an understanding informed in the main by observations of children engaged in free play experiences and research into the mental well-being of children.
>
> Has her vision for a new world been realized? Are there aspects of her vision which resonate with your vision for ECEC provision in the present day?
>
> *Edited from:* O'Donnell, M. (2013) *Maria Montessori: A Critical Introduction to Key Themes and Debates.* London: Bloomsbury, 1–4.

More than a century ago Maria Montessori's approach to education was completely out of step with everything done in schools. The Montessori method evolved through direct observations of 'free' children in a prepared environment. Montessori's success in 1907 with young children learning to write and read at 4 years was revolutionary.

Overshadowing all of Montessori's medical expertise as a clinical pediatrician was her interest in mental health. Her research focus before graduation was on nervous diseases when she worked in the psychiatric department of the University of Rome. She treated adult inmates, some of whom were mothers with children also living in the asylum. Soon, her focus turned to the causes of mental diseases in children. To Montessori it became clear that mental deficiency needed to be treated as a pedagogical problem rather than a medical problem.

Beginning with clinical observations, she conducted trials with special needs children [sic] in the asylum, and they succeeded in learning to care for their personal needs, caring for their environment and learning the 3Rs (writing, reading, arithmetic) using her special self-correcting materials. Some of these children were presented to sit an open examination and passed whereas children in schools failed the exam. With the success of her learners' learning, Montessori was keen to do trials with 'normal' children attending schools where so many failed to learn, to read and to write.

It was 1907 before Montessori had her opportunity to work with 'normal' children aged 3 to 6 years. She had no theory but began with practice. She planned to observe children who were free to move about and choose what they would do. A few materials were available to them which she had used with the children in the asylum. There were two rules to follow. First, children were shown how to respect the materials. Second, they were not allowed to interrupt anyone using a piece of material. Montessori observed the children using didactic materials and activities she had designed to help them gain control of their own movements and meet with success. Success was a key to happiness, to a positive state of mental health. Observation of children revealed their natural tendencies. They liked to choose what to do, repeat the experience and then put the material back on the shelf. All their tendencies became the principles of Montessori education. Children learned to care for their own needs and their environment, becoming independent of adults – a key aim of Montessori education. Observations revealed some children were excessively anxious, tired, worried or had hostile feelings towards others. This meant these children were not 'free' (in mind) to perform their chosen tasks. Children were to become masters of themselves, not masters of others. Montessori considered mastery of the environment along with positive relationships to be indications of good mental health. The Montessori teacher, a 'directress', presented each piece of material to each child individually using a short three-period lesson. She then moved away to allow the child to make discoveries. This could be referred to as 'directed discovery', whereby the child was able to explore and make new discoveries for himself.

The directress was to be a researcher and keep detailed notes of children's discoveries. Montessori demonstrated how to keep records of observations about progress in development. This was a very new role for teachers. Montessori urged teachers in 1907 to be researchers by using observation skills, taking notes, reflecting and taking action. The teacher prepared the environment and was responsible for providing conditions for learning and an interpersonal climate. Included in the conditions was an anxiety free environment with no tests, no exams, no prizes, no punishments, no competition among students' standards, no timetables and no homework. Establishing a friendly interpersonal climate contributed to good mental health which had everything to do with each child's feelings towards his learning environment and his feelings about his own ability and self-esteem. Providing conditions conducive for each child to be successful led to happiness which Montessori believed to be a key to the life of the mind.

Montessori's vision of a new world

In *Education and Peace* (1972), *Education for a New World* (1974) and other writings, Montessori spoke of her vision for a better world in which education would be the catalyst and principal agent for global harmony, peace and happiness. This new world would be realized not through adults but by way of children. There was a need for all humans to uplift themselves to the laws that govern (human) nature, she argued, and to reconnect to the laws of the universe which for millions of years had been a prerequisite for harmony among mankind (Lecture, late 1930s). Montessori envisaged a world where all people experienced social justice precisely as children in Montessori schools. She spoke of the 'universal child' growing into a young adult able to make wise choices in a free democratic world. Every graduate from school would be a cultured young adult fully prepared to adapt to an increasingly technological society no matter where he found himself as a world citizen. Her plan for new education for a new world involved helping the development of each child's unique personality from birth enabling him to become literate and equipping him to adapt and care for an unknown, fast changing technological world. Civilization, she felt, was at risk because while man had developed material things, he had in the process 'forgotten himself' (Lecture, India, 1946). The implication was that man's development had not kept up with material development, and little or no thought was given to the cosmic construction of one whole human society based on mutual help among men (ibid.). 'Humanity was on the down', she declared categorically, and all efforts in education needed to be directed towards raising humanity to a higher level (Lecture, Rome, 1951). That particular ideal of Montessori appears especially important today in a world where globalization and multiculturalism are realities. Montessori had considered relationships to be the crux of education and in today's unsettled global village it would appear that relationships among peoples of the world are increasingly vital for its very survival. As long as there are nations living with conflicts and turmoil in their everyday life there can be no world peace. She saw people as being world citizens and considered herself to be one.

At its heart, Montessori philosophy of education embraces mental health in general, especially peace of mind in each individual, peaceful homes and above all peaceful classrooms. Montessori saw all of these things as an indispensable preparation leading towards a peaceful world. Montessori education will be relevant and valuable in the future and merits closer attention by education practitioners and policymakers. The fundamental value of the Montessori Method lies in its origin, a thorough, clinical examination of the development of each unique child.

Reading 9.4

Rudolf Steiner and the Waldorf Pre-School

Heiner Ullrich

> Rudolf Steiner's concept of education is often seen as controversial and more can be read about this in the translation of Heiner Ullrich's work by Janet Duke and Daniel Balestrini. In this extract Ullrich describes the emergence of Steiner Waldorf pre-schools, work with children with 'special needs' and the historical context of this work which offers insight into the influences of the approach.
>
> *Edited from:* Ullrich, H. (2008), *Rudolf Steiner*, Translated by Janet Duke and Daniel Balestrini. London: Continuum, 110–15.

Historically the Waldorf School did not emerge from a pre-school but rather the pre-school emerged as an optional appendage after the school was in existence. Over Easter 1926 – one year after Steiner's death – Elisabeth von Grunelius (1895–1985) began working as an educator in the first Waldorf preschool, integrated into the Waldorf School in Stuttgart. Together with the original Waldorf teachers (Herbert Hahn, among others) she developed the practices of anthroposophical pre-school education based on a Steinerian view of man, also inspired by the pre-school tradition that stemmed from educational principles of the German Romantic movement.

Before working at the Stuttgart school she had received intensive social-educational training, for example at the renowned 'Pestalozzi-Fröbel-House' in Berlin. After fleeing from Nazi Germany in the 1940s, she later founded the first Waldorf pre-school in the USA and the first one in France after her later return to Europe. She is considered the 'primordial pre-school teacher' of Waldorf preschools, but to this day her work remains in the shadow of Rudolf Steiner, who never explicitly applied his ideas to pre-school education.

The transformation of the Fröbelian 'kindergarten' through the spirit of anthroposophy

For Waldorf educators the goal of pre-school is not preparation for later scholastic demands such as reading, writing, calculating and researching. Very much in the tradition of its founder Friedrich Fröbel, the pre-school (German Kindergarten means 'child's garden') should truly be the garden of Eden given back to children, a place in which they can play happily and freely under the watch of caring adults. Here children should find the conditions that support their development. The basic tenets in pre-school education stem from the anthroposophical view of the 'child's nature', which in the first seven-year period – in line with the ascending line of the educational process – sees the senses unfold, thereby – in line with the descending movement of reincarnation – living in this early stage in close connection with the higher spiritual world. The child takes an active part in its direct environment through imitation. It is therefore educationally desirable to give the child as many opportunities as possible to imitate meaningful activities which are perceived through the senses. For pre-school teachers this means that they have to both live up to Critical Exposition of Steiner's Philosophical and Educational Work the fact that they are role models and provide the children with a wide variety of activities which cultivate the senses and train the will. One the other hand, for Steiner, children in their early years have a much closer connection to the spiritual world than they do later when the incarnation process up to 'earth maturity' is complete and the connection to pre-birth existence has been cut off completely. The Waldorf educator therefore sees the child as the 'messenger from a higher world' (Herbert Hahn), in whose fantasy and creative play a spiritual message is relayed. In the three phases of the first seven-year period the spiritual I, which is descending from the higher worlds, takes hold of the physical body and helps the child to stand upright and in acquiring languages. It later aids in imaginative fiction and role-playing before it receives a closer connection to reality in planned constructional play. To the Waldorf pre-school educator, the child is not an incomplete person, but rather an imaginative, religious being that is closer to spiritual reality and can therefore lead adults to reflection and reverence. The Romantic image of the godly child through which adults may become young again inspired not only Fröbel and Montessori in their pedagogical teachings, but also the anthroposophical reasoning for early education. The dual view of the 'child's nature' results in four pedagogical guidelines for Waldorf pre-school practice with imitation and rhythm on the one hand and playing and religious education on the other:

1 Imitation and role model

What the female pre-school teacher [sic] does and how she does it should be a model for the child and worth imitating. The pre-school therefore resembles a pre-modern household in which the female pre-school teacher cooks, bakes, washes, irons, sews, and cleans just as the mother would in a large family. In one corner there is a weaving loom and cotton. In another there is a workbench with a hammer, screws and small tools. In the garden one finds a rake, a hoe and a wheelbarrow. Every morning the children enter a pedagogical space in which they are drawn to objects and activities and are encouraged to take part. In the Waldorf pre-school the tasks of tradesmen and farmers which have disappeared from everyday life in the urban world are to be learned and practised in in order provide them with primary sensory experiences. The direct experiencing of such tasks, which follow one another in a meaningful order and which lead to concrete results, is thought to be a crucial prerequisite for the acquisition (in a later developmental phase) of logical thought and problem solving.

2 Rhythm and repetition

For Waldorf educators a rhythmic lifestyle is the guarantee for healthy development. The 'cosmic' rhythms of the day, week, month, and seasons therefore determine the pedagogical schedule. Every child is to experience the pre-school morning in two large breaths between which they enjoy a joint breakfast. The first major inhalation phase in which the child may more or less pursue its own drives is the free playing time with joint cleaning up and the washroom visit. Then there is a brief exhalation phase during the 'morning circle' or rhythmic games and breakfast. A second inhalation phase encompasses free playing in the garden or a short excursion, before the second chair circle with fairy tales, puppets or music wraps up the day with the next exhalation phase. For those children who remain for the afternoon, this is followed by the joint lunch and midday nap, followed by another phase for free playing until the parents come and pick the children up.

3 Religious education

Annual celebrations should not only make the children acquainted with nature's rhythms, but also with the world of Christian religion. Fairy tales told by the pre-school teachers represent a major component of religious education. For the child, who still has his original faith in religion as well as a rich fantasy world, fairy tales can provide 'answers to all things' (Kugelgen, 1991: 67).

4 Fantasy playing

In the different forms of child's play – from the sensory-motor exercises to symbolic role playing right through to planned construction games – the anthroposophical educator is convinced of the spiritual force which, step-by-step, becomes more strongly united with the body. The encouraging of play through the providing of development appropriate toys represents an important incarnation aid for the child's spiritual being (cf. Hahn 1929).

When playing the child should – first internally then externally – acquire the activities of adults (such as gardening, baking, building, and handicrafts), and should do so creatively in a manner that allows expression of both the imagination and allows imitation. In order to encourage imaginative play, they should be surrounded by as few 'completed' objects as possible. Therefore, in addition to useful household objects (such as benches, pails, brooms, pots, cloths, blankets, and clothespins), in the Waldorf pre-school one also finds numerous untreated natural materials, many colorful, handmade cloths and the consciously primitive textile Waldorf puppets. All mechanically produced, technical, or electronic toys – be it Lego blocks or computer games – are strictly banned from the pre-school because they hinder the imagination and paralyze the etheric forces being built up in the child's body.

Anthroposophical pre-school education specialists are also opposed to television and computer games in the child's world; convinced that television prevents children from taking an active interest in their real environment and from developing their own imagination. While listening to a story, children create their own inner images, but this imaginative activity is hindered through the hectic images of television. Their need to communicate with adults about the stories they have heard is also diminished.

Looking back now at the presented conception and practices of the Waldorf pre-school one may conclude that the central focus on free playing, the notion of the warm, motherly environment, and the focus on the child's own right to autonomy are in line with the Fröbelian tradition; the main differences lie in the focus on rhythms and ritualization of daily activities, in rejection of modern toys and technology and in the implementation of religious education.

Reading 9.5

HighScope
Sheila Nutkins, Catriona McDonald and Mary Stephen

HighScope began as a research project in 1962 in response to concerns over the low achievement rates of Afro-American students in the then racially segregated education system in Michigan, USA. The study identified short and long-term socio-economic benefits from a high quality preschool education.

Note how research plays a key role in both the development of practice and in accessing the impact of such practice.

Edited from: Nutkins, S., McDonald, C. and Stephen, M. (2012) *Early Childhood Education and Care.* London: Sage Publications Ltd, 217–32.

Weikart's HighScope curriculum did not magically appear overnight, but evolved gradually through reflection on practice over a period of five years, always with the child's learning as the central focus, Schweinhart et al. (2005). This moved over time from a position of experimentation and not being guided by developmental theory or objectives to an eventual model of early childhood education with a strongly explicit Piagetian base. This views the child as an intentional learner – a view now promoted at an even earlier stage, in babies, Goswami (2008) and has a clear focus on meeting the needs and interests of the individual.

The curriculum provided by HighScope has a strong emphasis on active learning on the part of the children and over time the focus shifted from measuring the child's attainment to being able to view the child's developmental status and provide a variety of materials from which active learning could arise, Blackwell (1994). He describes this as '*moving away from a deficit model to an asset model*' and teachers were aided in this by moving their thinking away from curriculum content to viewing the curriculum as a developmental tool which could provide children with opportunities to exploit their strengths.

This also changed the role of the teacher from leading to allowing the child to lead. This encouraged the child to do the talking and the adult role to become very much to listen and respond appropriately. This provided an enhanced teacher – child dialogue. From the child's point of view, this meant that they had to discuss with an adult what they planned to do that day, followed by carrying out the planned activity and then further discussion supported by an adult about how the activity had progressed. This developed into the Plan / Do / Review approach and is a fundamental principle of the HighScope curriculum.

For Weikart, it was also very important that there was a consistency in the daily routine. This is easily justified by the fact that young children need predictability and stability in terms of provision. For some children this might be the opposite from what they experience at home. This type of routine will help to promote the security that young children need. However, the consistency of the routine did also allow for flexibility too, in order to support children's interests and be able to adapt in a spontaneous way.

The layout of the classroom had to be well planned with thought given to the nature of the materials available – a balance of natural and commercial – and storage considered so as to be attractive and accessible to the young child. This helps to promote independence, using initiative and importantly, making choices. This type of approach is also favoured by Ferre Laevers and is an important aspect of the Reggio Approach.

Daily routine

The HighScope typical day would comprise:

- Greeting time
- Large group time 10–15 mins
- Small group time 15–20 mins
- Planning time 10–15 mins
- Work time 45–60 mins
- Tidy up 10 mins
- Recall 10–15 mins
- Outside 30–40 mins

Wiltshire (2012) comments on the importance of viewing these as maximum time periods for the various components listed above. She states that more than 15 minutes of a large groups time will result in fidgety children and that work time in excess of two hours will lose momentum. Compare this with the long hours that we expect 5 year olds to be able to cope with in primary schools in the UK.

The role of the adult is clearly defined within the HighScope programme; to guide and scaffold learning and to engage the child in meaningful conversations at the planning stage. These will encourage the child to be able to articulate their own ideas and make choices and solve problems. All of this contributes to the child developing self-esteem and competence, but key to this is the relationship between the child and the adult. Knowing that your thoughts and opinions are valued and that you are being encouraged is an intrinsically motivating factor in taking control of your learning. Understandably, this is particularly important for children from disadvantaged backgrounds, where adult-child dialogue may be unlikely to promote this.

Curriculum content

The adult role for HighScope teachers was to provide activities and experiences to meet the interests and needs of the child, but this was not at random. A range of 'key experiences', 58 of these, would be provided within five curriculum content areas:

- Creative representations
- Language and literature
- Initiative and social relations
- Movement and music
- Logical reasoning

Nowhere is the HighScope programme described as a 'preparation for school'. Although language and literature is a clear heading above, activities were provided to promote a 'caught not taught' approach to learning. However, all the available literature does support this as a 'preparation for life'. Compare this with the formal approach to phonics and language 'training' that is prevalent today. What was important was to be able to provide experiences and materials to help children to develop the broad language and logical abilities that form the foundation of future learning (OECD, 2004).

An analysis of the programme, Wiltshire (2012), would show that the key principles involve:

- children having active engagement with people, materials and ideas;
- children plan and carry out activities of their own choosing and reflect on them;
- children's work is supported by adults who share control with children.

Neaum and Tallack (2000) describe this as the adult having to be aware of the balance between encouraging, demonstrating and assisting, but not dominating, in order to balance instruction with children's initiatives which reflect the children's own interests.

Staff were also encouraged to use a problem-solving approach to resolving social conflict with children from an early age, so that by the time the children reached adulthood, they would have many of the necessary social skills, understand how to use them and the confidence to use them, gained from many years of practice and support, Wiltshire (2012).

Qualifications of staff

One other very significant point to bear in mind concerns the staff employed to work with the children in the original project. According to Slaughter-Defoe (2005), not much is known about the personal attitudes and values of the original teachers, who would be concerned with educational attainment rather than future lifetime effects, but that an aim was to support children to come to appreciate, enjoy and love learning for its own sake, to value education as a vehicle for the development of critical thinking skills and, to grow to be the kind of person who is respectful and caring of others.

Weikart used graduate teachers to staff the project and most importantly, all had to have a Certificate of Education. This is another significant aspect in terms of provision today, where in the UK many of those who work with young children have few, if any, academic qualifications. The necessity of the teaching qualification was justified by Schweinhart et al. (2004) as staff needed to be able to understand and support:

- children being intentional learners;
- adults being able to introduce ideas but to know that their role is to observe, support and extend learning;
- provide carefully set out areas of interests;
- add complex language, use of an appropriate questioning style, be able to expand vocabulary;
- encourage children to make choices, solve problems;
- promote an appropriate language model for adult – child and child – child;
- interaction as thinkers and doers rather than teacher initiated and child responding.

Overall research from the project has shown that children's language performance at age 7 compares as teachers' years of full time schooling increase. In other words children's language skills are better if they are taught by a more experienced teacher. Cognitive performance improves for children as they spend less time in whole group activities. This could also inform practice by planning for more individual activities rather than whole class 'lessons'. Children's cognitive performance at age 7 improves as the number and variety of equipment and materials available to children in preschool settings increase, Schweinhart et al. (2004). This highlights the longer term or cumulative benefits to the child of rich experiences in pre-school.

There is much discussion currently amongst politicians of the importance of early intervention programmes and there is much about the HighScope programme which could be found in current high quality pre-school provision. A pre-school programme that raises education and skills levels may be an important way to raise economic well-being through enhanced employment prospects for individuals. This must surely present compelling motivation for wider public investment in highly effective pre-school provision. There is a danger, however, that politicians might choose to cherry-pick certain aspects of the programme without fully understanding how interdependent all aspects of the programme are and that cost-cutting or diluting certain aspects would be very likely to affect the desired outcomes.

Reading 9.6

The Te Whāriki approach
Wendy Lee, Margaret Carr, Brenda Soutar and Linda Mitchell

This reading taken from Lee, Carr, Soutar and Mitchell considers the four principles behind the central ideas of the *Te Whāriki* (woven mat 'for all to stand on') curriculum with its holistic and inter-connected approach.

How does this align and contrast with the curriculum you work with?

Edited from: Lee, W., Carr, M., Soutar, B. and Mitchell, L. (2012) *Understanding the Te Whāriki Approach: Early years education in practice*, London: Routledge, 22–4.

Theoretical underpinnings

This collaborative and open-ended approach to the development of the curriculum was reflected in the title of the curriculum. The term Te Whāriki, introduced to the project by Tamati Reedy, was 'a central metaphor'. In Māori, Te Whāriki is a woven floor mat. It is translated in the document as follows:

> The early childhood curriculum has been envisaged as a whāriki, or mat, woven from the principles, strands, and goals defined in this document. The whāriki concept recognises the diversity of early childhood education in New Zealand. Different programmes, philosophies, structures, and environments will contribute to the distinctive patterns of the whāriki (New Zealand Ministry of Education, 1996: 11).

Four principles provide the central ideas of the Te Whāriki approach together they describe a sociocultural view of learning as empowering, relational, interconnected and holistic, see figure 9.6.1 below.

In an unusual condition for a national curriculum document, an ecological theoretical position is explicitly stated with an entire page on Urie Bronfenbrenner's ecology of human development (Bronfenbrenner, 1979), acknowledging that a child's learning environment 'extends far beyond the immediate setting of the home or early childhood programmes beyond the home' (New Zealand Ministry of Education, 1996: 19). This describes Bronfenbrenner's depiction of the child's early learning environment as a nested arrangement of the structures, like a set of Russian dolls with the individual (in this case, the child or the child and the family) in the centre.

The Te Whāriki approach therefore looks beyond the local setting to the wider context of family, culture and society, to ask 'How do we connect with the other contexts in the children's lives?'

Te Whāriki can be described as taking a sociocultural position on learning and development. This is reflected in Bronfenbrenner's ecological assumptions and the four

Figure 9.6.1
Te Whāriki: The
weaving

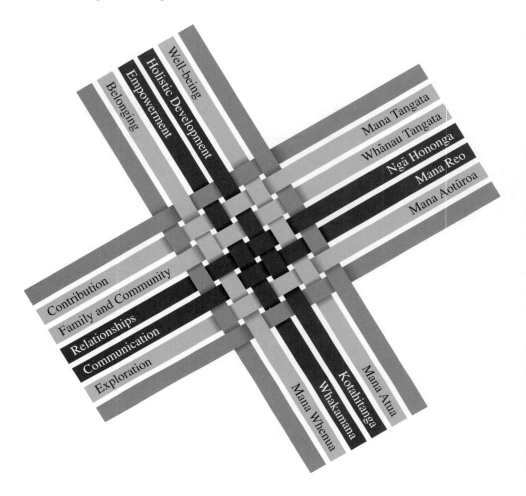

principles that emphasise empowerment (the aspiration for children and families to have some authority or authorship in their lives), relationships (learning is definited in terms of responsive and reciprocal relationships), family and community (the wider the world of family and community is seen as an integral part of the curriculum) and holistic frame (for defining education, beyond traditional categories, for instance, of physical cognitive social and emotional skills). In these principles the definition of education as being about relationships and participation rejected a stage or levelled view of development. However, in an elaboration of each of the goals, three age groups (infants, toddlers and 'young children') provide, in particular, reminders of environments for the especially vulnerable under-twos. This has anticipated a more recent rapid growth in demand for ECE provision for infants and toddlers (Dalli and White, 2011) reflecting in part the woefully poor parental leave provision in Aotearoa New Zealand (one of the lowest in the OECD countries). Mixed age provision is common and the setting out in Te Whāriki of three age groups has been controversial.

The framework

The framework for Te Whāriki included in this chapter is shown in Table 9.6.1. It begins with the four *curriculum principles* and the *aspirations for children* statement. The aspirations statement is elaborated in detail as five *strands* of learning outcome: in English, these are belonging, well-being, exploration, communication and contribution. In the document, but not here (there are 117 of them), the strands are further elaborated as 'indicative' (not prescribed) learning outcomes. In between the principles and the outcomes for children are the features of a facilitating learning environment, the *goals*.

Readers will recognise synergies between Te Whāriki's aspiration statement, principles and strands of outcome and other early childhood curriculum documents developed in the twenty-first century. The title of the first national curriculum for Australia, the 2007 early years' learning framework, 'Belonging, being and becoming' (Australian Government Department of Education, Employment and Workplace, 2007), signifies an interest in early childhood in its widest sense as a space where learner identities are constructed and diversity is respected.

Its five broad learning outcomes are:

- children have a strong sense of identity;
- children are connected with and contribute to their world;
- children have a strong sense of well-being;
- children are confident and involved learners;
- children are effective communicators.

'Pre-birth to three' for Scotland (Learning and teaching Scotland, 2010) include four key principles for best starts and positive outcomes:

- rights of the child;
- relationships;
- responsive care;
- respect.

The areas of learning in the British Columbia early learning framework (British Columbia Ministry of Health and Ministry of Children and Family Development, 2008) are:

- well-being and belonging;
- exploration and creativity;
- languages and literacies;
- social responsibility and diversity.

Table 9.6.1 The framework in Te Whāriki

Four principles An aspirations statement Five strands Eighteen goals 117 Indicative outcomes			
Relationships – Ngā hononga Children learn through responsible and reciprocal relationships	**Holistic development – Kotahitanga** The early childhood curriculum reflects the holistic way children learn and grow	**Family and community – Whānau tangata** The wider world of family and community is an integral part of the early childhood curriculum	**Empowerment – Whakamana** The early childhood curriculum empowers the child to grow and learn
Aspirations statement This curriculum is founded on the following aspirations for children: to grow up as competent and confident learners and communicators, healthy in mind, body and spirit, secure in their sense of belonging and in th knowledge that they make a valued contribution to society (Te Whāriki p.9)			
Well-being – Mana atua	Belonging – Mana whenua	Contribution – Mana tangata	Communication – Mana reo	Exploration – Mana aot roa
Children will experience an environment where: Goal 1: their health is promoted (4 outcomes) Goal 2: their emotional well-being is nurtured (7 outcomes)	Children and their families will experience an environment where: Goal 1: connecting links with the family and the wider world are affirmed and extended (6 outcomes) Goal 2: they know they have a place (5 outcomes)	Children will experience an environment where Goal 1: there are equitable opportunities for learning, irrespective of gender, ability, age, ethnicity, or background (8 outcomes) Goal 2: they are affirmed as individuals (5 outcomes)	Children will experience an environment where Goal 1: they develop non-verbal communication skills for a range of purposes (5 outcomes) Goal 2: they develop verbal communication skills for a range of purposes (8 outcomes)	Children will experience an environment where Goal 1: their play is valued as meaningful learning and the importance of spontaneous play is recognised (6 outcomes) Goal 2: they gain confidence in and control of their bodies (4 outcomes)

Well-being – Mana atau	Belonging – Mana whenua	Contribution – Mana tangata	Communication – Mana reo	Exploration – Mana aot roa
Goal 3: they are kept safe from harm (7 outcomes)	Goal 3: they feel comfortable with routines, customs and regular events (5 outcomes) Goal 4: they know the limits and boundaries of acceptable behaviour (6 outcomes)	Goal 3: they are encouraged to learn with and alongside others (7 outcomes)	Goal 3: they experience the stories and symbols of their own and other cultures (9 outcomes) Goal 4: they discover and develop different ways to be creative and expressive (9 outcomes)	Goal 3: they learn strategies for active exploration, thinking, and reasoning (5 outcomes) Goal 4: they develop working theories for making sense of the natural, social, physical, and material world (11 outcomes)

The four themes of learning and development in Ireland's 2009 early childhood curriculum framework (National Council for Curriculum and Assessment, 2009) are:

- well-being;
- identity and belonging;
- communicating;
- exploring and thinking.

Early childhood educators will refer to their own official espoused or enacted curricula and policies, comparing these with Te Whāriki in order to provoke discussion and to articulate their own position on the principles and outcomes that matter in the early years.

Key points

1 Dialogue and negotiation characterised the processes of curriculum development and early implementation of Te Whāriki.

2 The collaborative and open-ended approach to the development of the curriculum is reflected in the title of the curriculum, Te Whāriki, translated as a woven mat for all to stand on.

3 The principles, strands and goals provide the framework which allows for different programmes perspectives to be woven into the fabric.

4 Te Whāriki is not a curriculum that prescribes aims and content in detail; it expects Early Childhood Care and Education services to create their curriculum in a culturally and locally situated way.

5 Te Whāriki describes a sociocultural view of education, and assumes that education and learning will be empowering, holistic, ecological and relational.

6 The curriculum document emphasises an ecological position; this is unusual for a national curriculum document.

7 Te Whāriki has attracted international interest.

Planning

How are we implementing the curriculum?

10

Readings

10.1 Lilan G. Katz
A developmental approach to the curriculum in the early years (p. 198)

10.2 Peter Moss
Listening to young children (p. 203)

10.3 Phil Jones
Assumptions about children and young people (p. 207)

10.4 Kathy Brodie
Curriculum planning (p. 210)

10.5 Trisha Lee
The wisdom of Vivian Paley (p. 214)

The following readings begin with a consideration of the planning of curricula and the questions which ought to be asked in their planning: what should be learned, when should it be learned and how is it best learned?

We then move on with readings which help us to consider how children might be consulted and have a voice in the design and delivery of their education, some of the challenges this presents, and how our views of children might impact upon the design and delivery of curricula. This is followed by some practical guidance on planning for curriculum delivery in the short, medium and long term.

The final reading considers the inspiring work of Vivian Paley, which reminds us of the benefits of being open to children's views and of reflecting on and in practice.

Reading 10.1

A developmental approach to the curriculum in the early years

Lilan G. Katz

> This reading is of particular interest for the way it grounds principles of curriculum planning in what is known about children's development.
>
> *Edited from:* Katz, L. G. (1998) 'A Developmental Approach to the Curriculum in the Early Years'. In *S. Smidt The Early Years: A Reader.* London and New York: Routledge, 11–16.

Everyone responsible for planning a curriculum must address at least the following three questions:

1 What should be learned?

2 When should it be learned?

3 How is it best learned?

Responses to the first question provide the *goals of* the programme for which pedagogical practices are to be adopted. The second question is the *developmental* one in that it draws upon what is known about the development *of* the learner. In other words, child development helps to address the *when* questions *of* programme design. The third question turns specifically to matters of appropriate *pedagogy* itself., it includes consideration of all aspects of implementing a programme by which the programme's goals can be achieved, depending, of course, on what is to be learned, and when it is to be learned. In other words, responses to one of the three questions are inextricably linked to responses to the other two.

Thus *what* should be learned and *how* it is best learned depends on *when* the learning is to occur. Similarly, *how* something is learned depends upon *what* it is, as well as upon the developmental characteristics of the learner. For example, virtually all stakeholders in early childhood education would place literacy high on the list of answers to the question, 'What should be learned?' However, they are likely to diverge considerably upon the question of when as well as how it should be learned – the latter considerations being related to each other. Terms such as emergent literacy and preliteracy have recently appeared in the early childhood literature, partly in order to address the confounding of the when and how questions. Even though the three questions are clearly linked, for the sake of discussion, they are taken up separately below.

What should be learned?

The values and preferences of the parents served by the programme would seem to have first claim among criteria for determining what should be learned. However, parents are rarely a homogeneous or monolithic group with a clear consensus about the goals of their children's education. While the community and parents' preferences contribute to determining the goals, the special expertise of professional educators should be brought to bear on addressing the questions of when and how the goals can be best implemented.

Whatever specific learning goals and objectives are identified by clients and educators, they are all likely to fit into each of four types of learning goals: knowledge, skills, dispositions and feelings.

Knowledge: During the preschool period, this can be broadly defined as ideas, concepts, constructions, schemas, facts, information, stories, customs, myths, songs and other such contents of mind that come under the heading of what is to be learned. Three Piagetian categories of knowledge – social, physical and logically mathematical – are often used in discussions of the knowledge goals in early childhood education.

Skills: These are defined as small, discrete and relatively brief units of behaviour that are easily observed or inferred from behaviour (for example, skills such as cutting, drawing, counting a group of objects, adding, subtracting, friendship-making, problem solving skills, and so on).

Dispositions: These are broadly defined as relatively enduring 'habits of mind', or characteristic ways of responding to experience across types of situations (including persistence at a task, curiosity, generosity, meanness, the disposition to read, to solve problems). Unlike an item of knowledge or a skill, a disposition is not an end state to be mastered once and for all. It is a trend or consistent pattern of behaviour and its possession is established only if its manifestation is observed repeatedly. Thus a person's disposition to be a reader, for example, can only be ascertained if he or she is observed to read spontaneously, frequently and without external coercion.

Feelings: These are subjective emotional or affective states, e.g. feelings of belonging, or self, esteem, confidence, adequacy and inadequacy, competence and incompetence, and so forth. Feelings about or towards significant phenomena may range from being transitory or enduring, intense or weak, or perhaps ambivalent. In early childhood education attitudes and values can also be included in this category; in education for older children they merit separate categories.

In principle, pedagogical practices are developmentally and educationally appropriate if they address all four categories of learning goals equally and simultaneously. Pedagogical practices are not appropriate if they emphasise the acquisition of knowledge and the mastery of skills without ensuring that the dispositions to use the knowledge and skills so learned are also strengthened. Similarly, if the desired knowledge and skills are mastered in such a way that dislike of them or of the school environment itself develops throughout the learning process, then the pedagogy may be judged inappropriate. Similarly, if a pedagogical approach succeeds in generating feelings of joy, pleasure, amusement, or excitement, but fails to bring about the acquisition of desirable knowledge and skills, it cannot be judged appropriate.

Most stakeholders in early childhood education are likely to agree on broad goals in all four categories of learning. For example, most education authorities' curriculum guides list such goals as knowledge and skills related to literacy and numeracy and various items of cultural knowledge, plus such dispositions as the desire to learn, creativity, cooperativeness, and so forth; the list of goals related to feelings usually includes 'positive feelings about themselves', or 'self-confidence'.[2]

Once the knowledge, skills, dispositions and feelings to be learned have been agreed upon, the next question is when they should be learned.

When should it be learned?

Learning in the four categories of learning goals proposed above occurs constantly, whether intentional or incidental. However, a developmental approach to curriculum planning takes into account both dimensions of development: the normative and the dynamic dimensions. These two equally important dimensions of development are defined as follows:

The normative dimension of development addresses the characteristics and capabilities of children that are typical or normal for their age group (e.g. the typical size of vocabulary of four-year-olds, the average age of first walking or of understanding numerical concepts). Age norms also provide useful starting points for curriculum planning. Knowledge of age, typical interests, activities and abilities can provide a basis for preliminary planning of a general programme of activities, and the selection of equipment and materials. For example, norms of development provide a basis for assuming that most two-year olds need daytime naps, most four year-olds do not understand calendar concepts, or that, typically, most five year-olds can begin to write their own names, etc. Age norms are also useful for alerting teachers to individual children whose patterns of development depart noticeably from their age group and who warrant close observation by which to ascertain whether special curriculum and teaching strategies are required.

The dynamic dimension of development deals with an individual child's progress from immaturity to maturity. This dimension addresses changes over time within an individual and the long, term effects of early experience, rather than the normality of behaviour and abilities of an age group. For example, sequence refers to the order or stages of development through which an individual passes, e.g. in achieving mastery of first language. The curriculum and teaching practices consider what learning and developmental tasks have to be completed before the next learning can occur. Delayed effects refer to the potential positive and negative effects of early experience that may not be manifested at the time of occurrence, but may influence later functioning (e.g. early infant-caregiver attachment may influence later parenting competence).

A developmental approach to curriculum and teaching practices takes into account both dimensions of development. What young children *should* do and *should* learn is determined on the basis of what is best for their development in the long term (i.e. the dynamic consequences of early experience) rather than simply what works in the short term.

How is it best learned?

This question takes us directly to matters of pedagogy, such as consideration of teaching methods, activities, materials and all other practical matters designed to achieve the learning goals, and to take into account what is known about learners' development.

Learning in the four categories of goals is facilitated in different ways. In the case of both knowledge and skills, learning can be aided by instruction as well as by other processes, but dispositions and feelings cannot be learned from direct instruction. Many important dispositions are inborn – e.g. the disposition to learn, to observe, to investigate, to be curious, etc. Many dispositions appear to be learned from models, are strengthened by being manifested and appreciated, and are weakened when unacknowledged or ineffective.

Feelings related to school experiences are learned as by-products of experiences rather than from instruction. Both dispositions and feelings can be thought of as incidental learning in that they are incidental to the processes by which knowledge and skills are acquired. To label feelings as incidental is not to belittle them, or to devalue the role of pedagogy in their development; rather, it is to emphasise that they cannot be taught didactically. Children cannot be instructed in what feelings to have.

Recent insights into children's development suggest that in principle, the younger the child, the more readily knowledge is acquired through active and interactive processes; conversely, with increasing age children become more able to profit from reactive, passive-receptive pedagogical approaches or instructional processes. In other words, pedagogical practices are developmentally appropriate when the knowledge to be acquired or constructed is related to the child's own first-hand direct experiences and when it is accessible from primary sources. This is not to say that children do not acquire knowledge and information from such secondary sources as stories, books and films. The extent to which they do so is related to whether young children can connect the materials within the secondary sources to the images and knowledge they already possess. With increasing age and experience children become more able to profit from second-hand indirect experiences and secondary sources.

Thus pedagogical practices are appropriate if they provide young children with ample opportunity to interact with adults and children who are like and unlike themselves, with materials, and directly with real objects and real environments.

However, interactions cannot occur in a vacuum; they have to have content. Interactions must be about something ideally something that interests the interactors.

What criteria can be used to determine what knowledge or content is appropriate for young children? For example, should young children spend up to ten minutes per day in a calendar exercise? Should young children in southern Florida be making snowflake crystals out of Styrofoam at Christmas time? Should substantial amounts of time be allocated to observance of public holidays and festivals? Why? And why not? What factors, data or other matters should be taken into account in answering questions such as these? One way to approach these questions is to derive principles of practice from what is known about the nature of children's intellectual development.

In principle, a substantial proportion of the content of interaction should be related to matters of actual or potential interest to the children served by the programme. Since not all of children's interests are equally deserving of attention, some selection of which interests are the most worthy of promotion is required. Current views of children's learning and their active construction of knowledge suggest that those interests most likely to extend, deepen and improve their understanding of their own environments and experiences are most worth strengthening during the early years.

Reading 10.2

Listening to young children

Peter Moss

Moss begins his paper by looking at the growing interest in listening to children, and the influences behind this: the children's rights issue (particularly Articles 12 and 13 of the UN Convention) and the growing interest in the academic world, with children increasingly seen as subjects to be listened to rather than objects to be studied. He also mentions the growing interest of the commercial world as children are recognized, increasingly, as consumers. Moss believes these and other influences have 'come together from different directions and with different objectives in mind'. In this reading Moss looks at methods, benefits and risks of listening to young children.

Do the children in your practice have a voice? Have you moved beyond the idea that 'listening involves one person talking and the other one listening'? Was Malaguzzi right? Are children born with 100 languages but have lost 98 of them by the age of 6? We begin this extract from Moss's paper at the point he talks about his work at the Coram Institute with Alison Clark.

Edited from: Moss, P. (2006) 'Listening to Young Children – Beyond Rights to Ethics'. In *Let's talk about Listening to Children: Towards a Shared Understanding for Early Years Education in Scotland.* Learning and Teaching Scotland.

A lot of our work at the Thomas Coram Research Unit has been around the development of what Alison has called 'The Mosaic Approach' The first publication, called *The Mosaic Approach* (Clark and Moss, 2001) was developed as a result of researching issues important to young children in nurseries. The approach aimed to discover children's perspectives of the nursery, and what was important for them in a nursery. *Spaces to Play* (Clark and Moss, 2005) came out earlier this year. This publication is an account of a fascinating project in which young children have been involved in designing their outdoor environment. Alison is currently working on the 'Living Spaces' project, where young children under five and a practice of architects are working together on the design of a new children's centre.

The 'mosaic approach'

Why use the term 'mosaic approach'? A mosaic is made up of many small pieces that need to be put together to make a picture. Likewise, the mosaic approach gives young children the opportunity to demonstrate their perspectives in a variety of ways, calling on their hundred languages. So the mosaic approach brings together various forms of documentation and evidence. And it starts from a very specific view or image of children as experts in their own lives. This is, I think, a very powerful phrase, and one that is used a lot by researchers as well as practitioners. And it makes sense – if you want to find out about childhood, why not go and ask the people who are living it? Children are skilful communicators, particularly if you think about the hundred languages and you don't think about just speech and writing. Children are rights-holders, as Kathleen Marshall has pointed out. And children are also meaning makers – they are constantly trying to construct meaning out of their lives.

To sum up, the mosaic approach is multi-method and multilingual. It uses a variety of tools that play to young children's strengths and build on them.

Methods used in the mosaic approach

One of the methods used in this approach is to observe children. Another method – child conferencing – is an adapted form of interviewing children. Alison uses another interesting method. She gives digital cameras to two-, three- and four-year-olds, and they go off and take photographs. Or yet another method is where children go on tours of their environment and make maps. There could be a hundred methods, as well as a hundred languages. And it's a two-stage process. Firstly you document – the children document – using a variety of methods, such as those just mentioned, then the children and adults reflect on this documentation, enter into a dialogue, reflect, act and interpret what they have discussed. Listening is always an interpretive process, and we need to recognise its essentially subjective nature.

The benefits and risks of listening to children

This work on listening is of the utmost importance. I think it is actually potentially subversive and enormously transformational. And I think it has enormous benefits. But it is important to remember the cautionary words of the French philosopher Michel Foucault – 'Not everything is bad' he says, 'but everything is dangerous'. (Bernauer and Rasmussen, 1988). And there are, I think, many risks as well as benefits arising from this listening to children that I think we need to confront and think about. We need to keep a balance here. Many of these risks arise because of power relations, which Linda Kinney has already flagged up. As Foucault says, 'Human relations, whatever they are, whether it is a question of communicating verbally or a question of a love relationship, an institutional or an economic relationship, power is always present. I mean the relationship in which one wishes to direct the behaviour of another.' And all of us, children and adults, are implicated in power relations.

In my opinion, some of the most interesting work on early childhood today is being inspired and influenced by the work of Michel Foucault. Although he didn't write specifically about childhood, he explored principles and ideas that people in the early years field are really taking up. In the book *Doing Foucault in Early Childhood Studies: Applying Poststructural Ideas* (MacNaughton, 2005), students and practitioners write about how they are working with Foucauldian theories which, on the surface, might seem very abstract and difficult, but are really opening up all sorts of fascinating possibilities. I think in the early childhood field we really benefit from border-crossing into areas where we haven't often thought to look before.

Three risks

I now want to flag up three risks. Gaile Cannella, an American researcher, sums up the first risk very well: 'When voice is conferred upon the other without recognising or attempting to alter the inequities that created the original distinctions, the giving of voice or listening to just becomes another colonising apparatus.' (Cannella and Viruru, 2004). Even within a group of children there will be differences of power and inequalities. Glenda MacNaughton, for example, looks at some examples around gender, analysing how boys and girls are differently positioned in a group.

Because there is a lot of work currently being done about participation of communities in the development process, some very relevant and interesting literature is being written in this field. This, in turn, is developing a stimulating and interesting set of ideas about how you can engage with these power issues. For example, imagine that you are sending aid to a village in Asia. You will need to discuss how to spend the aid, but in doing so you will find that some people will be more vociferous than others. How do you deal with this?

The second risk is that these days listening has become very much a political or managerial tactic – a sort of tokenism – where listening is part of spin. So that instead of subverting or resisting power, listening becomes a means for reinforcing power.

And then thirdly, listening can become a way of managing behaviour more effectively, a means for governing more effectively – because if I listen to what you say, I can find out what I need to know to make sure you achieve the outcomes that I want you to have. I can find out what makes you happy, what makes you sad and what interests you.

Beyond rights to ethics

In the final part of this paper, I want to argue that 'rights' provide only one basis to justify listening. I want to discuss the idea that we can practise listening as a way of being and a way of living that should permeate everything we do in life – not just when we are at work from nine to five. This was first brought home to me very vividly, more than a decade ago, when I was editing a book called *Valuing Quality in Early Childhood Services* (Moss and Pence, 1994). I asked for a contribution from a very interesting Danish researcher – Ole Langsted – who had been doing work in the eighties, listening to children in kindergartens. The Danes were well ahead of us in this area of research, and used some fascinating methods, including tours and mapmaking. Ole wrote his contribution, and I asked him to spell out how to listen using bullet points. He is a very gentle, nice man, and I remember his patient reply. 'You need to want to listen in the first place and no amount of bullet points will help you if you don't have a culture of listening.'

This is what he wrote:

> More important [than structures and procedures] is the cultural climate which shapes the ideas that the adults in a particular society hold about children. The wish to listen to and involve children originates in this cultural climate.

And that has been with me ever since. Of course there are tools and there are procedures and these are very important – but the question you have to ask is 'As a culture, as a society, do we want to listen to each other? Do we want to conduct democratic relationships?'.

In our book, *Ethics and Politics in Early Childhood Education* (Dahlberg and Moss, 2005) Gunilla and I argue that the ethics of an encounter put listening at the heart of education and we use a pedagogy of listening to illustrate how this happens. This pedagogy of listening has been developed very much by Carlina Rinaldi (Rinaldi, 2005) and her colleagues in Reggio Emilia. The pedagogy of listening understands learning as a process, whereby we develop interpretative theories, provisional theories, about the world. We are always doing this – young or old. And these theories are generated through sharing, dialogue and listening. In her new book, Carlina puts it like this: 'Our theories need to be listened to by others … any theorisation, from the simplest to the most refined, needs to be expressed, to be communicated, and thus to be listened to, in order to exist'. It is here we recognise the values and foundations of the pedagogy of listening. So we construct our theories, we have a dialogue with others about them, others listen and respond and then we construct yet new theories. This is the process of learning as the Reggio Emilia practitioners understand it – and I think the theory is a challenging one.

Conclusion

To conclude, my argument has been that listening is an expression of rights, and that rights have an important part to play. But listening, I think, is also an expression of an ethical practice. Listening is the ethics of an encounter. It is also the expression of democratic practice. Because if we are able to recognise difference, to accept different interpretations and engage in dialogue, then we are conducting democratic practice. And if we bring listening into our work and our practice, then we are making ethics and politics first practice in early childhood education.

Reading 10.3

Assumptions about children and young people

Phil Jones

> When we think of childhood and adolescence, do we foreground what children and young people can do, or what they can't? Do we see capability or deficiency? Do we respect their agency or impose controls? How are the issues and dilemmas resolved?
>
> The stance taken by adults makes an enormous difference to the opportunities to learn which children and young people experience. It is reflected in the 'folk pedagogies' described by Bruner (**Reading 11.3**) and profoundly influences the development of children's attitudes to learning (see Dweck, **Reading 2.5**).
>
> What are your preconceptions about children and young people?
>
> *Edited from:* Jones, P. (2009) *Rethinking Childhood: Attitudes in Contemporary Society.* London: Continuum, 54–7.

A common way of seeing the period which we name as 'childhood' is that it is a time of maturation and growth, where needs for food and shelter cannot be fully met by the individual without support, and a time where cognitive and emotional development occurs.

The idea of competence in childhood has been defined from a number of different perspectives in relation to this time of maturation, need and development. France, for example, has argued that 'the young are seen as being in a "stage of deficit", where they lack morality, skills and responsibility' (2007: 152). The ideas have become associated with powerful adult definitions often associated with negative images of children. These perspectives are realised through language, attitudes and ways of behaving.

These perspectives regulate the ways in which adults see and treat children, and the ways children see themselves. They define adult-child relationships and the services provided by organizations surrounding the processes or growth, need and maturation of children. They can seem fixed, whereas in fact they are constructions largely made by adults.

One of the central ideas is that adults, often unconsciously, prepare children to be dependent. How do adults encourage children to see themselves in this way?

- Through creating laws that confine children.
- Through creating policies that confirm adults' attitudes that children need adults to make decisions for them.
- Through interacting with each other, and with children, in ways that do not allow children to express themselves or to participate in decision making.
- By using adulthood as a measure that is set as a norm against which other states, such as childhood, are seen as lacking, or in terms of being a deficit.
- By seeing and treating children as incapable and inadequate.

Such practices create a vicious circle for children. Adults have a framework within which children are raised and responded to. This framework sees and treats them as not capable. One of the effects of this is that children's own expectations and ways of seeing themselves are constructed within this incapability. In turn, the way they behave reflects this, which fulfils and confirms adult expectations. This can create situations that are unhelpful and harmful. Bluebond-Langner (1978), in her research with terminally ill children, found that children as young as three years of age were aware of their diagnosis and prognosis without ever having been informed by an adult.

If adult attitudes and the reality of children were congruent, then there would be no need or occasion for tension, challenge and change. However, the rise of different attitudes from children and young people, and from some adults who live and work with children, has created change. In the UK, for example, a series of decisions and counter-decisions regarding the notion of children's competence have occurred. One of the key arenas concerns health-related practices in areas such as medical, dental and surgical treatment. In the UK, from a legal challenge, the notion of the 'Gillick competent' child has arisen.

> Unlike 16- or 17-year-olds, children under 16 are not automatically presumed to be legally competent to make decisions about their healthcare. However, the courts have stated that under 16s will be competent to give valid consent to a particular intervention if they have 'sufficient understanding and intelligence to enable him or her to understand fully what is proposed'. In other words, there is no specific age when a child becomes competent to consent to treatment: it depends both on the child and on the seriousness and complexity of the treatment being proposed. (Department of Health, 2001)

These views of children affect different aspects of their lives. They connect to the way children are subordinated, and to the ways in which children relate to the world they live in.

Increasingly, such attitudes have been challenged. The critique points to constraining, traditional ways of perceiving children, and offers a new approach which is appreciative of children's competence. The contrast is illustrated in Figure 10.3.1.

Figure 10.3.1 Traditional and emerging positions

Traditional position	Emerging position
• Incapable	• Capable
• Not able to make valuable decisions	• Active decision-makers with opinions that matter
• Incomplete adults	
• As a threat to themselves and others due to deficits in reasoning and experience	• Seen in terms of own capacities
	• As able to contribute usefully

This emerging position is not without its challenges and difficulties. The issue of how competence and capability can be defined and seen is complex. The situations within which issues of capability arise also raises questions: Does a child have different competencies in relation to different spheres of their lives? How is competency to be involved in family decision making to be compared to making decisions needing to be made in medical or educational contexts? Questions arise out of the issue of differences regarding capability: How is the issue of age regarded? Are such questions irrelevant if you view the child from a point of view that sees them as capable, and that stresses their right to make decisions about their own, and others' lives?

Reading 10.4

Curriculum planning

Kathy Brodie

Planning should enhance rather than hinder children's learning, enabling them to access the curriculum fully while following their interests. To be of use, planning needs to be flexible and responsive; it needs to be understood and used by practitioners, and able to be explained to inspectors, families and other stakeholders. In this reading, Brodie points out that most of the planning in the EYFS is done in the short term. She provides practical advice to ensure planning is relevant and looks at the 'daunting' task of planning for every child.

Reflect on the planning in your setting. Is it used and understood by practitioners or do you (or someone else) spend hours on an attractive document that is seldom referred to? Does your planning ensure that every child can access the curriculum?

Edited from: Brodie, K. (2013) *Observation, Assessment and Planning in the Early Years: Bringing It All Together.* Maidenhead: Open University Press, 86–90.

Short-term planning

Most of the planning under the EYFS is done in the short term. This means different things to different settings, from planning a week in advance to a few hours in advance. It should always be responsive and flexible, changing to suit the children's needs at that time. Practitioners should be reflective and consider how each activity is progressing, making adjustments as necessary. There are many ways of recording short-term planning. One popular method is the 'cheese wedge' method: activities are planned in full for the whole of the first day; a few activities are planned for the second day, with maybe one or two activities planned for the third day. The fourth and fifth days are left blank. So, looking at the planning on the planning sheets, it looks like a cheese wedge, with the thick end being closest chronologically.

During the first day activities would be entered into the planning ready for the second day. These may be activities that the children have enjoyed, or ideas that have been sparked from activities during that day. This is repeated for each day, so that planning is completed on a rolling daily basis. The beauty of this method is that it is immediately responsive to the children's interest at that time. It can also demonstrate personalized planning, by adding the children's name or initials next to the activity. The ideas are fresh in the practitioner's minds.

Suggestions for activities suitable for a particular group of children, for example children that only attend on certain days can be put on the planning in advance. If the activity doesn't work as well as expected, or the children themselves change it, or the children are interested in something else that day, then the planning sheet is simply altered by putting a line through the activity and writing in the replacement activity. This demonstrates flexibility and being responsive to the children's interests. Short term planning sheets may also include a range of other information, as well as the actual activities. This could include:

- resources required for the activity;
- physical area where the activity is to take place (e.g. outdoors, sand tray, construction area);
- staff involved with the activity;
- areas linking to the EYFS;
- links with home;
- next steps and follow-on activities

Short-term planning should be displayed somewhere in the room, easily accessible by all practitioners, so that everyone is aware of the plans for the day. This also means that practitioners can update and modify planning quickly and easily. Everybody should be encouraged to participate in the planning process so they have ownership of the activities in the room. It also ensures that practitioners are able to plan for each of their key children. Encouraging practitioners to review and alter the planning accordingly is a good way to encourage reflective practice.

Planning for every child

It can be quite a daunting task to think that you have to plan for every child in a room of 12 or a class of 30! However, this can be achieved in a number of ways.

Multiple aspects of one activity

One activity may satisfy the needs and interests of many different children. For example the activity may be dinosaurs in the sand tray. This would be interesting for children who like to find hidden objects under the sand; children who like small world role-playing; children who like dinosaurs; children who like pouring and tipping sand and children who like burying objects. So in this one simple activity five different children could each have their needs met. Practitioners do need to be aware of how the activity is meeting their children's needs and be able to support this with suitable scaffolding. This could be through use of language, demonstrating play or provoking responses ('what do you think would happen if we did ...?)

Grouping of children

Think carefully about how you can group the children together. It may be useful to group those who have similar interests, for example schema. The planning should include resources to support the schema, suitable activities and provocations. Children could be grouped in mixed ages and/or abilities, to encourage peer support and peer-to-peer learning. The practitioner's role is to model interactions, support learning and encourage co-operation. The practitioner gives individualized support to each child, offering more or less support as required. For example, the practitioner may let more able children climb the climbing frame by themselves, but would give more support to a less confident or less able child.

Making planning accessible to all

The planning for any room or child should be understood by and accessible to all practitioners. This means that planning should be included as part of staff induction, even if the member of staff is in the room temporarily, and should not be 'something the room manager does'. The reason for this is that practitioners have to understand not only what to do, but also why. So the bubbles in the water tray may be to support the language development of one child, gross motor skills of another and creative development of a third child. Once the practitioner knows this they can support the children in an appropriate manner. Accessible planning can be accomplished by having regular staff meetings to discuss the current planning. These do not need to be formal, recorded meetings, but could be a 10-minute get together so that everyone understands what is on the planning sheet for the next few days. Invariably Ofsted inspectors will ask to see a sample of planning, and maybe how it fits with a child's learning journey or why these particular activities have been chosen. Hence, it is essential that all practitioners are able to explain how the observations, next steps, children's interests and personalized provision are represented on the planning.

Parents could also be part of the planning process, fostering true parent partnership, helping to suggest activities that their child enjoys for example, Whalley (2007) suggests that parents should be engaged as 'decision-makers in the planning and implementation of childcare at the setting. At the very least, it is good practice to give parents and carers access to the planning, so they can appreciate the sorts of things their child may be enjoying at the setting. If the setting's planning is reasonably complicated, or has lots of early years jargon, it may be worth displaying a simplified version. Further details could then be discussed with parents as questions arise.

Monitoring planning

If you are in a small setting, or a childminder, it is relatively easy to monitor yourself and keep planning relevant and up to date. However, if you are part of a larger team it may be necessary to have formal monitoring systems in place. It is likely that part of every practitioner's job description will be to do planning, keep it up to date and display it appropriately. Similarly, the room manager's role should involve an element of monitoring and the setting manager can do spot checks to support this.

Final thoughts

Planning is intended to support children's development, and as a tool to help practitioners ensure they are meeting the needs of the children. As with any tool, it should only be used in the right circumstances. If there is a fall of snow, or a baby is brought into the setting, or a child comes back after a particularly exciting trip at the weekend, then this must take priority over the 'planned' activities. Planning should be flexible and responsive, working to meet the working to meet the needs of and for the benefit of the children, not the children working to the planning. This can be frustrating for practitioners, but it is essential to meet the children's needs before the planning requirements. Planning can always be kept to be used another day. Planning depends on good quality, regular observations and assessments. Making this part of the ethos of the setting is essential, so it is seen as adding value to the practitioner's work and valuable for the children's development. With this in mind, staff should have regular training on the setting's observation, assessment and planning systems, especially as the systems grow and evolve. The induction of new staff must include detailed instructions on the observation, assessment and planning methods, to ensure that bad habits are not accidentally introduced.

Where there may be problems, such as practitioners who may have dyslexia or a lack of confidence or practitioners with English as an additional language, the practitioner should be supported and helped, rather than being left to struggle or omitted from doing observations.

Key learning points

Long-term planning and short-term planning are the most commonly used elements within early years. Long-term planning provides for an overview of the year with, for example, fixed dates for festivals. Short-term planning reflects the particular interests and needs of the children at that time, and must be responsive, on a daily basis, to the changes in children's ideas. It is paramount that planning reflects individual children's needs, (Whalley, 2007).

Reading 10.5

The wisdom of Vivian Paley
Trisha Lee

Vivian Paley taught in pre-schools in the USA. She spent much of her career reflecting upon the possibilities of play for children's development. In the reading which follows, Trisha Lee considers the benefits that story-telling and story-acting have for children's learning and relationships. In the piece, she draws attention to the benefits of being open to children's views and of reflecting on practice and being willing to develop your own thinking.

Edited from: Lee, T. (2011) 'The Wisdom of Vivian Gussin Paley'. In L. Miller and L. Pound (eds) *Theories and Approaches to Learning in the Early Years.* London: Sage Publications Ltd, 119–22.

The potential of story-telling and story-acting lies in the following qualities.

Immediately engaging all children regardless of ability

Story-telling and story-acting have an immediacy that sets them apart from many other activities within a classroom. As soon as a teacher begins to demonstrate the process of gathering stories, the children understand how to do it. They don't need long descriptions or complicated explanations; they intuitively know how it works. The whole process is so closely connected with what children do already in the fantasy play that it needs no teaching. Children are instantly empowered as the experts, they know what is expected of them and they eagerly embrace this play. In *In Mrs Tully's Room* Paley (2001: 5) describes 2-year-olds dictating and acting out their stories. She concludes that even at this young age children demonstrate 'an ability to bring a character to life and reveals something about themselves'.

Demonstrating a child's understanding of narrative structures

Paly's story-telling curriculum enables the teacher to interact with children and to witness first hand the profound comprehension of story that lies intuitively within them. This is the privilege of only those adults who are prepared to listen meticulously to the everyday narratives of the children around them. Paly observed children reinventing mythology, generating new versions of old tales and acting out legends (Paley, 1990: 4). For example, in one class a group of children recreate the story of Ngali and the hot Hippo that was forbidden to eat the fish. The children consider what would happen if Ngali grew angry and commanded the hippo to eat every animal, or if Ngali died and the hippo became the new god? In their ongoing narratives, Paley watched a class spontaneously investigating the possible endings, whilst at the same time examining compelling universal themes.

Creating a way of supporting children in exploring conflicts and emotions

Payley discovered that children often use story as a way of this understanding that fantasy playing enables us to put every thought and feeling into story form and to use story as a way to resolve, is a powerful insight into the potential we have when we allowed to tap into tools we are born with.

In *Mollie is Three* (Paley, 1986: 1–11), Fredrick has problems following some of the classroom rules. He grabs paintbrushes and play dough from other children, he knocks over a ship made from blocks and does a lot of furious yelling. Learning from three-year-old Libby, who uses story form to engage Fredrick as a father rather than a robber (because robbers can't play in the dolls corner), Paley finds herself using the same approach, asking frustrated Fredrick who he is pretending to be. It stops his tears immediately. 'Do you want to be a bad guy or a good guy?' Paley repeats (1986: 10). Fredrick wants to be a good guy and sits contentedly watching as the rest of the children continue to play. Later at the snack table, Christopher asks if Paley is still mad with Fredrick and when she says 'no', he questions further: Mollie steps in:

'Because now Fredrick is nice.'
'And before?' I ask.
'That's because he was a robber.'

Fredrick, she knows, plays many different roles. She can better explain his behaviour as a character portrayal than in terms of classroom rules (1986: 11).

In *White Teacher* (Paley, 2000) it is a girl named Sylvia who sometimes has problems conforming to the rules of play. One day she takes on the role of 'bad baby' and begins to pull out all of the dishes and pots from the dolls corner cabinet and throws them over the floor. Rena tries shouting at her in her role as mother, but Sylvia screams back. Anya steps in, threatening Sylvia with not playing together if she doesn't pick up the dishes. Sylvia wants to play and begins reluctantly to pick them up. Ruthie saves the day, turning Sylvia's actions into a game:

'Pretend we just move in…the moving van dropped all the boxes and now we have to put everything away on the shelf.'

'Rena dials the telephone. 'Mr Moving Boss, we won't pay you because it was a bad job.'

'Everyone was laughing as she hung up. The equilibrium was re-established (Paley, 2000: 81).

Promoting inclusivity and turn taking

In *You Can't Say You Can't Play,* Paley (1993) investigated inclusivity within her classroom and interviewed older children throughout the school to uncover memories of rejection by classmates. She solicited the opinions of all ages about the wisdom of introducing a rule of 'you can't say you can't play' throughout the book Paley demonstrates her unerring faith in the wisdom of the children she talks to. She is also honest and open about their own uncertainties. Is she right in this exploration? Is it possible to legislate for fairness and still allow children to be creative and free in their fantasy play?

You Can't Say You Can't Play was a radical book for Paley as it changed her thinking as to how she engaged with her story-telling curriculum. Prior to this investigation, children had chosen who acted in the stories with them. But following on from this, she began inviting children to participate in stories from their place around the stage. This turn-taking activity eliminated friendship groups cliques and resulted in all children having the chance to be involved in acting out the stories. An added bonus of this changed approach was that gender barriers were broken down; for example, boys became princesses and girls became 'baddies' and random chance dictated the story they acted in and the roles they played.

As children waited to get on the stage, they love to understand the process of turn taking. If they didn't get to play the character that inspired them in someone else's story, this motivated them to tell a story next time with this new character, adding their own 'take' to the plot. Paley considers it vital that children have the choice of which character to play in their own stories as they might not have this option in their own lives; but in fantasy play even the shyest child can be a superhero.

Breaking down the inequalities of narrative language

We know there are inequalities between the personal experiences of children. Some children are read to every night, or or are taken on amazing holidays, or visit galleries or museums. Some children have very little in the way of these experiences; their initial stories might involve a journey on the number 47 bus. But in story-telling and story-acting all children get to hear the stories of others. For example, if one child tells a story about a magic star that you have to touch to enter into another realm, their images and imagination are shared with the whole class. It may then be that suddenly all the children's stories begin with a magic star that leads to another realm. The possibilities for this re-wording of 'Once upon a time' can be endless. As the class developed a narrative language so they learn from each other, creating smiles and metaphors together as they grow a shared narrative experience.

So story dictation is a shared experience and a creative process and Paley recognises that in order to maximize its full potential, story-telling needs to be an activity that takes place in situations where children can drop in and out as they choose. One person's story inspires thoughts and images in another and this opens all the children's eyes, allowing them to see the hidden potential for their own version of events. As each child dictates, they add on their own 'supposings' and 'what ifs'. They twist and turn over the stories of each other; examining them from all sides as they strive to find their own story, their own invisible connection to the narrative that is unfolding within their classroom. As Paley says:

> Our kind of story-telling is a social phenomenon, intended to flow through all other activities and provide the widest opportunity for communal response. Stories are not private affairs; the individual imagination plays host to all the stimulation in the environment and causes ripples of ideas to encircle the listener (Paley, 1990: 21).

Developing an understanding of the properties of a story

In her story-telling curriculum, Paley allows the children to teach her new ideas about the properties of stories. Fredrick wanted to tell a story; it is his first story. He has been listening to the older boys telling stories for a while now, and today is his day. He turns to Paley and says the word 'Fredrick'. Hayley tries to elicit more from the story – what does Fredrick do? She suggested he could go school, but Fredrick isn't interested – the story is Fredrick, no more, no less. Paley talks to the children around her, and tells them that she wonders about a one word story.

> John, nearly five, responds quickly, 'It's not one word. It's a person'.
> Paley responds. 'Of course. A person is a story'. (Paley, 1986: 12)

Paley's openness in accepting the ideas and solutions suggested to her by the children is the strength that runs through all her enquiries. She says that Fredrick needs a justification for his presence in the story and helps to provide one. She appreciates how easily children accept ideas that she might find challenging and how things that don't make sense to her adult world often do make sense to the children.

Pedagogy
How can we develop effective strategies?

11

Readings

11.1 The General Teaching Council for England
What is pedagogy and why is it important? (p. 220)

11.2 Iram Siraj-Blatchford, Kathy Sylva, Stella Muttock, Rose Gilden and Danny Bell
Pedagogy in effective settings (p. 223)

11.3 Jerome Bruner
Folk pedagogy (p. 227)

11.4 Roland Tharp and Ronald Gallimore
Teaching as the assistance of performance (p. 229)

The readings in this chapter begin by exploring what pedagogy is – a term often used but misunderstood – drawing on the work of the General Teaching Council in England we ask you consider whether thinking pedagogically is an essential feature of reflective practice. We build on this idea in Reading 11.3, provided by Bruner, which considers how intuitive beliefs impact upon teaching practices.

Reading 11.2, the seminal work of the REPEY project, considers what effective pedagogy looks like in early years settings and how different forms of assistance support learning. Such work support pedagogic thinking in early years practice.

The final reading by Tharp and Galimore encourages us to reflect upon the influences to our pedagogy – how our own experiences and beliefs shape our practice.

Reading 11.1

What is pedagogy and why is it important?
The General Teaching Council for England

> Pedagogy, according to Alexander (2000), combines both the act of teaching and its rationale. In Europe, this conceptualization goes back at least to the 1630s when Comenius published his *Didactica Magna*, and it remains well established today. Understanding has been more limited in some parts of the UK, but is changing rapidly – and this reading explains why. To move forward, it is essential to establish beneficial synergies between theory and practice, research and application.
>
> Do you agree that, to be a really effective practitioner, it is necessary to think pedagogically?
>
> Edited from: GTCE (2010) 'Introduction'. In A. Pollard (ed.) *Professionalism and Pedagogy: A Contemporary Opportunity.* London: TLRP, 4–6.

International evidence is clear that the single most significant means of improving the performance of national educational systems is through excellent teaching (e.g. Barber and Mourshed, 2007; OECD, 2005). The quality of pedagogy, of what teachers actually do, is thus firmly on the contemporary agenda. Since the UK already has a qualified and trained teaching workforce, relatively modest investment in supporting teachers' professionalism could be very cost-effective. There is both a need and an excellent opportunity for the profession to demonstrate and strengthen its expertise and to improve its status in the public mind.

The relative lack of reference to pedagogy in educational discussion in the UK, compared with practice in many other successful countries, has been the focus of academic debate for the best part of thirty years. The concern was first raised by Brian Simon's 1981 paper, 'Why no pedagogy in England'?

In a world-class educational workforce – Finland might be used as an example – teachers are the ones who initiate discussions about pedagogy, and then evaluate and critique the ideas they develop. This 'pedagogic discourse' aspires to be explicitly grounded in the scrutiny of ideas, theories, ethical values and empirical evidence. It goes well beyond simplified prescription, for instance of 'what works', and supersedes reliance on centrally-imposed performance targets. In their place is greater trust in teachers' capacity for self-improvement as an inherent element of their professional identity. However, this trust has to be earned – hence the focus on the nature of pedagogic expertise.

Teaching is a professional activity underpinned by qualifications, standards and accountabilities. It is characterised by complex specialist knowledge and expertise-in-action. In liberal democratic societies, it also embodies particular kinds of values, to do with furthering individual and social development, fulfilment and emancipation.

'Pedagogy' is the practice of teaching framed and informed by a shared and structured body of knowledge. This knowledge comprises experience, evidence, understanding moral purpose and shared transparent values. It is by virtue of progressively acquiring such knowledge and mastering the expertise – through initial training, continuing development, reflection and classroom inquiry and regulated practice – that teachers are entitled to be treated as professionals. Teachers should be able and willing to scrutinise and evaluate their own and others' practice in the light of relevant theories, values and evidence. They should be able to make professional judgements which go beyond pragmatic constraints and ideological concerns, and which can be explained and defended.

Furthermore, pedagogy is impoverished if it is disconnected from the capacity and responsibility to engage in curriculum development and to deploy a range of appropriate assessment methodologies. Indeed, in most European countries, these elements are treated as a whole, enabling a broad conception of pedagogy. Teachers should be knowledgeable about curriculum and assessment principles as a part of their pedagogical expertise. To promote the further development of professional expertise in the UK, we have included these dimensions, and the interrelationships between them, in the conceptual framework later in the Commentary.

Pedagogic expertise can be thought of as a combination of science, craft and art (see Figure 11.1.1)

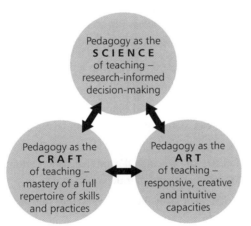

Figure 11.1.1
The science, craft and art of pedagogic expertise

This representation helps us to understand the complementary needs for collectively created knowledge, professional skills and personal capacities. It is also important to remember that all these are grounded in ethical principles and moral commitment – teaching is never simply an instrumental activity, a question just of technique.

One of the challenges for pedagogical discourse is to distinguish between what is known in a scientific sense of being explicit, cumulative and generalisable, and what are the irreducibly intuitive and creative elements of teaching.

It is generally accepted now that good teaching requires strategic decisions informed by evidence. But it also requires a large number of implicit and often instantaneous judgements and decisions. These are responses to the dynamic situation in the classroom, often shaped by the 'community of practice' to which the teacher belongs. They are also expressions of each teacher's individual relationship with his or her pupils: how s/he generates a positive classroom climate or takes advantage of unexpected teaching and learning opportunities. This is the 'craft' and the 'art' of teaching.

And we all need to acknowledge this paradox of teaching – that the more expert a teacher becomes, the more his or her expertise is manifested in sensitivity to contexts and situations, in imaginative judgements in-the-moment sourced from tacit knowledge. The importance of these forms of expertise is often underestimated. Indeed, they often become so embedded, instinctive and taken-for-granted that they are barely recognised.

Such behaviours need to be analysed and discussed, so that the profession can become more confident about its expert practice, its professionalism. The development of a conceptual framework for the discussion of pedagogy is a contribution to that goal (see Chapter 16 of *Reflective Teaching for Schools*).

The GTCE believes that teaching should be based on the development of a pedagogic discourse that arises from teachers sharing and scrutinising the practices and kinds of knowledge which they build, and the values in which these are rooted. The issue is not about theorising about practice since many teachers naturally do this. It is more about whether:

> 'The theories they espouse … have been justified and developed by being exposed to the critical scrutiny of other practitioners, whether they are based on a consideration of evidence from research…whether they have been interrogated in terms of the values and assumptions on which they are based' (Furlong, 2000: 13).

This integration of theory, practice and values into a discourse of pedagogy would mean amongst other things:

- strengthening the shared professional language for talking about teaching, learning and children so that it can stand up to scrutiny in terms of argument, evidence and espoused values;
- developing communities of 'warranted' practice which contribute to the development of this language in dynamic ways; and
- enabling teachers to present their theories, practices and language in more confident and accessible ways.

Reading 11.2

Pedagogy in effective settings

Iram Siraj-Blatchford, Kathy Sylva, Stella Muttock, Rose Gilden and Danny Bell

> The REPY project provides an insight into practitioner pedagogy and the impact that different ways of approaching teaching impact upon children's learning. In this reading the focus is on interactions and how practice can support developmental processes.
>
> *Edited from:* Siraj-Blatchford, I., Sylva, K., Muttock, S., Gilden, R. and Bell, D. (2002) *Researching Effective Pedagogy in the Early Years.* Nottingham: DCSF.

The term Pedagogy is applied here to refer to the instructional techniques and strategies which enable learning to take place. It refers to the interactive process between teacher/ practitioner and learner, and it is also applied to include the provision of some aspects of the learning environment (including the concrete learning environment, and the actions of the family and community).

For most practitioners, the declared priorities in the early years are on the development of positive dispositions to learning, self-confidence and independence. Staff and parents normally give priority to social development, but our evidence suggests that those settings which see cognitive and social development as complementary, achieve the best profile in terms of child outcomes.

Our analysis has also gone a long way to provide explanations for the statistical relation-ships which were found in the EPPE project data analysis. Four areas of impact were identified for special attention. Our close analysis of the Early Childhood Environment Rating Scale suggested that we needed to investigate each of the following practices further, to identify how some practitioners supported the children in making a great deal of developmental progress while others were less effective in this respect:

- adult-child verbal interactions;
- differentiation and formative assessment ;
- parental partnership and the home education environment;
- discipline and adult support in talking through conflicts.

Adult-child verbal interactions

If learning comes from a process of cognitive construction that is only achieved when the child is motivated and involved, we have argued that it is entirely consistent to treat the part played by the effective educator in the same way. The cognitive construction in this case is mutual, where each party engages with the understanding of the other, and learning is achieved through a process of reflexive 'co-construction'. A necessary condition is that both parties are involved and for the resultant learning to be worthwhile, that the content should be in some way instructive. Our analyses of the qualitative and quantitative data have substantiated this model. Our research has also shown that adult-child interactions that involve some element of 'sustained shared thinking', or what Bruner has termed 'joint involvement episodes', may be especially valuable in terms of children's learning.

We found that the most effective settings encourage 'sustained shared thinking' but we also found that this does not happen very frequently. The research found that, even in these effective settings, there were examples of inadequate knowledge and understanding of curriculum areas, especially in the teaching of phonological skills. Our study shows that early years staff may need support in developing their pedagogical content knowledge in the domains of the *Early Learning Goals*.

In 'excellent' settings there were significantly more 'sustained shared thinking' interactions occurring between staff and children than in the 'good' settings. When it did occur, it extended children's thinking. Our investigations of adult-child interaction have led us to view that periods of 'sustained shared thinking' are a necessary prerequisite, especially where this is also encouraged in the home through parental support settings, the analysis has shown that practitioners' knowledge and understanding of the particular curriculum area that is being addressed are vital.

A good grasp of the appropriate 'pedagogical content knowledge' is a vital component of pedagogy and it is shown to be just as important in the early years as at any later stage of education encouraged in the home through parent support. Parent interview data suggest that in some of our very middle class case study settings (notably the private day nurseries), it is less the staff's interventions and more the parents' pro-active behaviour towards their children's learning, in the embedded, cultural context of the home, that has provided a good basis for 'sustained shared thinking'. The analysis has shown that practitioners' knowledge and understanding of the particular curriculum area that is being addressed are vital as well. A good grasp of the appropriate 'pedagogical content knowledge' is a vital component of pedagogy and it is shown to be just as important in the early years as at any later stage of education. The research found that, even in these effective settings, there were examples of inadequate knowledge and understanding of curriculum areas. Our study shows that early years staff may need support in developing their pedagogical content knowledge in the domains of the *Early Learning Goals*.

In the most effective (excellent) settings, the importance of staff members extending child-initiated interactions was also clearly identified. In fact, almost half of all of the child-initiated episodes which contained intellectual challenge, included interventions from a staff member to extend the child's thinking. The evidence also suggests that adult 'modelling' is often combined with sustained periods of shared thinking, and that open-ended questioning is also associated with better cognitive achievement. However, open-ended questions made up only 5.1 per cent of the questioning used in even these 'effective' settings.

In the excellent and good settings, the balance of who initiated the activities, staff or child, was very equal, revealing that the pedagogy of these effective settings encourages children to initiate activities as often as the staff. The children in reception classes experienced a different balance of initiation, with a much greater emphasis upon staff initiated episodes. In all of the case study settings we found that the children spent most of their time in small groups. But our observations show that 'sustained shared thinking' was most likely to occur when children were interacting 1:1 with an adult or with a single peer partner. Freely chosen play activities often provided the best opportunities for adults to extend children's thinking. It may be that extending child-initiated play, coupled with the provision of teacher initiated group work, are the main vehicles for learning.

We found that qualified staff in the most effective settings provided children with more experience of academic activities (especially language and mathematics) and they encouraged children to engage in activities with higher cognitive challenge. While we found that the most highly qualified staff also provided the most direct teaching, we found that they were the most effective in their interactions with the children, using the most sustained shared thinking. Further, we found that less qualified staff were significantly better as pedagogues when they were supervised by qualified teachers.

Differentiation and formative assessment

Our teacher observations suggest an association between curriculum differentiation, formative assessment, and curriculum matching in terms of cognitive challenge, and 'sustained shared thinking'. The interviews, teacher observations and documentary evidence suggest that the better the setting does on each of these dimensions of good pedagogic practice, the more effective it will be in supporting children's cognitive progress.

Evidence confirms the importance of formative assessment to meet children's particular needs, especially formative feedback during activities.

Parental partnership

The case studies suggest that where a special relationship in terms of shared educational aims has been developed with parents and pedagogic efforts are made at home to support children, sound learning can take place even in the absence of good pedagogic practice in the pre-school setting. The most effective settings shared child related information between parents and staff, and parents were often involved in decision making about their child's learning programme.

In more disadvantaged areas, staff in effective settings had to be proactive in influencing and supporting the home education environment in order to support children's learning.

Discipline and adult support in talking through conflicts

The most effective settings adopted discipline/behaviour policies that involve staff in supporting children in being assertive, while simultaneously rationalising and talking through their conflicts. In settings which were less effective in this respect, our observations showed that there was often no follow up on children's misbehaviour and, on many occasions, children were 'distracted' or simply told to stop.

Organization

Three major approaches to early education were identified in a review of the literature:

- The teacher-directed, programmed learning approach.
- An open framework approach where children are provided with 'free' access to a range of instructive learning environments in which adults support children's learning.
- A child-centred approach where the adults aim is to provide a stimulating yet open-ended environment for children to play within.

We argue that effective pedagogy in the early years involves a balance of the first two approaches, both the kind of interaction traditionally associated with the term 'teaching', and also the provision of instructive learning environments and routines traditionally associated with 'open' approaches. Where young children have freely chosen to play within an instructive learning environment, adult interventions are especially effective. However, we have also noted that these interactions are not as frequent as they should be – even in settings we have classified as "effective" on the basis of child outcomes.

Reading 11.3

Folk pedagogy

Jerome Bruner

Bruner, from the perspective of an educational psychologist and strongly influenced by Vygotsky, is interested in how theories of the mind affect teachers' practice. He argues that teachers who theorize about learning need to take into account intuitive beliefs (which he terms 'folk pedagogy') because such beliefs may be deeply ingrained. However, teachers will also seek to change them in the light of their developing understanding of theories of mind. In this extract, he sets out why it matters that teachers understand how their perceptions of learners' minds affect how they teach.

Edited from: Bruner, J. S. (1996) *The Culture of Education.* 2nd edn. Cambridge, MA: Harvard University Press, 45–50.

Our interactions with others are deeply affected by everyday, intuitive theories about how other minds work. These theories are omnipresent but are rarely made explicit. Such lay theories are referred to by the rather condescending name of *folk psychology*. Folk psychologies reflect certain 'wired-in' human tendencies (like seeing people normally as operating under their own control), but they also reflect some deeply ingrained cultural beliefs about 'the mind'. Not only is folk psychology preoccupied with how the mind works here and now, it is also equipped with notions about how the child's mind learns and even what makes it grow. Just as we are steered in ordinary interaction by our folk psychology, so we are steered in the activity of helping children learn about the world by notions of *folk pedagogy*. Watch any mother, any teacher, even any babysitter with a child and you'll be struck by how much of what they do is steered by notions of 'what children's minds are like and how to help them learn', even though they may not be able to verbalize their pedagogical principles.

From this work on folk psychology and folk pedagogy has grown a new, perhaps even a revolutionary insight. It is this: in theorizing about the practice of education in the classroom (or any other setting, for that matter), you had better take into account the folk theories that those engaged in teaching and learning already have. For any innovations that you, as a 'proper' pedagogical theorist, may wish to introduce will have to compete with, replace, or otherwise modify the folk theories that already guide both teachers and pupils. For example, if you are convinced that the best learning occurs when the teacher helps lead the pupil to discover generalizations on her own, you are likely to run into an established cultural belief that a teacher is an authority who is supposed to *tell* the child what the general case is, while the child should be occupying herself with memorizing the particulars. And if you study how most classrooms are conducted, you will often find that most of the teacher's questions to pupils are about particulars that can be answered in a few words or even by 'yes' or 'no.' So your introduction of an innovation in teaching will necessarily involve changing the folk psychological and folk pedagogical theories of teachers – and, to a surprising extent, of pupils as well.

Teaching, in a word, is inevitably based on notions about the nature of the learner's mind. Beliefs and assumptions about teaching, whether in a school or in any other context, are a direct reflection of the belief and assumption the teacher holds about the learner. Of course, like most deep truths, this one is already well known. Teachers have always tried to adjust their teaching to the backgrounds, abilities, styles, and interests of the children they teach. This is important, but it is not quite what we are after. Our purpose, rather, is to explore more general ways in which learners' minds are conventionally thought about, and pedagogic practices that follow from these ways of thinking about mind. Nor will we stop there, for we also want to offer some reflections of 'consciousness raising' in this setting: what can be accomplished by getting teachers (and students) to think *explicitly* about their folk psychological assumptions, in order to bring them out of the shadows of tacit knowledge.

To say only that human beings understand other minds and try to teach the incompetent, is to overlook the varied ways in which teaching occurs in different cultures. The variety is stunning. We need to know much more about this diversity if we are to appreciate the relation between folk psychology and folk pedagogy in different cultural settings.

Understanding this relationship becomes particularly urgent in addressing issues of educational reform. For once we recognize that a teacher's conception of a learner shapes the instruction he or she employs, then equipping teachers (or parents) with the best available theory of the child's mind becomes crucial. And in the process of doing that, we also need to provide teachers with some insight about their own folk theories that guide their teaching.

Folk pedagogies, for example, reflect a variety of assumptions about children: they may be seen as wilful and needing correction; as innocent and to be protected from a vulgar society; as needing skills to be developed only through practice; as empty vessels to be filled with knowledge that only adults can provide; as egocentric and in need of socialization. Folk beliefs of this kind, whether expressed by laypeople or by 'experts', badly want some 'deconstructing' if their implications are to be appreciated. For whether these views are 'right' or not, their impact on teaching activities can be enormous.

A culturally oriented cognitive psychology does not dismiss folk psychology as mere superstition, something only for the anthropological connoisseur of quaint folkways. I have long argued that explaining what children *do* is not enough; the new agenda is to determine what they *think* they are doing and what their reasons are for doing it. Like new work on children's theories of mind, a cultural approach emphasizes that the child only gradually comes to appreciate that she is acting not directly *on* 'the world' but on beliefs she holds *about* that world. This crucial shift from naive realism to an understanding of the role of beliefs, occurring in the early school years, is probably never complete. But once it starts, there is often a corresponding shift in what teachers can do to help children. With the shift, for example, children can take on more responsibilities for their own learning and thinking. They can begin to 'think about their thinking' as well as about 'the world'.

Advances in how we go about understanding children's minds are, then, a prerequisite to any improvement in pedagogy.

Reading 11.4

Teaching as the assistance of performance
Roland Tharp and Ronald Gallimore

This reading is an elaboration of Vygotsky's ideas (see **Reading 2.3**), and sets out with particular clarity a four-stage model of learning in which different types of assistance in performance are characteristic: support from others; from self-regulation; from internalization; and where performance declines and new learning is necessary.

How does Tharp and Gallimore's four-stage model relate to your own learning? Think, for instance, about how you learned to swim, ride a bicycle or speak a language. And how does it relate to your teaching?

Edited from: Tharp, R. and Gallimore, R. (1988) *Rousing Minds to Life: Teaching, Learning and Schooling in Social Context.* New York: Cambridge University Press, 28–39.

To explain the psychological, we must look not only at the individual but also at the external world in which that individual life has developed. We must examine human existence in its social and historical aspects, not only at its current surface. These social and historical aspects are represented to the child by people who assist and explain, those who participate with the child in shared functioning:

> Any function in the child's cultural development appears twice, or in two planes. First it appears on the social plane, and then on the psychological plane. First it appears between people as an interpsychological category, and then within the child as an intrapsychological category. This is equally true with regard to voluntary attention, logical memory, the formation of concepts, and the development of volition (Vygotsky, 1978: 163).

The process by which the social becomes the psychological is called *internalization*: The individual's 'plane of consciousness' (i.e. higher cognitive processes) is formed in structures that are transmitted to the individual by others in speech, social interaction, and the processes of cooperative activity. Thus, individual consciousness arises from the actions and speech of others.

However, children reorganize and reconstruct these experiences.

Indeed, the child is not merely a passive recipient of adult guidance and assistance; in instructional programs, the active involvement of the child is crucial (Bruner, 1966).

In summary, the cognitive and social development of the child proceeds as an unfolding of potential through the reciprocal influences of child and social environment. Through guided reinvention, higher mental functions that are part of the social and cultural heritage of the child will move from the social plane to the psychological plane, from the socially regulated to the self-regulated. The child, through the regulating actions and speech of others, is brought to engage in independent action and speech. In the resulting interaction, the child performs, through assistance and cooperative activity, at developmental levels quite beyond the individual level of achievement. For skills and functions to develop into internalized, self-regulated capacity, all that is needed is performance, through assisting interaction. Through this process, the child acquires the 'plane of consciousness' of the society and is socialized, acculturated, made human.

Assisted performance defines what a child can do with help, with the support of the environment, of others, and of the self. For Vygotsky, the contrast between assisted performance and unassisted performance identified the fundamental nexus of development and learning that he called the zone of proximal development (ZPD).

The development of any performance capacity in the individual thus represents a changing relationship between self-regulation and social regulation. We present progress through the ZPD in a model of four stages. The model focuses particularly on the relationship between self-control and social control.

Figure 11.4.1
Genesis of performance capacity: Progression through the ZPD and beyond

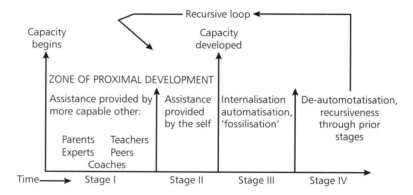

Stage I: Where performance is assisted by more capable others

Before children can function as independent agents, they must rely on adults or more capable peers for outside regulation of task performance. The amount and kind of outside regulation a child requires depend on the child's age and the nature of the task: that is the breadth and progression through the ZPD for the activity at hand.

Such assistance of performance has been described as *scaffolding*, a metaphor first used by Wood, Bruner and Ross (1976) to describe the ideal role of the teacher.

During Stage I, we see a steadily declining plane of adult responsibility for task performance and a reciprocal increase in the learner's proportion of responsibility. This is Bruner's fundamental 'handover principle' – the child who was a spectator is now a participant (Bruner, 1983: 60). The developmental task of Stage I is to transit from other-regulation to self-regulation.

Stage II: Where performance is assisted by the self

If we look carefully at the child's statements during this transition, we see that the child

> has taken over the rules and responsibilities of both participants in the language-game. These responsibilities were formerly divided between the adult and child, but they have now been taken over completely by the child, (Wertsch, 1979: 18)

Thus, in Stage II, the child carries out a task without assistance from others. However, this does not mean that the performance is fully developed or automatized.

During Stage II, the relationships among language, thought, and action in general undergo profound rearrangements. Control is passed from the adult to the child speaker, but the control function remains with the overt verbalization.

The phenomenon of self-directed speech reflects a development of the most profound significance. According to Vygotsky, and his follower Luria, once children begin to direct or guide behaviour with their own speech, an important stage has been reached in the transition of a skill through the ZPD. It constitutes the next stage in the passing of control or assistance from the adult to the child, from the expert to the apprentice. What was guided by the other is now beginning to be guided and directed by the self.

Stage III: Where performance is developed, automized, and 'fossilized'

Once all evidence of self-regulation has vanished, the child has emerged from the ZPD into the *developmental stage* for that task. The task execution is smooth and integrated. It has been internalized and 'automatized'. Assistance, from the adult or the self, is no longer needed. Indeed 'assistance' would now be disruptive. It is in this condition that instructions from others are disruptive and irritating; it is at this stage that self-consciousness itself is detrimental to the smooth integration of all task components. This is a stage beyond self-control and beyond social control. Performance here is no longer developing; it is already developed. Vygotsky described it as 'fossilized', emphasizing its fixity and distance from the social and mental forces of change.

Stage IV: Where de-automatization of performance leads to recursion back through the ZPD

The lifelong learning by any individual is made up of these same regulated, ZPD sequences – from other-assistance to self-assistance – recurring over and over again for the development of new capacities. For every individual, at any point in time, there will be a mix of other-regulation, self-regulation, and automatized processes. The child who can now do many of the steps in finding a lost object might still be in the ZPD for the activities of reading, or any of the many skills and processes remaining to be developed in the immature organism.

Furthermore, once children master cognitive strategies, they are not obligated to rely only on internal mediation. They can also ask for help when stuck or during periods of difficulty. Again, we see the intimate and shifting relationship between control by self and control by others. Even for adults, the effort to recall a forgotten bit of information can be aided by the helpful assistance of another so that the total of self-regulated and other-regulated components of the performance once again resembles the mother and child example of shared functioning. Even the competent adult can profit from regulation for enhancement and maintenance of performance.

Indeed, a most important consideration is that *de-automatization* and *recursion* occur so regularly that they constitute a Stage IV of the normal developmental process. What one formerly could do, one can no longer do. The first line of retreat is to the immediately prior self-regulating phase. A further retreat, to remembering the voice of a teacher, may be required, and consciously reconjuring the voice of a tutor – is an effective self-control technique.

But in some cases no form of self-regulation may be adequate to restore capacity, and a further recursion – the restitution of other regulation – is required. Indeed, the profession of assisting adults (psychotherapy) is now a major Western institution. In all these instances, the goal is to reproceed through assisted performance to self-regulation and to exit the ZPD again into a new automatization.

Communication
How does language support learning?

Reading

12.1 Pat Broadhead
Interactions and social development (p. 236)

12.2 Julia Manning-Morton
Talking babies (p. 238)

12.3 Belinda Buckley
The role of the linguistic environment in early language development (p. 242)

12.4 Tözün Issa and Alison Hatt
The bilingual learner (p. 245)

12.5 Colin Harrison
Why is reading so important? (p. 249)

12.6 Sandra Smidt
Narrative in the lives of children (p. 252)

Throughout this book and the parallel text *Reflective Teaching in Early Education* a common theme across all chapters has been communication. To build relationships, to support the learning of others, to work collaboratively, to convey what we know, to have an inclusive setting, we absolutely must be able to communicate effectively.

The first two readings explore the importance of interacting with others for personal development and for developing a sense of self. Readings 12.3 and 12.4 consider the linguistic environment and bilingualism and how this impacts upon children's learning.

In the final two readings, the relationships between reading and language and stories and children's early communication skills are examined, reminding us of the role of language and communication in children's cognitive development.

Reading 12.1

Interactions and social development
Pat Broadhead

In this reading, Pat Broadhead considers the relationship between learning and play in the early years by looking at our earliest interactions, the links between these interactions and intellectual development, and growth of language and concept of 'self' and knowledge and understanding of the world.

How effectively are the children in your care supported to develop effective communication skills?

Edited from: Broadhead, P. (2004) *Early Years Play and Learning: Developing Social Skills and Cooperation.* London: RoutledgeFalmer, 39–42.

Face-to-face interactions are among our earliest experiences of social interaction. From two months onwards this is a primary means of socializing and, as visual efficiency improves, this mode of interaction provokes responses and then initiation by the infant (Schaffer, 1996). From about five months of age, the emergence of manipulative abilities allows the young infant to examine and explore objects and these objects become an increasingly important part of the baby's social interactions with familiar adults as maturation occurs (Kaye and Fogel, 1980). There is no doubt that the very young infant is totally dependent on the willingness of those around her/him to initiate and sustain their socializing opportunities, but these 'self-regulating others and personified things indicate the degree to which the subjective world of infants is deeply social' (Stern, 1998: 123).

Stern argues that infants are already experiencing a sense of their core self and are bringing this sense of self-being to their social experiences with others.. He argues that these forms of 'being with' are active constructions by the young child. This sense of self grows out of regular contact with a significant other person or persons. This sense of self and others are fused initially but, over time, the sense of self becomes distinguished and differentiated (Main et al., 1985). There is some support for the view that securely attached infants develop their self-concept faster than insecurely attached infants (Schneider-Rosen and Cicchetti, 1984; Pipp et al., 1993). From these earliest months, the interconnections between the growth of concepts that begin to shape our knowledge and understanding of the world, the emergence of self-identity and opportunities for socialization are a fundamental yet essential part of the child's natural development.

Shared frameworks of meaning become increasingly important, Stern (1998) argues, as the child's theory of mind begins to develop from seven to nine months onwards. Realization grows and the infant gradually begins to recognize that inner (subjective) experiences can be shared with those familiar to us. Over the following months and into the second year of life, the young child increasingly recognizes their own capacity to initiate, share, demand and reject. The young child comes to recognize that their actions provoke responsive actions and that they can have some control, through their initiated actions, over the directions that these interactions might take. They begin to shape their social experiences more actively, sometimes to prolong them when others might want to end them and to initiate them more easily when they want to play with others. Physical mobility rapidly expands their universe and the 'personified things of the relatively immobilized infant give way to the persistent exploration and investigation of a world of exciting (and sometimes dangerous) objects to stimulate and engage.

The rapid development of language from the second year of life and beyond brings as important dimension on the connections between conceptual growth, self-identity and socialization. Not only does their sense of self acquire new attributes, but there is a new medium through which others and self create new meanings (Stern, 1998). During this period, emotional expression expands. Pride and shame may appear by the end of the second year as the young child learns to self evaluate. Joy and anger will usually (and often) be expressed before self-control can begin to emerge. Self-control takes time to develop, tantrums can be commonplace and regulation can only emerge through socialization processes that help the child to see greater benefits from being in control rather than out of control (Chorpita and Barlow, 1998). While the sense of self might sometimes scream for satisfaction and gratification, signs of helping, sharing and sympathy are also evident in this second year (Rhinegold, 1982; Zahn-Waxler et al., 1992; Hay, 1994). Children are capable of such pro-social behaviours at an early age and a key question for adults is in what kinds of conditions and in what kinds of circumstances are young children most likely to act in pro-social ways with their peers?

As children move from family-based settings into the wider world of pre-school and childcare, their relatively unlimited access to a key adult changes. Depending on their age and the setting, they will be sharing adults with other children to some degree. Dowling (2000), equates it with an adult starting a new job, but the child has far less experience of life on which to draw. This move to a group is momentous and will impact, for better or worse, on the child's self-concept and self-esteem. However, the growing child's capacity for interacting with more than one person simultaneously has already started to develop by age three, more especially when the child is in a secure and familiar environment with adults and children s/he has come to know.

Rapidly growing language skills, increasing self-control, desires for autonomy independence and knowledge can each assist the child in their participation in and active contribution to a more complex and demanding social environment. However, there are still a considerable number of skills to be developed and steps to be taken to be successful in this new world. The growth of self in relation to a limited number of 'others' needs expansion as those, now multiple 'others' also exert their desires and interests simultaneously with one's own. The growing child must learn to compromise if s/he is to engage with others, one of the earliest forms of which is turn taking. Here the child delays instant gratification because s/he comes to understand how the wait, usually in the company of others, can be exciting and socially meaningful. Anticipation becomes a time for reflection as well as interaction. Plans are made, decisions are taken. Conscious thought begins to have impact on subsequent action. Friendships begin to be formed and early friendships are an important part of social understanding and communicative intelligence (Faulkner and Miell, 1993).

Reading 12.2

Talking babies

Julia Manning-Morton

> This article, written by Julia Manning-Morton, considers communication with babies. The premise of the paper is that being social and communicating is fundamental for children's social development and that adults are key to supporting this development.
>
> *Edited from:* Manning-Morton, J. (2004) 'The importance of non-verbal interactions for under-threes'. Available from http://www.literacytrust.org.uk/talk_to_your_baby/news/1616_the_importance_of_non-verbal_interactions_for_under-threes

Communicating with others is fundamental to being a social being. As developing language relies on social interactions, the most important resource for very young children learning to communicate is the consistent, continuous care of responsive, familiar adults.

Children who are enabled to build trusting relationships develop self-confidence in expressing themselves and sharing their ideas. In such relationships of mutual respect there is powerful motivation to interact, communicate and use language.

A lot of learning about communication takes place around familiar routines such as nappy changing, sleeping and mealtimes. Consequently, carers must be responsive and attentive both physically and verbally.

Rocking or gently massaging a baby, for example, are ways of communicating that underpin early language development. Holding out your arms and asking a baby if they would like to have their nappy changed instigates a conversation as well as showing a child respect.

Karmiloff-Smith (1994) says that the sensitivity of the parents/carers to their baby in the first few months of life has a direct correlation to the linguistic ability of the baby at 12 months. Babies in daycare need carers with that same sensitivity. In this way we can see how the relationship between the baby and caring adult is central to their communication and learning.

Ways of communicating

Babies are communicators from birth. They recognise human voices that they have heard in the womb, and after birth they pay more attention to human voices than other auditory stimuli (Karmiloff-Smith, 1995).

Babies communicate their needs in different ways but crying is the primary means by which they communicate fear, pain, hunger, boredom or loneliness. The better a practitioner knows a baby, the more they are able to differentiate the type of crying that the baby uses to convey a particular need. It is useful for practitioners to remember that although a baby's crying makes us tense, this discomfort makes us act, which is what the baby needs. This in itself is a conversation and an early experience of cause and effect for the baby.

But babies also express their interest in communicating with us by gazing at adults' faces, searching with their eyes, smiling, babbling, reaching, laughing and shouting. These interactions usually take place with people they know. With strangers, or if they want to stop an interaction, babies show their displeasure by looking away, tilting their heads away, grimacing, whining and pushing away with their arms and legs (Manning-Morton and Thorp, 2001). Use of facial expression, body language, gesture and vocalisations are then all important ways in which babies and young children make themselves understood, long before language emerges.

Acredolo and Goodwyn (2000) suggest that almost all babies use signs and gestures such as pointing, waving and shaking their heads. Their research identified that where babies were supported in using signs to communicate their needs, they had more spoken language at two years old than non-signing peers. Toddlers in their study also experienced less frustration, as signing enabled them to communicate more effectively with their parents/carers, so enhancing relationships and consequently the children's self-esteem. Similarly, key persons who are tuned in to each of their babies' and toddlers' ways of communicating also lessen the times of intense frustration for the children and the consequent emotional collapse that they may experience.

Developing understanding

Before babies and toddlers develop language they develop an understanding of how language and communication works. They engage in turn-taking of conversation. For example, babies suck vigorously at the breast or bottle when feeding, then pause, gazing at their carer, who talks to and maybe jiggles the baby in the pauses, then the baby starts sucking again. Colwyn Trevarthan calls such exchanges 'proto-conversations' (Trevarthn, 1979), which also take place in many games we play with babies. He describes babies as young as two months engaging in these communications and says they provide children with a good understanding of their cultural vocabulary of communication.

Babies also show that they know what the adult intends to do when environments and routines are predictable. For example, babies look towards the fridge as you prepare their lunch. This ability to follow the adult's attention means the practitioner can show the baby interesting things and also follow the baby's attention and talk about what they are looking at or pointing to.

In this way babies make links between objects and events and language. This is further assisted by the attention that babies pay to the human voice, especially the exaggerated intonation, higher pitch and restricted vocabulary typical of 'motherese' or Infant Directed Speech.

Babies are also developing an awareness of the links between actions and language. Motherese, for example, also uses exaggerated facial expressions and actions that gain the babies' attention, such as tickling. As noted earlier, this develops into babies using their own gestures to communicate. Toddlers understand and use many expressions, gestures and imitate many language-related actions, such as shrugging their shoulders or putting their fingers to their lips for 'shh'.

As in the adult world, words for babies and toddlers mean far less if their meaning is not also communicated by facial expression, tone, pitch and gesture.

Implications for practice: The practitioner's role

Practitioners who support babies' and toddlers' communications effectively:

- spend time in conversation with their key children, echoing their vocalisations and pausing for replies
- respond to the meaning in young children's communications
- are knowledgeable about each child's interests, the words or events that trigger memories and the repeated conversations that are related to these
- are tuned in to each child's language, gestures and expressions and use them consistently in response.

Working with parents

To understand effectively the communications of babies and toddlers, practitioners and parents need to communicate well themselves. Daily exchanges are necessary, through conversation or a diary, for all adults to be able to interpret a child's actions or words. This means telling each other:

- the meaning of particular words or gestures that a child uses
- about a child's idiosyncratic words or rituals and what they mean
- about the child's experiences at home and in the setting so each understands what the child is referring to and can talk more about it.

Prime care times

Physical care times are prime times for conversation. To support communications at these times, key persons should be primarily responsible for changing, feeding and settling their key children to sleep.

Environment

Practitioners who know how hard it is to communicate, say, in a noisy club or quiet library, will understand how environment impacts on young children's efforts to communicate. Babies and toddlers can become fractious when the noise level in a group rises. This is just one reason why groups should not be too large or noisy or have too wide an age range for good communication to take place. Childminders' homes do not usually have large echoing spaces, but group settings should consider having sound-absorbing surfaces and quiet areas to reduce background noise and ensure that babies and toddlers can hear and be heard.

Play experiences/resources

There are many social communication games that birth to three-year-olds enjoy. For babies these mostly involve play with the adult. Older babies enjoy lively games with songs and comical teasing games such as 'round and round the garden'. Babies will show pleasure and excitement in this play with someone that they know well but not with a stranger. However, even a trusted adult must know to stop the game as soon as excitement turns to anxiety, or the developing trust will be damaged.

Reading 12.3

The role of the linguistic environment in early language development

Belinda Buckley

The following reading, provided by Belinda Buckley, focuses on the linguistic environment and its role in the development of children's language and communication skills. She refers to the highly influential work of Basil Bernstein.

Edit from: Buckley, B. (2003) *Children's Communication Skills – From Birth to Five Years.* London: RoutledgeFalmer, 19–23.

The British educational sociolinguist Basil Bernstein (1975) characterized two key styles of speech among speakers of English, which he referred to as 'elaborated code' and 'restricted code'. Elaborated code contains more unusual words, passives ('the bone was gnawed by the dog' instead of 'the dog gnawed the bone'), modals (should, ought, would) and proliferation of subjective phrases such as I think', 'In my opinion', 'Personally'. Bernstein identified elaborated code as a style of speech used by many (middle and upper class) Standard English speakers. Labov (1972) drew a contrast between speakers who use elaborated code and who appear knowledgeable while not dealing precisely with abstract ideas, and the more effective narrative, reasoning and debating skills illustrated by users of restricted code. This style of speaking involves a more direct style of expression, using the immediate context to express meanings. The restricted code was identified by Bernstein as a style of speech characteristic of working classes in the United Kingdom.

The role of the linguistic environment in early language development

Related to Bernstein's restricted and elaborated codes is the question of the role of the linguistic environment in children's language development. In a most basic form, linguistic input functions as the language model which most children eventually achieve, in that most grow up speaking the language of their environment. Input is thus clearly necessary. Two key questions have arisen concerning how language input might influence children's language acquisition:

Does the language that children hear act merely as a trigger, catalyzing children's predisposition to learn language and through this assist them in working out the rules of their language (such as the need in English to invert the subject and *verb* in order to transform a statement into a question, for example 'John likes blue shoes' 'Does John like blue shoes?'); and if so, to what extent'? Do the special features present in so much speech directed to babies and young children serve to facilitate language development, and if so, how'?

Many adults and older children (especially from western cultures) use simplifying, clarifying and affective features in speech addressed to babies and young children, distinguishing it from adult-to-adult speech. This form of speech, or register, has variously been termed '*motherese*' (Newport, 1976) and '*child directed talk*' (Warren-Leubecker and Bohannon III, 1989). The 'Motherese Hypothesis' resulted from research looking at the effect of adult (usually maternal) speech on language development. Ferguson (1977) claimed that many simplifying processes in motherese assisted in teaching language, which she maintained was the primary function of the register. Such processes include a smaller, simplified vocabulary, a rudimentary grammar with restricted, structurally simple sentence types, and fewer sound types and combinations of words. Ferguson noted that simplified language is accelerated in terms of complexity as the child's language progresses, drawing the conclusion that a cause and effect relationship existed between such features and language development, Garnica (1977) concluded that exaggerated use of features such as *vocal* pitch, pausing and longer duration of some words in motherese assisted children in deriving grammatical information about the language.

It is plausible that special features of this register have some function with regard to language learning, but opinion is divided concerning the degree to which functions are based in 'teaching' language and enabling communication.

A major tenet of the Motherese Hypothesis, that 'restrictive sentences' (i.e. in structure) are a requirement for language learning, has been challenged by Gleitman et al. (1984).

Against this background of claims and challenges regarding the role of adult speech in facilitating children's language development, the following research findings are worthy of note:

A shared focus of attention between the baby or young child and the adult, which is a basic principle of shared communication, increases the likelihood of early vocabulary growth (Tomasello and Ferrar, 1986; Garton, 1992).

An extended pitch range, including whispering and high pitch especially, particularly at the end of adult utterances, cues the child as to when she's expected to respond. This, together with frequent repetitions of the child's name, serves to establish and maintain the child's attention (Garnica, 1977).

Children exploit some of the linguistic input some of the time (Gleitman et al., 1984): i.e. children make use of the language they hear in different ways at different points of their development, and depending on their stage of language development at that time.

'Simple' input may be more facilitative for younger (18 to 21 month-old) children's task of learning vocabulary and producing simple phrases for a basic range of purposes, whereas more complex input may be required for older (24 to 27 month-old) children's task of acquiring word endings and grammatical rules (Snow, 1986).

The restricted range of vocabulary spoken by mothers to young children, focusing on words with the simplest and most unambiguous meanings, for example kin, the body, qualities, animals, games and food, constituting the here and now, enables children to figure out the meanings of words (Ferguson, 1977).

Adults' ability to match and anticipate a child's cognitive level is observed at the level of word meanings (semantic fine tuning), which benefits semantic development (Myers Pease et al., 1989). For example, an adult might label both lorries and cars as 'car' for a child at an early stage of language development. Later on, they might label them in such a way as to facilitate understanding of the relations that exist between word meanings and the entities they represent, for example 'lorries, cars, buses … they've all got wheels!'

A positive relation was identified between gradually increasing complexity of language spoken to children and children's language growth (Gleitman et al., 1984).

Better formed sentences by young children result from adults requesting clarification rather than making grammatical corrections (Garton, 1992).

Parents tend to correct the factual accuracy of children's language rather than how it is said (Snow, 1986).

Children of mothers whose language contained many commands designed to control their behaviour were described by Folger and Chapman (1977) as being 'more inclined to act than talk', and their vocabulary contained a greater number of personal and social words (for example, hello, bye, yeah, no, mine) than descriptive words (for example, big, more, wet, sticky).

Children of mothers whose language contained more descriptions of the environment and requests for information had a greater number of object names in their vocabulary (Della-Corte et al., 1983).

Reading 12.4

The bilingual learner

Tözün Issa and Alison Hatt

Tözün Issa and Alison Hatt explore language acquisition and learning and how to effectively support 'young learners' multiple identities and languages'. This reading is taken from Chapter 6 of their book, which begins by looking at the traditional perceptions of bilingualism in the late nineteenth century as negative and harmful. Bilingualism was thought to be 'a burden on cognitive processes, which would lead to mental confusion, inhibit the acquisition of the majority language and might even lead to a split personality'. The following extract looks at current perceptions of bilingualism, its effect on language acquisition and growth. It also looks at the role of the home language in second language acquisition, and the role of the early years practitioners as 'instigators of language'.

Edited from: Issa, T. and Hatt, A. (2013) *Language Culture and Identity in the Early Years.* London: Bloomsbury, 126–30.

First and subsequent language acquisition

A growing body of research appears to support the validity of co-operative learning strategies as: 'Extremely valuable instructional strategy for promoting participation and academic growth in culturally and linguistically diverse classrooms' (Cummins, 1996: 82).

Co-operative learning strategies involve small groups of pupils working together for a common objective though activities based on interdependent co-operation (Abrami et al., 1995; DeVillar and Faltis, 1991; Holt, 1993; Kessler, 1992). One of the effective programmes of research on the levels of achievement in collaborative programmes was carried out by Garcia (1991) on Latino speaking pupils in the United States. The instruction was organized in a way to facilitate maximum pupil interaction. Heath and Mangiola (1991) show how peer tutoring can result in academic gains for both children. Heath (1993) highlights how concentrating on another child's learning helps children to 'decompose what is involved in learning language' (p. 188).

It is useful to remind ourselves that there are aspects of children's home backgrounds, for example, family run businesses, business related talk at home and certain characteristics of speech patterns used. It is argued that because culturally specific talk takes place in the child's home language, it is useful to look at children's interaction in bilingual home language – English medium. Children's cultural experiences need to be looked at in informal settings as there are opportunities for children to use their naturally occurring language and work collaboratively to meet the challenges presented to them.

Cummins' (2009) more recent work on using learners' home language for bilingual literacy development can be shown as an example. He demonstrates how allowing children to articulate their linguistic and cultural experiences through their first language results in highly motivated individuals and high quality work in English. As Cummins talks about Tomer's – new arrival from Israel – 'Identity text', *Tom Goes to Kentucky*, he provides useful insights into his feelings about using Hebrew in the classroom. 'The first time I couldn't understand what she [Lisa – his teacher] was saying except the word Hebrew, but I think it's very smart that she said for us to do it in our language because we can't just sit on our hands doing nothing.' Cummins goes on to talk about how allowing Tomer to express his emotions in Hebrew enhances his thinking and subsequent written work in English. Similarly, Cummins shares the experiences of Madiha, Kanta, Baswa and Sulmana, four children who have recently arrived from Pakistan. They provide a touching account of their departure from their country, talking about how hard it was for them to leave Pakistan and adjust to a new way of life in Canada. The children produced an impressive account of their experiences in Urdu and English.

Cognitive benefits of bilingualism in early years settings

One of the important aspects of promoting multiculturalism in early years is its creation of a cohesive learning environment and helping young children to understand about 'each other'. This helps children to start to move away from their own egocentric world, beginning to see the values and the cultures of others as different but equally enriching as their own. Here the values of the mainstream English society are promoted equally as all the others: focusing on 'English' cultural and linguistic values as other communities. One of the most visible aspects of the EYC in our study was its promotion of children's culture and languages as 'something to be clever about'. Children as young as two and a half were openly talking about their own languages as well as that of their friends in the Centre. Different scripts colourfully displayed around the Centre were readily identified and associated with particular children by their friends. Everyone proudly talked about their own families, their languages and customs at home in their own books titled '…'s book' preceded by their name. 'Here it says Aysha can speak Turkish', Aysha proudly informed us. English was also promoted alongside other languages as an equally useful language to learn. Furthermore, it was accepted by all as the language everyone was going to learn before starting the other school. The explicit message given was that all languages were equal and part of who children were, part of their developing identities.

Exploring the role of the home language in second language acquisition
Some psychological considerations

It would be a wrong assumption to make if we were to claim that schools are discouraging young children to value and develop their home languages in the early years contexts; however, it may be fair to say that not all of them are actively involved in promoting them alongside English. One of the reasons for this is the commonly held belief among some policy makers, senior managers and practitioners that children starting school need to learn English as fast as they could in order to catch up with their peers. For this reason, any attempt to explore and develop their home cultures and languages will be detrimental to this. We have already explored the benefits of maintaining young children's home languages and cultures. What we will explore in this part of the chapter is the impact on young learners' emotional development of not supporting the natural development of the home languages.

We mentioned in earlier chapters that despite successive government claims young linguistic minority children start school with having been exposed mainly to their home languages. This would not imply that these children are conceptually inactive because of their lack of English, but they have already developed concepts as the result of their home experiences. It is useful to bear in mind that conceptual development occurs in relation to children's particular cultural experiences and such experiences are embedded in children's home languages. If we accept the findings of research on second language acquisition that the second language does not develop independently but in relation to the first language, we would expect the facilitation of the use of the first language by adults working in early years settings. The important question is how is this to be done. There is a big debate around this area.

The first of such debates defends a view that this can only be done effectively if the language of the child is spoken by the adult working with the child/ren concerned. Having a bilingual member of staff working with targeted children is an excellent strategy; however, we do not live in an ideal world and although the number of bilingual adults working in early years settings is increasing, the present day early years settings are linguistically enriched environments where up to 10–15 languages can be represented by children attending them. Our project Centre had 22 languages represented by its intake including English. Another view on this looks the role of professional adults working in early years settings as instigators of language use. The main thrust of this argument is its claim that one does not need to have the knowledge of a particular language in order to facilitate its use. This requires further attention as this was the positive practice we saw taking place at the EYC. Positive language use was actively encouraged by monolingual English speaking staff. For example, we frequently saw staff uttering odd words in children's home languages which seemed meaningful and acted as a good starting point for interactions.

Children were happy not only talking about their own languages but the languages of others including some adults around them. Morning greetings in different languages were a familiar sight. Children responded positively to this. Staff frequently chose a particular word that fitted the social reality of the learning context. For instance, when TI was talking to Selma about her book, the word torta (cake) was mentioned by Selma. Andrew, a member of staff who happened to be passing by joined the discussion briefly by saying 'torta – I know that word, it means cake. I also know it in Arabic but I will tell you later.' From his response we were not sure whether Andrew actually knew the Arabic equivalent of torta but it was his contextualization of the learning environment that is worthy of a mention here. Selma was tuned in to what seemed to be a worthwhile learning experience that had herself at the centre of it. Children were frequently allowed to develop their imagination by exploring their previous experiences further. A 'reflection tent' is where children could see their own reflections in the mirror and pretend to be anything they wanted to be. It was here that we found children's creativity in language use at its best. Children role-played and experimented with different language varieties quite happily as shown by the following example by Selma pretending to be one of the adults in the household informing the other adult that she was 'going to a meeting'.

Johnson and Newport (1989) point out that between the ages of 2 and 5 language learning is effortless with young children.

As part of the induction programme, we organize language learning sessions for our students on our teacher training course at the university. As a starter activity, we deliver lessons in different languages which are unfamiliar to students and are delivered by specialist teachers in that language. At the end of a 40-minute session, students are asked how they felt about the experience. Some of the responses we get from them are: 'Anxious, bored, frustrated, fed up, desperate'. Students are also asked about their feelings when the teacher or someone else accidentally used English during the session. Their responses were often summarized with one word: 'relief'.

If this is the reaction of grown-up mature students with teachers then we can imagine how young bilingual children feel when they first start the nursery. As adults it may make perfect sense to rationalize the need to learn English in order to pass exams and be successful in the education system. However, to a young bilingual learner starting an early years setting having been exposed mainly to another language can be quite traumatic. Of course, we are not suggesting that adults working in early years settings actively discourage young children from speaking their home languages. We know that we have come a long way in preparing our teachers for working in early years settings. However, walking into a new learning environment can be challenging enough for any young child, starting a predominantly English speaking setting can be pretty daunting if not catastrophic for a young bilingual learner. It creates a negative self-concept – what's wrong with my language? Our colleagues working in early years settings may recall a period of silence when a child does not speak for several days even weeks. The reasons for this may be complex, however, we should not rule out the anxiety factor as one of the causes for this. Adults need be actively encouraging children to think and use their home languages in relation to all purposeful talk which takes place in English. Failure to do so will give out wrong signals to an already worried young bilingual mind, leading to further anxiety and more serious consequences.

Reading 12.5

Why is reading so important?
Colin Harrison

> In this extract from *Understanding Reading Development*, Harrison reminds us to think about why reading is so important and hence why it forms a central part of any teacher's practice. Drawing on Bruner, he argues that narrative is crucial to human development, but that information books are equally important, because from both, young readers learn how texts – like people – can communicate.
>
> Why, in your view, is reading so important across the curriculum? What does this mean for the ways in which you support young learners and the development of early literacy skills?
>
> *Edited from:* Harrison, C. (2004) *Understanding Reading Development*. London: Sage Publications Ltd, 3–8.

Why should teachers devote so much time to supporting children in becoming confident and fluent readers? My starting point in answering this question is not taken from government statements identifying national goals in reading; rather, it is a quotation from a letter written by Gustave Flaubert in 1857:

> Do not read, as children do, to amuse yourself, or like the ambitious, for the purpose of instruction. No, read in order to live. (Flaubert, 1857, in Steegmuller, 1982)

Teachers can be forgiven for forgetting sometimes the joy and delight that most young children experience as they discover what words can do. But I want to make no distinction between reading stories and reading for information in relation to the question of what we gain from reading. I want to affirm that reading not only increases our life skills and extends our knowledge, but goes much deeper. Indeed, I want to argue that in many respects reading determines how we are able to think, that it has a fundamental effect on the development of the imagination, and thus exerts a powerful influence on the development of emotional and moral as well as verbal intelligence and therefore on the kind of person we are capable of becoming.

Many teachers of my generation were influenced by Barbara Hardy's essay on 'Narrative as a primary act of mind', taken from the book *The Cool Web* in which she argued that 'inner and outer storytelling' plays a major role in our sleeping and waking lives. She wrote:

> … For we dream in narrative, daydream in narrative, remember, anticipate, hope, despair, believe, doubt, plan, revise, criticize, construct, gossip, learn, hate, and love by narrative. In order really to live, we make up stories about ourselves and others, about the personal as well as the social past and future. (Hardy, 1977: 13)

The importance of narrative, she argues, is not simply about enjoyment of stories, or even about understanding ourselves; narrative is a fundamental tool in the construction of inter-subjectivity – the ability to recognize mental states in ourselves, and through imagination and projection, to recognize the potential reciprocity of mental states in others – their beliefs, intentions, desires, and the like. It is this (and not simply the existence of language) that makes us distinctive as human beings. Jerome Bruner put this point very powerfully:

> I want to propose that this deep, primitive form of human cognition [ie: inter-subjectivity] is captured linguistically in the form of narrative (Bruner, 2000: 33).

Bruner was arguing here that inter-subjectivity, our very ability to relate to other people in characteristically human ways, is fundamentally related to our use of the linguistic form of narrative.

If narrative is fundamental to human development, then reading is about much more than gaining a skill: it is about learning to be. And it is precisely because this is such a difficult and sensitive subject to talk about that we avoid talking about it, and this leaves an enormous vacuum. Because reading is so important, that vacuum becomes filled by other discourses, and often these have an emphasis on skills, on employment, on the economy and on reading for practical purposes. Of course, these practical purposes are extremely important, but I would nevertheless wish to emphasize that, when we are looking at reading development, we are talking about giving people tools to be human. Indeed, if learning to read opens significant additional possibilities in terms of understanding how we might live, then we can argue that we have a moral duty to read, and, therefore as teachers, a moral duty to teach reading.

It is enormously valuable for all teachers to have some understanding of how children learn to read, and of the remarkable potential of early literacy experiences to influence children's development.

In a nursery that I visit regularly, I heard the following story from the mother of Henry, then a cheerful little boy of 22 months. His language was developing well, which is to say that he was beginning to talk confidently, even though he was sometimes frustrated because he did not yet have the words to explain everything he wanted to say. But the remarkable incident which followed his being bitten by another child showed that Henry could use a book to communicate his feelings, even before he had learned the words to utter them.

One afternoon, when Henry's mum arrived to pick him up from nursery, Henry's key worker took her aside and asked her to sign her section of an accident form. 'Everything's alright,' said the key worker, 'but I have to tell you that I'm afraid Henry was bitten this afternoon by another child. I have had a conversation with the other child and explained how serious it is to bite someone, and have asked him not to do it again.' Naturally, this being a modern nursery, there was no mention of the name of the biter. When Henry's mum went to pick up Henry, there was no sign of anguish, anger or upset, but Henry proudly rolled up his sleeve and revealed a fine set of teeth marks on his forearm. He then became increasingly agitated and clenched his little fists with frustration, as he realized he could not tell his mum what had happened. Suddenly, he rushed over to the book corner, and fetched a book, ran back to his mum and opened it. The book had a number of pictures of reptiles, and Henry turned the pages determinedly until he found the picture he wanted. It was a photograph of a very large crocodile with its jaws wide open revealing a full set of sharp teeth. Henry pointed to the photograph, then he pointed to the bite on his arm. Then he pointed to his best friend, another little boy, who was sitting across the room, working with great concentration on a drawing. 'Snap! Snap!' said Henry as he pointed to his pal. His mum understood.

What is intriguing about this anecdote are the connections between the infant's intentionality, his communication strategies, and his emergent literacy. Henry understood, even before his speech was anything like fully developed, that books, as well as people, can communicate, and he used this understanding to make an announcement that was richer and far more dramatic than would have been possible without access to the book. What exactly was happening here? First, Henry was initiating a literacy event: a child who was not yet two was demonstrating an awareness that a book could be used as a bridge – a third possible world that might be used to link his own mental world to the mental world of his mum. Second, he already understood the potential of metaphor that one event or object which had a partial set of correspondences with another event or object could be used to stand proxy for that event or object, and could evoke a set of associations in the mind of another. Third, he implicitly understood how powerful a metaphor could be: his little pal, the biter, had not sprung from a jungle river and torn off his arm but Henry used the evocative image of the crocodile to striking effect, and to call up in his mother's mind associations with the atavistic fear of being attacked by a giant reptile. And these things did not just happen: they occurred because Henry inhabited a world surrounded by books – in the kitchen of his home, in his bedroom, at his grandparents' house, and in the nursery that he had attended daily since he had been six months old. They happened because since before he had been just a few months old, adults had been sharing books with him, and initiating him into the awareness of possible worlds that are accessed through books, and into the visual and linguistic representations that made up those worlds.

It is interesting that this example of developing inter-subjectivity used an information book. Indeed, whilst narrative and story are important in distinctive ways in human development, information books are important, too. Historians tell us that the first written texts were not stories or poetry, but information texts – facts about ownership, law, the permanent recording of important details and events. Stories offer us models of how to live, but information books give us the power to store, to name, to retrieve, to share, to explore, to wonder at, and to bring order to our representations of the world.

Reading 12.6

Narrative in the lives of children
Sandra Smidt

Sandra Smidt, drawing on the key concepts of the work of Jerome Bruner, identifies the role narrative plays in children's communication. She explores how children's communication skills can be supported through the use of stories and offers some practical guidance on how this can be achieved.

Edited from: Smidt, S. (2011) *Introducing Bruner: A Guide for Practitioners and Students in Early Years Education*. London: Routledge, 98–106.

Bruner tells us that children enter the world of narrative early in life. Those of us who have children or who have spent time with children will find this no surprise. Almost as soon as children begin to use spoken language they combine what words they have together with facial expression and gesture and intonation into tiny proto-narratives. Here are some examples:

The child looks at her empty ice-cream cone and says, in a mournful tone of voice, 'All gone!' (The child tells the sad story of how she has eaten all the ice cream so that now there is none left.)

Arturo, given a present on his birthday, beams and says ammi me (ammi is what he calls his aunt). (Arturo tells the happy story that his aunt has given him a present and he is happy.)

The urge to make sense of experience through story seems to arise from the child's earliest conversations with adults within the context of the culture. In these exchanges it seems that the adult's intention can be seen to be narrative in the sense of turning any exchange into a story to help the infant make sense of it. One clear example of this comes from the work of Catherine Snow (1977), who, in her analysis of the speech used by mothers even in the first few months of life, noted that they commented on everyday events in a remarkably narrative way, imputing motives and emotions and the rudiments of a plot.

Gordon Wells offered the example of a child called Mark, just short of his second birthday, who engaged in a real conversation with his mother, taking turns and being able to comment on what the birds were doing outside his window. The conversation started with Mark drawing his mother's attention to the birds and his mother then asking him what they were doing. His answer was intelligible only to his mother: 'Jubs bread.' (Jubs was his word for 'birds'). Wells tells us that two weeks later he was involved in an extended conversation with his mother and as they talked about an imagined shopping trip he gradually took over the role of principal narrator (Wells, 1981).

Bruner (2002) himself wrote about what he called the narrative precocity of infants and in doing this he cited the studies of the tape recordings of Emmy's musings to herself in bed before she fell asleep. The tapes were all recorded before Emmy reached the age of three. In his wonderfully entitled paper with Joan Lucariello 'Monologues as Narrative Recreation of the World' (1989) he showed how this small child used narrative. In his later book he discussed some surprising findings. For example, Emmy talked not only about the routines of the day but seemed to be very attracted by and interested in something strange or unexpected that had happened. She then mused on how she had perhaps dealt with similar things in the past or how she would deal with them if they should happen again. Bruner concluded that she was so intent on getting her story right that she seemed to have a narrative sensibility that enabled her to look for and often find the correct syntactic forms. So Bruner suggested we may have a predisposition to tell stories in order to make sense of reality. The reason children become narrators, is because they explore the expectations they have developed about how the world should be. They develop these expectations through their experiences and their interactions and the ways in which they look for patterns and regularities in the world. But they also love the unexpected, the fantastic and the surprise.

Here are some examples of narratives told or written by young children in which the strange or the fantastic mingle with the ordinary and everyday.

The first was told by four-year-old Octavia. It is a beautiful example of a child mixing book language and everyday language in a tiny narrative.

'Once upon a time when I was little in my garden, there were a earthworm coming out of my plant.'

The second is written by Sam when she was five years old:

'This is a witch who has caught a clown and she has stuck a knife into the clown. She mixes the magic powder to kill the funny clown. She is killing him just because he is funny. But there was reason why she is going to kill the funny clown because she doesn't like funny things and all clowns are funny and specially that one. Everyone like him but that witch. Even the other witches loved him dearly. They all thought he was great except for that one who was the only witch in the wild world who didn't like funny things. She really did hate funny things …'

And this is written by Peter when he was seven years old. It is called 'The Boy who Broke his Laser beam':

'Long ago, before motor cars were invented, there was this little boy and his name was John. This boy named John liked to go in the forest to see his grandparents and on this particular day he was walking through the forest when, just when he walked through a clearing of four trees, a giant net sprang on to him. The next thing he knew was that he was flying to a nearby cave in the claws of a bat …'

The implications for practice

You will almost certainly already use story and narrative in your class or setting as part of your everyday offer. You may have one or more story sessions or circle times a day, and you may plan these carefully in terms of selecting the books, stories or rhymes, thinking about what, if any, visual aids you will use to draw those children for whom English is an additional language into the meaning. But there is more you can do.

1. You will want to read to children and tell them stories, and, more than that, you will want to find ways of allowing children to create, tell and act out their own stories. We have seen in this book how Vivian Gussin Paley did that with the children in her kindergarten, and you may enjoy reading the book by Anne Hass Dyson called *Writing Superheroes* (1997). In this book, Dyson analysed work with older children, and her interest was in classes where the teachers were focused on getting the children to know that they were allowed to bring their interests into the classroom. Their interests at the time involved superheroes and other figures drawn from popular culture. The children did this through telling stories. Some practitioners use physical devices to encourage the telling of stories – something like 'the author's chair', for example, where the children can take turns to occupy a particular chair which then allows them to be in charge of the story for the day.

2. As you read stories to the children or listen to the stories they tell, pay attention to the opportunities within the stories for children to express their feelings. Sometimes children don't reveal the things that concern, frighten or delight them until they are given permission to do so. Narrative is a wonderful way of doing this. Here is an example, drawn from the work of Paley again. In *The Kindness of Children*, Paley writes about eight-year-old Carrie telling her what she calls a riddle.

> 'Every day you look for someone who likes you and sometimes you think you found a friend, but the next day you have to start again' – a complete and sad story about her struggle to make friends. (1999: 120–1)

3. You will remember Bruner's insistence that stories and narrative allow children and others to explore universals such as love and hate, fear and anger, right and wrong, jealousy and rivalry and so on. It is important for you to think carefully about the stories you tell the children and even more carefully about the stories they tell you so that you can identify what serious issues concern them so that you can follow up if necessary. In the example of Carrie cited above, this is how Paley responded.

> I put an arm around Carrie and waited. She has more to say but once the words are spoken they can no longer be disguised as a riddle ... 'The kids hate me,' she says simply. Four decades of teaching do not lessen the shock of her words ... 'Here's why they hate me so much. The way I talk. And my laugh is stupid. And I never get a joke so I have this dumb look on my face they can't stand ...' (Paley, 1999: 121)

Paley's ability to tune into the real theme of Carrie's little riddle enabled her to take steps to help the child deal with bullying

4. Another feature of narrative is that of things not having to be spelled out. If you are asking children to write something factual you need all the details. But narrative allows the writer, the author, to force the reader to do some work. I recently took some children to the theatre. They are children used to television, DVDs, computers, Wiis and other wonders of the technological world. And I was amazed to find that these children were unable to suspend disbelief. When one of the characters pointed to the ceiling of the theatre and said, 'Oh, look at the birds flying overhead', the children did not look up and were amazed that I did. They said, 'We didn't look up because we knew there couldn't be any birds inside

the building.' We need to give children the chance to imagine and to make us imagine with them. So develop your confidence in telling stories as well as reading them. And when you tell stories use complex language that uses metaphor and simile and that paints pictures in the minds of the children. Of course you need to be sensitive to the need for some children to have visual clues, and this could be one reason for organising some story sessions with visual resources and some without.

5. Geertz, the anthropologist, talked of using 'thick description' and meant that different points of view can give a more nuanced view of something. This is particularly true of young children, who will reveal different aspects of themselves and their development to different people or in different contexts. You will know this and in all probability already ensure that all those involved with the child are involved in contributing to developing a clear picture of how each child is progressing.

6. Another rather obvious implication is that relating to the expectations you have of the children in your care. It is really important to keep reminding yourself that all children however young, whatever home they come from, whatever languages they speak are competent, curious, hypothesis-making, social and interactive beings, eager to communicate and to learn. Having high expectations means that you will ensure that you offer a curriculum that allows all children to build on their prior experience and to raise and answer questions and to communicate.

Assessment

How can assessment enhance learning?

13

Readings

13.1 Margy Whalley
Creating a dialogue with parents (p. 258)

13.2 Patricia Broadfoot
Assessment: Why, who, when, what and how? (p. 262)

13.3 Andrew Burrell and Sara Bubb
Teacher feedback in the reception class (p. 268)

13.4 Scottish Government
Reporting on progress and achievement (p. 271)

13.5 Andrew Pollard and Ann Filer
The myth of objective assessment (p. 275)

13.6 Cathy Nutbrown
Watching and listening: The tools of assessment (p. 281)

The readings in this chapter provide clarification of types of assessment and suggest the positive contribution assessment can make to teaching and learning in the early years.

We begin with a reading from Margy Whalley, which discusses working with parents and creating relationships with them through which it becomes possible to include them in assessment processes. This is followed by a reading which asks the important questions about why assess? who ought to be conducting any assessments? and how this ought to be done. The third reading reports on a small-scale study which focused on the nature of the feedback given to two children. The authors take some of the big issues in assessment and ground them in reception classroom practice.

We then turn to government and policy perspectives on assessment with a reading from the Scottish Government, alongside a reading which argues that National Curriculum Assessment procedures cannot produce 'objective' evidence of pupil, teacher or school performance. Finally, we return to the tools at the heart of assessment processes in ECEC-watching and listening.

On *reflectiveteaching.co.uk*, updated sources for further study are provided in *Notes for Further Reading*.

Reading 13.1

Creating a dialogue with parents
Margy Whalley

> The need for settings to work more closely with parents was recognized by the School Curriculum and Assessment Authority in 1996. However – as pointed out by Margy Whalley in this reading – parents are not a homogenous group; they are as diverse in their needs and abilities as their children. Drawing on her experience at the Pen Green Centre, Whalley reminds us not to judge parents and to recognize that, although most want the best for their children, there are often external financial, health or social pressures which can affect them and their children. This extract supports practitioners in recognizing and building on the positive aspects of different parenting styles. It includes a case study of Janet, a parent using the setting in a holistic way. Does this resonate with any of your experiences of working with parents?
>
> *Edited from:* Whalley, M. (1997) *Working With Parents.* London: Hodder Education, 5–9.

… when we draw children, parents and families into our early childhood centres I think we should be sure that what we are about is making these people strong, providing them with the means to reshape their destinies, giving them a measure of control and influence about what goes on, encouraging them to stop accepting their lot and start creating the world they would like to be part of. (Chris Pascal, April 1996)

Working in partnership with parents can be painful and difficult for us as early childhood educators but it can also be enormously rewarding. Most parents are deeply committed to their children's learning and development. Also, parents have a critical role as their child's primary educator in the early years. Children are much happier and achieve more when early years educators work together with their parents.

Since parents are not an homogenous group they all have different needs and different starting points. They will want to get involved in their children's early years settings in very different ways. They will need to make their own priorities, negotiate their own learning and do this in their own time.

Focusing on their children

Some parents may want to know more about their children's learning. Many of the parents who have worked with us at Pen Green over the last fourteen years have been very interested in their children's development. When parents are first offered a nursery place for their child they are encouraged to watch and record their child's persistent concerns at home. Many become fascinated by the repeated patterns they observe within their children's play. Some parents, supported by experienced staff, have kept diaries, others record what they see their children doing on audio tapes or using camcorders. Over the last few years parents have become very involved in a nursery-based research project. They have attended daytime and evening sessions to compare notes with nursery staff and watch video tapes of their children playing in nursery and at home. Together parents and staff have built up information about their children's learning which has supported our curriculum planning in the nursery.

Focusing on parents' own learning needs

For some parents getting their child a place in a nursery or day care centre is a very important first step in that it gives them the time and the space to consider their own learning needs. It may be that they are interested in attending a group on assertiveness, or massage and aromatherapy, or perhaps a short course on basic typing skills. They may want to develop their numeracy or literacy skills as a way to get back into work. Parents sometimes want to undertake GCSEs and A levels in a supportive environment or perhaps want to undertake longer-term Open University Community Education courses such as the new *Confident Parents, Confident Children* study pack. Other parents may want to attend groups that help and support them and keep them informed, such as a single parents' support group or a support group for parents with children who have special educational needs. In these groups parents get time and space to discuss their own concerns and their children's issues.

Focusing on other people

Parents may want to start their involvement careers in your setting by doing things that help your centre or by doing things for other people in the community. Having been at home for years doing things for their children and their families they are most comfortable and confident in the role. Parents successfully run services such as playgroups, parent and toddler groups, toy libraries and nursery bookshops in many early years settings. It is important to offer parents training and support if they are running services of this kind. It will also be important sometimes to make a member of staff available from your own setting of from another agency to work alongside them.

Parents can have a vital role in the management committee. Parent representatives are elected by other parents and represent their views and make policy alongside senior officers from funding agencies. In many early years settings parents now act as governors and managers. This is a very positive way for parents to express their own commitment both to the local community and to improving services for children and families.

Working in a holistic way

The most effective parenting programmes in early years settings combine at least some aspects of all three of these approaches.

1 **Action for children** – when the focus is on children and the parents are encouraged to watch their children, learn more about their children's learning process and perhaps work towards a qualification as an early years educator themselves.

2 **Action for parents** – when the focus is on parent's own learning and doing things for themselves. This could mean claiming their own right to an education second time around, or building up their own self-esteem.

3 **Action for others (citizenship)** – when the focus is on parents coordinating groups and activities that help other people, or when parents take responsibility for managing and running early years services.

In the past, professionals often assumed parents would start in one particular way, gain confidence and gradually get more involved in what was going on in a setting, following a kind of linear 'route'. This is only one way that parents can use parenting programmes. Figure 13.1.1 provides an example of such routes. Many other parents, it is now recognised, want to access more than one kind of experience at the same time.

Figure 13.1.1
Parents' routes
through the Centre

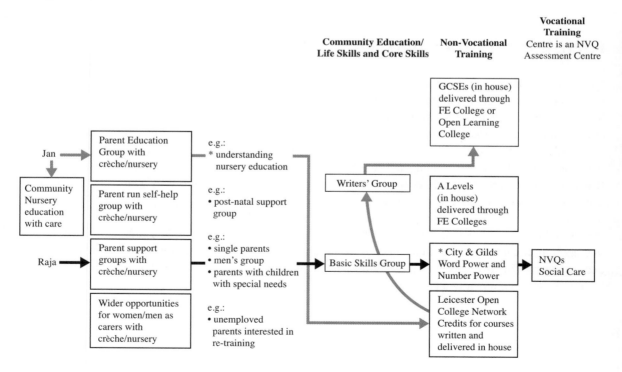

Janet is a good example of a parent who uses early childhood settings in this kind of holistic way.

Janet was a single parent with four daughters under six years. When she started using the Centre she always kept her coat on, ready for a quick getaway. She always looked down when she talked to adults. Janet was very vulnerable: she had just moved into the estate and knew no-one.

Action for herself as a parent

During the first few months she began using a support group where she was able to talk about what was going on in her life to other women experiencing similar pressure. When she became pregnant she joined the Great Expectations group run by a parent and a midwife. (This group offers support to parents who have experienced stillbirth and/or miscarriage.)

Action for her children

Two of Janet's children were attending the nursery. Cath, her key worker, invited Janet to start sharing information about both her daughters' development and play at home. For a whole year, Janet kept audio tapes of her children's experiences at home. She identified the patterns in her daughters' play and shared her observations with the nursery staff. Particularly, she commented on her daughter Katey's preoccupation with putting things inside other things and playing with bag, baskets and boxes. The nursery staff were able to tell her that Katey loved putting herself inside things when she was in nursery, e.g. the toy washing machine, the tent, the parachute or enclosing herself with the building blocks. Janet decided to support her child's learning at Christmas by buying her a big pink bag instead of the usual gifts from toy shops. Katey loved the bag and filled it with objects both at home and at nursery.

Janet got very excited by and involved in her daughters' learning so she joined an informal parent education group to find out more about children's educational needs.

Janet made all the decisions about the level, nature and timing of her involvement in the adult community education programme. Most recently, after watching videos of her daughter in the nursery she and her partner made a video of their four daughters and new baby playing at home. This home video has informed the nursery staff's planning for children's learning.

Janet has taken herself seriously as a student. She has also gained confidence as a parent and recognises the major contribution she has made as her children's first educator.

Reading 13.2

Assessment: Why, who, when, what and how?
Patricia Broadfoot

This reading provides a wide-ranging overview of most of the key issues in the use of assessment in education. It demonstrates that beyond the apparent simplicity of the results, with which we are all familiar, lie crucial issues about purposes, processes and effects. Assessment is also powerful – in measuring or accrediting performance, enhancing or distorting learning, and in many other ways. Expert practitioners need to understand it, and use it beneficially.

Which aspect of assessment, as reviewed by Broadfoot, are most relevant to your practice?

Edited from: Broadfoot, P. (2007) *Assessment Policy and Practice: The 21st Century Challenge For Educational Assessment.* London: Continuum, 3–14.

Introducing assessment

Assessment should be 'the faithful servant and not the dominating master' of teaching and learning (Mortimore and Mortimore, 1984). An essential first step to achieving this is the development of 'assessment literacy' amongst all those with responsibility for teaching and learning in institutions. Teachers, lecturers and education professionals of all kinds now readily accept that an understanding of the central issues around assessment and an ability to use assessment constructively is a key element of their professional repertoire of skills.

The scope of assessment

In seeking to understand the role that assessment plays in educational activity, it is convenient to divide the discussion in terms of five central questions. The first of these is the most profound, namely: why do we assess? For it is in the light of the decision about purpose that we may consider other options – who is to be assessed and who is to do the assessing, what is to be assessed, when is it to be assessed, and how is the assessment to be undertaken?

Why assess?

Four generic purposes of assessment were identified by the Task Group on Assessment and Testing for England and Wales – the body which provided the blueprint for the original national assessment system. These were:

- diagnostic assessment to identify students' learning needs;
- formative assessment to support and encourage learning;
- summative assessment to identify learning outcomes
- evaluative assessment which is directed at assessing the quality of provision in institutions and in the system as a whole. (DES, 1988)

A more sociological way of looking at the question of assessment purposes identifies the four functions of educational assessment as:

- certification of achievement (competence)
- selection (competition)
- the evaluation of provision (content)
- the control of both individual aspirations and systemic functioning (control) (Broadfoot, 1996)

Clearly, assessment serves a number of different purposes. Many of the purposes for which assessment is used are based on assumptions about its utility and effect which are rarely questioned. Our schools and universities, colleges and training centres are increasingly driven by assessment requirements. Yet, despite the enormous impact of this culture on all our lives, its desirability is rarely questioned, its effects rarely debated. The undoubted convenience of tried and tested assessment procedures underpins a web of assumptions and practices that seems almost inevitable.

In the past, it would have been possible to make a broad distinction concerning the overall purpose of assessment between its retrospective role in measuring and reporting past learning and achievement as in, for example, exam certificates, and its prospective role in identifying future potential and aptitudes when it is used as the basis for selection. However, recently there has developed a great deal of interest among academics and teachers about the ways in which assessment can be used to support the learning process itself. This is often expressed as a distinction between assessment for, rather than assessment of, learning. It is a development that has considerable significance in terms of how we think about assessment in that it has opened up the spectrum of assessment purposes much more widely.

Central to such considerations is the distinction between 'formative' and 'summative' assessment.

- Formative assessment is intended to contribute directly to the learning process through providing feedback which models success and guides future efforts, as well as giving encouragement.
- Summative assessment is a point in time measure. It is for 'checking up' or 'summing up' what an individual learner has achieved. It is often associated with reporting, certification and selection.

In discussing the purposes of assessment, it is also useful to make a distinction between assessment for curriculum, that is assessment which is an integral part of the ongoing teaching and learning process and assessment for communication which concerns all those aspects of assessment which have to do with providing information for potential users, whether this is about students, teachers, institutions or systems. Although there are many parallels here to the distinction between formative and summative assessment, the distinction between assessment for curriculum and assessment for communication makes more emphatic the fundamental tension between the different roles of educational assessment.

At one extreme of the continuum of assessment purposes is the 'diagnostic discourse' – the private evaluative conversation that both teachers and students engage in their heads as they monitor the learning process on an on-going basis. 'How am I doing? This is so boring! Will I be finished first?' are some of the thoughts that may typically be going through learners' minds. 'Is she paying attention? He looks unhappy – he may need me to explain this again' – are some of the many monitoring observations teachers will make as part of their internal 'diagnostic discourse'.

By contrast, the collection of marks and grades that typically sits in books and on record forms and reports is much more likely to be 'dead data'. It often makes very little contribution to the business of teaching and learning itself where its primary function is reporting progress, accountability and selection. (Broadfoot, 1996)

It should already be apparent that there is a fundamental tension between the two broad roles of assessment – for curriculum and for communication.

Who assesses?

This question is closely related, clearly, to the previous one of 'why assess'? The purpose of assessment will dictate who carries it out. The decision will also be influenced by who is paying for the assessment. A moment's thought will serve to highlight the inherent tensions between the purposes that teachers and other professionals might have for assessment as opposed to the candidates themselves, parents, the government and society as a whole. There will be aspects of common ground between these various groups in their shared concern with quality and with the need for fairness, but there will be important differences of emphasis too. For Government, for example, the acceptability of the assessment, its perceived legitimacy by the public, is usually paramount. For parents, by contrast, the priority may be that of motivation or minimizing the degree of stress the assessment causes for their children. However, traditionally and still today, most assessment has been conducted by those responsible for teaching.

More recently, however, two other partners have joined the ranks of the assessors. The first of these is the students themselves who, increasingly, are being called upon to engage in self-assessment and also assessment of each other, as a means of helping them understand their own learning. The other new member of the assessment team is the government. Although school inspectors are a familiar feature of most education systems, in recent years the activities of these individuals have been greatly strengthened by the advent of various new kinds of monitoring device aimed at enhancing both the accountability and the overall performance of the education system. It is the advent of the government as a major source of assessment which is fundamental to the advent of assessment as a key policy tool.

What is assessed?

Traditionally, most forms of formal student assessment have involved reading and writing – the so-called 'paper and pencil tests'. However, traditional tests and exams cover a very small portion of the potential range of skills, competencies and aptitudes that might usefully be included. As long ago as 1992, an influential report suggested that all the following aspects are potential areas for assessment:

- written expression, knowledge retention, organization of material, appropriate selection...
- practical, knowledge application, oral, investigative skills...
- personal and social skills, communication and relationships, working in groups, initiative, responsibility, self-reliance, leadership...
- motivation and commitment, perseverance, self-confidence, constructive acceptance of failure... (Hargreaves, 1992)

Hargreaves subsequently stressed the particular importance of 'learning how to learn' (Hargreaves, 2004).

Perhaps the most central point to bear in mind in any consideration of what is to be assessed is that the assessment tail tends to wag the curriculum dog. Teachers and students both know very well that what is assessed will be likely to form the priorities for learning, just as governments have recently realised that what is assessed in terms of institutional quality and subsequently translated into the indicators which form the basis of public judgement and league tables, is also likely to be a key driver of institutional priorities. This phenomenon, often called 'the washback effect', is one of the most important, yet least often studied aspects of assessment.

When to assess

At first sight this may seem a less important question. However, the issue of when to assess closely reflects the underlying purpose of the assessment. Clearly, teachers' monitoring of students' understanding and engagement is likely to be continuous. If the major purpose of assessment is to encourage better learning, the need for good quality feedback is likely to be frequent.

However, assessment which is more about communication and accountability, is likely to be more spasmodic and come at the end of a particular unit of learning. This might be, for example, for coursework assessment or school reports. Assessment for certification and/or national monitoring might take place at the end of a key stage of schooling. Assessment for selection is likely to take place when there is the need for a choice to be made, either because there is a requirement to ration among those potentially qualified, and to choose the best of this group, or because such assessment is needed to help students themselves make choices about where to go next.

Where the focus is not student learning but institutional performance, the decision about when to assess is likely to be driven as much by practicalities such as cost and the availability of suitable personnel, as by more educational concerns. School inspections, for example, demanding as they are in terms of preparation and time, are likely not to take place more often than every few years. However, internal self-evaluation for the same purpose, given its more formative character, is likely to be a much more ongoing process.

It should, therefore, be clear that there is a subtle interaction between decisions about what the assessment is for, what is to be assessed and when the assessment should take place.

How to assess

Reference has already been made to the various forms that evidence for assessment purposes might take. This includes insights gained from informal questioning, from diagnostic tests, from various kinds of observation, self-assessment documents, portfolios and appraisal reports, as well as more conventional teacher assessments and tests and external examinations. Formal public examination is the most visible expression of assessment activity, but it is certainly the tip of a much larger iceberg.

Fundamental to any decision regarding 'how to assess' is the issue of purpose, as this will drive the kind of comparison for which the data generated will be used. Perhaps the most familiar type of assessment is norm-referenced, in which candidates are compared with one another. This is an approach that is closely associated with competition. Apart from the widespread belief that such competition is motivating for learners, as in, for example, sport, it has also arisen because of the need for assessment that discriminates between individuals where a selection has to be made.

However, a great deal of assessment has always been, and remains, what is called 'criterion-referenced assessment', that is, assessment in relation to a standard. Some of the earliest forms of assessment were of this kind. In practice, of course, many tests have elements of both. The process of deciding, for example, the appropriate level children ought to achieve in a national curriculum assessment, has been initially identified by some exercise in norm-referencing, although the assessment itself will be criterion-referenced. Driving tests are often cited as the classic example of a criterion-referenced test since they lay down the competencies an individual needs to demonstrate if they are to be allowed a driving license. However, here again, the decision about what constitutes competence has, at some point, been made on a more norm-referenced basis.

The key distinction here is that, where the emphasis is on criterion-referenced assessment, the goal is that the assessed, whether this is an individual student, a group of students, a teacher or an institution, should be capable of being successful and that all those who do meet this defined standard should pass the test. In contrast, a norm-referenced test is almost inevitably associated with a number of candidates failing, in that it distributes those being assessed in terms of the best to the worst.

More recently, a third basis for comparing performance has become widely recognised. This is so-called ipsative assessment in which the standard for comparison is that of the individual learner with himself or herself. Here the concern is to identify an individual learner's progress in relation to their own previous performance. Ipsative assessment is an approach that is, of course, just as relevant for institutions and systems as it is for individuals. It is closely associated with the more recent development of interest in assessment for learning as part of the overall concern with formative assessment.

Two other crucial concepts are needed in the toolbox of the assessor when thinking about 'how to assess'. These are the concepts of reliability and validity. These terms are now very widely used and have become a familiar part of professional vocabulary. Reliability simply relates to the dependability of an assessment. It reflects the degree of confidence that if a different test was to be used or a student was to be re-tested on some future occasion, the result would be broadly similar.

Validity, on the other hand, concerns the degree to which an assessment is a faithful representation of what it purports to be assessing. There are several ways of looking at validity. 'Face validity' refers to whether the assessment being used is convincing in terms of its content as a test of the skill or knowledge in question. 'Construct validity' is by contrast, a more technical term that refers to the extent to which the assessment represents the underlying knowledge or skill that it is intended to.

Validity has been a particular problem in relation to standardised multiple choice testing. This is because such tests cannot easily represent a real-life performance situation. As a result there is now a powerful trend towards more teacher assessment in the pursuit of more 'authentic evidence' of student achievement through more 'performance-based' assessment. It is increasingly being recognised that a great deal of important information about student competencies has not, in the past, been captured because of the limitations of so-called 'objective' tests. Unfortunately, efforts to introduce more complex and authentic tasks which are capable of capturing some of the more ephemeral learning objectives, such as 'creativity', have often been bedevilled by the almost inevitably low levels of reliability.

The tension between reliability and validity is one of the most enduring features of contemporary educational assessment as it weaves its way through many of the debates that take place around the questions of why, who, when, what and how.

Reading 13.3

Teacher feedback in the reception class
Andrew Burrell and Sara Bubb

> This reading takes some of the big issues in assessment and grounds them in reception classroom practice. It reports on a small-scale study which focused on the nature of the feedback given to two children, Richard and Jane, in a reception class. Teacher feedback was observed and categorized using a typology developed by Caroline Gipps and her colleagues (1996). This is thus also a nice example of the application of research for professional reflection.
>
> Are there any significant patterns in the forms of feedback that you offer children?
>
> *Edited from:* Burrell, A. and Bubb, S. (2000) 'Teacher feedback in the reception class', *Education*, 3–13 (28), 3.

Children in school need to feel secure and happy in order to meet the challenges presented to them through the school curriculum, particularly learning to read and write. The class teacher and other adults are likely to play a particularly important part in achieving this. One aspect of their interaction with the children concerns the kind of feedback given. Such feedback might contribute to the children's emotional and social adjustment. Moreover, it may affect their attitude and behaviour in response to the intellectual demands that are made on them.

Research conducted by Gipps et al. (1996) observed the process of feedback to children by primary teachers. It was suggested that the feedback serves three functions. First, as part of the classroom socialisation process. This would seem to be particularly important in the child's first year in school. Second, it serves to encourage the children and maintain motivation and effort. Finally, it identifies specific aspects of attainment or good performance in relation to a specific task. Through their research, Gipps et al. (1996) were able to generate a typology of teacher feedback. Details of this typology are provided in Table 13.3.1.

Table 13.3.1 Teacher feedback typology: A summary

	Type A	Type B	Type C	Type D	
1 POSITIVE FEEDBACK	A1 Rewarding	B1 Approving	C1 Specifying attainment	D1 Constructing achievement	1 ACHIEVEMENT FEEDBACK
	rewards	positive personal expression; warm expression of feeling; general praises; positive non-verbal feedback	specific acknowledgement of attainment/use of criteria in relation to work/behaviour; teacher models; more specific praise	mutual articulation of achievement; additional use of emerging criteria child role in presentation; praise integral to description	
2 NEGATIVE FEEDBACK	A2 Punishing	B2 Disapproving	C2 Specifying improvement	D2 Constructing the way forward	2 IMPROVEMENT FEEDBACK
	punishing	negative personal expression; reprimands; negative generalisations; negative non-verbal feedback	correction of errors; more practice given; training in self checking	mutual critical appraisal	

We conducted a small-scale study to examine the nature and frequency of verbal feedback in the reception class in relation to adjustment to school. The class teacher was asked to nominate two children, one who they thought had adjusted poorly to school and the other who they considered had adjusted very well. This required her to make a personal judgement based on her own construct of 'adjustment'. In the case study Jane was considered by her class teacher to be very well adjusted to school. In contrast, Richard was considered to be poorly adjusted to school. These two children were in a class of 27 pupils, 15 of whom were full-time from September. The data were collected using a form of semi-structured observational event sampling. This required the observer to focus on the two children throughout the day and to record the types of feedback that each received. The observation was divided into five minute intervals, in which significant events were recorded.

The structured observations were then considered in relation to the typology of feedback suggested by Gipps et al. (see Table 13.3.2). Striking differences can be observed. In terms of positive feedback, Jane who is considered by her class teacher to be well adjusted, received feedback which is both rewarding and approving. In contrast, Richard, the child considered by his class teacher to be poorly adjusted receives no positive feedback from any of the adults he comes into contact with in the classroom during the course of the day. If we consider negative feedback, the poorly adjusted child receives a high proportion of feedback which can be regarded as 'disapproving'. In addition to this there were also two occasions of feedback in which the child was punished. The well adjusted child received no such negative feedback.

Table 13.3.2 Frequency of teacher feedback

	Type A	Type B	Type C	Type D	
1 POSITIVE FEEDBACK	A1 Rewarding	B1 Approving	C1 Specifying attainment	D1 Constructing achievement	1 ACHIEVEMENT FEEDBACK
Richard	0	0	0	0	
Jane	3	4	0	1	
2 NEGATIVE FEEDBACK	A2 Punishing	B2 Disapproving	C2 Specifying improvement	D2 Constructing the way forward	2 IMPROVEMENT FEEDBACK
Richard	2	14	7	2	
Jane	0	0	0	2	

Richard, the poorly adjusted child, did receive feedback of the 'improvement' kind (C2). This was mainly in the form of descriptive feedback whereby the teacher specified how something being learned could be corrected. Feedback of this kind is specific to a particular task or aspect of behaviour and is focused on where mistakes lie. Both children received feedback which prompted and supported them to examine their work and to make comparisons with their previous performance. This was usually in the form of a dialogue between the teacher and child.

Overall, tracking the children over the course of the day provided only one example of feedback of the 'constructing achievement' kind. This was targeted to Jane, the child who was considered by the class teacher to be well-adjusted. It is interesting to note the absence of feedback which was concerned with attainment and achievement.

The child's first year at school marks for most children the transition from home into a school setting. Research supports the need for an early positive adjustment to school and the benefits this has on future learning. Teacher feedback has a crucial role in such adjustment. In our child-focused observations, sharp differences existed in the kinds of feedback given to those children who had, according to the class teacher, adjusted very well to school and those who had not. We might speculate that if this was representative of the feedback they received on a daily basis there would either be an upward spiral or, of more concern, a downward one in their attitudes towards school and learning.

Reading 13.4

Reporting on progress and achievement
Scottish Government

> The following reading, taken from the Scottish Government's 'Principles of Assessment in Curriculum for Excellence', considers the purpose of assessment, how assessment is linked to learning and teaching and the recording of progress.
>
> Consider the five points provided in section 1 in relation to the curriculum you work with. Do these points align with what you believe the purpose of assessment to be? Do you use assessment in each of these ways?
>
> *Edited from:* Scottish Government (2011) *Principles of Assessment in Curriculum for Excellence, Building the Curriculum 5: A Framework for Assessment.* Edinburgh: Scottish Government.

Reflecting the values and principles of Curriculum for Excellence

Curriculum for Excellence sets out the values, purposes and principles of the curriculum for 3 to 18. The revised assessment system is driven by the curriculum and so necessarily reflects these values and principles. *A Framework for Assessment* is designed to support the purposes of Curriculum for Excellence. The purposes of assessment are to:

- support learning that develops the knowledge and understanding, skills, attributes and capabilities which contribute to the four capacities
- give assurance to parents and carers, children themselves, and others, that children and young people are progressing in their learning and developing in line with expectations
- provide a summary of what learners have achieved, including through qualifications and awards
- contribute to planning the next stages of learning and help learners progress to further education, higher education and employment
- inform future improvements in learning and teaching

Designing, discussions, tasks and activities

Assessment is part of the process of directing learning and teaching towards outcomes through enriched experiences and needs to be planned as such. Staff need to design effective discussions, tasks and activities that elicit evidence of learning. They need to ensure that assessment is fit for purpose by carefully considering the factors outlined in the previous section.

Figure 13.4.1
Questions for
developing a
Curriculum for
Excellence

Staff should consider the following questions:

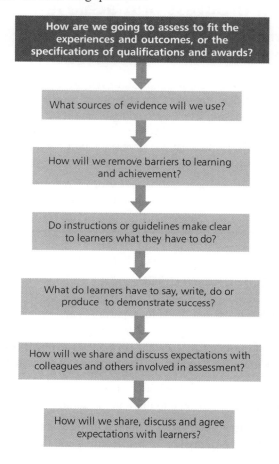

Staff should plan discussions, tasks and activities so that learners can provide evidence of their knowledge and skills from a range of sources and with choice of approach. These should include both in-school and out-of-school activities and should provide opportunities for learners to progress over time and across a range of activities. Staff should decide, with learners, on the most appropriate approach to assessment for a particular outcome or set of outcomes.

Sources of evidence can include:

- observations of learners carrying out tasks and activities, including practical investigations, performances, oral presentations and discussions
- records (oral, written, audio-visual) created by children and young people which may include self-assessment and/or peer assessment or may be assessed by the teacher

- information obtained through questioning in high quality interactions and dialogue
- written responses
- a product, for example, piece of artwork, report, project
- accounts provided by others (parents, other children or young people, or other staff) about what learners have done

Staff should consider ways to remove any unnecessary barriers including ensuring that language used to describe what is expected of learners is accessible. They should consider the amount of support required to ensure fairness and provide sufficient challenge.

In designing assessments staff should decide what would be appropriate evidence of achievement. This should involve reviewing exemplar materials, including those available through the National Assessment Resource, deciding on what learners would need to say, write, do or produce to demonstrate success and indicate, for example:

- expected responses to questions
- expected skills and attributes to be demonstrated
- success criteria for performances and products

Consideration should be given to how to reflect, share, discuss and agree these expectations with learners and with colleagues.

For specifically designed assessment tasks or tests, teachers should make sure that learners are clear about what they have to do. How assessment is carried out can provide opportunities for learners to demonstrate a number of skills, for example higher order thinking skills, working with others, enterprise and employability.

Assessment of interdisciplinary learning

Carefully planned interdisciplinary learning provides good opportunities to promote deeper understanding by applying knowledge and understanding and skills in new situations and taking on new challenges. Interdisciplinary learning can take place not only across classes and departments, but also in different contexts and settings involving different partners, including colleges and youth work organisations.

This requires careful planning to ensure validity and reliability. Interdisciplinary learning needs to be firmly focused on identified experiences and outcomes within and across curriculum areas, with particular attention to ensuring progression in knowledge and understanding, skills, attributes and capabilities.

Recording progress and achievements

It is important that staff keep regularly updated records of children's and young people's progress and achievements. These should be based on evidence of learning. Learners and staff will need to select whatever best demonstrates the 'latest and best' exemplars of learning and achievement.

Much recording will take place during day-to-day learning and teaching activities. In addition, staff will periodically complete profiles of individual and groups of learners when they have been looking in-depth at a particular aspect of learning.

Approaches to recording should be:

- manageable and practicable within day-to-day learning and teaching
- selective and focused on significant features of performance

Effective recording can be used as a focus for discussions during personal learning planning to identify next steps in learning. It also helps staff to ensure that appropriate support and challenge in learning is in place for each child and young person. It can be used to share success with staff, learners and parents.

Reading 13.5

The myth of objective assessment
Andrew Pollard and Ann Filer

This reading highlights the social factors that inevitably affect assessment processes, performance and the interpretation of assessment outcomes. The consequence, it is argued, is that National Curriculum Assessment procedures cannot produce 'objective' evidence of learner, teacher or school performance. While much assessment evidence may have valuable uses in supporting learning, it is thus an insecure source of comparative data for accountability purposes.

How do circumstances affect assessment in your setting? Do you see that the children in your care will move into these problems as they leave your setting and move on in statutory education?

Edited from: Pollard, A. and Filer, A. (2000) *The Social World of Pupil Assessment: Processes and Contexts of Primary Schooling*. London: Continuum, 8–11.

The assessment of educational performance is of enormous significance in modern societies. In particular, official assessment procedures are believed to provide 'hard evidence' on which governments, parents and the media evaluate educational policies and hold educational institutions to account; pupil and student learners are classified and counselled on life-course decisions; and employers make judgements about recruitment.

Underpinning such confident practices is a belief that educational assessments are sufficiently objective, reliable and impartial to be used in these ways. But is this belief supported by evidence? Can the results of nationally required classroom assessments be treated as being factual and categoric?

Our longitudinal, ethnographic research (Filer and Pollard, 2000) focused on social processes and taken-for-granted practices in schools and homes during the primary years. In particular, it documented their influence on three key processes: the production of pupil performance, the assessment of pupil performance and the interpretation of such judgements. On the basis of this analysis we argue that, despite both politicians' rhetoric and the sincere efforts of teachers, the pure 'objectivity' of assessment outcomes is an illusion. More specifically, we suggest that:

- individual pupil performances cannot be separated from the contexts and social relations from within which they develop;

- classroom assessment techniques are social processes that are vulnerable to bias and distortion;

- the 'results' of assessment take their meaning for individuals via cultural processes of interpretation and following mediation by others.

Our argument thus highlights various ways in which social processes inevitably intervene in assessment.

In this reading we confine ourselves to describing and selectively illustrating the core analytic framework which we have constructed. In particular, we identify five key questions concerned with assessment. These are set out in Figure 13.5.1.

Figure 13.5.1
Questions concerning social influences on assessment

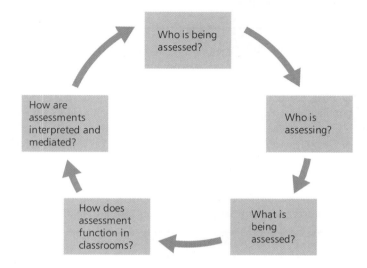

Who is being assessed?

The key issue here concerns the pupil's personal sense of identity. Put directly, each pupil's performance fulfils and represents his or her sense of self-confidence and identity as a learner.

We see self-perceptions held by individuals and judgements made about individuals as being inextricably linked to the social relationships through which they live their lives. Of course, there certainly are factors that are internal to the individual in terms of capacities and potentials, but realisation of such attributes is a product of external social circumstances and social relationships to a very significant extent (see Pollard with Filer, 1996). Amongst these are school assessments, of various forms, which constitute formalised, partial, but very powerful social representations of individuals. In our full account (Filer and Pollard, 2000), we provide extensive case-study examples of such influences on the development of children's identities – for instance, through the story of Elizabeth and her primary school career.

In the autumn of 1988, five-year-old Elizabeth entered Mrs Joy's reception class with about twenty seven other children and began her schooling at Albert Park. She was a physically healthy, attractive and lively child and assessments made during that first year relate to such characteristics, as well as to her intellectual and linguistic competence. Teacher records recorded a range of Elizabeth's communication, physical and intellectual skills.

Vocabulary good – a clear ability to express herself – confident – can communicate with adults. Can concentrate and talk about her observations.
Good language and fine motor skills – reading now enthusiastic – writing good.
Can organise herself, is able to take turns.
(Profile for Nursery and Reception Age Children, Summer 1989, Reception)

However, Mrs Joy perceived Elizabeth's classroom relationships in a more negative light, as her records from the time also show:

Elizabeth is loud during class activity time – she never looks particularly happy unless doing something she shouldn't be. Elizabeth is a loud boisterous child who needs constant correction of negative behaviour. When corrected she often cries and becomes morose for a short period. Elizabeth doesn't mix well with the girls and disrupts them at any given opportunity. (Teacher records, Reception, 1988–9)

Elizabeth's mother related to her daughter's identity as a girl and a wish that she was 'more dainty' and, in the opinion of her Year 2 teacher, a wish that she could have 'a neat, quiet child'. Certainly Eleanor Barnes held gendered expectations regarding the learning styles of girls and boys. Though, of course, she certainly wished for Elizabeth to do well at school, she revealed in many of her conversations in interview an expectation for a physical and intellectual passivity in girls that Elizabeth did not conform to. For instance:

… I mean, in some ways I think she should have been a boy because she's got so much energy, and she just wants to know about everything – How does this work? Why does it work like that? What do you do with this? – I mean, probably that is her. That is her personality. She wants to know everything and she wants to know what everybody else is doing. (Eleanor Barnes, parent interview with Ann Filer, July 1995, Year 6)

Even these brief illustrative snippets of data convey the interaction between the evolving identity of children and the views and actions of significant others in their lives. The data demonstrates just how diverse, complex and enduring such influences can be. However, variability in such social support for children is likely to be echoed by variability of their performance – with the result that this may not reflect their true potential. Performance is thus, in part, a social product which reflects self-belief and circumstances.

Who is assessing?

Having argued that pupil identity can only be understood in context, we clearly need to focus on teachers – since they are undoubtedly the most powerful classroom participants with whom pupils must interact.

In particular, we need a sociological conception of pedagogy and its link to each teacher's own sense of personal identity. For this, we have used the concept of 'coping strategy' and traced how satisfying role expectations and the constant pressures of teaching must be balanced with maintaining sense of personal integrity and fulfilment. In the immediacy of classroom dynamics, this can be seen as teachers juggle to resolve endemic dilemmas. At the level of the school, it is played out through negotiation between different interest groups and the formation of taken-for-granted institutional assumptions. In *The Social World of Pupil Assessment* (Filer and Pollard, 2000), we relate such issues to the context of the early 1990s in which the National Curriculum and new assessment requirements were introduced. A case study of Marie Tucker and her classroom practice demonstrates the detailed application of this analysis, showing how her coping strategies, classroom organisation and associated pedagogies produced particular contexts which satisfied her, but within which pupils such as Elizabeth then had to learn and perform. It also documents how Mrs Tucker began to perceive and assess pupils in terms of their actions in relation to her personal criteria.

Teachers thus mediate national policy, and this is likely to be a constructive process as requirements are adapted to particular classroom and pupil circumstances. However, whatever the settlement achieved by the teacher, the pupil has to respond to that situation and accept assessment in terms of his or her teacher's interpretation. This, we argue, will reflect both standard national requirements and local, or personal, adaptions.

What is being assessed?

An official answer to such a question might point to the subject content of a test, or to listed criteria of judgement, and would draw conclusions in terms of the 'attainment' of pupils. More colloquially, inferences about the particular 'abilities' of children may be legitimated by faith in the objectivity and categoric techniques of 'standardised assessment'. However, we argue that such confident conclusions are misplaced, because pupil knowledge, skills and understandings are embedded in particular socio-cultural understandings and further conditioned by factors such as gender, ethnicity and social class.

To put the problem simply, to what extent does National Curriculum Assessment measure the inherent capability of a pupil, and to what extent the influence of socio-economic and cultural factors on a child? Would we be assessing Elizabeth's performance as a distinct entity, or must we also recognise the circumstances that enable or restrict her capabilities? This could lead into an analysis of the material, cultural and social capital available to families, and the extent to which children embody such advantages or disadvantages and are thus more, or less, able to cope with the school curriculum. Similarly, at the level of the peer group, we could focus on the ways in which cultural factors can enable or constrain performance. Whilst the school performance of some children may be enhanced by being with a 'good group of friends', a well understood influence is also that of an anti-learning culture. In many comprehensive schools this is a very serious problem, through which 'swots', 'ear-oles', and 'keeners' are denigrated. Sadly, we also found signs of it in the primary schools we studied, with some children wanting to avoid achievement because 'it's so embarrassing when you get praised by everybody'.

Thus, whilst pupils' subject knowledge, skill or understanding may seem to be 'objectively' revealed by the neutral, standardisation technique of a test or assessment procedure, test results also reveal the facilitation or constraint of socio-cultural influences and forms of understanding. In *The Social World of Pupil Assessment* we illustrated the latter through a detailed analysis of a Year 3 'news' session at Albert Park Primary School. In particular, we showed how classroom meanings were created through interaction of circumstances, strategies and identities, and how language was used to satisfy pupil agendas as well as in response to teacher-led instruction.

Assessment, this analysis suggests, can never tap pure knowledge or capability – any result will also always reflect the wider socio-cultural circumstances of its production. Beyond the formal subject-matter, what else is being assessed?

How does assessment function in classrooms?

To really try to understand classroom assessment, we felt that we needed to trace the links between assessment and other sociologically important influences on classroom life – ideology, language and culture.

As a whole, these factors are played out through particular power relations between teachers and pupils, and have significant consequences for social differentiation. We have explored these ideas drawing on some of Basil Bernstein's work (1975) to analyse how assessment and other classroom processes are bound together in patterns of authority and control. We contrasted ways in which particular forms of assessment give rise to patterns of teacher-pupil relationships and interactions in the teaching process, and patterned goals for learning. In particular, we analysed ways in which testing and other assessment practices associated with 'performance goals' can act to polarise pupil attainment and thus, unwittingly, can promote 'learned helplessness' in some children. Additionally, we considered ways in which contrastive forms of teachers' assessment language can act to promote or inhibit pupils' responses. This highlights the ways in which classroom language is conditioned by patterns and forms of control, which are embedded in teachers' routine, everyday practices.

The consequence of this analysis, we would argue, is that it is not possible for teachers to be 'neutral' in their impact on pupil performance or in their assessment of pupil performance. Irrespective of intentions, each teacher's assessment practices generates a particular set of evaluative circumstances within which interaction with each child takes place. Elizabeth's experience was particular – it was not entirely shared by her classmates, nor was it consistent from year to year. The scope for variability in the overall effect of assessment practices is enormous.

How is assessment interpreted and mediated?

In following-through the assessment process, we needed to consider the various 'audiences' for assessments, with particular reference to families and, to a lesser extent, peers. How do they react to the assessment judgements that are made, and what effect does their reaction have?

For pupils such as Elizabeth, parents, siblings, families and peers are important 'significant others'. We traced their influence throughout our case-study children's lives from age 4 to age 11, and found that their response to seemingly official assessment results was particularly important. Most specifically, in The Social World of Pupil Assessment we analysed how families interpret, mediate and give meaning to assessment outcomes so that their impact on their child is shaped and filtered. Whilst a few parents appeared to take assessment results at face value, far more engaged in supportive conversations with their children. Knowing their children very well, they were able to explore the test outcomes in relation to their previous experiences, aptitudes and future interests. In this way, the personal meaning and significance of the tests was negotiated, endorsed and concluded as the latest episode in the family narrative of each pupil's childhood. Such meanings and conclusions were crucial for future self-confidence and engagement with new learning.

Once again then, we would argue that the outcomes of assessment cannot be seen as categoric and direct in their consequence. Rather, their meaning is malleable and is drawn into existing frames of reference, relationships and patterns of social interaction. For each learner, this is an extremely important process in the development of further phases of their personal narrative and in the construction of identity.

Conclusion

Overall then, in relation to each of the five major questions set out in our cyclical model, we emphasise the influence of social factors on assessment. In particular, learner, assessor, focus, process and interpretation are all embedded in particular socio-cultural contexts and caught up in webs of social relationships.

In such circumstances, we believe that the technical 'objectivity' of assessment is a myth too far. Certainly, it is an insecure foundation on which to base categoric and high-stakes measures of performance for teacher, school and LEA comparison. Indeed, we would go further and argue that because of these, and other, sociological factors, presently established assessment practices are likely to yield patterns and systematic effects which are fundamentally divisive. As a consequence, policy-makers' attempts to configure the education system to meet the demands of international competition, may also unwittingly reinforce social divisions and widen the life-chance gaps which many children already face. The relationship between performance and circumstances cannot be removed or wished away.

Reading 13.6

Watching and listening: The tools of assessment
Cathy Nutbrown

Having considered the wider context within which assessment processes are based, we return to the tools of assessment used within ECEC. Cathy Nutbrown reminds us of the need to assess and the benefits this can bring.

Edited from: Nutbrown, C. (2006), 'Watching and Listening: The Tools of Assessment'. In G. Pugh and B. Duffy (eds) *Contemporary Issues in the Early Years.* London: Sage Publications Ltd, 239–42.

What is assessment?

The word 'assessment' is used in different contexts and taken to mean different things. It refers to at least three different purposes, and there is no single shared understanding in policy or practice. Nutbrown (2006) has suggested three different purposes for assessment in the early years, arguing that different tools are needed for different purposes. Assessment for teaching and learning is the process of identifying the details of children's knowledge, skills and understanding in order to build a detailed picture of a child's development and subsequent learning needs. Assessment for management and accountability prefers scores over narrative accounts of children's learning. Such assessments included the Baseline Assessment system which measured children's progress in predetermined objectives (SCAA, 1997) and allowed the 'value added' by the school to be calculated. Assessment for research includes those assessments (and often tests of 'scales' involving numerical outcomes) which are used specifically in research projects where quickly administered measures are needed and where uniformity of approach is necessary. One such example is the Sheffield Early Literacy Development Profile (Nutbrown, 1997), which was developed to measure aspects of early literacy of 3–5-year-olds. Table 13.6.1 summarizes the characteristics of these three purposes of assessment. Assessment of young children raises a number of concerns in relation to their well-being and self-esteem. Roberts writes:

> Assessment and recording arrangements carry a world of hidden messages for children and parents. Is a positive model used, one which identifies children's special strengths as well as areas for support? Is there accurate and detailed information about children? Do adults make sure that children share their successes, both with their parents and with each other? These questions raise some of the issues which have a direct bearing on how children learn to see themselves. (Roberts, 1995: 115)

Table 13.6.1 Some characteristics of the three purposes of assessment

Assessment for teaching and learning	Assessment for management and accountability	Assessment for research
Focus on individuals	Focus on age cohort	Focus on samples
Concerned with details about each individual learner	Concerned with a sample of group performance	Concerned with performance of the sample
Is ongoing	Occurs within specific time frame	Takes place at planned points in a study
'Takes as long as it takes'	Is briefly administered or completed from previous assessment for teaching	Can be brief, depends on assessment and ages
Needs no numerical outcome to be meaningful	Numerical outcome provides meaning	Numerical outcomes often essential
Is open-ended	Often consists of closed list of items	Often consists of closed items
Informs next teaching steps	Informs management strategy and policy	Informs research decisions, and findings measures outcomes
Information relates primarily to individuals	Information relates Primarily to classes, groups, settings or areas	Information relates to the sample, not to individuals or schools
Assessments required for each child	Some missing cases permissible	Some missing cases permissible
Main purpose is teaching	Main purpose is accountability	Purpose is to add to knowledge
Only useful if information used to guide teaching	Only useful when compared to other outcomes (of other measures of cohorts)	Only useful as evidence of effectiveness of research study
Requires professional insight into children's learning	Requires competence in – administration of the test	Requires competence in administration of the test
Depends on established relationship with individual children to be effective	Can draw on information derived through interaction with individual children, but not dependent on relationship	Often requires no previous relationship, but the ability to establish a rapport with the child at the time of the assessment
Requires ongoing professional development, and experience	Requires short training session, learning the test and practice	Requires short training session, learning the test and practice.

Source: Nutbrown, 1999: 127

Why assess young children's learning and development?

This is a fundamental question in teaching young children. Children's learning is so complex, so rich, so fascinating, so varied, so surprising and so full of enthusiasm that to see it taking place every day, before one's very eyes, is one of the greatest privileges of any early childhood practitioner. The very process of observing and assessing children's learning is, in a sense, its own justification. Watching young children can open our eyes to the astonishing capacity of young children to learn, and shows us the crucial importance of these first few years in children's lives. But there is much more to say about assessing children's learning. Watching young children learn can, at times, make us marvel at their powers to think, to do, to communicate and to create. But observation points to more than our awe at young children's capacities. There is also an important piece of work for early childhood practitioners to understand, to really understand what they see. Several pioneers (Froebel, Piaget, Vygotsky and Isaacs) and more recent figures such as Donaldson (1983), Athey (1990), Elfer et al. (2003) and Nutbrown (1997) have illuminated children's learning and development and provided practitioners with strategies for reflecting upon and inter-preting their observations of children. The rich resource of research and commentary opens up to educators the meanings of children's words, representations and actions. Educators' personal experiences of individual children's learning can help them to see more clearly the general principles that other researchers and educators have established as charac-teristic of that learning. For example, those who work with babies and young children under 3 can draw on the work of Elfer, Goldschmied and Selleck (2003), Goldschmied and Jackson (2004), Abbott and Moylett (1997) and the Birth to Three Matters framework (DfES, 2002) in order to embellish their own understanding of the children with whom they work. When early childhood educators hold up the work of others as a mirror to their own, they can see the essential points of their own work reflected more clearly and better understand the learning and development of the children with whom they work. The published observations of some of the earlier pioneers can be useful to educators now as tools for reflection on children's processes of learning and as a means of moving from the specifics of personal experiences to general understandings about children's thinking. Susan Isaacs, for example, ran an experimental school, The Malting House, in Cambridge from 1924 to 1927. Her compelling accounts of the day-to-day doings of the children in the school show clearly how her analysis of children's intellectual development is the product of a mass of detailed anecdotal insights. For example, she describes (Isaacs, 1929) the development of the basic concepts of biology, change, growth, life and death, and illustrates the process with a rich body of observational evidence as the following show:

18th June 1925

The children let the rabbit out to run about the garden for the first time, to their great delight. They followed him about, stroked him and talked about his fur, his shape and his ways.

13th July 1925

Some of the children called out that the rabbit was dying. They found it in the summer-house, hardly able to move. They were very sorry and talked much about it. They shut it up in the hutch and gave it warm milk.

14th July 1925

The rabbit had died in the night. Dan found it and said: 'It's dead its tummy does not move up and down now'. Paul said, 'My daddy says that if we put it in water it will get alive again'. Mrs I said 'shall we do so and see?' They put it into a bath of water. Some of them said. 'It's alive, because it's moving.' This was a circular motion, due to the currents in the water. Mrs I therefore put a small stick which also moved round and round, and they agreed that the stick was not alive. They then suggested that they should bury the rabbit, and all helped to dig a hole and bury it.

15th July 1925

Frank and Duncan talked of digging the rabbit up – but Frank said, 'It's not there – it's gone up to the sky.' They began to dig, but tired of it and ran off to something else. Later they came back and dug again. Duncan, however, said, 'Don't bother – it's gone – it's up in the sky' and gave up digging. Mrs I therefore said, 'Shall we see if it's there?' and also dug. They found the rabbit, and were very interested to see it still there.

Isaacs's diary entries about the play and questioning of young children formed the basis of her analysis of children's scientific thinking and understanding, and offer rich evidence of the development of children's theories about the world and the things they find in it. Isaacs was able to learn about children's learning through her diligent and meticulous study of her own detailed observations of their play and other activities. Observation as a tool for assessing children's learning is not new, though for some who have not had the opportunity to continue to practise their skills of observation or had time to reflect with colleagues on those observations, these tools may have become a little blunt and may need to be sharpened and polished. However, many researchers and practitioners have followed Isaacs's observational practices; indeed, my own work on young children's learning has been informed by my daily journal jottings (made while working with young children) of children's words, actions and graphic representations (Nutbrown, 1999). Similarly, the pioneering practice of Reggio Emilia in northern Italy is developed largely through careful documentation which includes observations, notes, photographs and reflections upon the children's work as it unfolds in their learning communities (Filippini and Cecchi, 1996; Abbott and Nutbrown, 2001). Goldschmied's (1989) work with babies illustrates the importance of close observation. Watching babies playing with the Treasure Basket can give the adult valuable insights into their learning and development and interactions with others. The following extract from an observation of Matthew shows the fine detail of this 9-month-old's persistent interests:

> Kate places Matthew close enough for him to reach right into the basket. He immediately reaches in with his right hand and selects a long wooden handled spatula. 'Oohh, ahh' he says and looks directly at his mother. She smiles at him in approval. Still holding the spatula he proceeds to kneel up and lean across the basket in order to reach a long brown silk scarf. He pulls at the scarf and squeals in delight as he pulls the fabric through his fingers, 'oohh, ahh' he repeats. He lets go of the spatula and abandons the scarf to his side, his eyes rest on a large blue stone, he picks up the large stone with his right hand and turns it over on his lap using both hands. Still using both hands he picks the stone up and begins to bite it, making a noise as his teeth grind against the hard surface. He smiles; looking at his mother as he repeatedly bites the stone over and over again. He stops, holds the stone up to his face and looks at it intently then puts it to his mouth once more. He then picks up the wooden spatula again and whilst holding it firmly in one hand, he turns the contents of the basket over with his other hand, squealing loudly with delight as he discovers the matching long handled fork. Matthew looks at his mother and waves both items in the air smiling and rocking on his knees saying 'oohh, ahh'. He turns away from the basket and waves the long handled implements, up and down in his hands, first one then the other then both together. He turns back to the basket with a puzzled expression and for a few seconds stops waving the items. He drops the fork and reaches back into the basket and randomly picks up items one at a time, looks at them and then discards them on the floor beside him. He continues this pattern for several seconds until he comes upon a long handled brush. He picks up the brush, pauses and then waves it in his left hand, all the time continuing to hold the wooden spatula in his right hand. For several seconds he proceeds to bang items together, smiling as the two wooden items make a sound together. He then spots the wooden fork he had disposed of earlier and letting go of the brush picks up the wooden fork and bangs it together with the spatula. 'Baba, baba, da, da, da' he says, then a little more loudly he repeats 'baba, baba, da, da, da'. (Nutbrown, 2005: 153)

Assessment for teaching and learning

Effective and meaningful work with young children which supports their learning must be based on appropriate assessment strategies to identify their needs and capabilities. The fine mesh of learning requires detailed, ongoing and sensitive observations of children as they play. Observation is crucial to understanding and assessing young children's learning. The following example demonstrates the importance of involving parents in assessing their children's learning.

> Sean was three and a half years old. He attended a nursery class each morning, where he spent much of his time playing outdoors, on bikes, in tents, climbing, gardening and running. His nursery teacher was concerned that he did not benefit from the other activities available indoors – painting, writing, drawing, construction, sharing books,

jigsaws and so on. Even when some of these opportunities were placed outside, Sean still seemed to avoid them; The nursery teacher spoke with Sean's mother who said: 'We don't have a garden and there's nowhere for Sean to play outside he hasn't got a bike and there's no park for climbing, or swings around here, or a space to do outside things, but we have lots of books and jigsaws, Lego, play people, we draw and make things.' Sean was balancing his own curriculum but the adults involved needed to share what they knew in order to understand his learning needs and current capabilities. (Nutbrown, 1996: 49)

Key aspects in assessing young children

Several aspects need to be addressed if assessment is to work for children (Box 13.6.1).

Issues in Assessment

- Clarity of purpose – why are children being assessed?
- Fitness for purpose – is the assessment instrument of process appropriate?'
- Authenticity – do the assessment tasks reflect priorities of children's learning and their interests?
- Informed practitioners – are practitioners appropriately trained and supported?
- Child involvement – how can children be fittingly involved in assessment of their learning?
- Respectful assessment – are assessments fair and honest with appropriate concern for children's well being-and-involvement?
- Parental involvement – do parents contribute to their child's assessment?

(Adapted from Nutbrown, 2005: 14)

Respectful assessment can include the development of inclusive practices which seek to allow children to 'have their say' in the assessment of their own learning. Critchley (2002) explored ways of including children in the assessment of their achievements.

part four

Reflecting on consequences

14 **Outcomes** How do we capture learning achievements?

15 **Inclusion** How are we enabling learning opportunities?

Outcomes

How do we capture learning and achievements?

14

Readings

14.1 Guy Claxton
Learning and the development of resilience (p. 290)

14.2 Jenny Willan
Observing children (p. 292)

14.3 Margaret Carr and Guy Claxton
Learning dispositions and assessment (p. 295)

14.4 Anette Emilson and Ingrid Pramling Samuelsson
Observation and pedagogic documentation (p. 300)

14.5 Jonathan Glazzard
Involving parents and carers as partners in assessment (p. 304)

The readings in this chapter move us on from thinking about the purpose of assessment to help us consider where assessment processes can lead and which processes may help us on that journey.

In the first reading, Claxton considers the concept of resilience: what it is and how we lay the foundations for children to be resilient. We also consider aspects of assessment, including observation, in a reading provided by Willan, and pedagogic documentation in a reading provided by Emilson and Pramling Samuelsson. These readings draw our attention to the complexities of assessment in terms of what we collect, how we collect it, and how our personal values impact on both of these. The final reading provides a practical summary of assessment processes with a specific emphasis on working with parents as partners. In this reading Glazzard offers some practical examples of how this may be achieved.

Reading 14.1

Learning and the development of resilience
Guy Claxton

Guy Claxton has constructed an analysis of how young learners need to develop positive learning dispositions to support lifelong learning. He identifies his 'three Rs' – resilience, resourcefulness and reflection – as being crucial. This reading is focused on the first of these. Resilience is closely associated with having the self-confidence to face problems and the resolve to overcome them. It articulates well with Dweck's concept of 'mastery' (**Reading 2.5**).

How, through our classroom practices, could we support the development of resilience in our pupils?

Edited from: Claxton, G. (1999) *Wise Up: The Challenge of Lifelong Learning.* Stoke-on-Trent: Network Press, 331–3.

As the world moves into the age of uncertainty, nations, communities and individuals need all the learning power they can get. Our institutions of business and education, even our styles of parenting, have to change so that the development and the expression of learning power become real possibilities. But this will not happen if they remain founded on a narrow conceptualization of learning: one which focuses on content over process, comprehension over competence, 'ability' over engagement, teaching over self-discovery. Many of the current attempts to create a learning society are hamstrung by a tacit acceptance of this outmoded viewpoint, however watered down or jazzed up it may be. The new science of learning tells us that everyone has the capacity to become a better learner, and that there are conditions under which learning power develops. It is offering us a richer way of thinking about learning, one which includes feeling and imagination, intuition and experience, external tools and the cultural milieu, as well as the effort to understand. If this picture can supplant the deeply entrenched habits of mind that underpin our conventional approaches to learning, the development of learning power, and the creation of a true learning society might become realities. In this final chapter, let me summarize the lessons that the new science of the learning mind has taught us.

Learning is impossible without resilience: the ability to tolerate a degree of strangeness. Without the willingness to stay engaged with things that are not currently within our sphere of confident comprehension and control, we tend to revert prematurely into a defensive mode: a way of operating that maintains our security but does not increase our mastery. We have seen that the decision whether, when and how to engage depends on a largely tacit cost-benefit analysis of the situation that is influenced strongly by our subjective evaluations of the risks, rewards and available resources. These evaluations derive from our beliefs and values, our personal theories, which may be accurate or inaccurate. Inaccurate beliefs can lead us to over or underestimate apparent threats and to misrepresent to ourselves what learning involves.

So when you find people declining an invitation to learn, it is not because they are, in some crude sense, lazy or unmotivated: it is because, for them, at that moment, the odds stack up differently from the way in which their parents or tutors or managers would prefer. Defensiveness, seen from the inside, is always rational. If the stick and the carrot don't do the trick, it may be wiser to try to get a clearer sense of what the learner's interior world looks like. Often you will find that somewhere, somehow, the brakes have got jammed. Sensitivity to the learners' own dynamics is always smart.

Some of these beliefs refer to the nature of knowledge and of learning itself. For example, if we have picked up the ideas that knowledge is (or ought to be) clear and unequivocal, or that learning is (or ought to be) quick and smooth, we withdraw from learning when it gets hard and confusing, or when we meet essential ambiguity. Some beliefs refer to hypothetical psychological qualities such as 'ability'. The idea that achievement reflects a fixed personal reservoir of general-purpose 'intelligence' is pernicious, leading people to interpret difficulty as a sign of stupidity, to feel ashamed, and therefore to switch into self-protection by hiding, creating diversions or not trying. Some beliefs determine how much we generally see the world as potentially comprehensible and controllable ('self-efficacy', we called it). High self-efficacy creates persistence and resilience; low breeds a brittle and impatient attitude. Some beliefs forge a connection between self-worth on the one hand and success, clarity and emotional control on the other, making failure, confusion and anxiety or frustration induce a feeling of shame. All these beliefs can affect anyone, but there are a host of others that specifically undermine or disable the learning of certain groups of people, or which apply particularly to certain types of material. For example, girls and boys have been revealed as developing different views of themselves as learners of mathematics.

These beliefs are rarely spelt out, but are transmitted implicitly and insidiously through the kinds of culture that are embodied in the settings that learners inhabit, such as family, school or workplace. Learning messages are carried by a variety of media. The habits and rituals of the culture enable certain kinds of learning and disable others.

The implications of these conclusions for the kinds of learning cultures we create are self-evident. Parents, teachers and managers have to be vigilant, reflective and honest about the values and beliefs which inform the ways they speak, model and organize the settings over which they have control. Inadvertently create the wrong climate and the development and expression of learning power are blocked. Experience in childhood, at home and at school, is particularly important because these early belief systems, whether functional or dysfunctional, can be carried through into people's learning lives as adults.

Reading 14.2

Observing children
Jenny Willan

> Observing children is an integral aspect of any assessment process in the early years. Observers need to be mindful of the context of the observation, and to be aware of their own perspectives and expectations. In this reading Willan raises our awareness of the emotional dimension of observing others.
>
> *Edited from:* Willan, J. (2010) 'Observing Children'. In R. Parker-Rees, C. Leeson, J. Willan and J. Savage (eds) *Early Childhood Studies*. Exeter: Learning Matters, 63–6.

Observations and emotions

Observing children is not a neutral process. As we have seen, values, beliefs and expectations are all involved. So too are emotions. Both child and observer come with their own load of emotional baggage. The child being observed or assessed has feelings; so do the parents and carers and educators around him/her – and so of course does the observer. It is important to be aware of the emotional dimension of the observational context and to try to take it into account as part of the whole assessment process.

Not all emotions are easy to express in words. Much of our understanding of others is based on a reading of body language – a gesture, a flicker of the eyes, a facial expression, a stance, a way of moving, a tone of voice. Most children learn to respond to body language before and alongside spoken language and much of our understanding as adults involves reading the hidden messages behind words from the contextual cues provided by the speaker. But it is easy to get it wrong! Knowing the derivation of our own emotional reactions can alert us to our tendency to misapply them in certain situations. Take the sniff, for instance. In some families it denotes derision. In other families it merely indicated a runny nose. Some people have a powerful emotional reaction to the sniff; others barely register it!

Awareness of children's body language and of our own body language and its effects on the children we are observing is important. Some children such as those with visual or hearing impairment or non-verbal learning disorders or autistic spectrum disorders may learn body cues more slowly than their peers and may have difficulty in 'reading' the people around them and reproducing the relevant body language themselves. This can make communication and social relationships problematic and can skew our observations of what is going on.

We sometimes hear exasperated adults say 'Look at me when I'm talking to you!' They may be reading lack of eye contact as defiance or avoidance. But it may be related to something else. Boys are popularly reported to make less eye contact than girls. Some children, particularly those on the autistic spectrum, find eye contact painful (Diamond, 2002). Others avoid eye contact when they feel threatened. Others may avoid it when they feel shy and ill at ease. Work by Doherty-Sneddon (2003, 2004) on gaze aversion shows that young children (and adults) may need to break eye contact when they need to access internal representations, because the information from eye contact is too compelling (dazzling) to allow children to access the much dimmer images they are able to conjure up in their own minds such as memories, concepts, imagined scenarios.

As an observer or assessor, our role may be perceived as judgemental and this may set up a reaction in the child under scrutiny. We ourselves may react at an emotional level to the child under observation. To be fair in our observations, we need to take into account our own emotional context and that of the child.

Observation and language

As observers and writers of observational studies and reports, we have a duty to confront the way we employ our language. In communicating our observations to others we will need to choose our words carefully. This will be a particular concern to those of you who may find yourselves, in the wake of the Laming (2003) recommendations for multi-agency working, negotiating with parents and/or colleagues from other disciplines about referral reports in connection with a child.

Sometimes the purpose of observing children is to come to an assessment or evaluation – of their situation, of their understanding, of their ability, of their behaviour. As a consequence, we may have to categorise them in some way. The words we use can be powerful and emotive – they may even be damaging. Slotting people into tidy boxes, labelling them, summing them up in a few chosen words makes report writing quicker but it may not be helpful. Positive labels may help some children (not all), negative ones help no one. Labels are quick shorthand ways of summarising, but too often they can become substitutes for more sophisticated understandings. They may be equal opportunity issues. If interpretations seem to be based on stereotypical assumptions around sex, special needs, ethnicity, culture or class, then they must be challenged.

Where observational reports are passed around among colleagues and concerned professionals, they can quickly generate set responses and prejudice the way children are seen by others (Billington, 2006). They may even contribute to a self-fulfilling prophesy when readers of the report adopt a corresponding mindset towards a child. We can ameliorate some of the difficulties inherent in articulating our observations by checking them with the child or a carer or a colleague where it is appropriate. Through our exploration of differences in interpretation, we may come to discern our own values and attitudes and recognise how they affect the way we work. In order to become competent observers, we need to explore, acknowledge and confront our own values, beliefs, emotions and language. Testing our observations against another person's helps us refine our ideas and encourages us to be more objective and to stay alert to our duty of maintaining high standards of fairness.

Examining research perspective

When we study children, we start from a particular perspective, a theory that underpins the way we ask our questions. This perspective is sometimes referred to as our paradigm (Kuhn, 1970). The dominant or *hegemonic* paradigm within which we conduct our study of children can affect the way we impose a pattern or interpretation on what we observe. For example, in 1948 Esther Bick pioneered a system of infant observation at the Tavistock Clinic. The close observation of neonates and infants was a compulsory part of the training for child psychotherapists. Student psychotherapists observed the interaction between mothers and fathers and their newborn babies and continued their observations at weekly intervals for a year. In the observation below, the student psychotherapist is trying to understand the baby's emotions during feeding. Because of the particular psychoanalytic paradigm through which he views the incident, he attaches a very particular significance to the way a baby is suckling – first at his mother's breast and then on his fist:

Observations at 12 weeks

Oliver sucked vigorously at the breast then lay motionless. He jerked his head away from the nipple as if he had forgotten that he had it in his mouth. The jerking hurt the mother and she jokingly said that if he did it again she would give him a 'big cup and a straw'. After feeding, Oliver grabbed one fist with the other and vigorously sucked on his knuckle. Perhaps nipple and mouth were not felt to be separate, in that he may not have attributed a separate existence to the breast but felt it to be part of himself. Sucking on his knuckle may be evidence that he felt he possessed something like the nipple available whenever he wanted. This related to the devastating rage precipitated when Oliver woke up to find mother not there. Then, despite sucking his knuckle, fingers, and other parts of his body, he could not satisfy himself. It seemed hard for him to tolerate a space or the idea that he was dependent on something outside himself or the thought that he did not possess everything that mother had. (Miller et al., 1989: 180)

The way we view children influences the way we study them, and the way we study them influences the observations we make. The inferences we draw from our own observations are subject to a kind of metaphorical framing, depending on our own particular paradigm as observer.

Reading 14.3

Learning dispositions and assessment
Margaret Carr and Guy Claxton

> The following reading by Carr and Claxton provides detail of why it is important to assess learning dispositions and the constraints in doing this effectively and reliably. Many of these approaches align well with current thinking on assessment in the early years.
>
> *Edited from:* Carr, M. and Claxton, G. (2002) 'Tracking the development of learning dispositions', *Assessment in Education: Principles, Policy and Practice*, 9 (1), 9–37.

Why is assessment of learning dispositions important?

There are a number of reasons why it is important to generate valid and reliable methods for assessing learning dispositions and thus for tracking their development. First, if we are to help young people develop learning-positive dispositions, we need kinds of diagnostic and formative assessment that will enable us to relate to them appropriately. Though this need may well be relevant across their entire educational careers, such methods are particularly vital in early childhood, for it is here that the foundations of learning are being laid. Without some systematic way of keeping track of students' progress in this regard, it is all too easy for parents', teachers' and students' attention to be captured by the traditional goals of achievement and to lose sight of the more slippery, but even more important, development of dispositions. Second, assessment of learners' progress is necessary in order to evaluate the efficacy of the educational programme and the 'dispositional milieu' (Carr, 2001a) which schools offer. Without some systematic tracking of learners, educators cannot know whether their good intentions are being translated into the desired outcomes. Third, it is a truism that what is assessed is what is valued, by teachers, families and learners themselves. If the goal of developing positive learning dispositions is to be translated into practice, then there have to be assessment instruments which serve to keep teachers' and learners' eyes on this particular ball and prevent attention sliding back onto the mastery of content, with its long tradition of assessment. Fourth, it is necessary to be able to demonstrate the efficacy of 'education for the development of learning dispositions' in the face of either skepticism or a simplistic 'back to basics' agenda that, whatever its shortcomings, can at least point to (what appears to be) hard data about educational achievement. If it is to be effective, the rhetoric of learning to learn has to be backed with convincing evidence.

What constraints are there on an effective system of dispositional assessment?

In order to evaluate possible ways of trying to keep track of dispositional development, it is necessary to have some criteria against which to judge them. We suggest the following. First, any assessment procedure has to be manageable and practical. It has to be capable of being administered, interpreted and recorded by busy educational practitioners. Second, any procedure needs to be, in the conventional senses, reliable and valid. We need to agree that resilience, playfulness and reciprocity are indeed being captured by the assessments and that sequential assessments are capturing the same thing.

Third, and closely related to the second, an assessment procedure needs to contain some built-in flexibility, so that teachers at every level can adapt it to suit the realities of their own seminar rooms, classrooms or early childhood centres without losing the central features of the developmental 'trail'.

Finally, assessment procedures must, formatively, support the development of learning dispositions. The assessment procedures themselves must form part of a dispositional milieu that affords resilience, playfulness and reciprocity and encourages and values their development. And they will be situated in episodes of joint attention and reciprocal, responsive relationships. Messick (see for example Messick, 1994) expanded the definition of validity to include a consideration of social consequences, adding consequential to construct validity. Related to this, Ames (1992) argues that certain structures within the classroom make different goals salient. Her primary interest is in the development of resilience, but her analysis would apply equally well to playfulness and reciprocity. She identifies three characteristics of the relationship between the individual and the environment that affect how students approach and engage with learning: the evaluation (assessment), the authority pattern and the tasks. Writing about assessment, she concludes that: 'when evaluation is normative, emphasizes social comparison, is highly differentiated, and is perceived as threatening to one's sense of self-control, it contributes to a negative motivational climate' (Ames, 1992: 265). In other words, such features of assessment adversely affect the development of resilience, playfulness and reciprocity.

Candidate methods for the assessment of learning dispositions

We might divide possible methods for assessing learning dispositions into three groups: those based on direct observation of learners 'at work'; those based on information derived through interviews or questionnaires with teachers, parents or peers who know the learner; those based on self-report or self-assessment by learners themselves. In addition, portfolio approaches may combine a number of different methods.

Observational methods

These methods infer learning dispositions from observations of how people behave when actually confronted with learning challenges

Dynamic assessment

Thorndike (1922), for example, defined intelligence itself as 'the ability to learn', saying that estimates of intelligence 'should be estimates of the ability to learn. To be able to learn harder things or to be able to learn the same things more quickly would then be the single basis for evaluation' (Thorndike, 1922: 17 quoted in Guthke and Stein, 1996: 1). In recent years this approach has reappeared under the name of 'dynamic assessment', and it basically involves the assessor setting 'examinees' a task that is too hard for them and observing how they respond and how they make use of standardised prompts and hints as they are offered..

Experimental and customised challenges

Experimental tasks have been used by researchers to investigate children's learning dispositions and some of these may be adapted as customised challenges for assessment purposes. Jigsaw puzzle solving was used by Smiley and Dweck (1994) to investigate young children's resilience, for example.

These specially designed challenges largely rely on activities that are very different from many of those involved in normal curriculum implementation and, therefore, are less manageable by teachers because they have been separated from the process of teaching. Many of them look and feel like 'tests' and, therefore, run the risk of falling foul of Ames' (1992) criticisms of the formative or consequential validity of assessments that emphasise comparison, are highly differentiated (their criteria inflexibly defined) and normative. In their use, such tests are unlikely to advance the development of dispositions such as resilience, playfulness and reciprocity.

Learning stories

'Learning stories' have been developed as an assessment tool for use with the New Zealand early childhood education curriculum (Carr, 2001b). Learning stories are structured observations in everyday or 'authentic' settings, designed to provide a cumulative series of qualitative 'snapshots' or written vignettes of individual children displaying one or more of the target learning dispositions. The five key learning dispositions highlighted by Te Whaariki are translated into observable actions: 'taking an interest', 'being involved', 'persisting with difficulty', 'expressing an idea or a feeling' and 'taking responsibility or taking another point of view'. The latter two ('expressing an idea' and 'taking another point of view') roughly correspond with our 'reciprocity', 'being involved' has elements of 'playfulness' and 'persisting with difficulty' looks like 'resilience', but the correspondence between the two sets of dispositions is not exact.

Outsiders' questionnaires and interviews

Where the methods in the previous section aimed to track the development of learning dispositions through observations of specific learning episodes, those in this section rely on more cumulative, perhaps more impressionistic, judgements made by those who have had experience of learners over a period of time.

Self-reports

In the third category of assessments it is the learners themselves who offer a summary picture of their own learning styles, abilities and dispositions.

Questionnaires

Self-report assessments are exemplified by the California Critical Thinking Dispositions Inventory (CCTDI) (Facione and Facione, 1992) where students respond to 75 items using a six point Likert scale. Burden's (1995) 'Myself as a Learner' (MALS) test invites school-children to respond to a simple 20 item questionnaire that gives a single measure overview of their self-image as learners.

Situated projective interviews

Carr (2000b) devised an interview based around observations in an early childhood centre. An observer or a teacher uses children's own developing 'learning narrative' to construct an open-ended storybook that played back their own learning style and strengths to them and asks them for an ending and any comments.

Self-created learning stories

A number of educators have recently been exploring the educational value of students' keeping reflective 'learning logs': a kind of informal diary or journal within which they are encouraged to reflect regularly on their ups and downs as learners. Sometimes these logs are private, sometimes seen by the teacher and sometimes used as the basis for an interactive oral or written conversation between teacher and student around the topic of the students' developing learning power.

Interviews

A collaborative project in South Australia between the Salisbury Plains Coalition of Schools and the Faculty of Education at the University of South Australia has focused on issues of student resilience within an ecological framework (Dryden et al., 1998), using student interviews. The study initially investigated how children and their teachers constructed and understood the notion of childhood resiliency.

Portfolios

Students' portfolios can potentially include data from any or all of the above methods. For example, in a multi-cultural public secondary school in Harlem described in Meier (1995), five desirable 'habits of mind' are listed on almost every classroom wall, discussed every week in a newsletter, used to organise curricula and are the base criteria that teachers use for judging students' portfolios on graduation.

Reading 14.4

Observation and pedagogic documentation
Anette Emilson and Ingrid Pramling Samuelsson

In this reading Emilson and Pramling Samuelson extend the discussion around observation. They note the reflective element of generating pedagogical documentation from
observations is a vital aspect of developing understandings of children and their current
abilities and future potential.

Edited from: Emilson, A. and Pramling Samuelsson, I. (2014) 'Documentation and
communication in Swedish preschools', *Early Years: An International Research Journal*,
34 (2), 175–87.

Observation and documentation of practice

Traditional documentation is often confused with observation, although it may seem
obvious that there has to be an observation in order to document something. It is clear
that both observation and documentation are ways of working with children in preschool
(Johansson, 2007). On the other hand, observation can be done in many different ways,
which are more or less structured. However, observation and documentation have sprung
out of different traditions. The observation, as a notion and a phenomenon, has clear links
to developmental psychology, and it has emerged since it provided teachers with valuable
knowledge for adapting their work to the developmental level of the children (Johansson
2007). Studies within developmental psychology, according to Johansson, often aimed to
'improve the practical activities in working with children' (p. 148). The very term 'observation' refers to the psychological sense of systematic observations of children's behaviour,
which then form the basis for descriptions and explanations of children's behaviour and
their emotional reactions as well as their ways of thinking (Egidius, 2008). The observation
method has thus been employed in preschools to create an understanding of children, but
also to contribute to the improvement of the profession, and the development of the field.

Documentation as a phenomenon, on the other hand, derives from progressivism, and
like observation has a long tradition and an obvious role in preschool, which is pointed
out in the document 'Att erövra omvärlden' (To conquer the world), the background text
for the Swedish curriculum (SOU, 1997: 157).

The idea to document and evaluate pedagogical activity was important among representatives of educational progressivism. Both John Dewey and Elsa Köhler advocated a
reflective and problem-based approach to teaching activities and related tasks. Both also
claimed an approach to the child/student as an explorer of the world and the teacher as
a co-investigator. It was in the pedagogical communication of activities in practice, that
interaction and observation were put in the centre. (our translation, ibid., 95)

Observation and documentation are two sides of the same coin. In recent decades, theories of children's learning and development have undergone a paradigm shift (Sommer, 2005a, 2005b), in which the idea of a 'general child' has been rejected and the unique child has been highlighted. To catch sight of each child's uniqueness, preschool teachers must develop skills in becoming aware of children's abilities. It is in this sense that documentation has taken a central role in Sweden, while observations, seemingly unreflective, have been relegated to history, i.e. to the time when all children, at a specific age, were believed to be similar in their development.

The documentation of educational processes and children's learning is a high priority in Swedish preschools National Agency for Education (NAE, 2008). Significant resources have been invested in skills and technical equipment to provide teachers in preschool with the means to document using digital cameras, camcorders, computers, printers and related technical aids. The question is, however, what does documentation really mean?

The Bonnier dictionary (1985) defines documentation as: (1) evidence, authentication, documents required to prove an argument and (2) activity in support of technology, scientific research, etc. to collect, organize (classify), to make available all kinds of information. What does this mean in relation to preschool practice? In accordance with the definition above, documentation is to collect, analyse and categorize to make something visible to someone. The intention appears to be to find arguments for how something is represented or manifested. The question is, What? The government mandate to the preschool (U2008/6144/S) refers this 'what' to the clarification of the guidelines for monitoring and evaluation, as well as children's learning.

> Preschool activities should be planned, implemented, monitored and evaluated, and on this basis, comes the development in relation to defined goals in the curriculum In order to be able to do this, staff are required to monitor the children's learning and document this. The curriculum does not propose methods of documentation, but it is up to each teacher to choose the method that suits best. (p. 3)

The quote states that the government should not propose specific methods, but later, however, the memorandum emphasizes that pedagogical documentation can be an essential tool for visualizing processes in preschool, as the basis for the assessment of preschool quality, effectiveness and development. On the one hand, clearly the government does not want to control how activities are monitored and evaluated, but on the other hand, they suggest pedagogical documentation to be one way. Before we proceed, it is therefore essential to describe pedagogical documentation, since this kind of documentation has been very strongly and extensively promoted, and also prioritized by the NAE (2011).

Pedagogical documentation

The concept of pedagogical documentation differs from more general documentation, since the concept emphasizes the importance of the documentation leading to analysis, reflection and interpretation. The purpose of this type of documentation is, according to Rinaldi (2000), that the preschool teacher should catch sight of the child and his/her potential.

> Documentation, therefore, is seen as making listening visible, as the construction of traces (through notes, slides, videos, and so on), that not only testify to the children's learning paths and processes, but also show the relationships that are the building blocks of knowledge. (Rinaldi, 2000: 83)

Kennedy (1999 p. 10) who also advocates for pedagogical documentation, says, 'We want to show another way of looking at children. We want to show that children already are strong people who CAN much more than we adults have become accustomed to believe'. Pedagogical documentation is not only about generating knowledge about children, but also about making educational practice visible (Lenz Taguchi, 1997). The actual function of pedagogical documentation refers to the teacher's reflection and what this may lead to, according to Rinaldi (2001). She says, '... documentation as an integral part of the procedures aims at fostering learning and modifying the learning–teaching relationship' (p. 76). Åberg and Lenz Taguchi (2005) claim that this kind of documentation is a matter of the teachers learning to listen and reflect on what the child says and does to thus develop their teaching skills in preschool practice. They go a step further regarding documentation, arguing that listening can be made visible through documentation, which in turn can lead to a more democratic pedagogy.

It can be noted that there is a relatively large body of literature on pedagogical documentation (see e.g. Lenz Taguchi, 1997; Kennedy, 1999; Rinaldi, 2001; Picchio et al., 2012), but very little research in this area, either nationally or internationally. In a discourse analysis study by Bjervås (2011) examining how preschool teachers, in planning meetings, talk about and assess the children related to their own documentation, the results show that teachers talk about children as competent and with diverse abilities. These abilities are placed primarily within the child and not within the context that teachers provide, even if the context can appear as both supportive and limiting. The documentation situations were considered as valuable opportunities for children to be able to demonstrate their abilities to use their existing skills, but also to be able to develop new abilities. Several studies have shown that teachers who use pedagogical documentation as a tool stress the value not only of the joint reflection for visualizing children's learning, but also of the documentation procedure itself (Kocher, 2008; Buldu, 2010; Bjervås, 2011). Eidevald (2013) has shown how teachers struggle with analysing the observations and/or documentations they have collected.

It is worth noting that the available literature is predominantly positive about pedagogical documentation, and it is emphasized that, through pedagogical documentation, teachers can learn new ways of looking at children and their learning. Research shows that teachers see both advantages and disadvantages in using pedagogical documentation in preschool (Bjervås, 2011).

While considering the benefits, disadvantages have also been identified. Bjervås (2011) points out that there are critical aspects for each teacher to consider. Difficulties that emerged are that documentation takes a lot of time and there is a risk of accumulating too much documentation, which is then not used for joint reflection, analysis and the further development of the preschool. Further, it has been found that it may be difficult to be active in teaching at the same time that one is documenting (Buldu, 2010; Bjervås, 2011).

It may well be that pedagogical documentation arrived in the arena during the same period as the view of the child as competent and unique (see Bjervås, 2011), but it should be noted that documentation as a phenomenon, in the form of observations, had the same function, i.e. to understand children and their behaviour in order to adapt preschool so that it was suitable for different children. While pedagogical documentation has become central, children's perspectives and child interviews have also been emphasized, in order to view and to catch sight of the child's world and meaning (Sommer, Pramling Samuelsson, and Hundeide, 2010; Doverborg and Pramling Samuelsson, 2012).

Reading 14.5

Involving parents and carers as partners in assessment

Jonathan Glazzard

Jonathan Glazzard provides practical strategies for working with parents as partners in the assessment process. He notes that practitioners can learn from parents, particularly when they support parents to hone their skills of assessment.

Do you enable parents to participate in assessment processes?

Edited from: Glazzard, J. (2010), 'Involving Parents and Carers as Partners in Assessment'. In J. Glazzard, D. Chadwick, A. Webster and J. Percival *Assessment for Learning in the Early Years Foundation Stage.* London: Sage Publications Ltd, 143–6.

Communicating attainment and next steps to parents and carers

Parents and carers need to be informed about children's next steps in learning. It is considered to be good practice to work together with parents to formulate the next steps. Parents will often have their own thoughts about what they want their child to be able to do next. However, emphasise that the starting point must be where the child is. Stress that children are unique learners and they progress at different rates. It is also important to stress that children's attainment may not be consistent across all six areas of learning.

Enabling parents and carers to become confident assessors

It might be useful to share examples of practitioner observations and annotated photographs with parents before asking them to complete assessments themselves at home. Parents can therefore benefit from models of good practice. You could invite parents into the setting to observe practitioners observing young children's learning. You could then follow the observation with a debrief session. Parents and practitioners can discuss what they have both observed. In this respect, practitioners can act as mentors to parents. You could invite parents to informal training sessions where you train them in observational techniques. The key point is that in order to enable parents to become assessors, you will need to give them the confidence that they can do it, and they need to know that their observations are valuable and necessary.

The REPEY research (Siraj-Blatchford et al., 2002) acknowledges that staff may need to be more proactive in influencing and supporting a home learning environment, and some parents may be reluctant to engage with education or assessment of learning at home. Some parents will have formed assumptions about the role of home and school and created an artificial dividing line between the two. These parents will be more of a challenge in terms of developing effective partnerships. In these circumstances, it will be necessary to work harder at developing interactions and discussions with these parents. Take every opportunity to talk to parents informally and strike up a relationship. Ultimately, you will need to convince these parents why their knowledge of the child in the home environment should be shared with you. Once relationships are established and secure, you will then be able to develop partnerships focusing on learning and assessment.

Celebrating achievements at home

Finding time to meet with parents is never an easy task. Perhaps you could ask the parents to spend some time in the setting each morning. Encourage them to bring in photographs which evidence significant achievement at home and ask them to write short commentaries to accompany the photograph. This evidence can then be included in each child's personal learning journey. Try to spend some time talking to parents about their child's learning at home. You could ask them to write up some short observations that evidence significant achievement. However, you may need to run a session with them first on observational assessment. You might want to provide certificates that parents can freely access if they want to issue a reward for significant achievement. These could be displayed on a noticeboard and later included in the child's learning journey. However, it is important that parents understand the effects of overusing praise and the dangers of extrinsic motivation. In one setting recently visited, parents had been asked to complete Post-it notes to document evidence of their child's significant achievements at home. These were then displayed and used as a focus for generating a discussion with children about their learning at home.

The key point to stress is that practitioners should actively seek the contributions of parents and carers in the assessment process. Some parents will be more reluctant to contribute than others. The practitioner has an important role to play in encouraging parents and carers to be partners in the assessment process. Parents need to understand why their views and contributions are important and they need to recognise the importance of the learning which takes place in the home context. Equally, as a practitioner, you need to value this learning as much as the learning which takes place in the setting.

The National Assessment Agency (NAA) (2008) stresses that parental partnership in assessment is critical for families which frequently change location for example, Gypsy, Roma or Traveller children or children who have parents in the forces. In these circumstances, parents' extensive knowledge of their children's development will be extremely useful. Practitioners can use this knowledge and their own observations to gain a full picture of the child's development. Parental partnership is also critical in the case of children with English as an additional language. For these children, all scale points except scale points 4–9 on the four communication, language and literacy scales can be achieved in a child's home language (NAA, 2008). Therefore parent partnership is essential so that parents can inform the practitioner about their child's progress towards the first three scale points.

Practical strategies for facilitating parent partnership

Some strategies to facilitate effective parent partnership in assessment are documented below.

Training – Assessment is a complex process, particularly in the early years. Children's play and child-initiated interactions form a rich source of evidence of children's learning and development. Parents and carers will benefit from some training sessions which focus on the principles of assessment in the early years, and methods of evidencing significant achievement and linking assessment to the appropriate statutory framework. Parents and carers may also benefit from some training in the relevant framework. Initially, you may be happy to accept the evidence from parents without any links to developmental milestones or profile scale points. However, as the parents become more confident, you might wish to consider offering some training on making accurate judgements on learning and development by encouraging them to make reference to the framework. Parents will then be able to identify their child's next steps more accurately. You can then invite parents to termly meetings where day-to-day assessments are considered.

Home visits – Home visits before children join the setting provide a rich context for assessment. Spend some time talking to parents about the child's interests, dispositions and attitudes. Document this discussion, date it and add it to the child's learning journey. Try to take photographs of the child in the home environment and add these to the child's journal. Talk to the parents about the importance of play as a vehicle for learning and explain to parents the role of adult interaction in play. If parents understand what children are learning through play, they are more likely to be able to identify significant learning and achievement in the home context. This will be useful when you start to involve parents in observational assessments of their child in the home context.

Learning diaries, learning journeys and learning stories – Some settings use home school diaries to document evidence of a child's learning during the day. Practitioners may include photographs, observations of learning or quotes from conversations they may have had with the child. These can then be sent home to form a focus for discussion between the parent and the child. Parents can then add their own assessment evidence to the learning diary as a way of informing the practitioner about children's learning in the home context. Carr (2001) discusses the value of 'learning stories' and parental involvement with these. These stories document the learning which has taken place during the day. They can be shared with the parents, who can enjoy reading rich accounts about their child's daily experiences. The stories are a document of the child's holistic development and they can provide a catalyst for discussion between the child and the parent/carer. Learning stories are a valuable vehicle through which children can revisit learning which has taken place during the day. In settings with limited numbers of staff, learning stories are more difficult to manage, and in these situations staff may wish to document the child's significant achievements over time in a learning journey. This can be freely available in the setting for parents to refer to. However, it can also be sent home periodically and shared with the parents.

Achievement wall – This wall can be a celebration of a child's achievements, either in the home setting or in the context of the setting. Parents and practitioners can contribute to this jointly. You can encourage parents to add photographs and captions to the wall, or you might want to use special praise certificates or slips. These can be added to the child's learning journal at a later date.

Verbal evidence – Conversations with parents and carers provide rich sources of evidence for assessment. You will need to document and date the conversation, and this evidence can then be included in the child's learning journey. Conversations with parents can often be useful in terms of enabling practitioners to formulate a more holistic view of a child's achievements. For example, a child may be reluctant to initiate interactions in the setting but may demonstrate more confidence in the home. Remember to find the time and space to collect as much information from the parents as you can. The context of the activity needs to be clearly documented to make moderation easier.

Making learning visible – The NAA (2008) recommends that assessments of children's learning should be made visible to parents. This can be done in a variety of ways such as displaying photographs of children's learning on a wall and using the interactive whiteboard to display photographs of children's learning. This is particularly effective if the photographic images are played in a loop so that a cycle of images is repeated. This provides a powerful vehicle for discussion with parents about children's learning.

Moderation of parental assessments – There is a need to moderate assessment judgements and this is also the case for parental assessments. Therefore, you should include parental assessments in moderation events both within the setting and in cross-setting moderation. You might also want to consider involving parents in the moderation process.

The importance of values – Effective practitioners value parental contributions to assessment. They actively seek their involvement in the assessment process and empower them to contribute. These practitioners believe that parents are skilled and able to contribute equally to the assessment process. They form effective relationships with significant carers and thus help to break down barriers. Additionally, these practitioners believe that the child is a holistic learner and that learning takes place both within the setting and in the home. As a practitioner, it is important that you reflect on your own values. Do you believe that parents and carers can make valuable contributions to the assessment process, or do you place more emphasis on learning within the setting and do you value practitioner judgements over the judgements made by those closest to the child? This chapter challenges traditional notions of assessment and opens up new possibilities for practitioners to work in partnership with families and children.

Inclusion
How are we enabling opportunities?

15

Readings

15.1 Anastasia Liasidou
Defining inclusion (p. 310)

15.2 Penny Borkett
Supporting children with Special Educational Needs in the early years (p. 313)

15.3 Gary Thomas and Andrew Loxley
Difference or deviance? (p. 316)

15.4 Jonathan Rix
What's your attitude? Inclusion and early years settings (p. 319)

The readings in this chapter reflect how current thinking on inclusion and inclusive practices encourages us to move away from 'deficit models', which consider individuals as 'disadvantaged', to consider difference as a natural part of society.

We begin with a reading by Liasidou which requires us to consider what diversity is. Liasidou highlights how inclusion, as a term, does not carry the same meaning for all. The second reading, provided by Borkett, considers some of the specifics of how children with special educational needs can be supported in the early years. Together these readings provide some insight into the complex nature of inclusive practice within early years provision.

In the third reading, Thomas and Loxley challenge us to be clear about the nature of 'difference' and the diversity with which it is associated: is it to be welcomed, or feared?

Provided by RIx, the final reading considers these debates within the context of early years practice and provision. Rix encourages us to reflect upon our own perceptions and related practices.

Reading 15.1

Defining inclusion
Anastasia Liasidou

This reading encourages us to broaden their thinking about inclusion and diversity. Liasidou advocates a shift in thinking away from individuals, and what has been referred to as a 'deficit model' of the individual, to one of inclusivity for all.

Edited from: Liasidou, A. (2012) *Inclusive Education, Politics and Policymaking. Contemporary Issues in Education Studies*. London: Continuum, 5–7.

Defining inclusion: A semantic chameleon

Emanating from the social model of disability (Oliver, 1990), which puts the emphasis on disabling social barriers rather than individual deficits, inclusive education refers to the restructuring of social and, by implication, educational settings in order to meet the needs of all learners irrespective of their diverse biographical, developmental and learning trajectories. Inclusive education constitutes a radical paradigm shift and by no means should be considered as a linear progression from a special educational needs discourse. This said, inclusive education should never be a default vocabulary for Special Educational Needs. The moment we allow inclusive education to be special education for new times is the moment we submit to collective indifference … Inclusive education is code for educational reform at all levels. A new social imagination and congruent vocabulary is required that delivers us from the fortification of outdated traditions and practices of schooling. (Slee, 2011: 121–2)

Arguably, inclusion constitutes a response to the flawed ways in which the education of disabled students has been so far predicated, as it emanates from new theorizations of disability, whereby disability is not solely attributed to individual deficits. Rather, it is predominantly attributed to material and ideological disabling barriers that undermine the social, intellectual and emotional development of certain individuals. Within an inclusive context, children's atypical and diverse developmental trajectories are recognized and valued through a positive appreciation of difference for a socially just and fair society.

Nevertheless, despite its indisputable moral and ethical standing, the rhetoric advocating the realization of inclusion has been vociferously contested and characterized as a utopian pursuit (Croll and Moses, 2000) or a 'passionate intuition' (Pirrie and Head, 2007), while other analysts have pointed out the necessity to promote 'responsible inclusion' (Vaughan and Schumm, 1995).

Inclusion is a highly elusive notion whose interpretation, as well as implementation, are contingent on a vast array of discursive dynamics that give rise to varied and contradictory discourses, the latter defined as being the material effects of language-use, which constitute a coherent ensemble of ideas/regimes that exert social control by 'rendering some things common sense and other things nonsensical' (Youdell, 2006: 36). These discourses have according to Armstrong (1999: 76):

> Multiple meanings, used by different people in different contexts, and are commonly used in ways which mask the attitudes, social structures and processes which produce and sustain exclusions.

The ideological melange underpinning inclusion is extremely diverse, nebulous and occasionally contradictory, something that is subsequently reconfigured and regenerated through the social and institutional arrangements that purport to promote the realization of an inclusive discourse. As Graham and Slee (2008: 83) aptly put it, inclusion is 'troubled by the multiplicity of meanings that lurk within the discourses that surround and carry it'. It is not surprising then that some commentators talk about inclusion in the plural in order to denote its multiple facets and perspectives (Dyson, 1999).

Different people implicated in the debates around inclusion, as well as in the processes of policy formulation and implementation, have different understandings of inclusion and special educational needs. The field has been dominated by different theoretical camps holding diverse verdicts as to the feasibility of inclusion and its effectiveness to meet diverse needs. Quoting Clough and Corbett (2000: 6), '"Inclusion" is not a single movement; it is made up of many strong currents of belief, many different local struggles and a myriad of practices'. In a similar vein, Slee (2006: 111) suggests that: 'The theoretical and pragmatic imprecision of this thing we, and it is a very broad we, call inclusive education has permitted all manner of thinking, discourse and activity to pass off as inclusive'. The above statements denote the variegated nature of ideologically, culturally and historically grounded dynamics that bring to bear a prodigious impact on the ways in which inclusive education is conceptualized and acted upon.

The debates attract a disciplinarily heterogeneous group of people, who attempt to theorize inclusion according to their perceived optimal ways in which the latter can effectively meet learner diversity. Various models of inclusion are suggested and theorized in alignment with the ways in which difference is conceptualized and envisaged to be dealt with in mainstream schools (Booth and Ainscow, 1998; Rustemier, 2002; Farrell, 2009). In parallel with the debates around the social model of disability and the ways in which it can sufficiently explicate disability (Corker and French, 2001; Thomas, 2004), the debates have subsequently revolved around the different interpretations of inclusion, and the optimal educational arrangements that can effectively meet the needs of students designated as having special educational needs (Norwich, 2008a).

For instance, arguments in relation to inclusion revolve around its effectiveness, as well as its limitations, in meeting the individual needs of all students, and in particular, of those students with atypical developmental trajectories in terms of ability and attainment. The field has been an ongoing theoretical battlefield fraught with diverse perspectives and insights ranging from enthusiastic proclamations (e.g Stainback and Stainback, 1992; Thomas, 1997; Ainscow, 1997), to pessimistic and sceptical commentaries, as well as serious contemplations regarding the feasibility of inclusion as a means to providing the optimal learning environment for all students (Funch and Funch, 1994; Kauffman, 1995; Low, 1997; O'Brien, 2001; Farrell, 2009).

The contentious nature of inclusion and Special Educational Needs (SEN) has been recently reinforced in the United Kingdom by Baroness Warnock's (2005, 2010) assertions regarding the position and future of segregated special provision whereby the author characterizes inclusion as a dangerous legacy.

While denouncing pessimistic and unsubstantiated allusions about the utopian nature of inclusion, by no means is it suggested that inclusion is an easy and uncontested pursuit. Inclusion is a complex concept embedded in what Norwich (2010: 93) calls 'a plural values framework' whereby contradictory existing and emerging values are juxtaposed, repositioned, contested and negotiated. The interactionist values framework, and the tensions accrued, need to be thoroughly explored and understood if we are to go beyond unilateral and deficit-oriented understanding of special educational needs that prevent us from developing and fostering an inclusive framework in meeting students' capabilities and needs.

Inclusion has been debated and contested to such a great extent that it has been occasionally diluted to an empty linguistic construct (Benjamin, 2002a). As Armstrong et al. (2010: 29) write: 'The reality is not simply that inclusion means different things to different people, but rather that inclusion may end up meaning everything and nothing at the same time.' This said, in attempting to demystify and disentangle the conceptual complexity and semantic plurality of inclusion, it is important to theorize some of the ways in which inclusion has been conceptualized, theorized and enacted.

Reading 15.2

Supporting children with Special Educational Needs in the early years

Penny Borkett

> Building upon the reading provided by Liasidou, Borkett considers both how we view children with disabilities in the early years and how practitioners can support such young children in their first years of education.
>
> *Edited from:* Borkett, P. (2012) 'Diversity and Inclusion in the Early Years'. In J. Kay (ed.) *Good Practice in the Early Years*. London: Continuum, 91–4.

Models of disability

Models of disability are ways of thinking about how the child or adult with a disability is seen in society. The oldest model of disability is the medical model. This focuses on the need to 'label' the disability and to try to treat it. This model is very much a deficit model, which means that there is more of a focus on what the child or adult cannot do rather than what they can. It locates the disability in some form of problem for the individual. The term 'Down's syndrome child' is very much a sign of this model, whereby the disability is stated as the first and most significant aspect of the child. A better way of describing this would be 'a child with Down's syndrome', which acknowledges the child first and then the disability. Another feature of the medical model is the assumption that children with disabilities should be taught in special schools, and that there are significant limits to what they can achieve. This model prevailed for a long time and meant that, prior to the 1970s, many children with disabilities received little educational support and were not expected to participate fully in society.

The second model of disability is the social model, which is concerned with how society 'disables' the adult or child through inaccessible buildings, bureaucracies and education systems, stereotyping the needs of the person with the disability, or by assuming that the carer of the person will speak for them. This model locates the problem in societies response to disabled people, and suggests that it is an inflexible and prejudiced society that creates a disabling environment for some of its members. This is a more positive model because it does suggest that a child with disabilities should attend a mainstream setting that has adapted its facilities to the needs of the child. It also focuses more on the skills that the child has and the need for social change to better meet the needs of the child.

The third model is the affirmative model, which suggests that a disability is part of the fundamental identity of the person. This model suggests that a person with disabilities is completely responsible for their own life and needs, and has a voice to be able to make decisions relating to their own lives.

The role of the practitioner in supporting children with special educational needs

When working with all children, it is important to focus on the holistic needs of the child. This means that practitioners have a requirement to view all aspects of the child's life as being significant and having influence on the way the child grows and develops. So the practitioner needs to be aware of the child's family and social environment and other relevant factors, as well as any disability.

The emergence of SureStart programmes in 2001 sought to support children with disabilities in order that they may have greater access to mainstream early years provision. In the early days of SureStart, children received much greater access to speech therapy and other services such as Portage, in which professionals work in the home with very young children with disabilities, seeking to further the child's development through play-based activities. However, funding for some of these services has decreased over the years, although working with children with special needs is still one of SureStart's key activities.

So how can early years settings ensure that they meet the needs of all children? All children need to have access to practitioners who have a clear knowledge of child development. This knowledge will enable the practitioner to observe the child's developmental progress in all areas and, in partnership with parents and other professionals, to set new targets for the child's IEP in order to extend learning and development.

Some of the strategies highlighted in the previous section of this chapter, such as Makaton signs and symbols, are paramount to ensuring inclusion. Some parents may be concerned that, if their child is learning to sign, then they may not readily learn language, but it is emphasized that language must be used alongside the sign. This will ensure that the child receives a verbal clue to the word. Practitioners should be careful when working with children with a hearing impairment, as Makaton is not a visual-only language similar to British Sign Language (BSL). Children born with a hearing impairment usually have support from the local authority, with a teacher who works specifically with them, so consult with the teacher first before making the assumption that Makaton would be useful. Obviously a child with severe physical impairments may struggle to make the signs, so again you would need to consider this first.

Children with disabilities sometimes learn kinaesthetically (with all of their senses) and so relate better to sensory activities. Rather than giving the child a brush to paint with, let them explore the paint with their fingers. The use of cornflour, sand, water and bubbles is often a more engaging way into their learning. Games and activities that focus around a particular TV programme that the child may enjoy are sometimes a way into their learning. Lotto games, in which the child matches two characters from 'In The Night Garden', may be far more relevant to the child than random pictures which may have no interest to the child.

If the child has difficulty with speech it is good to encourage turn taking activities where the child can start to understand that communication is reciprocal e.g. rolling a ball to the child and calling their name when you roll it will be an enjoyable activity. Music is an activity which many children enjoy so at circle time produce a singing box where toys which relate to a song can be chosen by all children to indicate which song they would like to choose. As the child begins to learn what the toys represent you could then add photographs of the toy and when they recognize these, Makaton signs can be introduced. All of this will help to differentiate the learning for children with each stage encouraging new skills. If a child is not keen to look at books, you could try making a book using photographs that are familiar to the children, so one about their family or, again, featuring TV characters which they relate to, can help them to engage with books in a more specific and related way.

The EYFS states the need for activities to be child-initiated (chosen by the child alone), and this is absolutely vital for all children; however, sometimes children with a special need may have more difficulty choosing their activities. In this circumstance, a visual timetable may be introduced whereby practitioners suggest which activities the child may like to use during the session through pictures or symbols attached to a piece of Velcro. The child then removes the item from the Velcro when they have carried out the activity.

This approach was used to good effect with a child who loved bubbles. At the painting area, the child would paint bubbles, and draw them in the mark making area. Any book which had circles or bubbles in it was favoured, but encouragement to participate in other activities produced tears and tantrums. The timetable ensured that the bubble activities were interspersed with other activities to give the child access to a wider variety of learning.

Reading 15.3

Difference or deviance?

Gary Thomas and Andrew Loxley

This extract draws particular attention to the ways in which we respond to the characteristics of others, and how this works within educational institutions. It warns of how routine practices can 'create difference' and may even interpret it as deviance from an imagined norm. The quest for inclusion requires constant awareness of language, concepts, categories, statistics and other forms of representation.

Can you identify processes in your daily life which, in the terms of this reading, 'create difference'?

Edited from: Thomas, G. and Loxley, A. (2007) *Deconstructing Special Education and Constructing Inclusion*. Maidenhead: Open University Press, 76–8, 87.

To be called 'special' is to be given a new identity within the schooling system. How far this social identity becomes transferable to (or resisted by) other institutions or forms part of an individual's personal identity is highly debatable. However, it is clear that this accreditation of difference represents in practice two phenomena: first, a transition from one state to another – that is from the 'non-special' to the 'special'; second, a set of interventions which reinforces this state of difference. There is at work a process of re-ordering which positions a pupil into different and possibly new sets of social relations – with teachers, peers and support staff.

This is what Munro (1997) calls a continual 'labour of division', and it is characteristic of much activity of institutions, not just schools. This notion of labour of division is, of course, an inversion of Marx's (1995) concept of the division of labour, and it is used to signify the way institutions actively go about splintering and fragmenting previously given categories. It is about the drawing and continual redrawing of boundaries; of constructing points of demarcation which in turn are used as indices to 'map' individuals or groups into appropriate classifications. This making of difference seems almost to be an endemic part of the process of being an institution. If this is the case, it presents problems for those who wish to see more inclusion in social and institutional life.

What can be discovered about the process?

It is clear, first of all, that the recognition of difference is not necessarily anti-inclusional. Williams (1992), draws useful distinctions between diversity, difference and division:

> By *diversity* I mean difference claimed upon a shared collective experience which is specific and not necessarily associated with a subordinated or unequal subject position

... *difference* denotes a situation where a shared collective experience/identity ... forms the basis of resistance against the positioning of that identity as subordinate. By *division* I mean the translation of the expression of a shared experience into a form of domination. (Williams, 1992: 70)

Williams is arguing that we cannot assume that difference will automatically be translated into some anti-inclusive domination. Not all forms of difference automatically imply marginalisation and exclusion. Likewise, Munro (1997) points out that:

... considered as a feature of society, difference might be said to enjoy mixed fortunes. Sometimes difference is in vogue; it is a thing to be welcomed and may be referred to wholesomely in such terms as 'diversity'. On other occasions ... it is viewed as something more shadowy, even malevolent, with any difference being treated as deviant. (Munro, 1997: 14)

This then is the key issue: is difference something to be welcomed, or is it, in Munro's terms, to be made into something 'shadowy', 'malevolent', 'deviant'? There are clearly variations in the way that educators handle kinds of difference. In the case of certain systems of symbols – sexuality, clothing, patterns of speech and behaviour – there is strong evidence that exclusionary pressure associates itself with this kind of difference.

But it is not just with difficult behaviour at school that the process of making difference works. While it is not as conspicuous in other areas it nevertheless occurs, despite the outward impression that inclusion is happening. As Barnes et al. (1999) and Geertz (1973) remark, different cultural groups mark out and categorise social difference by reference to localised criteria. And this has been especially the case as far as education is concerned and the concept of 'need' has played its part in this. The mark of difference has been used as a rationale for segregation rather than celebration, even though the markers of that difference are subtle and elude definition. For instance, notions of 'need' in physical impairment or, even more relevantly, 'learning difficulties' may have referents which are difficult to be specific about outside a local context. There is certainly evidence of this as far as reading difficulty is concerned: Thomas and Davis (1997) showed that 'reading difficulty' is not a clear-cut, unambiguous label; teachers in different schools will have different ideas about what constitutes 'a child with reading difficulty', depending on their local experience.

With Warnock (DES, 1978), the number of children 'with special needs' rose from around two per cent of the school population – that is, those who were educated in special schools – to 20 per cent. People who were clever with numbers worked out that this meant that 18 per cent of children in ordinary schools had special needs, and this became a commonplace: 18 per cent of children in ordinary schools had special educational needs. It is extraordinary that this figure – 18 per cent – came to be accepted as uncritically as it was. The figure '18 per cent' even made its way into the title of a respectable book about special needs (Gipps, 1987). For 18 per cent to be accepted (not 17 per cent or 19 per cent, note) as the proportion of children with special needs in ordinary schools shows a faith in the power of statistics which has probably never been rivalled in the history of serious discourse on public policy.

As Giddens (1990) puts it:

> Concepts ... and the theories and empirical information linked to them, are not merely handy devices whereby agents are somehow more clearly able to understand behaviour ... they actively constitute what that behaviour is and inform the reasons for which it is undertaken. (Giddens, 1990: 42)

Giddens implies that as we 'discover' new ways of making sense of phenomena, these explanations in turn become inseparable from what those phenomena are. The empirical and epidemiological information drawn on by the Warnock Committee in 1978 (DES, 1978) did not merely hold a mirror up to some reality which could be used by educators. Rather, it actively generated a 'reality' which had to be lived up to.

Difference and identity are constructed in and through social relations. Whether difference is seen positively, as diversity, or negatively as deviance or deficit depends on the mindset of the person or group of people who observe that difference.

Various thinkers – Lyotard (1984), Foucault (1991), Bourdieu (1984), the labelling theorists – have helped to show how the words we use and the systems of thought and enquiry we employ, shape the interpretation of difference. One of their most important insights is that instruments of enquiry, including our very discourse, not only reveal the nature and extent of difference, but also go to construct that difference. They reveal also the imperative to seek homogeneity in institutional life and the corresponding imperative to delineate and differentiate those who differ from the norm. Their analyses, while in some ways depressing, are important for thinking about how to counteract the processes they reveal.

Reading 15.4

What's your attitude? Inclusion and early years settings

Jonathan Rix

Jonathan Rix provides a practical – and personal – insight into the experiences of children with SEN in early years settings, which requires us to consider how we see children and how inclusive practices can be developed.

Edited from: Rix, J. (2008) 'Inclusion and early years settings – What's your attitude?' in A. Paige-Smith and A. Craft (eds) *Developing Reflective Practice in the Early Years.* Maidenhead: Open University Press, 74–8.

Where do you start?

Early September, and a new intake of children arrives in your setting: twenty to thirty new characters to fill your working days. Who are they? How do you identify them? What behaviours grab your attention? What sorts of knowledge interest you? What appearances affect you? Do you quite quickly (consciously or subconsciously) categorize these children, putting an informal (or formal) label on them: the 'quiet one', the 'ball of energy', the one who's 'going to be a handful' …? All of us group and label others. As Foucault (1978) makes clear, we have to position ourselves within the dominant structure of the normalizing society. We constitute our own identities, and identify other's identities, in the context of social relationships and structures. A key factor in defining ourselves and others is positioning ourselves within social categories. We respond to others and their behaviours on the basis of whether we perceive them to be insiders or outsiders of the category in which we place ourselves (Waterhouse, 2004). This means that the same behaviour produces a different response in us dependent on how we perceive the individual.

Starting with your self

A good place to start is to consider your views about disability, ethnicity, class, gender, faith groups, sexual orientation and what constitutes appropriate social behaviours. Even if you feel that you are utterly fair-minded and treat all equally you are probably responding differently without being aware of it.

Look at the picture in Figure 15.4.1. What would your first thoughts be if these children arrived on that September morning? Would you immediately start to worry about practical problems? Would you immediately start thinking about opportunities for learning? Or would you want to get to know the children first? Such reflection can occur both in the moment and over longer periods of time. It can be both an internal, self-analytic act and an external one, involving discussion with others. It is both personal and communal.

Figure 15.4.1
Two children in
wheelchairs

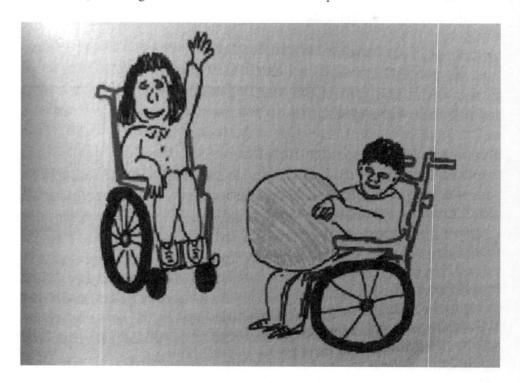

Thinking about a problem of inclusion

When you are reframing a problem, do you start by considering why you might feel it is a problem? Do you start with the child's difference or with your response to each child and the manner in which the context is supportive of that child? Many children – even at a very young age – are already used to being excluded by social systems: Even very young children may have been marginalized by a traumatic personal experience, or excluded by more everyday responses from people to such things as their size or looks or behaviours. Your response can easily reinforce this exclusion or challenge it. When you wish to explore the impact of your power within a relationship you could identify your role, identity and viewpoint within that context – your subject positions. This requires considering the external experiences and influences that shape and inhabit an individual's understanding of their situation and the wider context. Drawing upon Heron's (2005) work, you could consider the following questions.

- What power relations operate here?
- What subject positions do I and this other individual occupy?
- How are we 'empowered' and 'disempowered' in this relationship?

- What and how are we resisting – personally and within a wider context?

- What value and effort do I invest in understanding how to provide equal service to all? Why this level?

- How does this investment act as a barrier or facilitator for others?

- What self-image do I have as a result of my good intentions towards different social/ethnic/cultural/gender groups?

- What happens to my self-image if I see myself as having failed in respect to my good intentions?

- Have I failed? Have I, in fact, been unequal in my work with these individuals?

The purpose of asking such questions is not to make you feel guilty. They are a means of examining and challenging your unspoken biases and those that exist within the systems around you, and of identifying factors from which you and others can learn. Consider the actions of this reception class teacher, Susie, when her teaching assistant, Anna, takes control of a boy, Jared, in her class. Jared is a child with autism: Jared joins Susie at the literacy table but once again argues with her about her instructions, saying that she can't tell him to sit and that he won't if she asks. He leaves the table but Anna gets him back. It is clear that Susie now feels awkward and undermined. Susie controls her own sense of frustration, but tells off another distracted boy with more firmness than she might typically. (Rix, 2004) In this context Susie finds her typical power relations being usurped. She's the least powerful in this context. She's wishing to support her empowered teaching assistant. She's also aware that Jared is not at ease with a number of assumed social practices. It's important to her to be even-handed in her exchanges and so she allows herself to be potentially diminished in the eyes of those around her. Yet this leaves her feeling vulnerable.

Starting with the children

It is not just your assumptions that need consideration; children's behaviours and communications are affected by a range of possible physical, emotional, personal, social, cultural, intellectual and situational factors. These contextual factors frame the ways in which messages and meanings are expressed and interpreted. In some situations these factors can interfere with our ability to communicate (such as in the example of Susie above), and at other times they can ease the process of communication. This in turn affects the context for further messages.

The importance of listening

A central aspect of both inclusive and reflective practice is listening. Active listening is a particularly effective way for both adults and children to gain understanding of another person's ideas. It encourages the speaker to engage more fully in the communication.

It requires that you show that you are listening. It is not simply responsive, it is about engaging with the views of the individual, and taking the time to explore the meaning and the impact of that meaning. Listening is not just an aural activity, either. It can be seen as a holistic process, involving all our faculties to interpret the experiences being evidenced by others:

Seeing the child as active and knowledgeable

Children are neither static entities nor passive ones: Disabled children, like other children and adults, are flexible social beings whose behavioural patterns, communication abilities, level of involvement and level of interest will vary over the duration of an activity (Davis and Watson, 2000: 213). They bring with them understandings, skills and experiences. This social and cultural capital (Bourdieu, 1983) underlies the child's engagement with the social and cultural situations he or she faces

Avoiding assumptions, challenging fixed positions

How do you come to know the children you work with? Do you discuss them with their parents, with your colleagues, with outside practitioners, with the children themselves? Do you carry out detailed normative assessment or do you engage with children in the activity and explore their progress through formative assessment? Do you let them define their interests in a curricular context or do you impose what children do throughout their day? Do you seek out their views or rely upon your own experiences? It is not uncommon for practitioners to do the latter. For example, the rare questions teachers do ask about prior knowledge focus upon what has been taught in earlier lessons (Myhill and Brackley, 2004). This reinforces the notion that the knowledge children bring from outside the setting is less important than academic, taught knowledge. It also means that numerous learning opportunities are being missed. If we do not ask questions we must make assumptions about what children know. The chances are high that we'll make mistakes.

Starting with your practice

One of the challenges and pleasures of inclusion is that it is full of such possible contradictions. It is about tensions and rough edges. One of the most challenging is the need to respect and build upon a child's views and prior knowledge, yet at the same time confronting the biases that exist within them. Children from a very early age have many biases well established. Research in Australia (Davies, 1991, 1993), for example, demonstrated that within early years settings young people commonly respond to stories in a stereotypical, gendered manner, even if the stories remove stereotypical roles. Of course, much in our society and culture encourages negative stereotypes. For example, evil or tragic characters in classic children's books often have some sort of physical impairment (e.g. Long John Silver and Tiny Tim). If you wish children to move beyond these hidden (or not so hidden) biases then you have to encourage them to take a critical perspective on experiences. It may feel as if throughout this process you risk setting your values (and the education system's values?) against those of the child and the culture from which they come, creating the opportunity for exclusion. The lesson of inclusion, however, is that through encouraging children to engage in other people's perspectives, particularly through peer group interactive approaches, opportunities can be created to explore and reflect on such issues. Through this process children can come to see that possible contradictions are only contradictions if you see them from one fixed, unquestioning perspective.

Viewing it from another perspective

Another concern I have about this chapter is that it may have a negative tone. By encouraging you to question your attitudes and practices, it may feel as if it's suggesting there is something fundamentally wrong about them. This is not my intention. I hope that the reflective process helps you find much that is positive and provides you with inclusive opportunities. Susan Hart (1996) described how much that can enhance learning is overlooked because people are searching for the things that get in the way of the learning, or for things that they believe can be improved. She considers experiences and actions not because they are a source of difficulties but because they are a 'source of insight into possibilities'. She named this reflexive process 'innovative thinking'.

A key component of this innovative thinking approach is that it includes the context. The child is not the only focus. You move beyond your traditional response to explore other possibilities. Such an approach has value beyond the student/practitioner relationship, when considering issues related to anyone from a parent to a colleague to yourself!

Opening up to others

At the heart of inclusion practice is the collaboration that creates learning opportunities for both adult and child. Just as we support children within the setting, so too do we need to support and be supported by all those with whom we work and the systems we create. Research repeatedly shows that practitioners who are involved in good teamwork are more effective, enthusiastic and confident about inclusion.

Conclusion: Recognizing we are doing this together

Inclusion begins with an attitude. It only works if you believe it is your responsibility to make it work. Inclusion encourages you to reflect on your views about group identities, behaviours and roles, and your responses to them. It asks you to consider the manner in which you invest your own identity within such group identities, behaviours and roles. You can see the challenges you are presented with as opportunities. In so doing you try to shift perspectives, to engage with the views of others, and encourage them in turn to engage more widely. The great thing about children, however, is that they require very little encouragement to do all of this for themselves, and so in the process you too may learn far more than you ever expected.

part five

Deepening understanding

16 **Expertise** Conceptual tools for career-long fascination

17 **Professionalism** How does reflective teaching contribute to society?

Expertise
Conceptual tools for career-long fascination

16

Readings

16.1 Pat Collarbone
Contemporary change and professional development
(p. 328)

16.2 Tony Eaude
The development of teacher expertise (p. 332)

16.3 Marilyn Osborn, Elizabeth McNess, Andrew Pollard, Pat Triggs and Patricia Broadfoot
Creative mediation and professional judgement (p. 336)

16.4 Iiris Happo and Kaarina Määttä
The expertise of early childhood educators (p. 340)

The readings in this chapter offer perspectives on change and professional development.

We start with Pat Collarbone, whose experience in a national agency leads her to call on teachers to embrace professional development as part of workforce development to meet future needs. In the second reading, Tony Eaude considers the development of teacher expertise as the essence of professionalism. He draws particular attention to the structuring of knowledge. These readings are particularly useful in the context of change within which early years practitioners are currently operating.

In the third reading Osborn, McNess, Pollard, Triggs and Broadfoot consider the role of creative mediation and professional judgement and what it means to be a confident, reflective professional. The final reading focuses more specifically on what expertise and professionalism may include in the early years.

Reading 16.1

Contemporary change and professional development

Pat Collarbone

This reading explains the need to look forward, and to continually develop the individual and collective expertise of teachers. Collarbone argues that this is essential to respond to the pace of contemporary change, and this rationale certainly underpins the 'remodelling' policies of governments to enhance and focus the professionalism of the 'education workforce'.

Do you like being 'remodelled'? How can you take control of your own professional development in the contexts in which you work? What, if anything, can practitioners working within the early years sector learn from the experiences of practitioners in schools?

Edited from: Collarbone, P. (2009) *Creating Tomorrow: Planning, Developing and Sustaining Change in Education and Other Public Services.* London: Continuum, 2–5.

This is a time of profound and seismic global shifts. Our world is changing fundamentally; at an exhilarating, or terrifying, speed – depending on your perspective.

The changes and challenges we face today are even greater than those of the nineteenth century, when the industrial revolution exploded into being and fundamentally and permanently changed the way we work and live.

Today, the miracles and curses of the technological revolution are having a similar level of impact on our work and lives, only this time the change is even faster and the impact is even more ubiquitous. Today, things are becoming possible, even commonplace, on a daily basis that only a few short years ago seemed like outlandish science fiction.

The technological revolution isn't happening in isolation of course. At the same time, new economies are growing at an unprecedented pace, destabilizing the old economic status quo and creating uncertainty and conflict as well as opportunity: reserves of oil and other key resources are depleting at an alarming rate; our security is threatened by a real and sometimes over-imagined terrorist threat; and the earth itself is under dire environmental threat from our profligacy.

These momentous changes – and numerous others – are happening, here and now, whether we acknowledge them or do anything about them or not. They are affecting all our lives in a myriad of ways: political, economic, social, technical, legal, environmental … you name it. And the stakes are higher than at any other time in our history.

Such changes are fast making the old top-down organizational model that grew out of the industrial revolution a thing of the past. For effective organisations today, inclusively and collaboratively involving all staff in all aspects of planning, production and delivery, and putting the customer at the heart of delivery (and often development), is becoming the norm.

At the core of all this change is workforce development.

The movement to greater personalization is not only customer facing, it is also an internal process. A strong focus on individuals, both customers and staff, is becoming more and more important to success. To do this effectively, organizations need to become more demand led, reforming their staffing models and making them more inclusive and flexible. The following points illustrate the need for workforce development:

- Intellectual capital (and those that hold it) has become one of organizations' most valuable resources, if not the most valuable. This gives employees a great deal more power, importance and influence than they have ever previously had.

- The increasing mobility of all levels of workers, added to the importance of intellectual capital, is dramatically changing the way employees are viewed and treated.

- The nature of leadership is changing, from the 'hero' leader of old to a more democratic, inclusive and collaborative model.

- Organizations are looking more and more to develop new collaborative partnerships (locally, nationally and internationally), often supported by the efficiencies and capabilities of new technology, to enhance their work.

- The speed of change is increasing and this demands correspondingly flexible organizations – with flexible and talented staff – that are able to adapt and change equally quickly.

- Ongoing training and continual professional development for staff, i.e. a high level of staff expertise, is becoming increasingly key to organizations' long-term success.

These changes are not news. In fact, many of our more forward thinking organizations have already addressed them head on – and continue to address them. For example, in England, our schools, local authorities and range of support agencies and other organizations, have used and continue to use the remodelling change process to direct, manage and adapt to these changes in a successful and sustainable way of students, and students seeing teaching as the key to their ongoing learning. The remarkable feature of the evidence is that the greatest effect on student learning occurs when teachers become learners of their own teaching, and when students become their own teachers. When students become their own teachers, they exhibit the self-regulatory attributes that seem most desirable for learners (self-monitoring, self-evaluation, self-assessment, self-teaching).

A key premise is that the teacher's view of his or her role is critical. It is the specific mind frames that teachers have about their role – and most critically a mind frame within which they ask themselves about the effect they are having on student learning. Fundamentally, the most powerful way of thinking about a teacher's role is for teachers to see themselves as *evaluators* of their effects on students. Teachers need to use evidence-based methods to inform, change, and sustain these evaluation beliefs about their effect. These beliefs relate to claims about what each student can do as a consequence of the teacher's actions, and how every resource (especially peers) can be used to play a part in moving students from what they can do now to where the teacher considers they should be – and to do so in the most efficient, as well as effective, manner. It matters what teachers do – but what matters *most* is having an appropriate mind frame relating to the impact of what they do. An appropriate mind frame combined with appropriate actions work together to achieve a positive learning effect.

As I argued in *Visible Learning* (Hattie, 2009), when teachers see learning occurring or not occurring, they intervene in calculated and meaningful ways to alter the direction of learning to attain various shared, specific, and challenging goals. In particular, they provide students with multiple opportunities and alternatives for developing learning strategies based on the surface and deep levels of learning some context or domain matter, leading to students building conceptual understanding of this learning, which the students and teachers then use in future learning. Learners can be so different, making it difficult for a teacher to achieve such teaching acts: student can be in different learning places at various times, using a multiplicity of unique learning strategies, meeting different and appropriately challenging goals. Learning is a very personal journey for the teacher and the student, although there are remarkable commonalities in this journey for many teachers and students. It requires much skill for teachers to demonstrate to all of their students that they can see the students' 'perspective, communicating it back to them so that they have valuable feedback to self-assess, feel safe, and learn to understand others and the content with the same interest and concern' (Cornelius-White, 2007: 23).

The act of teaching requires deliberate interventions to ensure that there is cognitive change in the student; thus the key ingredients are being aware of the learning intentions, knowing when a student is successful in attaining those intentions, having sufficient understanding of the student's prior understanding as he or she comes to the task, and knowing enough about the content to provide meaningful and challenging experiences so that there is some sort of progressive development. It involves a teacher who knows a range of learning strategies with which to supply the student when they seem not to under- stand, who can provide direction and redirection in terms of the content being understood and thus maximize the power of feedback, and show the skill to 'get out the way' when learning is progressing towards the success criteria.

Of course, it helps if these learning intentions and success criteria are shared with, committed to, and understood by the learner – because in the right caring and idea-rich environment, the learner can then experiment (be right and wrong) with the content and the thinking about the content, and make connections across ideas. A safe environment for the learner (and for the teacher) is an environment in which error is welcomed and fostered – because we learn so much from errors and from the feedback that then accrues from going in the wrong direction or not going sufficiently fluently in the right direction. In the same way teachers themselves need to be in a safe environment to learn about the success or otherwise of their teaching from others.

To create such an environment, to command a range of learning strategies, and to be cognitively aware of the pedagogical means that enable the student to learn requires dedicated, passionate people. Such teachers need to be aware of which of their teaching strategies are working or not, need to be prepared to understand and adapt to the learner(s) and their situation, contexts, and prior learning, and need to share the experience of learning in this manner in an open, forthright, and enjoyable way with their students and their colleagues.

It is teachers with certain mind frames that make the difference. Powerful, passionate, accomplished teachers are those who:

- focus on students' cognitive engagement with the content of what it is that is being taught;
- focus on developing a way of thinking and reasoning that emphasizes problem-solving and teaching strategies relating to the content that they wish students to learn;
- focus on imparting new knowledge and understanding, and then monitor how students gain fluency and appreciation in the new knowledge;
- focus on providing feedback in an appropriate and timely manner to help students to attain the worthwhile goals of the lesson;
- seek feedback about their effects on the progress and proficiency of *all* of their students
- have deep understanding about how we learn; and
- focus on seeing learning through the eyes of their students, appreciating their fits and starts in learning, and their often non-linear progressions to the goals, supporting their deliberate practice, providing feedback about their errors and misdirections, and caring that the students get to the goals and that the students share the teacher's passion for the material being learnt.

This focus is sustained, unrelenting, and needs to be shared by all in a school.

Reading 16.2

The development of teacher expertise

Tony Eaude

> This excerpt is from a short summary of the literature on teacher expertise and addresses the background research, the structure of expert knowledge, practical flexibility and responsiveness and processes of expert development. The importance of practice is worth noting, as is the significance of conceptual understanding.
>
> Can you relate these ideas about expertise to practitioners you know?
>
> *Edited from:* Eaude, T. (2012) *How Do Expert Primary Class-teachers Really Work?* Knutsford: Critical Publishing, 8–10, 13, 61–2.

Berliner (2001) summarises research-informed propositions about expertise as follows:

- expertise is specific to a domain, developed over hundreds and thousands of hours, and continues to develop;
- development of expertise is not linear, with plateaus occurring, indicating shifts of understanding;
- expert knowledge is structured better for use in performance than is novice knowledge;
- experts represent problems in qualitatively different – deeper and richer – ways than novices;
- experts recognise meaningful patterns faster than novices;
- experts are more flexible and more opportunistic planners and can change representations faster, when appropriate, than novices;
- experts impose meaning on, and are less easily misled by, ambiguous stimuli;
- experts may start to solve a problem slower than a novice but overall they are faster problem solvers;
- experts are usually more constrained by task requirements and the social constraints of the situation than novices;
- experts develop automaticity to allow conscious processing of more complex information;
- experts have developed self-regulatory processes as they engage in their activities.

The list above was initially provided by Glaser (1999). It shows clearly that expertise is very difficult to develop, requiring a lot of practice over a long period of time. In many fields, such as music and sport, the figure of 10,000 hours is used and Berliner (2004) cites research that expert radiologists were estimated to have looked at 100,000 X-rays.

In relation to teaching, Berliner (2001) suggests at least four and a half years, though this depends on how expertise is defined and at what level.

Second, expertise develops at an uneven pace, as the individual's understanding changes; and separate aspects of expertise develop at different times and speeds. So a chess player's opening play and his tactical awareness may develop at different rates, probably according to which aspects he practises and concentrates on. And an engineer is likely to acquire expertise more in design, construction, maintenance or repair, according to which she focusses on. While all teachers can, and should be expected to, become increasingly expert, they are unlikely to have a high level of expertise in every respect.

Third, experts do not just do the same things as novices but better, or quicker, or more economically. They think and operate in different ways. Consider the hockey goalkeeper's expertise. Aspects such as body position, balance and timing are crucial, but this does not just entail doing what a club goalkeeper does, but much better. It involves using and combining varying aspects of knowledge to act in qualitatively different ways.

How experts structure knowledge

One key aspect of expertise is how the individual thinks about problems to be solved. Shulman (2004) provides valuable insights from his work on the thought processes of doctors when diagnosing a patient's medical condition. These processes are usually assumed to be rational, based on collecting all the evidence and then coming to a conclusion on the basis of this. However, Shulman's research suggests that, in practice, doctors intuitively formulate a series of tentative hypotheses, altering these, or formulating new ones, as fresh information becomes available.

A GP to whom I spoke recently stated that she relied heavily on intuition, but added that knowledge of the family often helps to make links which would otherwise be missed, though this could also be a hindrance if 'one loses the capacity to be surprised', in her words, or 'makes too many presuppositions', in mine.

Such processes are necessary to manage complex situations without oversimplifying. In Glaser's words, (1999: 91) expertise involves the selective search of memory or use of general problem-solving tactics, with an 'efficiency that derives primarily from this knowledge being structured for retrieval, pattern recognition and inferencing.' In other words, experts' knowledge is arranged so that what matters most can be recalled easily, possible patterns identified and reasonable hypotheses be formulated. Selecting which information or cues to take note of, and which to ignore, is one mark of the real expert.

Shulman (2004) emphasises that, in most fields, experts increasingly work in teams with other people who have specific skills or expertise that they do not have. So, for instance, a surgeon will rely on a whole team, including anaesthetists and specialist nurses; and an architect will work with engineers, quantity surveyors and others. One implication is that different sorts of expertise are – or should be – complementary. A second is that responsibility is collective rather than residing with one individual, helping to reduce the sense of isolation and of being on one's own which tends to make one more cautious, when faced with uncertainty. However, teachers rarely work in teams – at least when actually teaching – and so are often left isolated in the very situation where they most need the support of others.

How experts respond to events and feedback

Bereiter and Scardalmalia (cited in Berliner 2001: 473) distinguish between crystallized and fluid (or adaptive) expertise. The former 'consists of intact procedures that have been thoroughly learned through experience, brought forth and used in relatively familiar tasks. Fluid expertise consists of abilities that come into play when an expert confronts novel or challenging tasks.' Those working in complex situations and dynamic environments, such as teachers, require fluid expertise. This involves reliance on intuition and hunch, but supported by a deep knowledge both of the task and the context – and assessment of what might go well or otherwise and noticing signs that it is.

Glaser (1999: 89) writes that 'the central underlying properties or meaningful deep structure of the situation is key to experts' perceptions, whereas the surface features and structural properties organise the less-than-expert individuals' perceptions.' This indicates that experts recognise significant patterns and use these to inform practice; and that expertise involves models and routines based on an initial analysis of the situation, but adapted in the light of circumstances.

Glaser's list above included 'automaticity to allow conscious processing of more complex information.' Experts use routines to help cope with complexity and to decide quickly which information is relevant and which not. For example, the expert doctor or therapist will go through various routine checks and look out for symptoms or responses, especially unexpected ones. Experts know, and try to work at, the limits of their own expertise, but they do so economically, simplifying the situation to make it manageable but without oversimplifying. This allows them to concentrate on, and respond to, what is going on around them. Someone less expert tends to take too much account of what does not matter and either to oversimplify or to adopt an overcomplicated strategy. Oversimplifying limits the opportunities for novelty and improvisation, while overcomplicating leads to confusion and to wasted time.

Experts use self-regulatory processes with great skill, enabling them to step back at appropriate points and observe the process and outcomes of their actions. Their self-awareness is shown in the allocation of attention and sensitivity to what is happening, adapting their initial hypotheses in response to feedback of different types. This is because they need to, and do, see what is not going according to plan, so that they can adapt, with an expert being better than a novice at judging when, and to what extent, an activity or an approach should be modified.

As Sternberg and Horvath (1995: 16) suggest, an expert 'neither jumps into solution attempts prematurely nor follows a solution path blindly … and is able selectively to encode, combine and compare information to arrive at insightful solutions.' So, those with a high level of expertise are likely to move more rapidly to find the best way forward than non-experts when the situation or the problem is relatively simple. However, in complex or unfamiliar territory, they may move more slowly, more deliberatively, testing hypotheses against new evidence, though they are usually likely to be quicker overall and certainly more successful than non-experts. Experts sense when to act and when to hold off, neither panicking nor being indecisive, when faced with uncertainty. And when to stick by the rules and when to bend them.

Ways of developing expertise

When developing expertise, teachers gradually build better-informed and greater confidence in their own professional judgement.

Ideally, developing expertise is a collective as well as an individual process, where individuals can draw on the wisdom of others, from research and the practice of those with greater experience.

Teachers benefit from watching other teachers at work, or working alongside them, looking to identify and discuss dilemmas and successful patterns of resolution rather than concentrating on shortcomings.

Experts recognise the limits of their expertise and are prepared to call on others, where need be. In teaching, this involves drawing on the expertise of other people both within and beyond the school and sharing their own. This is much easier in a school context where others provide support. Just as the learning environment influences profoundly how children learn, the school and policy environment affects how teachers are encouraged, or otherwise, to exercise and develop their expertise. This requires headteachers and colleagues who encourage each other to explore, to risk, to innovate – and support each other through the successes and the difficulties.

Shulman highlights the value of case studies in developing professional expertise, suggesting (2004: 564) that these are valuable because 'participants are urged to elaborate on … what actually happened, what was said and done, how all that occurred made them feel … to dig deep into the particularity of the context because it is in the devilish details that practice differs dramatically from theory.'

Watching and discussing with others with a high level of expertise is a necessary part of teachers developing expertise. But it is not enough. Underlying how teachers act is how they think. So teachers have to challenge – and often try to change – how they think about ideas such as intelligence and inclusion, behaviour and breadth, curriculum and challenge. For instance, Twiselton's (2006) research into primary student teachers characterises some as 'task managers', with little emphasis on children's learning, some as 'curriculum deliverers' where the focus is more on learning but largely based on external demands, and some as 'concept/skill builders' where they understand and encourage patterns of learning beyond the task. If teachers are to see themselves as curriculum creators rather than deliverers, initial teacher education must at least open up this possibility; and continuing professional development must encourage it.

Reading 16.3

Creative mediation and professional judgement

Marilyn Osborn, Elizabeth McNess, Andrew Pollard, Pat Triggs and Patricia Broadfoot

This reading is drawn from one of the final reports from the PACE project – an independent analysis of the impact of the introduction of the National Curriculum and assessment on primary teachers and pupils. The study documented many teacher responses to new challenges, including simple compliance, resistance (and even retirement), but one of the most constructive was 'creative mediation'. This approach is what might be expected from a confident, reflective professional.

Edited from: Osborn, M., McNess, E. and Broadfoot, P., with Pollard, A. and Triggs, P. (2000) *What Teachers Do: Changing Policy and Practice in Primary Education.* London: Continuum, 81–3.

A central factor in determining teachers' ability to adopt a creative response to the imposed reforms was their level of professional confidence. As Helsby (1999: 173) argues:

Teachers who are professionally confident have a strong belief not only in their capacity but also in their authority to make important decisions about the conduct of their work … In order to be able to do this, the teacher needs to feel "in control" of the work situation. Thus professional confidence also implies that the teacher is not overwhelmed by excessive work demands that can never be properly met. The confident teacher has a sense of being able to manage the tasks in hand rather than being driven by them. Instead of crisis management, corner-cutting and ill-considered coping strategies, they are able to reflect upon, and make conscious choices between, alternative courses of action and can feel that they are doing "a good job".

The key question here is to be able to identify and foster those factors which contribute to a teacher's level of professional confidence. We have shown previously that, to some extent, teachers' personal biographies, their previous experiences and the values they have developed as a result influenced their level of professional confidence (Osborn, 1996a, 1996b). In our report of phase two of the PACE project we drew upon the examples of Sara and Elizabeth, two Key Stage 1 teachers of roughly the same age and level of teaching experience who worked in the same school. A comparison of these two teachers over the first few years of the reforms from 1990 to 1994, showed how personal biography and career trajectories can affect the level of professional confidence and a continued sense of satisfaction with the teaching role.

Both Sara Wilson and Elizabeth West were highly experienced teachers who had been working in the same infant school in the outskirts of a large southern city for well over ten years. Sara had been a teacher for 22 years and Elizabeth for 26 years. In 1990 both were feeling overloaded, stressed and anxious about the effect of the National Curriculum on the children in their class. They had considerable fears about how primary education would develop in the future and about the effect of national assessment on the quality of teaching and learning in their school. During the course of the study, Sara, who was responsible for a Year 2 class, had become Deputy Head. Elizabeth, who taught a mixed Year 1 and Year 2 class, had a point of responsibility for special needs. Strikingly, in spite of many similarities in terms of their experience in teaching, their commitment to the children, and the same school context, the changes impacted quite differently upon them during the course of the four years.

By the end of the four years, Sara felt she had emerged with a new sense of focus and clarity about her role and her practice. She saw the gains and rewards from teaching post-National Curriculum as clearly outweighing the losses, and was particularly confident that she had acquired improved skills in assessment. As she described it:

> I'm more focused now when I plan an activity.

Sara felt that a key factor in helping her to adapt to change was the support she derived 'from being in a school with a strong, stable staff, and from her own temperament which she defined as calm and practical, enabling her to "get hold of the changes and do them in the least damaging way, keeping hold of children's happiness and enthusiasm'. However, perhaps the key point in Sara's response to the changes, and the one which most differentiated her from Elizabeth, was the emphasis she placed on the importance of taking control of the changes, and finding ways of making them part of her thinking rather than simply seeing them as external targets which had to be met. She described this in the following way:

> I think that what I hope to do is to internalise myself as a teacher, internalise all this detail and to then be able to use it in good infant practice, etc. etc.

This striving after internalisation, taking control, and integration of new demands into what she defined as good infant practice was a hallmark of teachers whom we have described as 'creative mediators', those who feel able to take active control of educational changes and to respond to them in a creative, but possibly selective way.

Sara's emergence as a confident, post-ERA professional, who had successfully integrated the new requirements into her own identity as a teacher, contrasted with the unhappiness and sense of loss expressed by Elizabeth four years into the reforms. Although she also saw gains from teachers having a clearer idea and more awareness of what they were aiming for in their work with children, for her the losses outweighed the gains. She did not feel that she had been able to hold onto the creativity she had before.

> I've tightened up but also narrowed down. We are really missing the fun of the extra bits. As someone said in one of our staff meetings, "It's like walking through a wood and keeping to a pathway, not seeing the interesting things on either side ... For me the National Curriculum has narrowed my outlook as much as I have tried for it not to. There is still so much to get through and I still feel in a straitjacket. I do smashing work with the children and then I find it doesn't cover the Attainment Targets, so I realise that I still

have all that to do….It takes a lot of enjoyment from me. For me, teaching has always been a creative outlet. Now I'm constrained, I've lost a lot of creativity.

Her own identity as a teacher, her confidence, and her ability to be creative were perceived by her to be under threat. A key difference between Elizabeth and Sara seemed to be in their ability to take control and make choices about how to implement the changes. Elizabeth was, by her own description, a perfectionist. She felt that she must conscientiously cover every attainment target with every child no matter what the cost. Sara, on the other hand, saw herself as able to say 'no' to new demands. She was able to avoid the over-conscientiousness which has been a characteristic of many committed primary teachers (Campbell et al., 1991).

Another key difference was in the new roles taken on by both teachers in the course of the study. Sara had been able to move onto a new role as deputy head which arguably gave her a broader view of the reforms, new challenges, and new motivations. Rather than feeling de-skilled, she had been able to make the new demands build upon her strengths. Huberman, 1993, argued that a key factor in the professional satisfaction of teachers was a feeling of 'upward mobility and social promotion'. This characterised the career trajectories of many teachers in his sample of middle and high-school teachers who had remained the most energetic and committed throughout their careers.

Another factor for these teachers' continued satisfaction was the continuation of an enjoyable and good relationship with pupils. Whereas Sara had certainly gained a new role which involved 'upward mobility and social promotion', Elizabeth had lost her key 'satisfier', her relationship with the children, which she perceived to be increasingly under threat. Her post of responsibility for special needs children (sic) was particularly significant here and may have exacerbated this sense of loss. Of the Key Stage 1 teachers in the 1994 PACE sample, 44 per cent saw the National Curriculum as particularly disadvantaging children with special needs. It was clear from Elizabeth's responses that she shared this view. In primary teaching, there is a close link between a teacher's self or sense of identity as part of the professional role and the 'self' as a person (Cortazzi, 1991; Nias, 1989; Pollard, 1985). In Elizabeth's case it appears that the changes threatened not only her professional identity, but also her sense of 'self' as a person, since for her it was the emotional response of the 'personal self' reinforced by her relationships which made teaching worthwhile.

Both these teachers had been working under many constraints, not the least of which were large classes. The strategies which they evolved to cope with the constraints imposed by multiple change were influenced by their level of professional confidence which, in turn appeared to be influenced by their personal biographies and career trajectories and the level of satisfaction they continued to derive from their work.

Another key factor in the development of professional confidence, even within the constraints imposed by multiple change, is the context and culture within which a teacher works. As Chapter 3 suggested, the socio-economic catchment area of the school may lead to teachers experiencing very different pressures and consequently adopting different strategies for change. Research also suggests that the ability to adopt a response of 'creative mediation' to the National Curriculum is heavily influenced by the presence of a supportive school climate, in particular where a collaborative culture flourishes which gives teachers the confidence to assert their own interpretations upon situations (Helsby and McCulloch, 1997). In the case study drawn upon above, Sara commented upon the importance of the supportive environment provided by the head and the school in which teachers were encouraged to make their own decisions about how they selectively implemented change. Most of the teachers we identified as 'creative mediators' worked within a strong, collaborative school culture where they were given confidence that they could benefit from the structure and guidelines of the National Curriculum without letting it drive them or destroy what they knew to be good about their practice.

We have thus identified some areas where teachers can be seen to have mediated policy through professional practice in ways which may amount to policy creation. We have outlined four strategies of creative mediation; protective, innovative, collaborative, and conspiratorial by which teachers can be seen to have formulated classroom policy by acting in common, although not necessarily collective ways.

More recent evidence suggests that even with the introduction of the national literacy and numeracy strategies in schools, many schools and the individual teachers within them are seizing the potential for a margin of manoeuvre between such centralised policies and their implementation. Thus some teachers are finding creative ways of working within the guidelines imposed by these recent strategies and gaining a 'new professional discourse' (Woods and Jeffrey, 1997) as a result. The evidence presented here suggests that creative mediation by teachers is an important strategy which may have system-wide effects on policy and which will continue as long as there are teachers who feel sufficiently confident to adapt and develop practices that accord with their values and working situations.

Professional confidence may depend upon many variables at both institutional and individual level, including personal biographies and career trajectories, the gaining of an overview through moving to a new level of responsibility and a consequent sense of being re-valued and re-skilled, school context, and perhaps most significantly of all the existence of a supportive and collaborative school climate and culture.

Reading 16.4

The expertise of early childhood educators
Iiris Happo and Kaarina Määttä

In this final reading, Happo and Määttä consider what expertise is, how it is developed, and the professional expertise of early childhood practitioners, with a specific focus on practitioners in Finland.

Do you feel you are an expert? What supports this notion? Do you feel your expertise is valued?

Edited from: Happo, I. and Määttä, K. (2011) 'Expertise of early childhood educators', *International Education Studies*, 4 (3), 91–9.

Multidimensional pedagogical expertise

Expertise is a concept which is used in many different connections (Ericksson et al., 2006). Generally, it refers to the special know-how which is related to different professions (Burnard, 1992; Carter et al., 1987; Disch, 2002; Sim and Kim, 2010; Walker et al., 2010). A certain amount of education and work experience is usually needed for the development into the expert (see also Adelson, 1984). In order to understand the multidimensional pedagogical expertise, we should consider the character of expertise and its principal components. These essential components are practical, formal, and metacognitive knowledge and they complement each other. (Bereiter and Scardamalia, 1993; Eteläpelto, 1992; Eteläpelto, 1997; Tynjälä, 1999; Tynjälä, 2008, et al., 2006).

Practical knowledge is informal differing from theoretical knowledge (Bereiter and Scardamalia, 1993; Calderhead, 1984; Tynjälä et al., 2006). At the practical level, knowledge appears as a pragmatic action. It is based on experience and is often acquired in working life. Professionals learn much simply by doing. It means that teachers develop their expertise by teaching. (Tynjälä et al., 2006.)

When people talk about 'knowledge' they usually mean formal knowledge and refer to it loosely as 'the kind of thing that is found in textbooks'. Although it is found in textbooks, it is more than some kind of an abstraction existing in individuals' minds. Formal knowledge is important for communication, teaching, and learning. In order to communicate, experts need a common language with a conceptual similarity. Formal knowledge can also be created in social processes through critical thinking and argumentation. (Bereiter and Scardamalia, 1993; Tynjälä, 2008).

Formal knowledge provides the basis of the experts' practical skills. However, one of the major questions is how to translate formal knowledge into informal knowledge and skills. (Bereiter and Scardamalia, 1993) According to Bereiter and Scardamalia (1993), it seems plausible that formal knowledge is converted into a skill by using formal knowledge to solve procedural problems. Furthermore, formal knowledge is converted into informal knowledge by using formal knowledge to solve comprehension problems. (Bereiter and Scardamalia, 1993) Problem solving is an inseparable part of pedagogical expertise at every level of knowledge. Hatano and Inagaki (1986, 1992) distinguish routine expertise and adaptive expertise from each other. While a routine expert is able to make an efficient and high-quality performance in unchanging situations, the adaptive expert is able to acquit oneself well also in new, constantly changing situations.

The third component of the pedagogical expertise is metacognitive knowledge. It involves self-knowledge and self-assessment. It includes knowledge about where and when to use particular strategies; for example, for learning or problem solving. Rather, it is about knowing how to regulate oneself in order to do a task in a particular way than knowing how to do a task. It is a question of self-regulatory knowledge. (Bereiter and Scardamalia, 1993; Eteläpelto, 1997; Stenström, 2006; Tynjälä, 2008).

Expertise of early childhood educators

It is agreed that experts are people who have the ultimate skills and knowledge of their own field. They usually have a long working experience and they are able to use their professional ability in practice. (Eteläpelto, 1992.) In Finland, the experts of early childhood education are professionals in the pedagogical field working mainly in the day care sector in its various forms (National Curriculum Guidelines, 2003). Finnish early childhood education comprises care, education, and instruction. However, the know-how included in these areas can also be examined as the separate fields of competences. Early childhood educators' instructional knowledge includes curriculum, content, and pedagogical knowledge. Curriculum knowledge directs an educator to utilize appropriate contents and structure of teaching young children. In addition to a subject to be taught, content knowledge contains the competence of knowing how to teach young children. Pedagogical knowledge contains the choices made in the teaching situation as well as practical action. A pedagogically skilful teacher has exquisite interaction skills. She understands what makes learning easy or difficult and can choose developmentally appropriate practices flexibly during a teaching situation. (Guskey, 1986; Saracho and Spodekin, 2003).

Ryan and Cooper (2004) present that teachers' self-knowledge and enthusiasm have a significant implication for successful educating and teaching. Successful educational work requires a positive attitude towards children, colleagues, and parents. Especially, children are sensitive to perceive adults' behavior and emotions. (Ryan and Cooper, 2004) Also van Manen (1991) emphasizes interaction as a part of a good pedagogical process.

The expertise of an early childhood educator is apparently versatile and this phenomenon contains skills and competences of a different kind to be reviewed. According to Karila and Nummenmaa (2001), early childhood educators' competences are contextual knowledge, interaction and cooperation skills, and pedagogical knowledge. In order to improve as an educator, the critical reflection skills are needed as well.

Contextual knowledge contains the understanding about culture and society. Early childhood educators have to be aware of children's and families' living environment and take this into account in their educational work. Interaction and cooperation skills are needed in cooperation with children, families, and partners. A good relationship between parents and educators is an essential part of children's well-being and these social skills are an inseparable part of educators' work. (Karila and Nummenmaa, 2001; National Curriculum Guidelines, 2003).

Early childhood educators' core competence is pedagogical knowledge. In order to be able to improve children's well-being and development, early childhood educators should be aware of the values and goals of education as well as the concept of learning. They should understand the meaning of supporting interaction. However, the understanding of education and concept of learning constantly develops. (Karila and Nummenmaa, 2001; Hirsjärvi, 1997) Ryan and Cooper (2004) call the examination and evaluation of one's own work as reflective thinking and emphasize its importance for vocational development. Similarly Costigan and Crocco (2004) stress the significance of reflection for teachers' development. Furthermore, it would be important to use reflective thinking at work starting immediately from the first work year. However, vocational development should continue the whole career (Costigan and Crocco, 2004).

Professionalism
How does reflective teaching contribute to society?

17

Readings

17.1 Cathy Nutbrown
Qualifications: The Nutbrown Review (p. 346)

17.2 Margaret Archer
Thinking about educational systems (p. 349)

17.3 Frank Field
The Field report: Preventing poor children becoming poor adults (p. 351)

17.4 Jones Irwin
The philosophy of Paulo Freire (p. 355)

17.5 Tony Bertram and Chris Pascal
The impact of early education as a strategy in countering socio-economic disadvantage (p. 358)

The readings in this chapter are concerned with professionalism and society.

We begin with an excerpt form the Nutbrown Review in which Cathy Nutbrown lays out her vision for the future of the early years workforce, with a specific focus on the qualifications of those working within the sector – something which has undergone a great deal of scrutiny and change in recent years. The second reading looks at how educational systems are subjected to scrutiny and reminds us that policy and rhetoric must be questioned.

We then move on to a group of readings which consider the role of education in changing society, of supporting those who 'have less' or whose 'voice' may be marginalized – often related to wealth. Indeed, as these readings show, wealth plays a central role in determining children's futures, but they also remind us that education, and the early years of education in particular, have a key role in supporting children to realize futures which may not otherwise be possible.

Of course, there is a list of suggested Key Readings and further materials available at *reflectiveteaching.co.uk*.

Reading 17.1

Qualifications: The Nutbrown Review
Cathy Nutbrown

In the following reading Cathy Nutbrown lays out her vision for the future of the early years workforce with a specific focus on qualification levels and professionalism. A vision based upon careful review of research evidence.

Note how this is placed within the current economic climate. Do you feel that this vision is desirable, realistic? Why?

Edited from: Nutbrown, C. (2012) 'Foundations for Quality: The Independent Review of Early Education and Childcare Qualifications: Final Report [online]. Runcorn: Department for Education.' Available from https://www.education.gov.uk/publications/standard/publicationDetail/Page1/DFE-00068-2012 [accessed 12 July 2012].

At all times, throughout my Review, I have sought to be realistic in terms of what it might achieve and how change might be brought about. I recognise that the current economic climate means the sector, Government and parents are all under financial pressure. However, the many responses to my Call for Evidence and other events throughout my Review have demonstrated the increasing professionalism of the early years sector, which means it can, with support from Government, bring about change for higher quality experiences for young children. I believe the Government must have a role in demanding certain standards, and I have made recommendations for what these should be. I also believe that more can be asked of the sector in terms of a responsibility to enhance professionalism and ensure high quality provision.

This is a challenge for Government and for everyone working in and leading provision for young children. For me, the role of Government is to ensure the necessary standards are being met, but the sector must play a role in determining how these can be achieved as it strives for excellence. The sector is becoming more professional, and Government must support this diverse sector to make its own improvement. In all my recommendations I have specified high and achievable standards, and how Government might apply these. I have also aimed to allow flexibility in how the sector may work towards them.

A clear, rigorous system of qualifications

We need a rigorous set of qualifications in place to ensure a competent and confident workforce. But the current qualifications system is confusing: there are too many qualifications, and many are not equipping the workforce with the necessary knowledge and skills to provide high quality early education and care.

Starting out in the early years workforce: Entry and initial training

As a country we need to raise our expectations of what it means to work with young children, and attract the best people into the workforce.

An early years career: Progressing to and beyond level 3

If young children are to get the early education and care they need, there must be a substantial change in the way working with young children is perceived. An early years career should be just that: a career. There needs to be clear roles in the early years workforce, linked to qualifications, and clear routes for capable people to progress to more senior roles.

Raising our aspirations: Qualifications for leadership

Excellent pedagogical leadership is vital in improving the quality of provision, and all early years practitioners can aspire to be pedagogical leaders. Progression opportunities need to be accessible for all capable and committed women and men, and I recommend that the Department for Education conduct research to ensure Black and Minority Ethnic groups are not being excluded from more senior roles.

My vision for early childhood education and care is one where:

- every child is able to experience high quality care and education whatever type of home or group setting they attend;
- early years staff have a strong professional identity, take pride in their work, and are recognised and valued by parents, other professionals and society as a whole;
- high quality early education and care is led by well qualified early years practitioners; and
- the importance of childhood is understood, respected and valued.

There are examples of excellent practice that meet these aims, but this is not the case in all settings, and the time is right to set our sights higher and demand excellent work with all young children across the sector. This requires:

- An increase in the number of qualified teachers with specialist early years knowledge who lead practice in settings, working directly with babies, young children, and their parents, using their pedagogical expertise to support young children's learning, play and development.

- Early years teachers who lead, and are supported by, an effective team of early years practitioners, qualified at a minimum of level 3, with all staff taking professional pride in their work, and continually seeking to extend and develop their knowledge and skills.

- Those who are working towards early education and childcare qualifications to be taught and supported by qualified and knowledgeable tutors, who are experienced in the early years. Tutors, as much as the practitioners in the setting, must take pride in their professional development, and regularly engage in practice in settings, ensuring their skills and pedagogy are current.

- Only those candidates who are confident and capable in their literacy and numeracy are able to enrol on these level 3 courses. Level 3 qualifications must be rigorous and challenging, requiring high quality experiences in placements, giving students time to reflect on and improve their own practice.

- A rigour of qualification such that employers can have confidence that those who hold a recognised qualification have the necessary depth and breadth of knowledge and experience to be ready for work in the setting.

- Employers who support new members of staff, and take the time to induct them to the setting and their role, and ensure they have good support and mentoring in place for at least their first six months.

Reading 17.2

Thinking about educational systems
Margaret Archer

This reading comes from the introduction to Margaret Archer's analysis of the ways in which educational systems form, develop and change through time. She argues that such systems reflect the priorities and conceptions of those who have power. However, such power is likely to be contested and, in any event, those in a position to make policy must also relate their ambitions to the constraints of practical realities.

To what extent can you relate Archer's model, as expressed here, to the recent history of changing educational policy?

Edited from: Archer, M. (1979) *The Social Origins of Educational Systems.* London: Sage Publications Ltd, 1–3.

How do educational systems develop and change?

This question can be broken down into three subsidiary ones: Who gets education? What happens to them during it? Where do they go to after it? These enquiries about inputs, processes and outputs subsume a whole range of issues, many of which have often been discussed independently. They embrace problems about educational opportunity, selection and discrimination, about the management and transmission of knowledge and values and about social placement, stratification and mobility. At the same time they raise the two most general problems of all, namely those about the effects of society upon education and about the consequences of education for society.

The fundamental question here is, 'Why does education have the particular inputs, processes and outputs which characterize it at any given time?' The basic answer is held to be very simple. Education has the characteristics it does because of the goals pursued by those who control it. A second question asks, Why do these particular inputs, processes and outputs change over time?' The basic answer given here is equally simple. Change occurs because new educational goals are pursued by those who have the power to modify previous practices. As we shall see, these answers are of a deceptive simplicity. They are insisted upon now, at the beginning because, however complex our final formulations turn out to be, education is fundamentally about what people have wanted of it and have been able to do to it.

The real answers are more complicated but they supplement rather than contradict the above. It is important never to lose sight of the fact that the complex theories we develop to account for education and educational change are theories about the educational activities of people. This very basic point is underlined for two reasons. Firstly, because however fundamental, much of the literature in fact contradicts it and embodies implicit beliefs in hidden hands, evolutionary mechanisms, and spontaneous adjustments to social change. There education is still seen as mysteriously adapting to social requirements and responding to demands of society not of people. Secondly, and for the present purposes much more importantly, our theories will be *about* the educational activities of people even though they will not explain educational development strictly *in terms* of people alone.

The basic answers are too simple because they beg more questions than they solve. To say that education derives its characteristic features from the aims of those who control it immediately raises problems concerning the identification of controlling groups, the bases and processes upon which control rests, the methods and channels through which it is exerted, the extensiveness of control, the reactions of others to this control, and their educational consequences. Similarly, where change is concerned, it is not explained until an account has been given of why educational goals change, who does the changing, and how they impose the changes they seek. To confront these problems is to recognise that their solution depends upon analyzing complex forms of social interaction. Furthermore, the nature of education is rarely, if ever, the practical realization of an ideal form of instruction as envisaged by a particular group. Instead, most of the time most of the forms that education takes are the political products of power struggles. They bear the marks of concession to allies and compromise with opponents. Thus to understand the nature of education at any time we need to know not only who won the struggle for control, but also how: not merely who lost, but also how badly they lost.

Secondly, the basic answers are deceptively simple because they convey the impression that education and educational change can be explained by reference to group goals and balances of power alone. It is a false impression because there are other factors which constrain both the goal formation and goal attainment of even the most powerful group – that is the group most free to impose its definition of instruction and to mould education to its purposes. The point is that no group, not even for that matter the whole of society acting in accord, has a blank sheet of paper on which to design national education. Conceptions of education are of necessity limited by the existing availability of skills and resources. Another way of stating this is to say that cultural and structural factors constrain educational planning and its execution. Since this is the case, then explanations of education and educational change will be partly in terms of such factors.

Moreover, only the minimal logical constraints have been mentioned so far: in practice educational action is also affected by a variable set of cultural and structural factors which make up its environment. Educational systems, rarities before the eighteenth century, emerged within complex social structures and cultures and this context conditioned the conception and conduct of action of those seeking educational development. Among other things the social distribution of resources and values and the patterning of vested interests in the existing form of education were crucially important factors. Once a given form of education exists it exerts an influence on future educational change. Alternative educational plans are, to some extent, reactions to it (they represent desires to change inputs, transform processes, or alter the end products); attempts to change it are affected by it (by the degree to which it monopolizes educational skills and resources); and change is change of it (which means dismantling, transforming, or in some way grappling with it).

Reading 17.3

The Field report: Preventing poor children becoming poor adults

Frank Field

The following reading provides a summary of the findings of the Field Report. Frank Field notes the crucial role played by pre-schools and children's early experiences in influencing life-chances, thus supporting the case for investment into ECEC. Field also makes clear that parents need to be supported so that they, in turn, are enabled to support their children, starting from pregnancy.

Edited from: Field, F. (2010) *The Foundation Years: Preventing Poor Children Becoming Poor Edults. The Report of the Independent Review on Poverty and Life Chances.* London: Cabinet Office, 5–9.

Frank Field was commissioned by the Prime Minister in June 2010 to provide an independent review on poverty and life chances. The question the Review found itself asking was how we can prevent poor children from becoming poor adults. The Review has concluded that the UK needs to address the issue of child poverty in a fundamentally different way if it is to make a real change to children's life chances as adults.

We have found overwhelming evidence that children's life chances are most heavily predicated on their development in the first five years of life. It is family background, parental education, good parenting and the opportunities for learning and development in those crucial years that together matter more to children than money, in determining whether their potential is realized in adult life. The things that matter most are a healthy pregnancy; good maternal mental health; secure bonding with the child; love and responsiveness of parents along with clear boundaries, as well as opportunities for a child's cognitive, language and social and emotional development. Good services matter too: health services, Children's Centres and high quality childcare.

Later interventions to help poorly performing children can be effective but, in general, the most effective and cost-effective way to help and support young families is in the earliest years of a child's life.

By the age of three, a baby's brain is 80 per cent formed and his or her experiences before then shape the way the brain has grown and developed. That is not to say, of course, it is all over by then, but ability profiles at that age are highly predictive of profiles at school entry. By school age, there are very wide variations in children's abilities and the evidence is clear that children from poorer backgrounds do worse cognitively and behaviourally than those from more affluent homes. Schools do not effectively close that gap; children who arrive in the bottom range of ability tend to stay there.

The current poverty measure that is most commonly referred to is the 60 per cent median income measure. The previous government pledged to halve child poverty by 2010–11 and eradicate it by 2020. Its policies and programmes to achieve this ambitious target included very heavy investment in income transfers through tax credits, support to parents through its New Deal programme to help lone parents into work, and early years services, including the SureStart programme for under fives in the most deprived areas.

There has been significant improvement in building early years service provision over the last ten years. High quality, professionally led, childcare programmes to support parents, and some intensive programmes are well evidenced to show they can be cost effective. But, current services are also very variable and there is generally both a lack of clear evidence of what works for poorer children and insufficient attention to developing the evidence base.

Progress was made towards meeting the financial poverty targets in the early stages of the strategy, but it has become increasingly clear that not only has the 2010/11 target not been met but it would require very large amounts of new money to meet the 2020 target. Such a strategy is not sustainable in the longer run, particularly as we strive to reduce the budget deficit. But even if money were not a constraint there is a clear case to be made for developing an alternative strategy to abolish child poverty.

The evidence about the importance of the pre school years to children's life chances as adults points strongly to an alternative approach that focuses on directing government policy and spending to developing children's capabilities in the early years. A shift of focus is needed towards providing high quality, integrated services aimed at supporting parents and improving the abilities of our poorest children during the period when it is most effective to do so. Their prospects of going on to gain better qualifications and sustainable employment will be greatly enhanced. The aim is to change the distribution of income by changing the position which children from poor backgrounds will be able to gain on merit in the income hierarchy.

Overarching recommendations

There are two overarching recommendations in section 3.

- To prevent poor children from becoming poor adults the Review proposes establishing a set of Life Chances Indicators that measure how successful we are as a country in making more equal life's outcomes for all children. Nothing can be achieved without working with parents. All our recommendations are about enabling parents to achieve the aspirations that they have for their children.

- To drive this policy the Review proposes establishing the 'Foundation Years' covering the period from the womb to five. The Foundation Years should become the first pillar of a new tripartite education system: the Foundation Years leading to school years leading to further, higher and continuing education.

Additionally, recommendations for the Foundation Years include:

- The Review recommends that government, national and local, should give greater prominence to the earliest years in life, from pregnancy to age five, adopting the term Foundation Years. This is for several reasons: to increase public understanding of how babies and young children develop and what is important to ensure their healthy progress in this crucial period; to make clear the package of support needed both for children and parents in those early years; to establish the Foundation Years as of equal status and importance in the public mind to primary and secondary school years; and to ensure that child development and services during those years are as well understood.

- The Review recommends that the Government gradually moves funding to the early years, and that this funding is weighted toward the most disadvantaged children as we build the evidence base of effective programmes. The Fairness Premium, introduced in the 2010 Spending Review, should begin in pregnancy.

- The increased funding should be targeted at those factors we know matter most in the early years: high quality and consistent support for parents during pregnancy, and in the early years, support for better parenting; support for a good home learning environment; and, high quality childcare.

- The Review has focussed on the early years, but recognises that important changes can and do take place later in children's lives and that investment in the early years will not be fully effective unless it is followed up with high quality services for those who need them most later in childhood. The Review therefore recommends that the Government extends the life chances approach to later stages in childhood.

Summary findings

- Nobody would doubt the fact that parents play the most significant role in influencing their children's futures and the evidence backs up this instinctive belief. There is a weight of evidence which shows that a combination of positive parenting, a good home learning environment and parents' qualifications can transform children's life chances, and are more important to outcomes than class background and parental income.

- Pregnancy and the first five years of life shape children's life chances – the associations between cognitive development at age five and later educational outcomes are very strong. During the earliest years, it is primarily parents who shape their children's outcomes – a healthy pregnancy, good mental health, the way that they parent and whether the home environment is educational. 'What parents do is more important that who parents are'. Institutions such as health services, Children's Centres and childcare in particular also have an impact as do family background factors, such as the parents' level of education.

- It is in the early years that the socio-economic gaps in outcomes appear. Already by age three there are large and systematic differences between children from lower and higher income families and these gaps persist throughout childhood, as later attainment tends to be heavily influenced by early development.

- Later in childhood, parents continue to impact on their children's outcomes and their aspirations for their children start to rub off on the children themselves. Children's own attainment, social and emotional development and aspirations also have a significant impact on their future attainment. High achieving children reinforce the achievements that are formed by their background. For low achieving children the opposite is true as by this stage they do not have the resources to grow their achievements in a similar way. Schools can have an impact, albeit a smaller one, especially where good leadership and teaching provides an environment for poor children to thrive, but it has generally been found very difficult to undo the disadvantages carved out in the earliest years.

Reading 17.4

The philosophy of Paulo Freire

Jones Irwin

This reading provides an introduction to the life and work of Paulo Freire. It allows us to see how many of the things we have discussed throughout this book and Reflective Teaching in Early Education – the importance of personal experience, personal feelings and context – influence our work, how we see ourselves as practitioners and how we view education and its purpose.

Can you identify how your experiences have impacted upon our view of education?

Edited from: Irwin, J. (2012) *Philosophy of Education Origins, Developments, Impacts and Legacies.* London: Continuum, 1–4.

From life to philosophy: Exploring Freire's biography

The intimate connections between life and philosophy are nowhere more apparent than through an exploration of Paulo Freire's work. This symbiosis between life and philosophy is everywhere manifest in Freire's texts, early to late. It involves less a kind of edifying approach which would supplement his theories with more down-to-earth experience, and more an integral commitment of his overall philosophical vision. From the very beginning, Freire's texts develop organically from existential and political situations, often of acute terror and vulnerability, such as that of the military coup in Brazil in 1964. Freire's philosophy is thus fundamentally a philosophy of life and politics, in a way that often more supposedly practical philosophies could never be. His writing evolves from a sometimes fraught but oftentimes celebratory understanding of the possibilities of living, both the immense dangers but also the intense joys of human relationship and community. As Nietzsche declared, 'I love only what a person has written with his blood' (quoted in Derrida, 1978: 328) and Freire is, in this sense, very much a writer in the Nietzschean tenor.

'A land of contrasts and a pedagogy of contradiction'

As one of Freire's greatest commentators, Carlos Alberto Torres, has noted, in 'A land of contrasts and a pedagogy of contradiction', much of the verve and tension of Freire's thinking derives from the specifics of his Brazilian upbringing and socio-cultural context (Torres, 1994): 'Brazil is a land of contrasts. Land of wonderful Rio de Janeiro, with the beautiful sights of the Corcovado mountain and its splendid world-class beaches, but also land of the Amazonian Indians, harassed, haunted, and murdered in their own dominion by gold prospectors and entrepreneurs of many sorts' (Torres, 1994: ix). Freire's early texts, for example, resound with the echoes and moods of the political and educational conflicts of the early 1960s in Brazil, conflicts which will lead to Freire's enforced exile. While his most famous text Pedagogy of the Oppressed (Freire, 1996a) tends to opt for a more universalist-humanist perspective, it is clear, from a reading of Education as The Practice of Freedom (Freire, 2005a), that Freire developed these ideas and concepts very much out of the crucible of a Brazilian society struggling with the damaging legacy of Portuguese colonialism, and with its own complex internal politics.

Freire's own upbringing in Recife and Jaboatão in Northeastern Brazil (he was born in 1921) had already exposed him to the reality of poverty and oppression, as this was one of the poorest regions of the world. Freire's own relatively affluent family were thrown into disarray by the premature death of his father when Freire was just 13, and he only entered the ginásio (or high school) when he was 16, while his classmates were aged 11 or 12 (Gadotti, 1994: 3). This no doubt contributed to his 'great difficulty in assimilating any kind of formal education' (Gadotti, 1994: 3), a factor perhaps contributing to his uncommon sensitivity to the weaknesses of traditional education. His mother's strong religious faith was also central to Freire's formation, and he always remained a Catholic philosopher, although hardly orthodox. He consistently challenged and criticized what he saw as the oppression perpetrated by the traditionalist church, advocating instead what he termed the 'prophetic church' (Gadotti, 1994: 4), in a manner which drew him close to the Liberation Theology movements of Latin America (Gutierrez, 2001; Torres, 1993). His first wife Elza was also a constant source of inspiration to Freire, who acknowledges her 'solidarity' (Gadotti, 1994: 5) throughout the difficult years of imprisonment and exile, right up until her death in 1986. His second wife, Ana Maria Araújo Freire, also features as a key interlocutor and reader of his later work (Freire, 2004) and we can thus foreground the significance of inter-personal relationships in the intellectual formation of Freire. Marx's thinking, and especially the early Marx, is a constant recourse throughout Freire's texts this may be seen as paradigmatic in the development of Freire's criticisms of traditionalist or essentialist philosophy. Not the least of the enigmas surrounding Freire's thinking is, therefore, how he succeeds in being both a Christian and a Marxist at the same time.

Perhaps the key philosophical and political moment in Freire's early life is his development of a new method of adult literacy education, which he first presented at Pernambuco in 1958 (Gadotti, 1994: 8). This new approach, which was built on a strong criticism of existing methods of literacy and more general education, forms the basis of his more evolved work. We can trace its first systematic exposition in book form in *Education as the Practice of Freedom* (2005a) and, of course, it will also serve as the theoretical and practical foundation for Freire's theses in *Pedagogy of the Oppressed* (1996a).

A new approach to literacy

Gadotti draws out the story of how this evolution of Freire's method began to engender political conflict in Brazil – this was 'the method which took Paulo Freire into exile'

(Gadotti, 1994: 15). The emergence of this literacy method in Northeastern Brazil is not coincidental – in 1960 this area had an illiteracy rate of 75 per cent and a life expectancy of 28 years for men and 32 for women; in 1956, half of the land was owned by 3 per cent of the population; the income per capita was only 40 per cent of the national average (Elias, 1994). Of course, precisely at the heart of the threat this educational approach posed to the status quo was the fact that it went beyond the confines of ordinary methodologies – instead of being a 'method', we might describe Freire's approach as being rooted in an attempt to construct a new epistemology or theory of knowledge (Elias, 1994: 2, Gadotti, 1994: 16). Or, as Linda Bimbi notes, the Freirean approach to literacy is linked to a 'total change in society' (quoted Gadotti, 1994: 17). While the first experiments began in 1962 with 300 rural farm workers who were taught to read and write in 45 days (Gadotti, 1994: 15), the following year Freire had been invited by the President of Brazil to rethink the literacy schemes for adults on a national basis. By 1964, 20,000 cultural circles were set up for two million illiterate people (Gadotti, 1994: 15). But, as Gadotti notes, 'the military coup, however, interrupted the work right at the beginning and cancelled all the work that had already been done' (Gadotti, 1994: 16). The military coup thus attacks the literacy and political programme at its very roots: Freire, along with many others, was jailed. This incarceration lasted for 75 days, with many instances of torture and murder of prisoners (most of whom were teachers and community workers). After release, Freire was encouraged to leave the country and he fled to exile in Chile.

Again and again throughout his texts, Freire will return to this time as constitutive for his understanding of the relation between politics and education, but, we might also say, for his sensitivity to the relation between personal existence and philosophy. This emphasis is evident in early works such as 'Extension or Communication' (Freire, 2005b), which was written during his exile in Chile right up until later works such as *Pedagogy of Hope: Reliving Pedagogy of the Oppressed* (Freire, 1992), where Freire exactly 'relives' the initial attempts at political and educational transformation in Brazil. We will also explore how Freire's life and work can seen as coming full circle in his later return to Brazil. In 1980, 16 years after his initial exile, Freire is allowed to come back to Brazil where he becomes a Minister for Education in São Paulo. During this last period of his life, Freire teaches influentially at the University of São Paulo, while also being instrumental in the formation of the Brazilian Workers' Party (Partido dos Trabalhadores), led by later Brazilian President Lulu. His texts from this period constantly foreground the tensions of individual and collective freedom and responsibility. Freire died in 1997 but his legacy continues to be powerfully influential in Brazil and South and Latin America, as well as on a more worldwide level. Understanding Freire as philosopher, for us, will thus also be a process of coming to understand Freire a person, in an existential and political sense.

Reading 17.5

The impact of early education as a strategy in countering socio-economic disadvantage

Tony Bertram and Chris Pascal

This reading concludes this book with a consideration of poverty and social disadvantage in our society. It reminds us of the impact early years provision can have on children's lives and futures, reaffirming the importance of the sector and those professionals working within it.

Edited from: Bertram, T. and Pascal, C. (2013) *The Impact of Early Education as a Strategy in Countering Socio-economic Disadvantage.* London: Ofsted, 7–10.

The growing extent of child poverty, inequality and social immobility

The latest report from UNICEF, 'Measuring Child Poverty' (2012), acknowledges that there is almost no internationally comparable data available on the effect of the recent economic downturn on child poverty. However, it is evident everywhere that front line services in the UK are under strain as austerity measures increase the numbers in need while depleting the services available. The UNICEF report points out that 'worse is to come' and young children can be particularly vulnerable in times of recession. It demonstrates that there is always a time lag between the onset of an economic crisis and the full extent of its impact. Its current analyses reveal that in the UK the economic crisis is already beginning to threaten social protection programmes. Child benefits have been frozen for three years and child tax credits and other programmes designed to protect the poorest children have been cut back or reshaped. The report states that these changes are likely to throw into reverse the progress made on child poverty in recent years. Although currently stable at about 20 per cent, with a commitment to achieve 10 per cent by 2020 under the Child Poverty Act (2010), the child poverty rate in the UK is predicted to begin rising again in 2013 and to reach 24 per cent (relative) and 23 per cent (absolute) by 2020/21. This would mean a return to the relative child poverty levels of two decades ago, coincidently projecting a return to the same economic and social conditions identified in the influential 1993 OfSTED report, Access and Achievement in Urban Education. UNICEF states that these forecasts are the best available independent estimate of 'what might happen to poverty under current government policies'. This immediate economic and social context sets an urgent, challenging and timely agenda for this review of the power of early education to counter such disadvantage.

Even before the recession, the evidence in each of the reports we examined indicates that in the UK, especially, parents' socio-economic status continues to be the primary predictor of which children prosper in adult life. The data reveals that the UK remains at the bottom of international league tables for social mobility, as measured by income or earnings. Latest comparisons suggest British citizens are about half as socially mobile as people in Finland or Denmark, which means they are twice as likely to stay in the same income bracket as their parents when they become adults (see Figure 17.3.1).

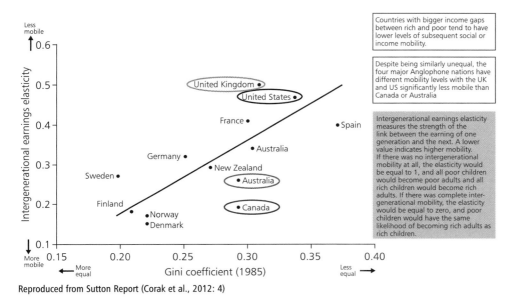

Figure 17.3.1
Social Mobility Trends

Reproduced from Sutton Report (Corak et al., 2012: 4)

UK social mobility is also significantly lower than in Canada and Australia, countries with whom we share much in common – economically, culturally and in the rich diversity of their populations. Amongst G20 richest nations, only the USA has poorer social mobility than the UK.

These findings challenge one of the fundamental assumptions of a meritocratic society, that large inequalities of income are acceptable as long as everyone has equality of opportunity to progress in life through their own talents and hard work. The UK's low social mobility levels show that this is not being realised and that those at the bottom of the income ladder in early life are far less likely to earn higher incomes as adults, when compared to those in most other countries of similar wealth.

Inter-generational social mobility patterns in the UK, over time, whether classified by social class or income, reinforce the life patterns of individuals. Wealthier parents are able to provide their children with advantages that less affluent parents cannot afford and a cycle for the poor is perpetuated and becomes chronic. The evidence shows that the role of education as a socio-economic leveller is clearly failing for the vast majority of children from less privileged backgrounds. Far from raising opportunities for all irrespective of background, our current education system seems to perpetuate inequalities.

As the Sutton Trust /Carnegie Corporation Summit Report (Waldfogel and Washbrook, 2008) points out, 'It is clear that for a fortunate few, education, and particularly higher education, can be a driver of upward mobility. Yet, the few talents from humble origins that do go on to realise their potential often do so despite the system, not because of it. Not only is this unfair for individuals unlucky enough to find themselves on the bottom rungs of society: it represents a tragic waste of talent to the British economy in an increasingly global economy'.

Their figures show that stark, persistent gaps, widening from pre-birth to post-graduation, characterise the UK, with students from the highest social class groups being three times more likely to enter university as those from the lowest social groups (see Figure 17.3.2).

Figure 17.3.2
Higher Education Rates

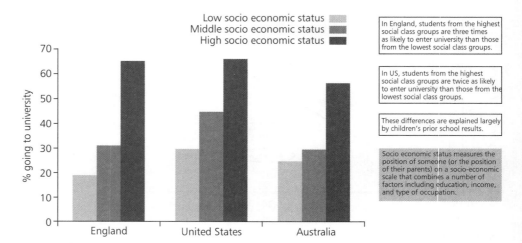

Low socio economic status
Middle socio economic status
High socio economic status

In England, students from the highest social class groups are three times as likely to enter university than those from the lowest social class groups.

In US, students from the highest social class groups are twice as likely to enter university than those from the lowest social class groups.

These differences are explained largely by children's prior school results.

Socio economic status measures the position of someone (or the position of their parents) on a socio-economic scale that combines a number of factors including education, income, and type of occupation.

Reproduced from Sutton Trust Report (Corak et al., 2012: 16)

Even starker gaps persist in entry to the elite academic institutions in the UK: less than one in five degree entrants in leading research universities come from the four lower class groups that make up half the UK population. This report continues by arguing that this is all the more concerning as education is now, perhaps more than ever, the gateway to better life prospects; this at a time when higher order skills and knowledge are increasingly the most valued commodities in the world's rapidly evolving labour market. The persistence of this underachievement gap has been quantified in economic costs as imposing the equivalent of a permanent national recession (McKinsey and Company, 2009) and is estimated to reduce the GDP of a country by between 9–16 per cent. The core question of how far education, and particularly early education, can improve mobility levels is an even more pressing issue amid an economic recession that will undoubtedly affect the lives of those on low incomes.

Our analysis of the evidence indicates that even the most successful education policy interventions can only reduce and not eliminate disparities in educational outcomes across income, social class or race. The Sutton Trust /Carnegie Corporation Report suggests that the most successful interventions will improve educational outcomes by no more than a quarter of a standard deviation, enough to pass a cost benefit test but not enough to equalise educational opportunity for all children. They argue that this should not mean despair but rather that we should recognise that schooling interventions by themselves should never be seen as a panacea for addressing deeply entrenched social class inequalities in the UK.

Educationalists should be realists but not defeatists there are real differences that can be achieved with high quality early intervention strategies.

List of figures

Figure 2.5.1   Achievement goals and achievement behaviour
Figure 3.6.1   Bloom's hierarchy of thinking processes
Figure 4.1.1   Principled Pedagogic Model
Figure 6.2.1   Belbin Team Role summary descriptions
Figure 9.6.1   Te Whāriki: The weaving
Figure 10.3.1   Traditional and emerging positions
Figure 11.1.1   The science, craft and art of pedagogic expertise
Figure 11.4.1   Genesis of performance capacity: Progression through the ZPD
                  and beyond
Figure 13.1.1   Parents' routes through the Centre
Figure 13.4.1   Questions for developing a curriculum for Excellence
Figure 13.5.1   Questions concerning social influences on assessment
Figure 15.4.1   Two children in wheelchairs
Figure 17.3.1   Social Mobility Trends
Figure 17.3.2   Higher Education Rates

Bibliography

Abbott, L. and Moylett, H. (eds) (1997) *Working with the Under Threes: Responding to Children's Needs*. Buckingham: Open University Press.

Abbott, L. and Nutbrown, C. (eds) (2001) *Experiencing Reggio Emilia: Implications for Pre-School Provision*. Milton Keynes: Open University Press.

Abbott, L. and Pugh, G. (eds) (1998) *Training Issues in the Early Years*. Buckingham: Open University Press.

Åberg, L. and Lenz Taguchi, H. (2005) *Lyssnandets pedagogik* [The pedagogy of listening]. Stockholm: Liber. [Bonniers large lexicon], 4. Ems-Gal. Stockholm: Bonnier fakta.

Abrami, P. C., Chambers, B., Poulson, C., De Simone, C., d'Apollonia, S. and Howden, J. (1995). *Classroom Connections: Understanding and Using Co-operative Learning*. Toronto: Harcourt Brace.

Acredolo, L. and Goodwyn, S. (2000) *Baby Signs. How to Talk with your Baby Before your Baby can Talk*. London: Vermilion: Ebury Press.

Adelson, B. (1984) 'When novices surpass experts: the difficulty of a task may increase with expertise', *Journal of Experimental Psychology: Learning, Memory, and Cognition*, 10 (3), 483–95.

Ainscow, M. (1997) 'Towards inclusive schooling', *British Journal of Special Education*, 24 (1), 3–6.

Ames, C. (1992) 'Classrooms: goals, structures, and student motivation', *Journal of Educational Psychology*, 84 (3), 261–71.

Anning, A. (2000) *New Deals and Old Dilemmas: Lone Parents of Young Children Balancing Work and Parenthood*. Paper presented at BERA Conference, Cardiff, September.

Anning, A. and Edwards, A. (1999) *Promoting Children's Learning from Birth to Five: Developing the New Early Years Professional*. Buckingham/Philadelphia: Open University Press.

Archer, M. (1979) *The Social Origins of Educational Systems*. London: Sage Publications Ltd, 1–3.

Argyle, M. (1994) *The Psychology of Interpersonal Behaviour*. 5th edn. London: Penguin.

Argyle, M. and Dean, J. (1965) 'Eye-contact, distance and affiliation', *Sociometry*, 28, 289–304.

Armstrong, A. C., Armstrong, D. and Spandagou, I. (2010) *Inclusive Education: International Policy and Practice*. London: Sage Publications Ltd.

Armstrong, D. (1999) 'Histories of Inclusion: Perspectives on the History of Special Education'. In L. Barton and F. Armstrong (eds) *Difference and Difficulty: Insights, Issues and Dilemmas*. Sheffiield: University of Sheffield.

Arnold, C. (2002) *Observing Harry*. Buckingham: Open University Press.

Arnold, M. (1874) *High Schools and Universities in Germany*. London: Association for Bilingual Education/Cambridge: Cambridge University Press.

Athey, C. (1990) *Extending Thought in Young Children*. London: Paul Chapman.

—(2002) *Extending Thought in Young Children: A Parent–Teacher Partnership*. 2nd edn. London: Sage Publications Ltd.

—(2007) *Extending Thought in Young Children: A Parent–Teacher Partnership*. 3rd edn. London: Sage Publications Ltd.

Australian Government Department of Education, Employment and Workplace (2007) 'Belong, Being and Becoming. Early years learning framework for Australia'. Canberra: DEEWR. Available from www.ag.gov.au/cca (accessed 14 August 2014).

Bacon, W., Groundwater-Smith, S., Nash, C. and Sachs, J. (2000) *Legitimating Professionalism?*. Paper presented at the British Educational Research Association Annual Conference, 7/10 September, Cardiff University, Wales.

Ball, S. (1981a) *Beachside Comprehensive*. Cambridge: Cambridge University Press.

—(1981b) 'Initial Encounters in the Classroom and the Process of Establishment'. In P. F. Woods (ed.) *Pupil Strategies*. London: Croom Helm.

—(2003) *The More Things Change: Educational Research, Social Class and 'Interlocking' Inequalities*, Professorial Inaugural Lecture, Institute of Education, University of London.

Ball, S. J. (2001) 'Performativities and Fabrications in the Education Economy'. In D. Gleeson and C. Husbands (eds) *The Performing School: Managing, Teaching and Learning in a Performance Culture*. London: RoutledgeFalmer.

Barber, M. and Mourshed, M. (2007) *How the World's Best-performing Schools Systems Come out on Top*. London: McKinsey and Company.

Barnes, C., Mercer, G. and Shakespeare, T. (1999) *Exploring Disability: A Sociological Introduction*. Cambridge: Cambridge University Press.

Bartlett, F. C. (1932) *Remembering: A Study of Experimental and Social Psychology*. Cambridge: Cambridge University Press.

Beardsley, G. and Harnett, P. (1998) *Exploring Play in the Primary Classroom*. London: David Fulton.

Belbin, R. M. (2010) *Team Roles at Work*. 2nd edn. London: Butterworth-Heinemann.

Benjamin, S. (2002a) 'Valuing diversity: a cliché for the 21st century?', *International Journal of Inclusive Education*, 6 (4), 309–23.

Bereiter, C. and Scardamalia, M. (1993) *Surpassing Ourselves. An Inquiry into the Nature and Implications of Expertise*. Chicago, IL: Open Court.

Berliner, D. C. (2001) 'Learning about and learning from expert teachers', *International Journal of Educational Research*, 35, 463–82.

—(2004) 'Describing the behavior and documenting the accomplishments of expert teachers', *Bulletin of Science, Technology and Society*, 24 (3), 200–12.

Bernauer, J. and Rasmussen, D. (1988) *The Final Foucault*. Cambridge, MA: MIT Press.

Bernstein, B. (1975) *Sources of Consensus and Disaffection in Education. Class, Codes and Control*. London: Routledge and Kegan Paul.

Bertram, T., Pascal, C., Bokhari, C., Gasper, M., Holtermann, S. J. and Nelson, C. (2002). *Early Excellence Centre Pilot Programme*. Third Annual Evaluation Report 2001–2, Birmingham: Centre for Research in Early Childhood.

Billington, T. (2006) *Working with Children*. London: Sage Publications Ltd.

Bjervås, L.-L. (2011) *Samtal om barn och pedagogisk dokumentation som bedömningspraktik i förskolan. En diskursanalys* [Dialogues about children and pedagogical documentation as a praxis of evaluation in preschool. a discourse analysis]. Göteborg: Acta Universitatis Gothoburgensis.

Black, P. and Wiliam, D. (1998) *Inside the Black Box – Raising Standards through Classroom Assessment*. London, King's College School of Education.

Blackwell, F. F. (1994) *Highscope – The First 30 Years*. Tyne and Wear: Highscope UK Publications

Bliss, L., Askew, M. and McCree, S. (1996) *Effective Teaching and Learning: Scaffolding Revisited*. Oxford: Oxford Review of Education.

Bloom, B. (1964) *Taxonomy of Educational Objectives: Handbok 1: Cognitive Domain*. London: Longman.

Bluebond-Langner, M. (1978) *The Private Worlds of Dying Children*. Princeton, NJ: Princeton University Press.

Booth, T. and Ainscow, M. (eds) (1998) *From Them to Us: An International Study of Inclusion in Education*. London: Routledge.

Bourdieu, P. (1983) 'Economic capital, cultural capital, social capital', *Sozialewelt, Supplement* 2, 183–98.

—(1984) *Distinction: A Social Critique of the Judgement of Taste*. London: Routledge and Kegan Paul.

Bowman, B., Donovan, M. and Burns, M. (eds) (2001) *Eager To Learn: Educating our Preschoolers*. Washington: National Academy Press.

Bredekamp, S. and Copple, C. (eds) (1997) *Developmentally Appropriate Practice in Early Childhood Programs*. 2nd edn. Washington, DC: National Association for the Education of Young Children.

British Columbia Ministry of Health and Ministry of Children and Family Development (2008) 'Early Learning Framework'. Available from http://www.bced.gov.bc.ca/early_learning/early_learning_framework.htm (accessed 6 June 2014).

British Education Technology Association (BECTA) (2006) *Evidence on the Progress of ICT in Education*. Coventry: Becta. Beastall.

Broadfoot, P (1996) *Education, Assessment and Society*. Buckingham: Open University Press.

—(2004) *Early Years Play and Learning: Developing Social Skills and Cooperation*. London: RoutledgeFalmer.

Brock, A. (2011) 'Perspectives on Professionalism'. In A. Brock and C. Ranken (eds) *Professionalism in the Interdisciplinary Early Years Team*. London: Continuum.

Brock, A., Frost, N., Karban, K. and Smith, S. (2009) *Towards Interprofessional Partnerships: A Resource Pack*. Leeds: Leeds Metropolitan University.

Brodie, K. (2013) *Observation, Assessment and Planning in the Early Years: Bringing it all Together*. Maidenhead: Open University Press.

Bronfenbrenner, U. (1979) *The Ecology of Human Development: Experiments by Nature and Design*. Cambridge MA: Harvard University Press.

—(1993) 'Ecological models of human development', *International Encyclopaedia of Education*. Oxford: Elsevier, 3.

Brophy, J. (1981) 'Relationships enhanced through confidence and effective use of praise teacher praise, a functional analysis', *Review of Educational Research*, 88 (2), 5–32.

Bruce, T., Findlay, A., Read, J. and Scarborough, M. (1995) *Recurring Themes in Education*. London: Paul Chapman Publishing.

Bruner, J. (1960) *The Process of Education*. Cambridge, MA: Harvard University Press.

—(1966) *Towards a Theory of Instruction*. Cambridge, MA: Harvard University Press.

—(1972) *The Relevance of Education*. London: George Allen and Unwin.

—(1983) *Child Talk*. London: Oxford University Press.

—(1996) *The Culture of Education*. 2nd edn. Cambridge, MA: Harvard University Press, 45–50.

—(1998) 'Some Specifications for a Space to House a Reggio Preschool'. In G. Ceppi and M. Zini (eds) *Children, Spaces, Relations: Metaproject for an Environment for Young Children*. Reggio Emilia, Italy: Reggio Children and Domus Academy Research Centre, 138.

—(2000) 'Reading for Possible Worlds'. In T. Shanahan and F. B. Rodriguez-Brown (eds) *49th Yearbook of the National Reading Conference*. Chicago: National Reading Conference.

—(2002) *Making Stories: Law, Literature, Life*. Cambridge, MA: Harvard University Press.

—(2006) *In Search of Pedagogy Volume II: The Selected Works of Jerome S. Bruner*. New York: Routledge.

Bruner, J. and Lucariello, J. (1989) 'Monologue as Narrative Recreation of the World'. In N. K. Nelson *Narratives from the Crib*. Cambridge, MA: Harvard University Press.

Buldu, M. (2010) 'Making learning visible in kindergarten classrooms: pedagogical documentation as a formative assessment technique', *Teaching and Teacher Education*, 26 (7), 1439–49.

Bull, P. (1987) *Posture and Gesture*. Oxford: Pergamon.

Bundy, A. C., Luckett, T., Tranter, P. J., Naughton, G. A., Wyver, S. R., Ragen, J. and Spies, G. (2009) 'The risk is that there is "no risk": a simple, innovative intervention to increase children's activity levels', *International Journal of Early Years Education*, 17 (1), 33–45

Burden, R. (1995) 'Assessing children's perceptions of themselves as learners and problem-solvers', *School Psychology International*, 19 (4), 291–305.

Calderhead, J. (1984). *Teachers' Classroom Decision-making*. Worcester: Billing & Sons Ltd.

Cameron, C. and Moss, P. (2007) *Care Work in Europe: Current Understandings and Future Directions*. London: Routledge.

Campbell, F. A., Goldstein, S., Schaefer, E. S. and Ramey, C. T. (1991) 'Parental beliefs and values related to family risk, educational intervention, and child academic competence', *Early Childhood Research Quarterly*, 6, 167–82.

Cannella, G. and Viruru, R. (2004) *Childhood and Postcolonization: Power, Education and Contemporary Practice*. New York: Routledge Falmer.

Carr, M. (2000), 'Seeking Children's Perspectives about their Learning'. In A. B. Smith, N. J. Taylor and M. M. Gollop (eds) *Children's Voices: Research, Policy and Practice*. Auckland: Pearson Education, 37–55.

Carr, M. (2001a) *Assessment in Early Childhood Settings*. London: Paul Chapman.

—(2001b) 'A sociocultural approach to learning orientation in an early childhood setting', *Qualitative Studies in Education*, 14 (4), 525–42.

Carter, K., Sabers, D., Cushing, K., Pinnegar, S. and Berliner, D. C. (1987) 'Processing and using information about students: a study of expert, novice, and postulant teachers', *Teaching and Teacher Education*, 3 (2), 147–57.

Castells, M. (1996) *The Rise of the Network Society*. Oxford: Blackwell.

Cheng, D. P. W. (2001) 'Difficulties of Hong Kong teachers' understanding and implementation of "play" in the curriculum', *Teaching and Teacher Education*, 17 (7), 857–69.

Chorpita, B. F. and Barlow, D. H. (1998) 'The development of anxiety: the role of control in the early environment', *Psychological Bulletin*, 124, 93–102.

Chung, S. and Walsh, D. (2000) 'Unpacking child-centredness', *Journal of Curriculum Studies*, 32, 215–34.

Clark, A. and Moss, P. (2001) *Listening to Young Children: The Mosaic Approach*. London: National Children's Bureau for the Joseph Rowntree Foundation.

—(2005) *Spaces to Play*. London: National Children's Bureau Enterprise Ltd.

Claxton, G. (1999)'The Anatomy of Intuition'. In T. Atkinson and G. Claxton (eds) *The Intuitive Practitioner: On the Value of Not Always Knowing What One is Doing*. Buckingham: Open University Press.

—(ed.) (1997) *Hare Brain, Tortoise Mind: Why Intelligence Increases When You Think Less*. London: Fourth Estate.

Clough, P. and Corbett, J. (eds) (2000) *Theories of Inclusive Education. A Students Guide*. London: Sage Publications Ltd.

Cockburn, J. (1905) 'Froebel's Spirit And Influence'. In T. Bruce, A. Findlay, J. Read and M. Scarborough *Recurring Themes in Education*. London: Paul Chapman Publishing.

Collarbone, P. (2009) *Creating Tomorrow Planning, Developing and Sustaining Change in Education and Other Public Services*. London: Continuum.

Corak, M., Waldfogel, J., Washbrook, L., Ermisch, J., Vignoles, A., Jerrim, J., Vignoles, A. and Jerrim, J. (2012) *Social Mobility and Education Gaps in the Four Major Anglophone Countries: Research Findings for the Social Mobility Summit*. Proceedings held at Royal Society, London 21–22 May of research sponsored by Sutton Trust & Carnegie Corporation of New York published on line by Sutton Trust, London. Available from http://www.suttontrust.com/research/social–mobility–summit–research–findings/ (accessed 6 December 2012).

Corker, M. and French, S. (1999) 'Reclaiming Discourse in Disability Studies'. In M. Corker and S. French (eds) *Disability Discourse*. Buckingham: Open University Press, 1–11.

Cornelius-White, J. (2007) 'Learner-centred teacher-student relationships are effective: a meta-analysis', *Review of Educational Research*, 77 (1), 113–43.

Cortazzi, M. (1991) 'Cultural and Educational Expectations in the Language Classroom'. In B. Harrison (ed.) *Culture and the Language Classroom*. London: Modern English Publications and the British Council, 54–65.

Costigan, A. T. and Crocco, M. S. (2004) *Learning to Teach in an Age of Accountability*. Hillsdale, NJ: Lawrence Erlbaum.

Coussée, F., Bradt, L., Roose, R. and Bouverne-De Bie, M. (2008) 'The emerging social pedagogical paradigm in UK child and youth care: deus ex machina or walking the beaten path?', *British Journal of Social Work*, 40 (3), 789–805.

Critchley, D. (2002) 'Children's Assessment of their own Learning'. In C. Nutbrown (ed.) *Research Studies in Early Childhood Education*. Stoke-on-Trent: Trentham Books.

Croll, P. and Moses, D. (1994) 'Policy–making and special educational needs: a framework for analysis', *European Journal of Special Needs Education*, 9 (3), 275–86.

Csikszentmihayli, M. (1979) 'The Concept of Flow'. In B. Sutton-Smith (ed.) *Play and Learning*. New York: Gardner, 257–73.

Cummins, J. (1996) *Negotiating Identities: Education for Empowerment in a Diverse Society*. California: Association for Bilingual Education/Cambridge: Cambridge University Press.

Dadds, M. (1997) 'Continuing professional development: nurturing the expert within', *British Journal of In-Service Education*, 23 (1), 31–8.

Dahlberg, G. and Moss, P. (2005) *Ethics and Politics in Early Childhood Education*. Oxfordshire: Routledge Falmer.

Dalli, C., White, E. J., Rockel, J., Duhn, I. with Buchanan, E., Davidson, S., Ganly, S., Kus, L. and Wang, B. (2011) *Quality Early Childhood Education for Under-two-year-olds: What Should it Look Like? A Literature Review*. Wellington, New Zealand: Ministry of Education.

David, T., Curtis, A. and Siraj-Blatchford, I. (1993) *Effective Teaching in the Early Years: Fostering Children's Learning in Nurseries and in Infant Classes*. Stoke-on-Trent: Trentham Books.

Davies, B. (1991) *Frogs and Snails and Feminist Tales: Preschool Children and Gender*. North Sydney Australia: Allen and Unwin.

—(2003). *Shards of Glass: Children Reading and Writing Beyond Gendered Identities*. Cresshill, NJ: Hampton Press.

Davis, J. and Watson, N. (2000) 'Disabled children's rights in everyday life: problematizing notions of competency and promoting self-empowerment', *International Journal of Children's Rights*, 8, 211–28.

Day, C. (1999) 'Researching Teaching Through Reflective Practice'. In J. Loughran (ed.) *Researching Teaching: Methodologies and Practice for Understanding Pedagogy*. London: Falmer Press.

Della Corte, M., Benedict, H. and Klein, D. (1983) 'The Linguistic Environment'. In D. Ingram (ed.) *First Language Acquisition*. Cambridge: Cambridge University Press.

Department for Children, Schools and Families (2009) *Breaking the Link between Disadvantage and Low Attainment*. Nottingham: DCSF.

Department for Education and Skills (DfES) (2003) *Birth to Three Matters*. Nottingham: DfES Publications.

Department of Health (DoH) (2001) *Seeking Consent: Working With Children*. London: DoH.

DeVillar, R. A. and Faltis, C. J. (1991) *Computers and Cultural Diversity*. Albany: State University Press.

Dewey, J. (1916) *Democracy and Education*. New York: Macmillan.

—(1933) *How We Think: A Restatement of the Relation of Reflective Thinking to the Educative Process*. Chicago: Henry Regnery.

Diamond, K. E. (2002) 'Social Competence in Children with Disabilities'. In P. K. Smith and C. H. Hart (eds) *Blackwell Handbook of Childhood Social Development*. Oxford: Blackwell.

Disch, J. (2002), 'From expert to novice', *Journal of Professional Nursing*, 18 (6), 310.

Doherty-Sneddon, G. (2003) *Children's Unspoken Language*. London: Jessica Kingsley Publishers.

—(2004) 'Don't look now… I'm trying to think', *The Psychologist*, 17 (2) (February), 82–5.

Donaldson, M. (1983) *Children's Minds*. Flamingo: London.

Donnelly, C. (2000) 'In pursuit of ethos', *British Journal of Educational Studies*, 48 (2),134–54.

Doverborg, E. and Pramling Samuelsson, I. (2012) *Att förstå barns tankar. Kommunikation – ens betydelse* [To understand young children's thinking. The role of communication]. Stockholm: Liber.

Dowling, M. (2000) *Young Children's Personal Social and Emotional Development*. London: Paul Chapman Publishing.

Dryden, J., Johnson, B., Hoeard, S. and Mcguire, A. (1998) *Resiliency: A Comparison of Construct Definitions Arising from Conversations with 9 Year Old – 12 Year Old Children and their Teachers*. Paper presented at AERA, San Diego, April 13–17.

Dunn, M., Harrison, L. J. and Coombe, K. (2008) 'In good hands: preparing research-skilled graduates for the early childhood and professional', *Teaching and Teacher Education*, 24 (3), 703–14.

Dweck, C. S. (2006) *Mindset. The New Psychology of Success*. New York: Ballantine.

—(1986), 'Motivational processes affecting learning', *American Psychologist*, 41 (10), 1040–6.

Dyson, A. (1999) 'Inclusion and Inclusions: Theories and Discourses in Inclusive Education'. In H. Daniels and P. Garner (eds) *World Yearbook of Education 1999: Inclusive Education*. London: Kogan Page, 36–53.

Dyson, A. H. (1997) *Writing Superheroes: Contemporary Childhood, Popular Culture, and Classroom Literacy*. Williston, VT: Teachers College Press.

Early, D. M., Maxwell, K. L., Burchinal, M., Alva, S., Bender, R. H., Bryant, D., Cai, K., Clifford, R. M., Ebanks, C., Griffin, J. A., Henry, G. T., Howes, C., Iriondo-Perez, J., Jeon, H. J., Mashburn, A. J., Peisner-Feinberg, E., Pianta, R. C., Vandergrift, N. and Zill, N. (2007) 'Teacher's education, classroom quality, and young children's academic skills: results from seven studies of preschool programs', *Child Development*, 78 (2), 558–80.

Eaude, T. (2012) *How Do Expert Primary Class-teachers Really Work?* Knutsford: Critical Publishing.

Edwards, C., Gandidi, L. and Foreman, G. (1993) *The Hundred Languages of Children, The Reggio Emilia Approach to Early Childhood Education*. New Jersey: Ablex Publishing.

Egidius, H. (2008) *Psykologilexikon* [Psychology dictionary]. Stockholm: Natur och Kultur.

Ekman, P., Frieson, W. V. and Ellsworth, P. (1972) *Emotions in the Human Face*. New York: Pergamon.

Elder, G. H. (1974) *Children of the Great Depression*. Boulder, CO: Westview Press.

Elfer, P., Goldschmied, E. and Selleck, D. (2003) *Key Persons in the Nursery: Building Relationships for Quality Provision*. London: David Fulton.

Elias, J. (1994) *Paulo Freire: Pedagogue of Liberation*. New York: Teacher's College Press.

Epstein, A. (1978) *Ethos and Identity*. London: Tavistock.

Eraut, M. (1994) *Developing Professional Knowledge and Competence*. London: Falmer Press.

Ericsson, K., Chairness, N., Feltovich, P. J. and Hoffman, R. R. (eds) (2006) *The Cambridge Handbook of Expertise and Expert Performance*. Cambridge: Cambridge University Press.

Erikson, E. (1980) *Identity and the Life Cycle*. New York: W. W. Norton.

Estyn (2002) *Excellent Schools: A Vision for Schools in Wales in 21st Century*. Cardiff: Estyn.

Eteläpelto, A. (1992) 'Asiantuntijuuden kehittäminen ammattikorkeakoulun haasteena' [The Development of Expertise as a Challenge for a Polytechnic]. In J. Ekola (ed.) *Johdatusta ammattikorkeakoulupedagogiikkaan* [Introduction to Pedagogy at Polytechnic]. Porvoo, Finland: WSOY, 19–42.

Eteläpelto, A. (1997) 'Asiantuntijuuden muuttuvat määritykset' [The Changing Definitions of Professionalism]. In J. Kirjonen, P. Remes and A. Eteläpelto (eds) *Muuttuva asiantuntijuus* [Changing Professionalism]. Jyväskylä, Finland: Finnish Institute for Educational Research, 86–102.

Evans, L., Packwood, A., Neill, S. and Campbell, J. (1994) *The Meaning of Infant Teachers' Work.* London: Routledge.

Evetts, J. (2009) 'New professionalism and new public management: changes, continuities and consequences', *Comparative Sociology*, 8 (2), 247–66.

Facer, K. (2009) *Towards an Area-Based Curriculum: Insights and Directions from the Research.* London: RSA.

Facione, P. A. and Facione, N. C. (1992) *The California Critical Thinking Dispositions Inventory.* Millbrae, CA: California Academic Press.

Farrell, M. (2009) *Foundations of Special Education.* Oxford: Blackwell.

Farson, R. (1996) *Management of the Absurd: Paradoxes in Leadership.* New York: Simon and Schuster.

Faulkner, D. and Miell, D. (1993) 'Settling into school: the importance of early friendships for the development of children's social understanding and communicative competence', *International Journal of Early Years Education*, 1, 23–45.

Feinstein, L. (2003) 'Inequality in the early cognitive development of British children in the 1970 cohort', *Economica*, 70, 73–97.

Feinstein L., Duckworth K. and Sabates R. (eds) (2008) *Education and the Family: Passing Success Across the Generations.* Oxford: Routledge.

Feinstein, L., Vorhaus, J. and Sabates, R. (2008) *Foresight Mental Capital and Wellbeing Project. Learning Through Life: Future Challenges.* London: The Government Office for Science.

Ferguson, C. (1977) 'Baby Talk as a simplified Register'. In C. Snow and C. Ferguson (eds) *Talking to Children.* Cambridge: Cambridge University Press.

Filer, A. and Pollard, A. (2000) *The Social World of Pupil Assessment.* London: Continuum.

Filippini, T. and Cecchi, V. (eds) (1996) *The Hundred Languages of Children: The Exhibit.* Reggio Emilia: Reggio Children.

Fisher, J. (1996) *Starting from the Child.* Buckingham: Open University Press.

Fisher, R. (1997) 'Building bridges in early literacy', *International Journal of Early Years Education*, 5 (3), 189–98

Folger, J. and Chapman, R. (1977) 'A Pragmatic analysis of spontaneous imitations', *Journal of Child Language,* 5, 25–38

Foucault, M. (1978) *The History of Sexuality.* Vol. 1. New York: Pantheon.

—(1991) *Discipline and Punish: The Birth of a Prison.* London: Penguin.

Freire, P. (1992) *Pedagogy of Hope: Reliving Pedagogy of the Oppressed.* Trans. R. Barr. London: Continuum.

—(1996) *Pedagogy of the Oppressed.* London: Continuum.

—(1999) *Pedagogy of the Heart.* New York: Continuum.

—(2005) 'Extension or Communication'. In P. Freire *Education For Critical Consciousness.* London: Continuum.

Friedman, R. (2007) 'Listening to Children in the Early Years'. In M. Wild and H. Mitchell (eds) *Early Childhood Studies: Reflective Reader.* Exeter: Learning Matters, 81–94.

Friedson, E. (1994) *Professionalism Reborn: Theory, Prophecy and Policy.* Oxford: Polity Press.

—(2001) *Professionalism: The Third Logic.* Cambridge: Polity Press.

Frost, N. (2001) 'Professionalism, change and the politics of lifelong learning', *Studies in Continuing Education*, 23, 5–17.

Fuchs, D. and Fuchs, L. (1994) 'Inclusive schools movement and the radicalisation of special education reform', *Exceptional Children*, 60 (4), 294–309.

Fukkink, R. G. and Lont, A. (2007) 'Does training matter? a meta-analysis and review of caregiver training studies', *Early Childhood Research Quarterly*, 22, 294–311.

Furlong, J. (1999) 'Intuition and the Crisis in Teacher Professionalism'. In T. Atkinson and G. Claxton (eds) *The Intuitive Practitioner: On the Value of Not Always Knowing What One Is Doing*. Buckingham: Open University Press.

—(2000) *Higher Education and the New Professionalism of Teachers: Realising the Potential of Partnership*. A Discussion Paper. London: SCOP/CVCP.

Gadotti, M. (1994) *Reading Paulo Freire: His Life and Work*. New York: State University of New York Press.

Galton, M., Hargreaves, L., Comber, C. and Wall, D. (1999) *Inside the Primary Classroom: 20 Years On*. London: Routledge.

Gandini, L. (1998) 'Educational and Caring Spaces'. In C. Edwards, L. Gandini and G. Forman (eds) *The Hundred Languages of Children: The Reggio Emilia Approach – Advanced Reflections*. New Jersey: Ablex Publishing, 161–78.

Garcia, E. E. (1991) 'Effective instruction for language minority students: the teacher', *Journal of Education*, 173 (2), 130–41.

Garnica, O. (1977) 'Some Prosodic and Paralinguistic Features of Speech to Young Children'. In C. S. Snow and C. A. Ferguson (eds) *Talking to Children*. Cambridge: Cambridge University Press.

Garton, A. (1992) *Social Interaction and the Development of Language and Cognition*. Hove: Lawrence Erlbaum.

Geertz, C. (1973) *The Interpretation of Cultures*. New York: Basic Books,

Gibbs, G. (1988) *Learning by Doing. A Guide to Teaching and Learning Methods*. London: Further Education Unit

Giddens A. (1990) *The Consequences of Modernity*. Stanford, CT: Stanford University Press.

Gill, T. (2007) *No Fear. Growing up in a Risk Averse Society*. London: Calouste Gulbenkian Foundation.

Gipps, C., Gross, H and Goldstein, H. (1987) *Warnock's Eighteen Per Cent: Children with Special Needs in Primary Schools*. London: Falmer Press.

Gipps, C., McCallum, B. and Brown, M. (1996) 'Models of teacher assessment among primary school teachers in England', *The Curriculum Journal*, 7 (2), 167–83.

Glaser, R. (1999) 'Expert Knowledge and Processes of Thinking'. In R. McCormick and C. Paechter (eds) *Learning and Knowledge*. London, Paul Chapman Publishing, 88–102.

Gleitman, L. R., Newport, M. and Gleitman, H. (1984) 'The current status of the motherese hypothesis', *Journal of Child Language*, 11, 43–79.

Goldschmied, E. (1989) *Infants at Work: The Treasure Basket Explained*. London: National Children's Bureau.

Goldschmied, E. and Jackson, S. (2004) *People Under Three: Young children in Day Care*. 2nd edn. London: Routledge.

Goleman, D. (1996) *Emotional Intelligence: Why It Can Matter More than IQ*. London: Bloomsbury.

Goswami, U. (2008) *The Learning Brain, Psychology Press*. London: Taylor and Francis.

Graham, J. A. and Argyle, M. (1975) 'A cross-cultural study of the communication of extra-verbal meaning by gesture', *International Journal of Psychology*, 10, 57–67.

Graham, L. J. and Slee, R. (2008) 'Inclusion?'. In S. L. Gabel and S. Danforth (eds) *Disability and the Politics of Education: An International Reader*. New York: Peter Lang, 81–100.

Great Britain Parliament (2010) *Child Poverty Act 2010*. London: HMSO.

Greenfield, C. (2003) 'Outdoor play – the case of risks and challenges in children's learning and development', *Safekids News* (21), 5.

GTCE (2010),'Introduction'. In A. Pollard (ed.) *Professionalism and Pedagogy: A Contemporary Opportunity*. London: TLRP.

Guskey, T. R. (1986) 'Staff development and the process of teacher change', *Educational Researchers*, 15 (5), 5–12.

Guthke, J. and Stein, H. (1996) 'Are learning tests the better version of intelligence tests?'. *European Journal of Psychological Assessment*, 12 (1), 1–13.

Hahn, H. (1929) *Vom Ernst des Spielens*. Stuttgart: Waldorfschul-Verlag.

Hall, E. T. (1966) *The Hidden Dimension*. New York: Double Day.

Hardy, B. (1977) 'Narrative as a Primary Act of Mind'. In M. Meek, A. Warlow and G. Barton *The Cool Web*. London: Bodley Head.

Hargreaves, D. (1992) 'Report of the Committee on the Curriculum and Organisation of ILEA Secondary Schools'. London: ILEA

—(2004) *Learning for Life: The Foundations of Lifelong Learning*. Bristol: The Policy.

Harrison, C. (2004) *Understanding Reading Development*. London: Sage Publications Ltd, 3-8

Hart, S. (1996) *Beyond Special Needs: Enhancing Children's Learning through Innovative Thinking*. London: Paul Chapman.

Hatano, G. and Inagaki, K. (1986) 'Two Courses of Expertise'. In H. Stevenson, H. Azuma and K. Hakuta (eds) *Child Development and Education in Japan*. New York: W. H. Freeman, 262–72.

—(1992) 'Desituating Cognition through the Construction of Conceptual Knowledge'. In P. Light and G. Butterworth (eds) *Context and Cognition: Ways of Knowing and Learning*. New York: Harvester Wheatsheaf, 115–33.

Hattie, J. (2009) *Visible learning: A Synthesis of Over 800 Meta-Analyses Relating to Achievement*. London: Routledge.

Hatton, N. and Smith, D. (1995) 'Reflection in teacher education', *Journal of Teaching and Teacher Education*, 11, 33–49.

Hay, D. F. (1994) 'Pro-social development', *Journal of Child Psychology and Psychiatry*, 35, 29–72.

Heath, S. B. (1993) 'Inner city life through drama: imagining the language classroom', *TESOL Quarterly*, 27 (2), 177–92.

Heath, S. B. and Mangiola, L. (1991) *Children of Promise: Literate Activity in Linguistically and Culturally Diverse Classrooms*. Washington, DC: National Education Association.

Heckman, J. J. (2005) 'Invited Comments'. In L. J. Schweinhart, J. Montie, Z. Xiang, W. S. Barnett, C. R. Belfield and M. Nores (2005) *Lifetime Effects – The High/Scope Perry Preschool Study Through Age 40*. Ypsilante: HighScope Educational Research Foundation.

Heiner, U. (2008) *Rudolf Steiner*. Trans. J. Duke and D. Balestrini. London: Continuum.

Helsby, G. (1996) 'Professionalism in English secondary schools', *Journal of Education for Teaching*, 22, 135–48.

Helsby, G. (1999) *Changing Teachers' Work: The Reform of Secondary Schooling*. Milton Keynes: Open University Press.

Helsby, G. and McCulloch, G. (eds) (1997) *Teachers and the National Curriculum*. London: Cassell.

Heron, B. (2005) 'Self-reflection in critical social work practice: subjectivity and the possibilities of resistance', *Reflective Practice*, 6 (3), 341–51.

Hill, E. (1980) *Where's Spot?* London: Heinemann.

Hirsjärvi, S. (1997) 'Kasvatustietoisuus' [Educational Consciousness]. In S. Hirsjärvi and J. Huttunen (eds) *Johdatus kasvatustieteeseen* [Introduction to the Science of Education]. 4th–5th edn. Porvoo, Finland: WSOY, 60–2.

Hodgkin, R. A. (1985) *Playing and Exploring: Education through the Discovery of Order*. London: Methun.

Holt, D. (ed.) (1993) *Co-operative Learning: A Response to Linguistic and Cultural Diversity*. Washington, DC: Center for Applied Linguistics.

Howard, A. W., MacArthur, C., Willan, A., Rothman, L., Moses-McKeag, A. and MacPherson, A. K. (2005) 'The effect of safer play equipment on playground injury rates among school children', *Canadian Medical Association Journal*, 172 (11), 1443–6.

Hoyle, E. and John, P. D. (1995) *Professional Knowledge and Professional Practice*. London: Cassell.

Huberman, M. (1993) *The Lives of Teachers*. New York: Teachers College Press.

Hughes, B. (2002) *A Playworkers Taxonomy of Play Types*. 2nd edn. London: PlayLink.

Ingram, D. (ed.) (1989) *First Language Acquisition*. Cambridge: Cambridge University Press.

Irwin, J. (2012) *Philosophy of Education Origins, Developments, Impacts and Legacies*. London: Continuum.

Issa, T. and Hatt, A. (2013) *Language Culture and Identity in the Early Years*. London: Bloomsbury.

Izard, C. E. (1975) *The Face of Emotion*. New York: Apple-Century-Crofts.

Johansson, E. (2003) 'Att närma sig barns perspektiv' [To approach the perspective of the child], *Pedagogisk Forskning i Sverige*, 8, 42–57.

Johansson, E. (2007) 'Etiska överenskommelser i förskolebarns världar' [Ethical agreements in preschool children's worlds], *Göteborg Studies in Educational Sciences*, 249. Göteborg: Acta Universitatis Gothoburgensis.

Johnson, H. G., Ekman, P. and Friesen, W. V. (1975) 'Communicative body movements: American emblems', *Semiotica*, 15, 335–53.

Johnson, J. S. and Newport, E. L. (1989) 'Critical period effects in second language learning: the influence of maturational state on the acquisition of English as a second language', *Cognitive Psychology,* 21, 60–99.

Jones, E. and Reynolds, G. (1992) *The Play's the Thing: Teachers' Roles in Children's Play*. New York: Teachers' College Press.

Jones, P. (2009) *Rethinking Childhood: Attitudes in Contemporary Society*, London: Continuum.

Karila, K. and Nummenmaa, A. R. (2001) *Matkalla moniammatillisuuteen Kuvauskohteena päiväkoti* [A the Way Towards Multiprofessionalism: Day Care Centre as the Target of Depiction]. Porvoo, Finland: WSOY.

Karmiloff-Smith, A. (1994) *Baby it's You*. London: Ebury Press

—(1995) 'The extraordinary journey from foetus through infancy', *Journal of Child Psychology and Psychiatry,* 36, 1293–315.

Kärrby, G. (1992) *Kvalitet i pedagogiskt arbete med barn: nya vägar inom barnomsorgen* [Quality in Pedagogical Work with Children: New Ways in Early Childhood Education]. Stockholm: Allmänna.

Katz, L. G. (1995) *Talks with Teachers of Young Children*. New Jersey: Ablex Publishing.

—(1998) 'A Developmental Approach to the Curriculum in the Early Years'. In S. Smidt *The Early Years: A Reader*. Routledge: London, New York, 11–16.

Kauffman, J. M. and Hallahan, D. P. (eds) (1995) *The Illusion of Full Inclusion: A Comprehensive Critique of a Current Special Education Bandwagon*. Austin, TX: Pro-Ed.

Kaye, K. and Fogel, A. (1980) 'The temporal structure of face-to-face communication between mothers and infants', *Developmental Psychology*, 16, 454–64.

Kennedy, B. (1999) *Glasfåglar i molnen* [Glass birds in the clouds]. Stockholm: Stockholms universitets förlag.

Kernan, M. (2007) *Play as a context for Early Learning and Development: A Research Paper*. Commissioned by the National Council for Curriculum and Assessment (NCCA).

Kessler, C. (ed.) (1992) *Co-operative Language Learning: A Teachers Resource Book*. New Jersey: Prentice-Hall Regents.

Kingston, D. and Melvin, J. (2012) 'Quality and Effectiveness in Working with Young People'. In N. Edmond and M. Price (eds) *Integrated Working with Children and Young People*. London: Sage Publications Ltd.

Kocher, L. (2008) *The Disposition to Document: The Lived Experience of Teachers Who Practice Pedagogical Documentation A Case Study*. Early Childhood Education. Toowomba: The University of Southern Queensland.

Kolb, D. (1984) *Experiential Learning: Experience as the Source of Learning and Development*. New Jersey: Prentice-Hall.

Kompf, M., Bond, W. R., Dworet, D. and Boak, R. T. (1996) *Changing Research and Practice: Teachers' Professionalism, Identities and Knowledge*. London and Washington, DC: Falmer Press.

Krathwohl, D. R., Bloom, B. S. and Masia, B. (1964) *Taxonomy of Educational Objectives, the Classification of Educational Goals – Handbook II: Affective Domain*. New York: McKay.

Kugelgen, Helmut von (ed.) (1991) *Plan und Praxis des Waldorfkindergartens: Beitr''age Erziehung des Kindes im ersten Jahrsiebt*. 11th edn. Stuttgart: Freies Geistesleben.

Kuhn, T. S. (1970) *The Structure of Scientific Revolutions*. 2nd edn. Chicago: University of Chicago Press.

Kunneman, H. (2005) 'Social work as a laboratory for normative professionalisation', *Social Work & Society*, 3 (2), 191–200.

Labov, W. (1972) *Language in the Inner City*. Pennsylvania: United Press.

Laevers, F. (2003) 'Experiential Education: Making Care and Education More Effective through Well-being and Involvement'. In F. Laevers and L. Heylen (eds) *Involvement of Children and Teacher Style*. Leuven: Leuven University Press.

Laming, H. (2003) *The Protection of Children in England: A Progress Report*. London: The Stationary Office.

Lankshear, C. and Knobel, M. (2004) 'Planning pedagogy for i-mode: from flogging to blogging via wifi'. Published jointly in *English in Australia*, 139 (February), 78-102 and *Literacy in the Middle Years*, 12 (1), 78–102.

Learning and teaching Scotland (2010) 'Pre-birth to three. Positive outcomes for Scotland's children and families', National Guidance. Available from http://www.educationscotland.gov.uk/earlyyears/prebirthtothree/nationalguidance/index.asp. (accessed 6 February 2013).

Lee. T. (2011) 'The Wisdom of Vivian Gussin Paley'. In L. Miller and L. Pound (eds) *Theories and Approaches to Learning in the Early Years*. London: Sage Publications Ltd.

Leitch, R. and Day, C. (2000) 'Action research and reflexive practice: towards a holistic view', *Educational Action Research*, 8 (1), 173–93.

Lenz Taguchi, H. (1997) *Varför pedagogisk dokumentation?* [Why pedagogical documentation?]. Stockholm: Stockholms universitets förlag.

Lindon, J. (1999) *Too Safe for Their Own Good*. London: National Children's Bureau.

Little, H., and Wyver, S. (2008) 'Outdoor play – does avoiding the risks reduce the benefits?', *Australian Journal of Early Childhood*, 33 (2), 33–40.

Low, C. (1997) 'Is inclusivism possible?', *European Journal of Special Needs Education*, 12 (1), 71–9.

Lyotard, J.-F. (1979) *The Postmodern Condition: A Report on Knowledge*. Minneapolis: University of Minnesota Press.

Main, M., Kaplan, N. and Cassidy, J. (1985) 'Security in Infancy, Childhood and Adulthood: a move to the level of representation'. In I. Bretherton and E. F. Waters (eds) *Growing Points of Attachment Theory and Research, Monographs of the Society for Research in Child Development*, 50 (1–2, serial no. 209).

Malaguzzi, L. (1996) *The Hundred Languages of Children*. Reggio Emilia: Reggio Children.

Malone, K. (2007) 'The bubble-wrap generation: Children growing up in walled gardens', *Environmental Education Research*, 13 (4), 513–27.

Manning-Morton, J. and Thorp, M. (2001) *Key Times: A Framework for Developing High Quality Provision for Children Under Three Years*. London: Camden EYDCP/University of North London.

Marsh, J. (2005) 'Ritual, Performance and Identity Construction: Young Children's Engagement with Popular Cultural and Media Texts'. In J. Marsh (ed.) *Popular Culture, New Media and Digital Literacy in Early Childhood*. London: Routledge Falmer, 12–38.

—(2007) *Digital Beginnings: Conceptualisations of Childhood*. Paper presented to the WUN Virtual Seminar, 13 February. Available from http://www.wun.ac.uk/download.php?file=2488_Childpaper13feb.pdf&mimetype=appliance/pdf (accessed 7 December 2013).

Marsh J., Brooks G., Hughes J., Ritchie L., Roberts S. and Wright K. (2005) *Digital beginnings: Young children's use of popular culture, media and new technologies*. Report of the 'Young Children's use of Popular Culture, media and New Technologies' Study. Sheffield: Literacy Research Centre, University of Sheffield.

Marx, K. (1995) *Capital*. Oxford: Oxford University Press.

Mathematics Enhancement Programme (1999) Presented at the American Educational Research Association Conference. Montreal, Quebec, 19 April. Cited in D. Muijs and D. Reynolds *30 Effective Teaching: Evidence and Practice*. London: Paul Chapman Publishing.

McKendrick, J. H., Bradford, M. G. and Fielder A. V. (2000) 'Kid customer? commercialization of playspace and the commoditization of childhood'. *Childhood,* 7 (3), 295–314.

McKinsey and Company (2009) *The Economic Impact of the Achievement Gap in America's Schools*. Washington, DC: Social Sector Office, McKinsey and Company.

McLaughlin, M. W. (1993) 'What Matters most in Teachers' Workplace Context?'. In J. W. Little and M. W. McLaughlin (eds) *Teachers' Work: Individuals, Colleagues and Contexts*. New York: Teachers College Press, 73–103. Cited in C. Day *Developing Teachers: The Challenges of Lifelong Learning* London: Cassell.

McPake, J., Stephen, C., and Plowman, L. (2007) 'Entering e-Society. Young Children's Development of e-Literacy. Stirling: Institute of Education', University of Stirling. Available from www.ioe.stir.ac.ukiresearchiproiects/esociety/ (last accessed 1 November 2008).

McPake, J. Stephen, C., Plowman, L., Sime, D. and Downey, S. (2005) *Already at a Disadvantage? ICT in the Nollic Children's Preparation for Primary School*. Coventry: BECTA.

Meadows, S. (1996) *Parenting Behaviour and Children's Cognitive Development*. Hove: Psychology Press.

Meier, D. (1995) *The Power Of Their Ideas*. Boston, MA: Beacon.

Messick, S. (1994) 'The interplay of evidence and consequences in the validation of performance assessments', *Educational Researcher*, 23 (2), 13–23.

Miller, L. (2008) 'Developing professionalism with a regulatory framework in England: challenges and possibilities', *European Early Childhood Education Research Journal*, 16 (2), 255–68.

Miller, L., Rustin, M. and Shuttleworth, J. (eds) (1989) *Closely Observed Infants*. London: Duckworth.

Mills, C. W. (1959) *The Sociological Imagination*. New York: Oxford University Press.

Ministry of Education and Science. U2008/6144/S. *Uppdrag till Statens skolverk om förslag till förtydliganden i läroplanen för förskolan* [Assignment to the national agency on proposed clarifications in the preschool curriculum]. Stockholm: Regeringskansliet.

Montessori, M. (1972 [1932]) *Education and Peace*. Chicago: Regnery.

—(1974 [1946]) *Education for a New World*. Madras: Kalakshetra.

Moon, J, (1999) *Learning Journals: A Handbook for Academics, Students and Professional Development*. London: Kogan Page.

Mortimore, J. and Mortimore, P. (1984) *Secondary School Examinations: Helpful Servant or Dominating Masters?* Bedford Way Papers, 18. London: Institute of Education.

Moss, P. and Pence, A. (eds) (1994) *Valuing Quality in Early Childhood Services*. London: Paul Chapman Publishing.

Moyles, J. (2001) 'Passion, paradox and professionalism in early years education', *Early Years: An International Research Journal*, 21 (2), 81–95.

Moyles, J. and Adams, S. (2001) *Statements of Entitlement to Play. A Framework for Playful Teaching*. Buckingham: Open University Press.

Moyles, J. and Suschitzky, W. (1997a) *Jills of All Trade?: Classroom Assistants in KS1 Classes*. Leicester: ATL/Leicester, University of Leicester.

—(1997b) *'The Buck Stops Here ...!': Nursery Teachers and Nursery Nurses Working Together*. Esmée Fairbairn Charitable Trust/University of Leicester.

Moyles, J., Adams, S. and Musgrove, A. (2002) S*PEEL Study of Pedagogical Effectiveness*, Norwich: Stationary Office. Department for Education and Skills ESRC funded project (R000238200), Universities of Leicester and Durham.

Muijs, D. and Reynolds, D. (2001) *Effective Teaching: Evidence and Practice*. London: Paul Chapman Publishing.

Munro, R. (1997) 'Ideas of difference: Stability, Social Spaces and the Labour of Division'. In K. Hetherington and R. Munro (eds) *Ideas of Difference: Social Spaces and the Labour of Division*. Oxford: Blackwell.

Myers Pease, D., Berko Gleason, J. and Alexander Pan, B. (1989) 'Gaining Meaning: Sematic Development'. In J. Berko Gleason (ed.) *The Development of Language*. 2nd edn. Columbus: Merrill Publishing Company.

Myhill, D. and Brackley, M. (2004) 'Making connections: teachers' use of children's prior knowledge in whole class discourse', *British Journal of Educational Studies*, 52 (3), 263–75.

National Agency for Education (NAE) (2008) *Tio år efter förskolereformen* [Ten Years after the Preschool Reform]. Stockholm: Fritzes.

—(2011) *Curriculum for Preschool, 1–5 Years*. Rev. edn. Stockholm: Fritzes.

National Assessment Agency (NAA) (2008) *Engaging Parents and Children in EYFS*. Profile Assessment. London: NAA.

National Council for Curriculum and Assessment (2009) 'Aistear: The Early Childhood Curriculum Framework, National Council for Curriculum Assessment'. Principles and themes. Dublin. Available from http://www.ncca.biz/Aistear (accessed 7 June 2011).

National Curriculum Guidelines on Early Childhood Education and Care in Finland (2003) 'Guidelines 56. Helsinki, Finland: Statistics Finland'. [Online] Available from http://kasvunkumppanit.thl.fi/thl-client/pdfs/267671cb-0ec0-4039-b97b-7ac6ce6b9c10 (accessed 6 February 2011).

Neaum, S. and Tallack, J. (2000) *Good Practice in Implementing the Pre-School Curriculum*. Cheltenham: Nelson Thornes.

Neisser, U. (1976) *Cognition and Reality*. San Francisco, CA: W. H. Freeman.

New Zealand Ministry of Education (1996) *Te Whāriki: He Whāriki Mātauranga mö ngä Mokopuna o Aotearoa: Early Childhood Curriculum*. Wellington: Learning Media.

Newman, D., Griffin, P. and Cole, M. (1989) *The Construction Zone: Working for Cognitive Change in School*. Cambridge: Cambridge University Press.

Newport, E. L. (1976) 'Motherese: The Speech of Mothers to Young Children'. In N. Castellan, D. Pisoni and G. Potts (eds) *Cognitive Theory*. Vol. II. Hillsdale, NJ: Lawrence Erlbaum.

Nias, J. (1989) *Primary Teachers Talking: A Study of Teaching at Work*. London: Routledge.

Noddings, N. (1994) 'An Ethic of Caring and Its Implication for Instructional Arrangements'. In L. Stone (ed.) *The Education Feminism Reader*. New York and London: Routledge.

Norwich, B. (2008) *Dilemmas of Difference, Inclusion, and Disability*. London: Routledge.

—(2010) 'A Response to Special Educational Needs: A New Look'. In L. Terzi (ed.) *Special Educational Needs: A New Look*. London: Continuum, 47–111.

Nutbrown, C. (1996) *Respectful Educators-Capable Learners. Children's Rights and Early Education*. London: Paul Chapman Publishers.

—(1997) *Recognising Early Literacy Development: Assessing Children's Achievements*. London: Sage Publications Ltd.

—(1999) *Threads of Thinking*. 2nd edn. London: Paul Chapman Publishing.

—(2005) *Key Concepts in Early Childhood Education and Care*. London: Sage Publications Ltd.

—(2006) *Threads of Thinking*. 3rd edn. London: Sage Publications Ltd.

—(2011) *Threads of Thinking: Schemas and Young Children Learning*. 4th edn. London: Sage Publications Ltd.

—(2012) 'Foundations for quality: the independent review of early education and childcare qualifications: Final Report' [online]. Runcorn: Department for Education. Available from https://www.education.gov.uk/publications/standard/publicationDetail/Page1/DFE-00068-2012 (accessed 12 July 2012).

Nutkins, S., McDonald, C. and Stephen, M. (2012) *Early Childhood Education and Care*. London: Sage Publications Ltd.

O'Brien, T (ed.) (2001) *Enabling Inclusion: Blue Skies... Dark Clouds*? London: TSO.

Oberhuemer, P. (2000) 'Conceptualizing the professional role in early childhood centres: emerging profiles in four countries', *Early Childhood Research & Practice*, 2 (2). Also available from http://ecrp.uiuc.edu/v2n2/oberhuemer.html (accessed 14 January 2008).

Ödman, P. J. (2004) 'Hermeneutik och forskningspraktik'. In I. B. Gustavsson (ed.) *Kunskapande metoder inom samhällsvetenskapen* [Methods of Knowledge in the Social Sciences]. Lund: Studentlitteratur, 71–93.

Oliver, M. (1990) *The Politics of Disablement*. London: Macmillan.

Organisation for Economic Co-operation and Development (OECD) (2004). *Starting Strong. Curricula and Pedagogies in Early Childhood Education and Care: Five Curriculum Outlines*. Paris: OECD.

—(2005) *Teachers Matter: Attracting Developing and Retaining Effective Teachers*. Paris: OECD.

—(2006) 'Starting Strong II: Early Childhood Education'. In J. Peeters and M. Vandenbroeck (eds) *Working Towards Better Childcare: Report over Thirteen Years of Research and Training*. Gent: RUG, VBJK, 39–79.

Osborn, M. (1996) 'Teachers Mediating Change: Key State 1 Revisited'. In P. Croll (ed.) *Teachers, Pupils and Primary Schooling*. London: Cassell.

Osborn, M., McNess, E. and Broadfoot, P. with Pollard, and Triggs, P. (2000) *What Teachers Do: Changing Policy and Practice in Primary Education*. London: Continuum.

Osgood, J. (2006) 'Deconstructing professionalism in early childhood education: resisting the regulatory gaze', *Contemporary Issues in Early Childhood*, 7 (1), 5–14.

Paley, V. G. (1999) *The Kindness of Childre*n. Cambridge, MA: Harvard University Press.

—(1986) *Mollie is Three: Growing up in School*. Chicago: The University of Chicago Press.

—(1990) *The Boy who Would be a Helicopter*. Cambridge, MA: Harvard University Press.

—(1993) *You Can't Say You Can't Play*. Cambridge, MA: Harvard University Press.

—(2001a) *In Mrs Tully's Room*. Cambridge, MA: Harvard University Press.

—(2001b) *White Teacher*. Cambridge, MA: Harvard University Press.

Parker, S. (1997) *Reflective Teaching in the Postmodern World: A Manifesto for Education in Post-modernity*. Philadelphia: Open University Press.

Parker-Rees, R. (1997) 'Making sense and made sense: design and technology and the playful construction of meaning in the early years', *Early Years*, 18 (1), 5–8.

—(1999) 'Protecting Playfulness'. In L. Abbott and H. Moylett (eds) *Early Education Transformed*. New Millennium Series. London, and New York: Falmer Press, 64–6.

Pascal, C. (April 1996) *Higher Education Partnerships with Early Childhood Services*. Pen Green Lecture. Unpublished.

Pascal, C. and Bertram, T. (1995) '"Involvement" and the Effective Early Learning Project: A Collaborative Venture'. In F. Laevers (ed.) *An Exploration of the Concept of 'Involvement' as an Indicator for the Quality of Early Childhood Care and Education*. Dundee: CIDREE, 25–38.

Pascal, C., Bertram, T., Hall. R. and Mould, M. (1998) 'Exploring the relationship between process and outcome in young children's learning: stage one of a longitudinal study', *International Journal of Educational Research*, 29, 51–67.

Perkin, H. (2002) *The Rise of the Professional Society: England Since 1880*. 3rd edn. London: Routledge.

Piaget, J. (1969) *The Mechanisms of Perception*. London: Routledge and Kegan Paul.

—(1953) *The Origin of Intelligence in the Child*. London: Routledge and Kegan Paul.

—(1961) 'A genetic approach to the psychology of thought', *Journal of Educational Psychology*, 52, 151–61.

Picchio, M., Giovannini, D., Mayer, S. and Musatti, T. (2012) 'Documentation and analysis of children's experience: an on-going collegial activity for early childhood professionals', *Early Years*, 32 (2), 159–70.

Pipp, S., Easterbrooks, M. A. and Brown, S. R. (1993) 'Attachment status and complexity of infants' self and other knowledge when tested with mother and father', *Social Development*, 1-14.

Pirrie, A. and Head, G. (2007) 'Martians in the playground: researching special educational needs', *Oxford Review of Education*, 33 (1), 19–31.

Plowman, L. and Luckin, R. (2003) *Summary of Research: Exploring and Mapping Interactivity with Digital toy Technology. Futurelab Conference paper Digital Childhoods: The Future of Learning for the under 10s*. Robinson College, March.

Pollard, A. (1985) *The Social World of the Primary School*. London: Cassell.

Pollard, A. with Filer, A. (1996) *The Social World of Children's Learning: Case Studies of Pupils from Four to Seven*. London: Cassell.

—(1999) *Social World of Pupil Career: Strategic Biographies Through Primary School*. London: Cassell.

Pollard, A. and Thiessen, D. (1996) *Children and Their Curriculum: The Perspectives of Primary and Elementary School Children*. Lewes: Falmer Press.

Pramling, I. (1994) *Kunnandets grunder: prövning av en fenomenografisk ansats till att utveckla barns sätt att uppfatta sin omvärld* [The Basic of Knowledge: A Phenomenographic Approach to Develop Children's Conceptions of the World]. Göteborg: Acta Universitatis Gothoburgensis.

Pring, R. (1976) *Knowledge and Schooling*. Open Books: London.

—(2000) *Philosophy of Educational Research*. London: Continuum.

Pugh, G. and Duffy, B. (2006) *Contemporary Issues in the Early Years*. 4th edn. London: Sage Publications Ltd.

Putnam, R. (1993) 'Prosperous community: social capital and public life', *The American Prospect*, 3 (13), 11–8.

Qualifications and Curriculum Authority (2009) *Research into Marking Quality: Studies to Inform Future Work on National Curriculum Assessment*. London: QCA.

Rankin, C. and Butler, F. (2011) 'Issues and Challenges for the Interdisciplinary Team in Supporting the Twenty-First-Century Family'. In A. Brock and C. Rankin (eds) *Professionalism in the Interdisciplinary Early Years Team*. London: Continuum.

Rhinegold, H. L. (1982) 'Little children's participation in the world of adults, a nascent pro-social behaviour', *Child Development*, 46, 459–63.

Rinaldi, C. (1994) 'Staff Development in Reggio Emilia'. In L. L. Katz and B. Cesarone (eds) *Reflections on the Reggio Emilia Approach*. Urbana, IL: ERIC EECE.

—(1998) 'The Space of Childhood'. In G. Ceppi and M. Zini (eds) *Children, Spaces, Relations: Metaproject for an Environment for Young Children*. Reggio Emilia, Italy: Reggio Children and Domus Academy Research Centre, 114–20.

—(2001) 'Documentation and Assessment: What is the Relationship?'. In C. Giudici, C. Rinaldi and M. Krechevsky (eds) *Making Learning Visible. Children as Individual and Group Learners*. Reggio Emilia: Reggio Children and Project Zero, 148–51 .

—(2005a) 'Documentation and Assessment: What is the Relationship?'. In A. Clark, A. Trine Kjorholt and P. Moss (eds) *Beyond Listening: Children's Perspectives on Early Childhood Services*. Bristol: Policy Press.

—(2005b) *In Dialogue with Reggio Emilia: Listening, Researching, and Learning*. London: Routledge.

Rix, J. with Tan, A. and Moden, S. (2004) 'A Balance of Power: Observing a Teaching Assistant'. In R. Hancock and J. Collins (eds) *Primary Teaching Assistants: Learners and Learning*. London: David Fulton, 193–99.

Roberts, C. (1995) *Self-esteem and Successful Early Learning*. London: Hodder and Stoughton.

Roose, R. and De Bie, M. (2003) 'From participative research to participative practice: a study in youth care', *Journal of Community & Applied Social Psychology*, 13, 475–85.

Rowling, J. K. (2000) *Goblet of Fire*. London: Bloomsbury.

Rustemier, S. (2002) *Social and Educational Justice: The Human Rights Framework for Inclusion*. Bristol: CSIE

Ryan, K. and Cooper, J. M. (2004) *Those who can, Teach*. 10th edn. Boston: Houghton Mifflin Company.

Salas, E., Goodwin, J. and Burke, C. S. (eds) (2008) *Team Effectiveness in Complex Organizations: Cross-disciplinary Perspectives and Approaches*. New York: Taylor and Francis.

Salonius-Pasternak, D. E. and Gelfond, H. S. (2005) 'The next level of research on electronic play: Potential Benefits and contextual influences for children and adolescents', *Human Technology*, 1 (1), 5–22.

Salzberger-Wittenberg, I., Gianna, H. and Osborne, E. (1983) *The Emotional Experience of Learning and Teaching*. New York: Routledge and Kegan Paul.

Saracho, O. N. and Spodek, B. (2003) 'The Preparation of Teachers for the Profession in Early Childhood Education'. In O. N. Saracho and B. Spodek (eds) *Studying Teachers in Early Childhood Settings*. Greenwich, CT: Information Age Publishing, 1–28.

Schaffer, H. R. (1996) *Social Development*. Oxford: Blackwell.

Scherer, K. R. (1981) 'Speech and Emotional States'. In J. K. Darby (ed.) *Speech Evaluation in Psychiatry*. New York: Grune and Stratton.

Schneider-Rosen, K. and Cicchetti, D. (1984) 'The relationship between affect and cognition in maltreated infants: quality of attachment and the development of self-recognition', *Child Development*, 55, 648–58.

Schön, D. (1983) *The Reflective Practitioner: How Professionals Think in Action*. London: Temple Smith.

School Curriculum And Assessment Authority (1997) *Looking at Children's Learning: Desirable Outcomes for Children's Learning on Entering Compulsory Education*. London: SCAA.

Schwebel, D. C. (2006) 'Safety on the playground: mechanisms through which adult supervision prevent child playground injury', *Journal of Clinical Psychology in Medical Settings*, 13 (2), 135–43.

Schwebel, D. C., Summerlin, A. L., Bounds, M. L. and Morrongiello, B. A. (2006) 'The Stampin Safety program: a behavioral intervention to reduce behaviors that can lead to unintentional playground injury in a preschool setting', *Journal of Pediatric Psychology*, 31 (2), 152–62.

Schweinhart, L. J. Montie, J., Xiang, Z., Barnett, W. S., Belfield, C. R. and Nores, M. (2005) *Lifetime Effects – The High/Scope Perry Preschool Study Through Age 40*. Ypsilante: HighScope Educational Research Foundation.

Scottish Government (2004) *A Curriculum for Excellence*. Edinburgh: The Curriculum Review Group, Scottish Executive.

Sestini, E. (1987) 'The Quality of Learning Experiences for Four Years Olds in Nursery and Infant Classes'. In *NFER/SCDC, Four Year Olds in School Policy and Practice*. Slough: NFER/SCDC.

Sheridan, S. (2000) 'A comparison of external and self-evaluations of quality in early childhood education', *Early Child Development and Care*, 164, 63–78.

—(2001) *Pedagogical Quality in Preschool: An Issue of Perspectives*. Göteborg: Acta Universitatis Gothoburgensis.

—(2007) 'Dimensions of pedagogical quality in preschool', *International Journal of Early Years Education*, 15 (20), 197–217.

Shulman, L. S. (2004) *The Wisdom of Practice – Essays on Teaching, Learning and Learning to Teach*. San Francisco, Jossey-Bass.

Sim, M. and Kim, J.-U. (2010) 'Differences between experts and novices in kinematics and accuracy of golf putting', *Human Movement Science*, 29 (6), 932–46.

Siraj-Blatchford, I. (1992) 'Why Understanding Cultural Differences is Not Enough'. In G. Pugh (ed.) *Contemporary Issues in the Early Years*. London: Paul Chapman.

—(1999), 'Early Children Pedagogy: Practice, Principles and Research'. In P. Mortimore (ed.) *Understanding Pedagogy and its Impact on Learning*. London: Paul Chapman.

Siraj-Blatchford, I., Sylva, K., Muttock, S., Gilden, R. and Bell, D. (2002). *Researching Effective Pedagogy In The Early Years*. London: DCSF.

Slaughter-Defoe, D. T. (2005) 'Life Begins at 40'. In L. J. Schweinhart, J. Montie, Z. Xiang, W. S. Barnett, C. R. Belfield and M. Nores *Lifetime Effects – The High/Scope Perry Preschool Study Through Age 40*. Ypsilante: HighScope Educational Research Foundation.

Slee, R. (2006) 'Limits to and possibilities for educational reform', *International Journal of Inclusive Education*, 10 (2–3), 109–19.

—(2011) *The Irregular School: Exclusion, Schooling and Inclusive Education*. London: Routledge.

Smidt, S. (2011) *Introducing Bruner: A Guide for Practitioners and Students in Early Years Education*. London: Routledge.

Smiley, P. A. and Dweck, C. S. (1994) 'Individual differences in achievement goals among young children', *Child Development*, 65, 1723–43.

Snow, C. (1977) 'The development of conversation between mothers and babies', *Journal of Child Language*, 4 (1), 1–22.

—(1986) 'Conversations with Children'. In P. Fletcher and M. Garman (eds) *Language Acquisition*. 2nd edn. Cambridge: Cambridge University Press.

Sommer, D. (2005a). *Barndomspsykologi. Utveckling i en förändrad värld* [Childhood Psychology. Development in a Time of Change]. Stockholm: Liber.

—(2005b) *Barndomspsykologiska fasetter* [Childhood Psychological Facets]. Stockholm: Liber.

Sommer, D., Pramling Samuelsson, I. and Hundeide, K. (2010) *Child Perspectives and Children's Perspectives in Theory and Practice*. Dortrecht.

Springer. SOU. (1997). *Att erövra omvärlden* [To conquer the world]. Förslag till läroplan för förskolan. Stockholm: Fritzes, 157.

Sheridan, S. (2007) 'Dimensions of pedagogical quality in preschool', *International Journal of Early Years Education*, 15 (20), 197–217.

Sorel, M. and Wittorski, R. (2005) *La Professionalisation en Actes et en Questions*. Paris: L'Harmattan.

Spencer-Woodley, L. (2014) 'Accountability: Tensions and Challenges'. In Z. Kingdon and J. Gourd (eds) *Early Years Policy: The Impact on Practice*. Oxon: Routledge.

Stainback, S. and Stainback, W. (eds) (1992) *Curriculum Considerations in Inclusive Classrooms: Facilitating Learning for all Students*. Baltimore: Brookes.

Steegmuller, F. (1982) *The Letters of Gustave Flaubert*. Cambridge, MA: Harvard University Press.

Steinberg, S. and Kincheloe, J. (1998) *Students as Researchers – Creating Classrooms that Matter*. London: Routledge.

Stenström, M. L. (2006) 'Polytechnic Graduates' Working-life Skills and Expertise'. In P. Tynjälä, J. Välimaa and G. Boulton-Lewis (eds) *Higher Education and Working Life: Collaborations, Confrontations and Challenges*. Amsterdam: Elevier, 89–102.

Stern, D. N. (1998) *The Interpersonal World of the Infant*. London: Karnac Books.

Sternberg, R. J. and Horvath, J. A. (1995) 'A prototype view of expert teaching', *Educational Researcher*, 24 (6), 9–17.

Stone, L. (ed.) (1994) *The Education Feminism Reader*. New York and London: Routledge.

Sugrue, C. (1997) *Complexities of Teaching: Child-centred Perspectives*. London: Falmer Press.

Sutton-Smith, B. (1997) *The Ambiguity of Play*. Cambridge, MA: Harvard University Press.

Sylva, K. (1992) 'Conversations in the Nursery: How They Contribute to Aspirations and Plans', Society of Arts, Start Right (The Ball Report). London: RSA, 84–96.

Sylva, K., Melhuish, E., Sammons, P. and Siraj-Blatchford, I. (1999) *The Effective Provision of Pre-school Education (EPPE) Project – a Longitudinal Study*. Funded by the DfEE (1997–2003). University of London: Institute of Education (IOE).

Sylva, K., Melhuish, E., Sammons, P., Siraj-Blatchford, I. and Taggart, B. (2004). *The Effective Provision of Preshool Education (EPPE), Project: Final Report*. Nottingham: DfES Publications/London: The Institute of Education.

Tarr, P. (2001) 'Aesthetic codes in early childhood classrooms: what art educators can learn from Reggio Emilia', *Art Education*, 54 (1), 33–9.

—(2004) 'Consider the walls', *Young Children*, 58 (3), 88–92.

Terzi, L. (2005) *Special Educational Needs: A New Look*. IMPACT Series No. 11. London: Philosophy of Education Society of Great Britain Publications.

Tharp, R. and Gallimore, R. (1988) *Rousing Minds to Life: Teaching, Learning and Schooling in Social Context*. New York, Cambridge University Press, 28–39

Thomas, C. (1997) 'Inclusive schools for an inclusive society', *British Journal of Special Education*, 24 (3), 103–7.

—(2004) 'How is disability understood?', *Disability and Society*, 19 (6), 569–83.

Thomas, G. and Davis, P. (1997) 'Special needs: objective reality or personal construction? judging reading difficulty after the code', *Educational Research*, 39 (3), 263–70.

Thomas, G. and Loxley, A. (2007) *Deconstructing Special Education and Constructing Inclusion*. Maidenhead: Open University Press.

Thorndike, E. L. (1922) 'Practice effects in intelligence tests', *Journal of Experimental Psychology*, 5, 101–7.

Thornton, L. and Brunton, P. (2009) *Understanding the Reggio Approach*. 2nd edn. London: Routledge.

Tomasello, M. and Ferrar, J. (1986) 'Joint attention and early language', *Child Development*, 57, 1454–63.

Trevarthan, C. (1979) 'Communication and Co-operation in Early Infancy: A Description of Inter-subjectivity'. In M. Bullowa (ed.) *Before Speech: The Beginning of Interpersonal Communication*. Cambridge: Cambridge University Press.

Turner-Bissett, R. (1999) 'The knowledge bases of the expert teacher', *British Educational Research Journal*, 25 (1), 39–55.

Turner-Bissett, R. (2001) *Expert Teaching: Knowledge and Pedagogy to Lead the Profession*. London: David Fulton.

Twiselton. S. (2006) 'The problem with English: the exploration and development of student teachers' English subject knowledge in primary classrooms', *Literacy*, 40 (2), 88–96.

Tynjälä, P. (1999) 'Konstruktivistinen oppimiskäsitys ja asiantuntijuuden edellytysten rakentaminen koulutuksessa' [The constructivist idea of learning and creating the prerequisites of expertise in education]. In A. Eteläpelto and P. Tynjälä (eds) *Oppiminen ja asiantuntijuus. Työelämän ja koulutuksen näkökulmia* [Learning and Expertise: Perspectives of Working Life and Education]. Porvoo, Finland: WSOY, 160–79.

—(2008) 'Perspectives into learning at the workplace', *Educational Research Review*, 3 (2), 130–54. [Online] Available from http://www.sciencedirect.com (accesed 16 February 2011).

Tynjälä, P., Slotte, V., Nieminen, J., Lonka, K. and Olkinuora, E. (2006) 'From University to Working Life: Graduates' Workplace Skills in Practice'. In P. Tynjälä, J. Välimaa and G. Boulton-Lewis (eds) *Higher Education and Working Life: Collaborations, Confrontations and Challenges*. Amsterdam: Elsevier, 73–88.

UNICEF Innocenti Research Centre (2008) *Report Card 8: The Child Care Transition*. Florence: UNICEF.

Urban, M. (2008) 'Dealing with uncertainty: challenges and possibilities for the early childhood profession', *European Early Childhood Education Research Journal*, 16 (2), 135–52.

Urban, M. and Dalli, C. (2008) 'Editorial', *European Early Childhood Education Research Journal*, 16 (2), 131–3.

Valentine, M. (1999) *The Reggio Emilia Approach to Early Years Education*. Dundee: Scotland's Consultative Council on the Curriculum.

Van Manen, M. (1991) *The Tact of Teaching. The Meaning of Pedagogical Thoughtfulness*. Albany, NY: State University of New York Press.

Vaughn, S. and Schumm, J. S. (1995) 'Responsible inclusion for students with learning disabilities', *Journal of Learning Disabilities*, 28 (5), 264–70.

Verenikina, I., Herrington, J., Peterson, R. and Mantei, J. (2008) 'The Affordances and Limitations of computers for play in early childhood'. Proceedings of the World Conference on Educational Multimedia, Hypermedia and Telecommunications, Vienna, Austria, 3–4 June, 2008.

Vygotsky, L. S. (1978) *Mind in Society: The Development of Higher Mental Processes*. Cambridge: Harvard University Press.

Waldfogel, J. and Washbrook, E. (2008) *Early Years Policy*. Paper prepared for the Sutton Trust– Carnegie Summit: Social Mobility and Education Policy. London. Available from http://www. bristol.ac.uk/media-library/sites/ifssoca/migrated/documents/waldfogeleyp.pdf (accessed 25 November 2014).

Walker, G. H., Stanton, N. A., Salmon, P. M., Jenkins, D. P., Rafferty, L. and Ladva, D. (2010) 'Same or different? genralism from novices to experts in military command and control studies', *International Journal of Industrial Ergonomics*, 40 (5), 473–83. DOI:10.1016/j. ergon.2010.04.003. Available from http://dx.doi.org/10.1016/j.ergon.2010.04.003 (accessed 6 July 2011).

Waller, T. (2008) 'ICT and Literacy'. In J. Marsh, and E. Hallet (eds) *Desirable Literacies: Approaches to Langauge and Literacy in the Early Years*. 2nd edn. London. Sage Publications Ltd.

—(2010a) 'Digital Play in the Classroom: A Twenty-first Century Pedagogy?'. In S. Rogers (ed.) *Rethinking Play and Pedagogy in Early Childhood Education: Concepts, Contexts and Cultures*. Abingdon: Routledge Falmer.

—(2010b) 'Special Educational Needs: A New Look'. In L. Terzi (ed.) *Special Educational Needs: A New Look*. London: Continuum, 32–43.

Warren-Leubecker, A. and Bohannon, J. N. (1989). 'Pragmatics: Language in Social Contexts'. In J. Berko-Gleason (ed.) *The Development of Language*. 2nd edn. Columbus, OH: Merrill.

Waterhouse, S. (2004) 'Deviant and non-deviant identities in the classroom: patrolling the boundaries of the normal social world', *European Journal of Special Needs Education*, 19 (1), 69–84.

Wells, G. (1981) *Learning through Interaction, Language at Home and at School*. Vol 1. Cambridge: Cambridge University Press

Wenger, E. (1998) *Communities of Practice: Learning, Meaning, and Identity*. Cambridge: Cambridge University Press.

Wertsch, J. (1979) 'From social interaction to higher psychological process; a clarification and application of Vygotsky's theory', *Human Cognition*, 2 (1), 15–18.

—(1991) *Voices of the Mind: A Sociocultural Approach to Mediated Action*. Cambridge: Harvard University Press.

Whalley, M (ed.) (2007) *Involving Parents in their Children's Learning*. 2nd edn. London: Paul Chapman.

Whitebread, D. and Bingham, S. (2012) 'School Readiness: A Critical Review of Perspectives and Evidence'. TACTYC. Available from http://scmeyegroup.weebly.com/uploads/1/8/4/9/1849450/readiness_review_12312.pdf (accessed 2 August 2014).

Williams, F. (1992) 'Somewhere over the Rainbow: Universality and Diversity in Social Policy'. In N. Manning and R. Page (eds) *Social Policy Review*. Canterbury: Social Policy Association.

Wiltshire, M., Brunton, P. and Thornton, L. (eds) (2012). *Understanding the HighScope Approach*. London: Routledge.

Wood L. and Bennett, N. (1998) 'The rhetoric and reality of play', *Early Years* 17 (2), 17–22.

Wood, D. (1998) *How Children Think and Learn*. Oxford: Blackwell Publishers.

Wood, D. Bruner, J. S. and Ross, G. (1976) 'The role of tutoring in problem solving', *Journal of Child Psychology and Psychiatry*, 17 (2), 89–100.

Wood, E. (2009) 'Developing a Pedagogy of Play'. In A. Anning, J. Cullen and M. Fleer (eds) *Early Childhood Education: Society and Culture*. 2nd edn. London: Sage Publications Ltd.

Wood, E. and Attfield, J. (1996) *Play Learning and the Early Childhood Curriculum*. Paul Chapman.

Wood, E. and Bennett, N. (1999) 'Progression and continuity in early childhood education: tensions and contradictions', *International Journal of Early Years Education*, 7 (1), 5–16.

Woodhead, M. (1998). '"Quality" in early childhood programmes – a contextually appropriate approach', *International Journal of Early Years Education,* 6 (1), 5–17.

Woods, P. and Jeffrey, B. (1996) *Teachable Moments: The Art of Teaching in Primary Schools*. Buckingham: Open University Press.

—(1997) 'Creative Teaching in the Primary National Curriculum'. In G. Helsby and G. McCulloch (eds) *Teachers and the National Curriculum*. London: Cassell.

Yelland, N. (ed.), (1998) *Gender in Early Childhood*. London and New York: Routledge.

Yelland, N. J. (2007) *Shift to the Future: Rethinking Learning with New Technologies in Education*. New York: RoutledgeFalmer.

Youdell, D. (2006) 'Diversity, inequality, and a poststructural politics for education', *Discourse*, 27 (1), 33–42.

Zahn-Waxler, C., Radke-Yarrow, M., Wagner, E. and Chapman, M. (1992). 'Development of concern for others', *Developmental Pschology,* 28, 126–36.

Zevenbergen, R. (2007) 'Digital natives come to preschool: implications for early childhood practice', *Contemporary Issues in Early Childhood*, 8 (1), 18–28.

Permissions

We are grateful to the authors and publishers listed below for permission to reproduce the following extracts:

1.1 'Passion, Paradox and Professionalism in Early Years Education', by Janet Moyles (2001), edited from *Passion, Paradox and Professionalism in Early Years Education in Early Years: An International Research Journal*, 21 (2), 81–95, reproduced by permission of Taylor & Francis.

1.2 'Perspectives on Professionalism', by Avril Brock (2011) in A. Brock and Ranken, C. (eds) *Professionalism in the Interdisciplinary Early Years Team*, reproduced by permission of Bloomsbury Publishing.

1.3 'Accountability: Tensions and Challenges,' by Lisa Spencer-Woodley, (2014) in Z. Kingdon and J. Gourd (eds) *Early Years Policy: The Impact on Practice*, reproduced by permission of Taylor & Francis.

1.4 'Practical judgement and evidence-informed practice', by Ruth Heilbronn, edited from 'The Nature of Practice-based Knowledge and Understanding', in R. Heilbronn and J. Yandell, (eds) *Critical Practice in Teacher Education: A Study of Professional Learning* (2010), published by IOE Press.

1.5 'Questioning the story of Quality', by Peter Moss, edited from *Transformative Change and Real Utopius in Early Childhood Education: A Story of democracy, experimentation and potentiality* (2014), reproduced by permission of Taylor & Francis.

1.6 'Improving Quality in the Early Years: A Comparison of Perspectives and Measures', by Sandra Mathers, Rosanna Singler and Arjette Karemaker in *Improving Quality in the Early Years: A Comparison of Perspectives and Measures* (2012), reproduced by permission of Daycare Trust and Sandra Mathers.

2.1 'The Science of Learning and the Art of Teaching', by Burrhus Skinner, in *The Science of Learning and the Art of Teaching* (1954), reproduced by permission of Harvard Educational Review.

2.2 'The genetic approach to the psychology of thought', by Jean Piaget, edited from 'A genetic approach to the psychology of thought', *British Journal of Educational Psychology*, 52 (1961), reproduced by permission of John Wiley & Sons Inc.

2.3 'Mind in Society: Development of Higher Psychological Processes' by L. S. Vygotsky, edited by Michael Cole, Vera John-Steiner, Sylvia Scribner and Ellen Souberman, pp. 84–90, Cambridge, MA: Harvard University Press, © 1978 by the President and Fellows of Harvard College.

2.4 The Spiral Curriculum', by Jerome Bruner, edited from 'The meaning of educational reform', *Journal of the National Association of Montesori Teachers* (1991), reproduced by permission of National Association of Montesori Teachers.

2.5 'Motivational processes affecting learning', by Carol Dweck, edited from 'Motivational processes affecting learning, American Psychologist', October (1986), reproduced by permission of American Psychological Association.

2.6 'Protecting playfulness', by Rodd Parker-Rees (1999) in L. Abbott and H. Moylett (eds)

Early Education Transformed: New Millennium Series, reproduced by permission of Taylor & Francis.

3.1   'The Role of Reflection in the Professionalization of the Early Years Workforce', by Jan Peeters and Michel Vandenbroeck edited from *Childcare Practitioners and the Process of Professionalization* (2011), reproduced by permission of Sage Publications Ltd.

3.2   'The Importance of Practitioner Research' by Lawrence Stenhouse, in *An Introduction to Curriculum Research and Development* (1975), reproduced by permission of Heinemann.

3.3   'Action Research and the Development of Practice', by Richard Pring, in *Philosophy of Educational Research* (2000), reproduced by permission of Bloomsbury Publishing.

3.4   'Measures of Quality', by Denise Kingston and Jane Melvin in *Quality and Effectiveness in Working with Young People* (2012), reproduced by permission of Sage Publications Ltd.

3.5   'Reflection-in-action', by Donald Schön, edited from The *Reflective Practitioner: How Professionals Think in Action* (1983), reproduced by permission of Perseus Books.

3.6   'Thinking and Reflective Experience', by John Dewey, edited from *How We Think: A Restatement of the Relation of Reflective Thinking to the Educative Process* (1933), and *Democracy and Education* (1916), published by Henry Regnery and Macmillan.

4.1   'Learning without Limits', by Mandy Swann, Alison Peacock, Susan Hart and Mary Jane Drummond, from *Creating Learning Without Limits* (2012), reproduced by permission of Open University Press.

4.2   'The Effective Provision of Pre-School Education (EPPE) Project: Findings from Pres-school to end of Key Stage 1', by Kathy Sylva, Edward Melhuish, Pam Sammons, Iram Siraj-Blatchford and Brenda Taggart (2004), Crown copyright, reproduced under Open Government Licence.

4.3   'Insights, Opportunities and Challenges of Educational Neuroscience', by The Royal Society in *Brain Waves Module 2: Neuroscience: Implication for Education and Lifelong Learning* (2011), reproduced by permission of The Royal Society.

4.4   'Playful Learning', by Rod Parker-Rees, in *Protecting Playfulness* (1999), reproduced by permission of Taylor & Francis.

4.5   'Schemas and Learning', by Cathy Nutbrown, in *Key Concepts in Early Childhood Education & Care* (2011), reproduced by permission of Sage Publications Ltd.

5.1   'Being an Educator in times of Change,' in *Teacher Development: Knowledge and Context,* (2007), reproduced by permission of Bloomsbury Publishing.

5.2   'The Sociological Imagination', by C. Wright Mills, edited from *The Sociological Imagination* (1959), reproduced by permission of Oxford University Press.

5.3   'Exploring the School Readiness Debate', in *School Readiness: A Critical Review of Perspectives and Evidence*, by D. Whitebread and S. Bingham (2012), reproduced by permission of D. Whitebread.

5.4   'Education, Opportunity and Social Cohesion', by Andy Green and Jan Janmaat, in *Education, Opportunity and Social Cohesion* (2011), published by LLAKES.

5.5   'Schooling, Social Class and Privilege', by Stephen Ball, edited from *The More Things Change: Educational Research, Social Class and 'Interlocking' Inequalities.* Professorial Inaugural Lecture (2004), published by IOE Press.

6.1   'The Importance of Relationships for Children's Development', by Maria Evangelou, Kathy Sylva, Maria Kyriacou, Mary Wild and Georgina Glenny edited from *Early Years Learning and Development Literature Review*.

6.2   'Working in Teams', by Carolynn Rankin and Fiona Butler, 'edited from *Issues and Challenges for the Interdisciplinary Team*, reproduced by permission of Bloomsbury.

6.3   'What is Self-esteem?', by Dennis Lawrence, edited from *Enhancing Self-Esteem in the Classroom* (1987), reproduced by permission of Sage Publications Ltd.

6.4   'Attachment, What it is, Why it is Important?', by Sir Richard Bowlby in *Attachment, What it is, Why it is Important and What we can do about it to Help Young Children Acquire a Secure Attachment.* (2008), reproduced by permission of Sir Richard Bowlby.

6.5 'The Role of the Preschool Practitioner in the Development of Children's Social Competencies' (2012) by Jennifer Colwell from *The Relational Approach to Group Work the Role of the Preschool Practitioner in the Development of Children's Social Competencies*, reproduced by permission of Jennifer Colwell.

7.1 'Measuring Involvement in the Early Years', by Ferre Laevers edited from *Experiential Education: Making Care and Education More Effective Through Well-being and Involvement* (2003), reproduced by permission of Leuven University Press.

7.2 'Understanding Children's Behaviour in Relation to their Development', by Pat Broadhead, Jane Johnston, Caroline Tobbell and Richard Woolley edited from *Personal, Social and Emotional Development* (2010), reproduced by permission of Bloomsbury Publishing.

7.3 'How Practitioner Behaviour Impacts upon Children's Behaviour', by Sonja Sheridan edited from *Dimensions of Pedagogical Quality in Preschool* (2007), reproduced by permission of Taylor & Francis.

7.4 'Non-verbal Communication', by Michael Argyle edited from *The Psychology of Interpersonal Behaviour,* 5th edn, 1994, published by Penguin.

7.5 'The Highscope Approach to Behaviour Management', by Michelle Graves and Ann Arbor edited from *Working With a Challenging Child* (2002), reproduced by permission of Highscope.

8.1 'The Learning Environment' by Janet Moyles, Siân Adams and Alison Musgrove edited from *SPEEL Study of Pedagogical Effectiveness* (2002), Crown copyright, reproduced under Open Government Licence.

8.2 'The Value of Providing for Risky Play in Early Childhood Settings' by Marie Willoughby edited from *Childlinks* (2001), published by Banardos.

8.3 'Respectful Environments for Children' by Tim Loreman edited from *Respecting Childhood* (2009), reproduced by permission of Bloomsbury Publishing.

8.4 'The ecology of social environments', by Urie Bronfenbrenner, edited from 'Ecological Models of Human Development', *International Encyclopaedia of Education,* Vol. 3 (1993).

8.5 'Digital Technology and Play' by Tim Waller, edited from *Digital Play in the Classroom: A Twenty-first Century Pedagogy?* (2010a), reproduced by permission of Taylor & Francis.

9.1 'Froebel's Spirit And Influence' by Tina Bruce, Anne Findlay, Jane Read and Mary Scarborough edited from *Recurring Themes in Education* (1995), reproduced by permission of Sage Publishing Ltd.

9.2 'The Reggio Emilio Approach', by Sheila Nutkins, Catriona McDonald and Mary Stephen edited from *Early Childhood Education and Care* (2012), reproduced by permission of Sage Publications Ltd.

9.3 'The Montessori Approach' by Marion O'Donnell edited from *Montessori: A Critical Introduction to Key Themes and Debates* (2013), reproduced by permission of Bloomsbury.

9.4 'Rudolf Steiner and The Waldorf Pre-School', by Heiner Ullrich edited from *Rudolf Steiner* (2008), reproduced by permission of Bloomsbury Publishing.

9.5 'The HighScope Approach', by Sheila Nutkins, Catriona McDonald and Mary Stephen edited from *Early Childhood Education and Care* (2012), reproduced by permission of Sage Publications Ltd.

9.6 'The Te Whāriki Approach' by Wendy Lee, Margaret Carr, Brenda Soutar and Linda Mitchell edited from *Understanding the Te Whāriki Approach: Early Years Education in Practice* (2013), reproduced by permission of Taylor & Francis.

10.1 'A Developmental Approach to the Curriculum in the Early Years', by Lilan G. Katz edited from *The Early Years: A Reader* (1998), reproduced by permission of Taylor and Francis.

10.2 'Listening to Young Children', by Peter Moss edited from *Let's Talk about Listening to*

Children: Towards a Shared Understanding for Early Years Education in Scotland (2006), Crown copyright, reproduced under Open Government Licence.

10.3   'Assumptions about Children and Young People', by Phil Jones edited from *Rethinking Childhood: Attitudes in Contemporary Society* (2009), reproduced by permission of Bloomsbury Publishing.

10.4   'Curriculum Planning' by Kathy Brodie edited from *Observation, Assessment and Planning in the Early Years: Bringing it all Together* (2013), reproduced by permission of McGraw Hill Education.

10.5   'The potential of Story-telling and Story-acting', by Trisha Lee edited from *Observation, Assessment and Planning in the Early Years: Bringing it all Together* (2011), reproduced by permission of Sage Publications Ltd.

11.1   'What is Pedagogy and Why is it Important?', by the General Teaching Council for England, edited from *Professionalism and Pedagogy: A Contemporary Opportunity* (2010), a TLRP Commentary, reproduced by permission of Teaching and Learning Research Programme.

11.2   'Pedagogy in Effective Settings', by Iram Siraj-Blatchford, Kathy Sylva, Stella Muttock, Rose Gilden, Danny Bell edited from *Researching Effective Pedagogy In The Early Years* (2002), Crown copyright, reproduced under Open Government Licence.

11.3   'Folk Pedagogy' edited from *The Culture of Education* by Jerome Bruner, pp. 45–50, Cambridge, MA: Harvard University Press, © 1996, reproduced by permission by the President and Fellows of Harvard College.

11.4   'Teaching as the Assistance of Performance', by Roland Tharp and Ronald Gallimore, edited from *Rousing Minds to Life: Teaching, Learning and Schooling in Social Context* (1988), reproduced by permission of Cambridge University Press.

12.1   'Interactions and Social Development', by Pat Broadhead edited from *Early Years Play and Learning: Developing Social Skills and Cooperation* (2004), reproduced by permission of Taylor & Francis.

12.2   'Talking Babies', by Julia Manning-Morton edited from *The Importance of Non-verbal Interactions for Under-threes* (2004), reproduced by permission of Nursery World.

12.3   'The Role of the Linguistic Environment in Early Language Development', by Belinda Buckley edited from *Children's Communication Skills – From Birth to Five Years* (2003), reproduced by permission of Taylor & Francis.

12.4   'The Bilingual Learner', by Tözün Issa and Alison Hatt edited from *Language Culture and Identity in the Early Years* (2013), reproduced by permission of Bloomsbury Publishing.

12.5   'Why is Reading so Important?', by Colin Harrison, edited from *Understanding Reading Development* (2004), reproduced by permission of Sage Publications Ltd.

12.6   'Narrative in the Lives of Children', by Sandra Smidt edited from *Introducing Bruner: A Guide for Practitioners and Students in Early Years Education* (2011), reproduced by permission of Taylor & Francis.

13.1   'Creating a Dialogue With Parents', by Margy Whalley edited from *Working with Parents* (1997), published by Hodder Education.

13.2   'Assessment: why, who, when, what and how?', by Patricia Broadfoot edited from *Assessment Policy and Practice: The 21ˢᵗ Century Challenge For Educational Assessment* (2007), reproduced by permission of Bloomsbury Publishing.

13.3.   'Teacher Feedback in the Reception Class', by Andrew Burrell and Sara Bubb edited from *Teacher Feedback in the Reception Class* (2000), reproduced by permission of Taylor & Francis.

13.4   'Reporting on Progress and Achievement', by the Scottish Government edited from *Principles of Assessment in Curriculum for Excellence, Building the Curriculum* (2011), Crown copyright reproduced under Open Government Licence.

13.5   'The Myth of Objective Assessment', by Ann Filer and Andrew Pollard, edited from *The*

Social World of Pupil Assessment (2000), reproduced by permission of Ann Filer, Andrew Pollard and Bloomsbury Publishing.

13.6   'Watching and Listening: The Tools of Assessment', by Cathy Nutbrown edited from *Contemporary Issues in the Early Years* (2006), reproduced by permission of Sage Publications Ltd.

14.1   'Learning and the Development of Resilience', by Guy Claxton, edited from *Wise Up: The Challenge of Lifelong Learning* (1999), reproduced by permission of Bloomsbury Publishing.

14.2   'Using Observation', by Rod Parker-Rees, edited from *Early Childhood Studies* (2010), reproduced by permission of Sage Publications Ltd.

14.3   'Learning Dispositions and Assessment', by Margaret Carr & Guy Claxton edited from *Tracking the Development of Learning Dispositions, Assessment in Education: Principles, Policy & Practice* (2002), reproduced by permission of Taylor & Francis.

14.4   'Observation and Pedagogic Documentation', by Anette Emilson and Ingrid Pramling Samuelsson edited from *Documentation and Communication in Swedish Preschools* (2014), reproduced by permission of Taylor & Francis.

14.5   'Involving Parents and Carers as Partners in Assessment', by Jonathan Glazzard edited from *Assessment for Learning in the Early Years Foundation Stage* (2010), reproduced by permission of Sage Publications Ltd.

15.1   'Defining Inclusion', by Anastasia Liasidou edited from *Inclusive Education, Politics and Policymaking Contemporary Issues in Education Studies* (2012), reproduced by permission of Bloomsbury Publishing.

15.2   'Disability, and Support Children with Special Educational Needs in the Early Years' by Penny Borkett edited from *Diversity and Inclusion in the Early Years* (2012), reproduced by permission of Bloomsbury Publishing.

15.3   'Difference or Diversity?', by Gary Thomas and Andrew Loxley, edited from *Deconstructing Special Education and Constructing Inclusion* (2007), reproduced by permission of McGraw-Hill Education.

15.4   'What's your Attitude?: Inclusion and Early Years Settings by Jonathan Rix, edited from *Inclusion and Early Years Settings – What's your Attitude?* (2008), reproduced by permission of McGraw-Hill Education.

16.1   'Contemporary Change and Professional Development', by Pat Collarbone, edited from *Creating Tomorrow: Planning, Developing and Sustaining Change in Public Services* (2009), reproduced by permission of Bloomsbury Publishing.

16.2   'The Development of Expertise', by Tony Eaude, edited from *How do Expert Primary Classteachers Really Work?* (2012), reproduced by permission of Tony Eaude and Critical Publishing.

16.3   'Creative Mediation and Professional Judgement', by Marilyn Osborn, Elizabeth McNess, Andrew Pollard, Pat Triggs and Patricia Broadfoot edited from *What Teachers Do: Changing Policy and Practice in Primary Education* (2000), reproduced by permission of Bloomsbury Publishing.

16.4   'The Expertise of Early Childhood Educators', by Iiris Happo and Kaarina Määttä edited from *International Education Studies Expertise of Early Childhood Educators* (2011), reproduced by permission of Iiris Happo and Kaarina Määttä.

17.1   'Qualifications: Nutbrown Review', by Cathy Nutbrown edited from *Foundations for Quality: The Independent Review of Early Education and Childcare Qualifications* (2012), Crown copyright, reproduced under Open Government licence.

17.2   'Thinking about Education Systems', by Margaret Archer, edited from *The Social Origins of Educational Systems* (1979), reproduced by permission of Sage Publications Ltd.

17.3   'Field Report: The Foundation Years: Preventing Poor Children Becoming Poor Adults', by Frank Field edited from *The Foundation Years: Preventing Poor Children Becoming Poor Adults* (2010), Crown copyright, reproduced under Open Government Licence.

17.4   'The Philosophy of Paulo Freire', by Jones Irwin edited from *Philosophy of Education Origins, Developments, Impacts and Legacies* (2012), reproduced by permission of Bloombury Publishing.

17.5   'The Impact of Early Education as a Strategy in Countering Socio-economic Disadvantage', by Tony Bertram and Chris Pascal edited from *The Impact of Early Education as a Strategy in Countering Socio-economic Disadvantage* (2013), reproduced by permission of Chris Pascal.

Index

This index categorises reflective settings, practitioners, children teaching and learning, and related concepts under different headings; it covers Chapters 1–17 but not personal names. An 'f' after a page number indicates a figure; page references in bold denote a table.

ability 66–9, 103
accommodation 30
accountability 12–13
achievement 103
    recording 273–4
    wall 307
Acredolo, L. 239
action research 46–8
actual development level 33
adult-child verbal interactions 223–5
Ames, C. 296
anthroposophy 181–4
appearance 144
Argyle, M. 143
assessment 262–7, 271–3, 281, 286 *see also*
    observation
    Baseline Assessment system 281
    classroom 279
    criterion referenced 266
    dynamic 297
    formative 225, 263–4
    ipsative 266–7
    learning dispositions and 295–9
    learning stories and 297–8
    for management and accountability 281, **282**
    norm-referenced 266
    objective 275–80
    parents and 280, 285–6, 304–7
    portfolios and 299
    reception class, and 268–70
    reliability and 267
    for research 281, **282**
    self-reports and 298–9
    socio-cultural influences and 278, 280
    summative 263–4
    for teaching and learning 281, **282**, 285–6
    validity and 267
assimilation 30
assisted performance 230
Athey, NC. 82
'Att erövra omvärlden' 300

attachment 118–23
Attentional Processes 126
Australia 191
aversive consequences 25

babies 351
    behaviour of 133
    communication with 238–41, 242–4
    interaction and 236
    observing 294
Bandura 126
Baseline Assessment system 281
behaviour management 145–7
behaviourism 24–7
Belbin, R. M. 109, 110f
'Belonging, being and becoming' 191
Berliner, D. C. 332–3
Bernstein, B. 242
Bick, E. 294
biography 91–2
bilingualism 245–8
Bjervås, L.-L. 302
Bloom, B. 58
body–image 115
body language 294
Bowlby, R. 118
brain, the 74–8, 123
'Brain Waves' reports 74
Brazil 355–7
British Columbia 191
Bronfenbrnner, U. 189
    Ecology of Human Development, The 160
Bruner, J. 35, 227, 250
    'Monologues as Narrative Recreation of the
        World' 253
    narrative and 252–3
    Process of Education, The 35
Butler 101

California Critical Thinking Dispositions Inventory
    (CCTDI) 298

carers *see* parents
CCTDI (California Critical Thinking Dispositions Inventory) 298
Ceppi 157
challenges 297
change 328–31, 336–9, 349–50
child-centred ideology 151
child directed talk 243 *see also* motherese
child poverty 358–61
children 283 *see also* pupils
     assumptions about 207–9
     behaviour of 133–7, 145–7
     communication and 314–15
     competency and 176, 207–91
     development and 106–7, 115, 133–7, 229–30, 236–9
     disadvantaged 72–3 *see also* inclusion
     grouping of 212
     interactions with professionals and 112–13
     interactions and 236–7
     language and 236–7, 242–4, 245–8
     life chances of 351–4
     movement and 155 *see also* playgrounds
     nature of 181–2
     performance and 230–2, 354
     perspectives of 203–4
     pro-social behaviour and 108
     relationships and 106–8
     social competencies of 124–6
     social skills of 134
     special educational needs (SED) and 314–15
Children of the Great Depression (Elder) 162
chronosystems 161–2
civic competences 98
Clark, A.
     Mosaic Approach, The 203
     Spaces to Play 203
Claxton, G. 5
cognitive development 79
cognitive enhancement 77
collaboration 153, 339 *see also* teamwork
committed compliance 108
communication 79, 314–15
     babies and 238–41
     inclusion and 321–2
     non-verbal 141–4
conflict resolution 145–7
conservation 29, 30
construct validity 267
content knowledge 341
contextual knowledge 341–2
continuous improvement 50
co-operative learning strategies 245
cooperation skills 341, 342
Cooper, J. M. 341
Creating Learning Without Limits (Swann, Peacock, Hart and Drummond) 67
Creating Learning Without Limits project 69

creative mediation 337, 338–9
criterion referenced assessment 266
critical reflection 58
crystallized expertise 334
cultural capital 103
Cummins, J. 246
curricula
     Australia and 191
     British Columbia and 191
     Froebel, F. and 170–2
     HighScope approach, and 185–8
     Ireland and 193
     Montessori approach, and 178–81
     National Curriculum 337–9
     planning and 198–202, 210–13
     Reggio Emilio approach, and 173–7
     Scotland and 191
     Te Whāriki approach, and 189–94
     Waldorf pre-schools 181–4
Curriculum for Excellence 271
curriculum knowledge 341

Dahlberg, G.: *Ethics and Politics in Early Education* 206
Day, C. 89
daycare 122 *see also* pre-schools
de-automatization 232
Deming 50
descriptive reflection 58
descriptive writing 58
development
     dynamic dimension of 199
     normative approach to 200
developmental stage 231
Dewey, J. 54, 298
diagnostic discourse 264
dialogic reflection 58
dictatorship of no alternatives (DONA) 17
difference 316–18
differentiation 225
digital immigrants 163, 164
digital natives 163, 164
digital technology 163–5
disability 310–11, 314
     models of 313
disadvantaged children 72–3
discipline 226
discourses 311
dispositions 198, 201
diversity 316
division 317
documentation 176, 300–3, 306–7
Doherty-Sneddon, G. 293
Doing Foucault in Early Childhood Studies: Applying Poststructural Ideas (Mcnaughton) 204
domain specificity 36
DONA (dictatorship of no alternatives) 17
Donnelly, C. 151

Drummond, M. J.: *Creating Learning Without Limits* 67
Dunne 14
Dweck, C. 37
dynamic assessment 297
dynamic of transformations 28–31
Dyson, A. H.: *Writing Superheroes* 254

early years practitioners 5–6 *see also* practitioners; teachers
    accountability and 12–13
    careers and 347
    expertise and 340–2
    paradox and 6
    passion and 4–6
    practical judgement and 15–16
    professionalism and 6–7, 10, 11
    qualifications and 346–8
ecological environment, the 160–2, 189
Ecology of Human Development, The (Bronfenbrenner) 160
economic crisis, the 97, 358
education
    economy and 360
    inequality and 97–9, 100
    religious 183
Education and Peace (Montessori) 179
Education as The Practice of Freedom (Freire) 356
Education for a New World (Montessori) 179
Education of Man, The (Froebel) 170
educational systems 349–50
Effective Provision of Pre-school Education (EPPE) 70–3
Ekman, P. 143
elaborated code 242
Elder, G. H.: *Children of the Great Depression* 162
emotions 89–90, 237
English 247–8, 305
environment 241
Environmental Rating Scales 20–1
EPPE (Effective Provision of Pre-school Education) 70–3
equilibration 30–1
ethics 15
Ethics and Politics in Early Education (Dahlberg and Moss) 206
ethos 150–2
Evans, L. 152
exosystems 161
expertise 332–5, 340–2
Extension or Communication (Freire) 357
eye contact 295–6

face validity 267
facial expression 141–2
families 101–2
feedback 268–70
feelings 198, 201
Ferguson, C. 243
Field, Report, The 351–4
Filer, A.: *Social World of Pupil Assessment, The* 278–81
Finland 341
flexibility 15

fluid expertise 336
folk pedagogy 227–8
folk psychology 227
formal knowledge 340–1
formative assessment 225, 263–4
Foucault, M. 204–5
Foundation Years, the 352–3
Freire, P. 5, 355–7
    Education as The Practice of Freedom 356
    Extension or Communication 357
    Pedagogy of Hope: Reliving Pedagogy of the Oppressed 357
    Pedagogy of the Oppressed 356
Friedson, E. 9
Friesen, W. V. 143
Froebel, F. 170–2
    Education of Man, The 170
Froebel Early Education Project 82

Gadotti, M. 356–7
gaze 142, 293
gestures 143
Gibbs, G. 57
Gipps, C. 268–9
Glaser, R. 332–4
Goleman, D. 5
Goodwyn, S. 239
government policy
    accountability and 12–13
    poverty and 352
Graham, J. A. 143
Grunelius, E. von 181

handover principle 230
Hardy, B.: *Narrative as a Primary Act of Mind* 249
Hargreaves, D. 88
Hart, S. 323
    Creating Learning Without Limits 67
Hatano, G. 341
Hattie, J.: *Visible Learning* 330
Hatton, N. 58
hazard 154
HighScope approach, the 185–8
history 91–2
home language 247–8
home learning 72–3, 245–6, 306
humanity 179–80

ideal self 116
identity 89
Inagaki, K. 341
inclusion 310–12, 319–24 *see also* difference; special
    educational needs individuals 91–2
inequalities
    education and 97–9, 100
    of income 97
    of skills distribution 98
informal knowledge 340–1

innovative thinking 323
intelligence 39
intensive mothering 103
intensive parenting 103
inter-subjectivity 250–1
interactions 236–7, 341–2
interdisciplinary learning 273
internalization 229
interviews 298, 299
invariants of groups 29
involvement 130–3
ipsative assessment 266–7
Ireland 193
Isaacs, S. 283–4

James 114
Johnson, H. G. 143

kaizen 50
Karila, K. 341
Kincheloe 5
Kindergarten, the 170, 181
Kindness of Children, The (Paley) 254
knowing-in-action 52
knowledge 51, 199, 340–1
Köhler, E. 300

labour of division 316
Labov, W. 242
land of contrasts and a pedagogy of contradiction, A (Torres) 355
Langsted, O. 205–6
language 34
    bilingualism 245–8
    development 237, 242–4, 305
    reports and 293
    sign 314
Law of Effect, the 24
learning 32–4, 283, 284, 330
    ability 66–9, 77
    curricula and 201–2
    home 72–3, 245–6, 306
    interdisciplinary 273
    neuroscience and 74–8
    processes 126
    psychology of 24–7
    recording 273–4
    Reggio Emilio approach, and 173–7
    resilience and 290–1
learning capacity 67
learning dispositions, assessment of 295–9
learning environments 150–2, 330–1
    cohesive 246
    Reggio Emilio approach, and 176
    respectful 157–9
    social environments 160–2, 189
learning goals 38–9

learning logs 298
learning stories 297–8, 306–7
Learning Without Limits project 67–9
Leuven Scale for Involvement, the 131, 132
Leuven Scale for Well-being, the 132
liberal societies 96
linguistics 242–5
listening 202–6, 321–2
literacy 356–7
'Living Spaces' project 203
local authorities 19–20
logical structure 30
logico-mathematical experience 30
Lucariello, J.: 'Monologues as Narrative Recreation of the World' 253
Luckin, R. 165

Mcnaughton, G.: Doing Foucault in Early Childhood Studies: Applying Poststructural Ideas 204
macrosystems 161
Makaton 314
Malaguzzi, L. 173, 174
MALS (Myself as a Learner) test 298
'Managing Risk in Play Provision' 154
mathematics 25–7
maturation 29
'Measuring Child Poverty' (UNICEF) 358
Measuring Outcomes for Public Service Users (MOPSU) 12
mental health 180
mesosystems 161
metacognitive knowledge 341
microsystems 160
middle class, the 101–3
models of disability 313
Mollie is Three (Paley) 215
'Monologues as Narrative Recreation of the World' (Bruner and Lucariello) 253
Montessori, M. 178
    Education and Peace 179
    Education for a New World 179
Montessori approach, the 178–80
Moon, J. 57
MOPSU (Measuring Outcomes for Public Service Users) 12
mosaic approach, the 203–4
Mosaic Approach, The (Clark and Moss) 203
Moss 11
Moss, P.
    Ethics and Politics in Early Education 206
    Mosaic Approach, The 203
    Spaces to Play 203
Moteric Reproduction Processes 126
motherese 239–40, 243
Motherese Hypothesis, The 243
mothers 103, 118–23
motivation 37–9
Motivation Processes 126
Mrs Tulley's Room (Paley) 214

multiculturalism 152
Myself as a Learner (MALS) test 298

narrative 249–50, 252–5
Narrative as a primary act of mind (Hardy) 249
National Curriculum 337–9
nature/nurture debate 75
neuroplasticity 75–6
neuroscience 74–8, 123
New Zealand 189–94
non-verbal communication 141–4
norm-referenced assessment 266
Nummenmaa, A. R. 341
Nutbrown, C. 281
Nutbrown Review, the 346–8

observation 179, 284–5, 292–4, 297–8
    pedagogic documentation and 300–3
Ofsted (Office for Standards in Education, Children's Services
    and Skills) 20–1, 49
Office for Standards in Education, Children's Services and Skills
    (Ofsted) 20–1, 49

PACE project 336
Paley, V. 214–17
    Kindness of Children, The 254
    Mollie is Three 215
    Mrs Tulley's Room 214
    White Teacher 215
    You Can't Say You Can't Play 216
paradigms 294
paradox 6
parents 19–20, 101–2, 258–61, 351–4
    assessment and 280, 285–6, 304–7
    communication and 240
    curricula and 199
    pedagogy and 225
    planning and 212
    Reggio Emilio approach, and 173–5
passion 4–6
Peacock, A. 69
    Creating Learning Without Limits 67
pedagogical documentation 301–2
pedagogical knowledge 341, 342
pedagogical quality 138–40
pedagogy 220–2, 223–6
    folk pedagogy 227–8
Pedagogy of Hope: Reliving Pedagogy of the Oppressed (Freire)
    357
Pedagogy of the Oppressed (Freire) 356
performance 230–2
performance goals 38–9
Perkin, H. 9
personal rootedness 15–16
phronesis 14
physical experience 30
Piaget, J. 28

PISA (Programme for International Student Assessment) 98–9
play 79–80, 121–2, 151–2
    communication and 241
    risk and 154–7
    technology and 163–5
    Waldorf pre-schools and 181–4
Play Safety Forum 154
playgrounds 158–9
Plowman, L. 165
Pollard, A.: *Social World of Pupil Assessment, The* 278–81
Portage 314
portfolios 299
positive reinforcement 25, 39
posture 143
poverty 358–61
power 204–5, 319–21, 350
practical judgement 14–16
practical knowledge 340
practitioners 4, 42–3 *see also* early years practitioners; teachers
    change and 88–90
    children's social competencies and 124–6
    communication and 240
    inclusion and 319–24
    planning and 212
    research and 44–5
    special educational needs (SEN) and 314–15
'Pre-birth to three' 191
pre-schools 70–3 *see also* daycare
    Froebel, F. and 170–2
    HighScope approach, and 185–8
    Montessori approach, and 178–81
    quality and 139–41
    Reggio Emilio approach, and 173–7
    Te Whāriki approach, and 189–94
    Waldorf pre-schools 181–4
Prensky 164
private schools 101
Process of Education, The (Bruner) 35
professional development 328–31
professional self-development 44
professionalism 6–7, 8–10, 11
    change and 88–9
    research and 42–3, 44–5
Programme for International Student Assessment (PISA) 98–9
providers 19–20
psychology 24–7, 28–31
punishment 25
pupils *see also* children
    identity and 276–7, 316–18

qualifications 42, 187–8
quality 17–18, 19–21
    quality assurance (QA) 50
    quality control 49
    quality improvement 50
    total quality management (TQM) 50
quality assurance schemes 20–1

readiness 94–5
reading 116, 249–515, 317
ready to learn 93
reception class, the 268–70
recording 273–4
recursion 232
recycling 176
reflecting-in-action 51–3
reflection 42–3, 56–7
reflective practice 54–5
reflective writing 56–62
Reggio Emilio approach, the 173–7, 206, 284
regime of truth 13
reinforcement 24–6, 39
relationships 152
        children and 106–8
        Reggio Emilio approach, and 175
reliability 267
religious education 183
research 42–3, 46 *see also* action research
        Montessori approach, and 179
        perspectives 294
resilience and 290–1, 296
restricted code 242
Retention Processes 126
Rinaldi, C. 206
risk 153–6 *see also* playgrounds
Robson 101
routine 185–6
Ryan, K. 341

Salas, E. 111
scaffolding 230
schemas 81–3
Schön, D. 51
school readiness 93–5
Schwebel, D. C. 158–9
Scotland 191
second language acquisition 247–8, 305
self-concept 114–15, 236
self-control 76
self-efficacy 291
self-esteem 114–17
self-image 115
self-regulation 231–2
self-reports 298–9
SEN (special educational needs) 310, 312, 316, 317
        role of practitioners and 314–15
Sheffield Early Literacy Development Profile 281–2
Shulman, L. S. 333
sign language 314
Simons, B.: 'Why no pedagogy in England?' 220
situational compliance 108
skills
        curricula and 199
        distribution 98
Skinner, B. F. 24

Smith, D. 58
Snow, C. 252
social class 100–3, 360–1
social cohesion 96–9
social democratic regime 97
social environments 160–2
social interaction 30–1
Social Learning Theory 126
social market regime 96–7
social mobility 359–61
Social World of Pupil Assessment, The (Filer and Pollard) 278–81
society 88–90, 91–2, 349–50
socio-economic status 358–9
sociological imagination, the 91–2
Spaces to Play (Clark and Moss) 203
spatial behaviour 144
special educational needs (SEN) 310, 312, 316, 317
        role of practitioners and 314–15
SPEEL framework, the 150–2
spiral curriculum 35–6
state of flow 130
Steinberg, S. 5
Steiner, R. 181
Stenhouse, L. 44
stereotypes 322–3
Stern, D. N. 236
story-telling 214–17
summative assessment 263–4
SureStart programmes 314, 352
sustained shared thinking 224–5
Swann, M.: *Creating Learning Without Limits* 67
Sweden 300–1

Tarr, P. 157
Te Whāriki approach, the 189–94
teacher expectancy effect 39
teachers 88–90, 330–1 *see also* practitioners
        assessment and 277–8
        confidence and 336–9
        emotions and 89–90
        as evaluators 329–30
        expertise and 332–5
        feedback and 268–70
        identity and 89–90, 338
        professional development and 328–31
        professionalism and 88–9
        qualifications and 42, 187–8
        quality and 139–40
        reflection and 58
        roles of 89–90
        satisfaction and 338
teaching 220–2, 227–8, 330 *see also* pedagogy
        Froebel, F. and 170–2
        Montessori approach, and 178–80
        psychology of 25–7
        Reggio Emilio approach, and 173–7

values and 15, 307
Team Roles 109, 110f, 111
teamwork 109–13, 323–4, 333–4 *see also* collaboration
technology 163–5
The Malting House 283–4
thick description 255
thinking 28–9, 54–5, 58
Thorndike, E. L. 297
time 161–2
Torres, C. A. 355
    land of contrasts and a pedagogy of contradiction, A 355
touch 143–4
transformability 67–9
Twiselton, S. 335

UNICEF: 'Measuring Child Poverty' 358

validity 267, 296
value for money 12–13
Verenikina, I. 164–5
Visible Learning (Hattie) 330
voice 142

Vygotsky, L. 32, 135, 230–1

Waldorf pre-schools 181–4
Warnock Committee 317–18
washback effect, the 265
Wells, G. 252
West, E. 336–8
White Teacher (Paley) 215
Why no pedagogy in England? (Simons) 220
Williams, F. 316–17
Wilson, S. 336–8
Wiltshire, M. 186
women 7, 11, 173
workforce development 329
Writing Superheroes (Dyson) 254

You Can't Say You Can't Play (Paley) 216

Zini 157
zone of proximal development (ZPD) 32–4, 230–2
ZPD (zone of proximal development) 32–4, 230–2

The reflective teaching series

This book is one of the *Reflective Teaching Series* – applying principles of reflective practice in early, school, further, higher, adult and vocational education. Developed over three decades, the series books, companion readers and website represent the accumulated understanding of generations of teachers and educationalists. Uniquely, they offer *two* levels of support in the development of teacher expertise:

- *Comprehensive, practical guidance* on key issues – including learning, relationships, curriculum, teaching, assessment and evaluation.
- *Evidence-informed principles* to support deeper understanding.

The Reflective Teaching Series thus supports both initial steps in teaching and the development of career-long professionalism.

The series is supported by a website, **reflectiveteaching.co.uk**. For each book, this site is being developed to offer a range of resources including reflective activities, research briefings, advice on further reading and additional chapters. The site also offers generic resources such as a compendium of educational terms, links to other useful websites, and a conceptual framework for 'deepening expertise'. The latter draws on and showcases some of the UK's best educational research.

Underlying these materials, there are three key messages.

- It *is* now possible to identify teaching strategies which are more effective than others in most circumstances. Whatever the age of the learners for whom we have responsibility, we now need to be able to develop, improve, promote and defend our expertise by marshalling such evidence and by embedding enquiry, evaluation and improvement within our routine practices.

- All evidence has to be interpreted – and we do this by 'making sense'. In other words, as well as deploying effective strategies, we need to be able to pick out the underlying principles of learning and teaching to which specific policies and practices relate. As well as being practically competent, we need to be able to *understand* what is going on.

- Finally, we need to remember that education has moral purposes and social consequences. The provision we make is connected to our future as societies and to the life-chances of those in our care. The issues require very careful consideration.

The series is coordinated through meetings of the volume and series editors: Paul Ashwin, Jennifer Colwell, Maggie Gregson, Yvonne Hillier, Amy Pollard and Andrew Pollard. Each volume has an editorial team of contributors whose collective expertise and experience enable research and practice to be reviewed and applied in relation to early, school, further, higher, adult and vocational education.

The series is the first product of the Pollard Partnership, a collaboration between Andrew and Amy Pollard to maximise the beneficial use of research and evidence on public life, policy-making and professional practice.

Andrew Pollard, Bristol, February 2015